IRELAND
ROAD ATLAS

CONTENTS

Layout of Map Pages	See Opposing Page
Legend	2
Distance Chart	3
Road Maps of Ireland	4-35
Street Map of Dublin	36-37
Street Map of Belfast	38
Street Map of Cork	39
Street Map of Limerick	40
Street Map of Galway	41
Street Map of Londonderry	42
Index of Place Names	43-64
Counties of Ireland	Inside Back Cover

Legend to Road Maps

Symbol	Description	Symbol	Description
M50	Motorway	—•—	Railway line with station
7	Motorway with junction number	Glencree River	Lake, lough, river
········	Motorway under construction	～—～⌒	Irish border
N11 — A55	Dual carriageway	▨ ○	Large town / small town
N3 — A2	National Primary Road / A Road	⊕	Airport, airfield
N82	National Secondary Road	⚑	Golf course
········	Road under construction	Round Tower •	Monument
R121 — B147	Regional Road / B Road	647 ▲	Height in metres
——	Other Roads	▬	Beach

Scale of road maps is 1:300,000 (1cm = 3km or 1 inch = 4.7 miles)

© Causeway Press (N.I.)

The maps on pages 4 to 42 are based upon Ordnance Survey of Northern Ireland and Ordnance Survey Ireland data.

Northern Ireland mapping is based upon data licensed from the Ordnance Survey of Northern Ireland with the permission of the Controller of Her Majesty's Stationery Office. Crown Copyright 2005. Permit number 50155.

Republic of Ireland mapping is based upon data licensed from Ordnance Survey Ireland. Permit number 8020. Copyright Ordnance Survey Ireland and Government of Ireland 2005.

Many place names in the Index of Place Names are given both in English and in Irish. The names given are those approved by the Ordnance Survey of Northern Ireland and Ordnance Survey Ireland.

All rights reserved. No part of this publication may be reproduced, stored in a retrieval system, or transmitted in any form or by any means electronic, mechanical, photocopying, recording or otherwise, without prior permission of Causeway Press (N.I.). Great care has been taken throughout this publication to be accurate but the publishers cannot accept responsibility for any errors which appear, or their consequences.

Printed by The Universities Press (Belfast) Ltd.

Compiled by Paul Slevin. Published by Causeway Press (N.I.), 17 Osborne Park, Bangor, N.Ireland BT20 3DJ. Phone 07768 172442. E-mail paulslevin@talk21.com

DISTRIBUTION: Distributed by Eason Wholesale Books. ISBN 1 872600 83 2

Distance Chart

The distance between two places can be found at the intersection of their respective row and column. For instance, the distance between Belfast and Dublin is 104 miles, or 167 kilometres, as indicated by the highlighted squares below.

1 mile = 1.61 kilometres

1 kilometre = 0.62 miles

Distance in Miles

Distance in Kilometres

4

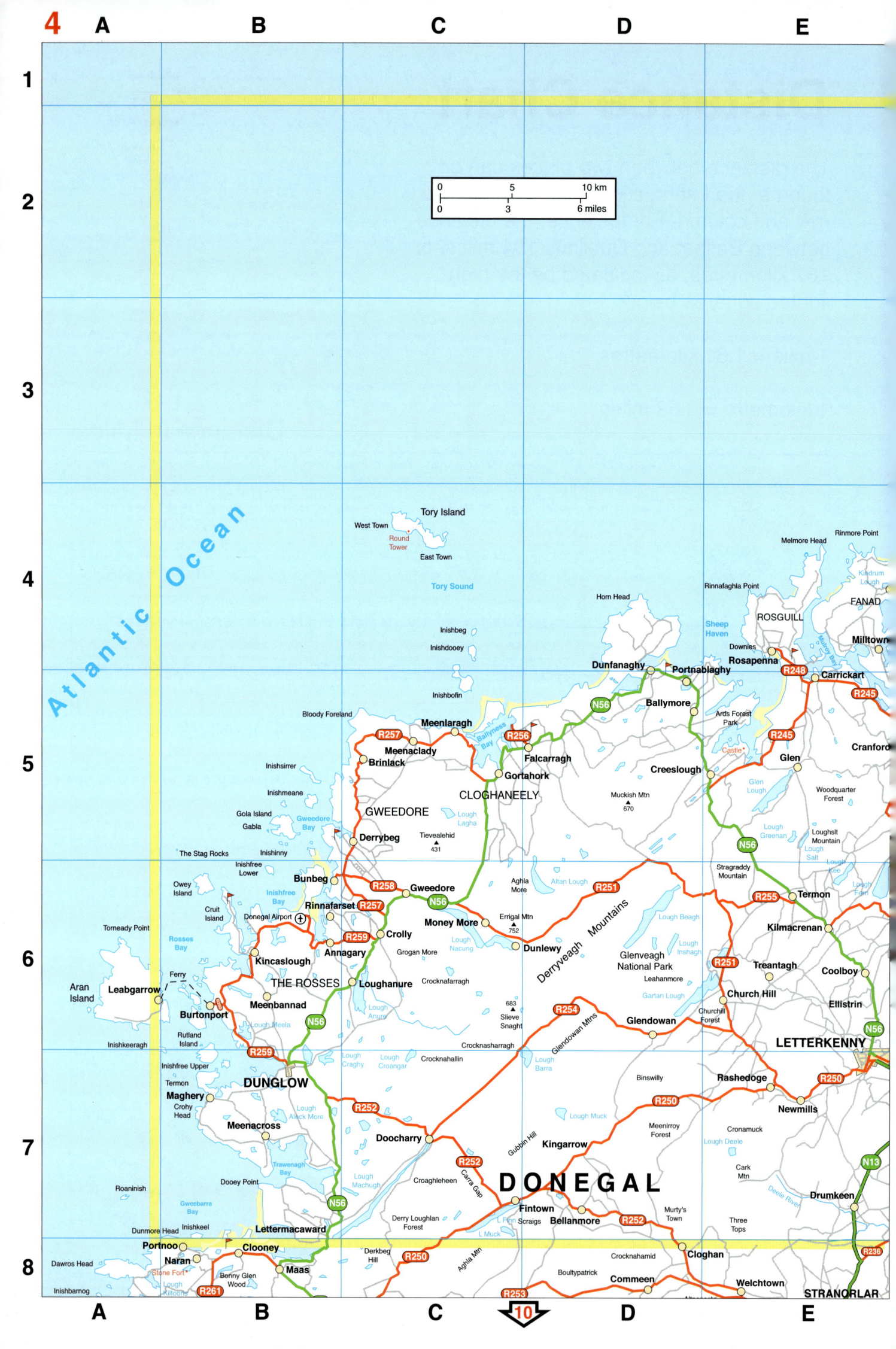

Map grid: A B C D E / 1–8

Atlantic Ocean

Tory Island — West Town, Round Tower, East Town
Tory Sound
Inishbeg
Inishdooey
Inishbofin

Horn Head
Melmore Head, Rinmore Point
Rinnafaghla Point
FANAD
Kindrum Lough
ROSGUILL
Sheep Haven
Downies
Dunfanaghy — **Portnablaghy** — **Rosapenna** — Mulroy Bay — **Milltown**
R248
Carrickart
R245
N56
Ballymore
Ards Forest Park
Castle
R245
Creeslough
Glen
Cranford

Bloody Foreland
R257
Meenlaragh
Meenaclady
R256
Ballyness Bay
Brinlack
Falcarragh
Gortahork
CLOGHANEELY
Muckish Mtn 670
Woodquarter Forest

Inishsirrer
Inishmeane
GWEEDORE
Lough Lagha
Tievealehid 431
Gola Island
Gabla
Gweedore Bay
Derrybeg
Lough Greenan
Loughslt Mountain
Lough Salt
Lough Kee

The Stag Rocks
Inishinny
Inishfree Lower
Bunbeg
R258
Gweedore
N56
Altan Lough
R251
Stragraddy Mountain
Lough Fern
R255
Termon

Owey Island
Cruit Island
Inishfree Bay
Rinnafarset
R257
Donegal Airport
R259
Money More
Errigal Mtn 752
Lough Nacung
Lough Inshagh
Kilmacrenan

Torneady Point
Rosses Bay
Crolly
Annagary
Grogan More
Dunlewy
Derryveagh Mountains
Lough Beagh
R251
Treantagh
Coolboy

Aran Island
Leabgarrow
Ferry
Kincaslough
THE ROSSES
Loughanure
Crocknafarragh
Glenveagh National Park
Leahanmore
Gartan Lough
Churchill Forest
Church Hill
Ellistrin

Burtonport
Meenbannad
Lough Meela
N56
Lough Anure
683 Slieve Snaght
R254
Glendowan
Glendowan Mtns
N56
LETTERKENNY

Inishkeeragh
Rutland Island
Inishfree Upper
R259
Lough Craghy
Lough Croangar
Crocknahillin
Lough Barra
Binswilly
Lough Muck
R250
Rashedoge
R250
Newmills

Termon
Maghery
DUNGLOW
Crocknasharragh
Gubbin Hill
Kingarrow
Meenirroy Forest
Cronamuck
Lough Deele
N13

Crohy Head
Meenacross
Doocharry
R252
Carra Gap
Cark Mtn
Drumkeen

Roaninish
Dooey Point
Trawenagh Bay
Croagleheen
Derry Loughlan Forest
L Finn
Scraigs
DONEGAL
Murty's Town
Three Tops
R236

Dawros Head
Dunmore Head
Inishkeel
Gweebarra Bay
N56
Fintown
Bellanmore
R252
Cloghan

Inishbarnog
Portnoo
Naran
Stone Fort
Clooney
Bonny Glen Wood
Maas
Lettermacaward
R250
Derkbeg Hill
Aghla Mtn
Crocknahamid
Boultypatrick
Commeen
Welchtown
STRANORLAR
R261
R253

Scale: 0—5—10 km / 0—3—6 miles

→ 10

F G H J K

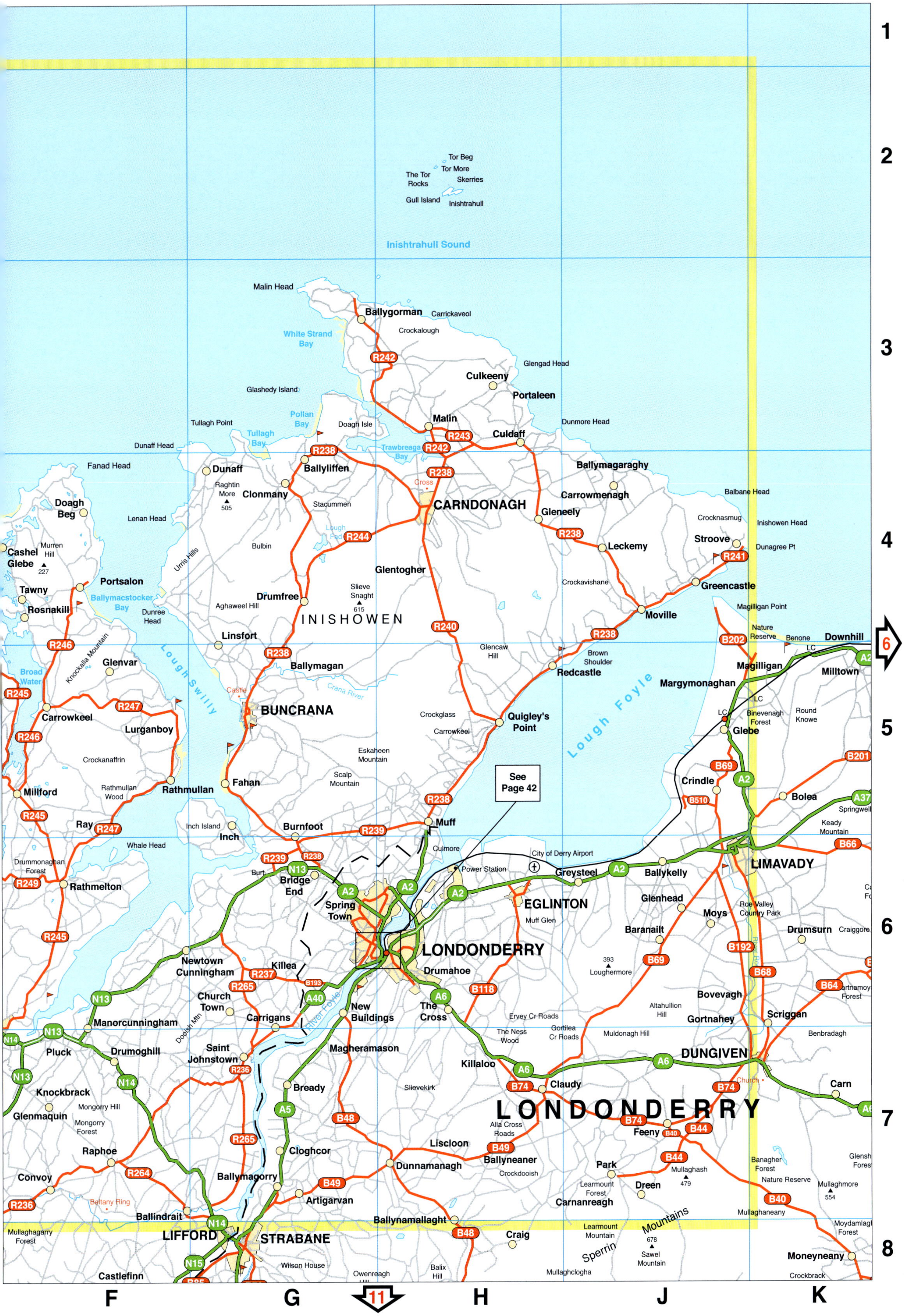

1 2 3 4 5 6 7 8

F G H J K

6

Grid references
A B C D E (top and bottom)
1 2 3 4 5 6 7 8 (sides)

Scale: 0–10 km / 0–6 miles

Locations

Coastal / Northern area:
- Carrowmenagh, Balbane Head, Crocknasmug, Inishowen Head
- Leckemy, Stroove, Dunagree Pt
- Greencastle, R241
- Moville, R238
- Magilligan Point, Benone, Downhill, Castlerock
- Portstewart, Portrush, Ramore Head Coastguard Stn, The Skerries
- Dunluce Castle, Portballintrae, Bushmills, Distillery
- Giant's Causeway Causeway Centre, Benbane Head, White Park Bay, Sheep Island
- Dunseverick, Ballintoy, Carrickarede Island & Rope Bridge, Kinbane or White Head
- Lagavara, Clare Wood, Ballycastle, Ballycastle Marina, Ballycastle Bay, Ballyvoy
- Glentaisie, Glenshesk, Ballycastle Forest
- Rathlin Island, Bruce's Cave, Slieveard, Bull Point, Church Bay, Rue Point, Rathlin Sound

Central area:
- Margymonaghan, Magilligan, Milltown, Articlave, Coleraine, Blagh, Revallagh
- Castlecat, Moss-Side, The Dry Arch, Moyarget, Knocklayd 514
- Ballyrashane, Ballybogy, Derrykeighan, Dervock, Garry Wood, Conogher Cross Rds
- Kirkhills, Stranocum, Cape Castle, A44
- Glebe, Crindle, Bolea, Macosquin, Letterloan, Springwell Forest, Keady Mountain
- Ballywildrick, Round Knowe, Binevenagh Forest
- Damhead, Ballymoney, Armoy, Breen Wood, Agangarrive Hill
- Limavady, Ballykelly, Glenhead, Baranailt, Moys, Drumsurn, Craiggore
- Roe Valley Country Park, Carn Forest
- Ringsend, Mullan, Agivey, Milltown, Balnamore, Kilraghts, The Drones
- Slieveanorra or Orra Head 508, Loughguile, Slieveanorra Forest, Altnahinch Dam, Slievenahanaghan 540
- Ballylintagh, Crossgare, Aghadowey, Boleran, Killykergan, Caheny
- Bendooragh, Garryduff, Finvoy, Dunloy, Mullan Head, Craigs Wood
- Clogh Mills, Newtown-Crommelin, Clogh, Martinstown
- Altahullion Hill, Bovevagh, Gortnahey, Scriggan, Benbradagh
- Gortnamoyagh Forest, Brockagh, Garvagh, Garvagh Forest, Moneydig
- McLaughlins Corner, Rasharkin, Glenvale, Glarryford, McGregor's Corner
- Muldonagh Hill, Dungiven, Carn, Carntogher
- Bovedy, Kilrea, River Bann, Craig's Cross, Craigs, Antrim
- Correen, Quarrytown, Broughshane
- Londonderry, Feeny, Park, Dreen, Mullaghash 479, Banagher Forest Nature Reserve
- Glenshane Pass, Glenshane Forest, Mullaghmore 554
- Swatragh, Moran's Cross Rds, Aughnacleagh, Cullybackey, Galgorm, Ballymena, M2
- Tamlaght O'Crilly, Upperlands, Clady, Inishrush, Portglenone, Ahoghill, Gracehill
- Sperrin Mountains, Sawel Mountain 678, Mullaghaneany
- Lisnamuck, Moydamlaght Forest, Glen, Culnady, Maghera
- Moneyneany, Tobermore, Gulladuff, Knockcloghrim, Bellaghy, Newferry, Killybegs
- Chesney's, Whitesides, Kells, Connor

Roads: A2, A6, A26, A29, A37, A42, A43, A44, A54, M2, B15, B16, B17, B18, B40, B41, B42, B44, B52, B62, B64, B66, B67, B68, B69, B70, B74, B75, B86, B93, B94, B96, B98, B146, B147, B182, B185, B186, B188, B190, B192, B201, B202, B207, B238, B510, R238, R241

7

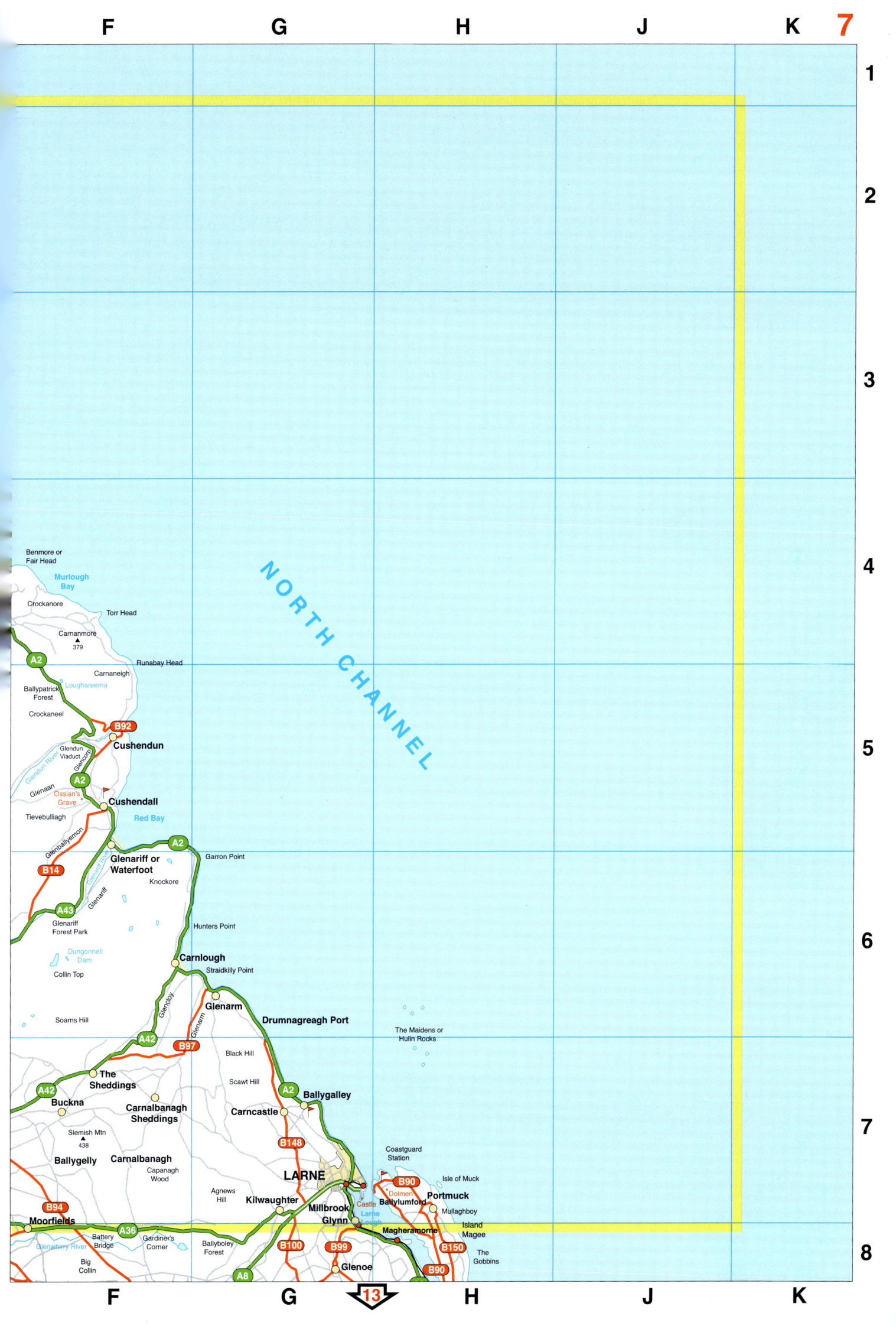

F G H J K

Grid row 1-4 (sea area)
NORTH CHANNEL

Coastal features and locations (rows 4-8):

- Benmore or Fair Head
- Murlough Bay
- Crockanore
- Carnanmore ▲379
- Torr Head
- A2
- Carnaneigh
- Runabay Head
- Ballypatrick Forest
- Loughareema
- Crockaneel
- B92
- Glendun Viaduct
- Glendun River
- Glencorp
- Cushendun
- Glenaan
- A2
- Ossian's Grave
- Cushendall
- Tievebulliagh
- Red Bay
- Glenballyemon
- B14
- Glenariff Bay
- A2
- Garron Point
- Glenariff or Waterfoot
- Knockore
- A43
- Glenariff
- Glenariff Forest Park
- Dungonnell Dam
- Collin Top
- Hunters Point
- Carnlough
- Straidkilly Point
- Soarns Hill
- Glencloy
- Glenarm
- Drumnagreagh Port
- A42
- B97
- Glenarm
- Black Hill
- The Maidens or Hulin Rocks
- The Sheddings
- Scawt Hill
- A42
- A2
- Ballygalley
- Buckna
- Carnalbanagh Sheddings
- Carncastle
- Slemish Mtn ▲438
- Ballygelly
- Carnalbanagh
- Capanagh Wood
- B148
- Coastguard Station
- Isle of Muck
- Agnews Hill
- LARNE
- B90
- Portmuck
- B94
- Kilwaughter
- Millbrook Glynn
- Castle
- Dolmen
- Ballylumford
- Mullaghboy
- Moorfields
- A36
- Battery Bridge
- Gardiner's Corner
- Ballyboley Forest
- Larne Lough
- Magheramorne
- Island Magee
- Glenwhirry River
- B100
- B99
- B150
- The Gobbins
- Big Collin
- A8
- Glenoe
- B90

↓ 13

F G H J K

8

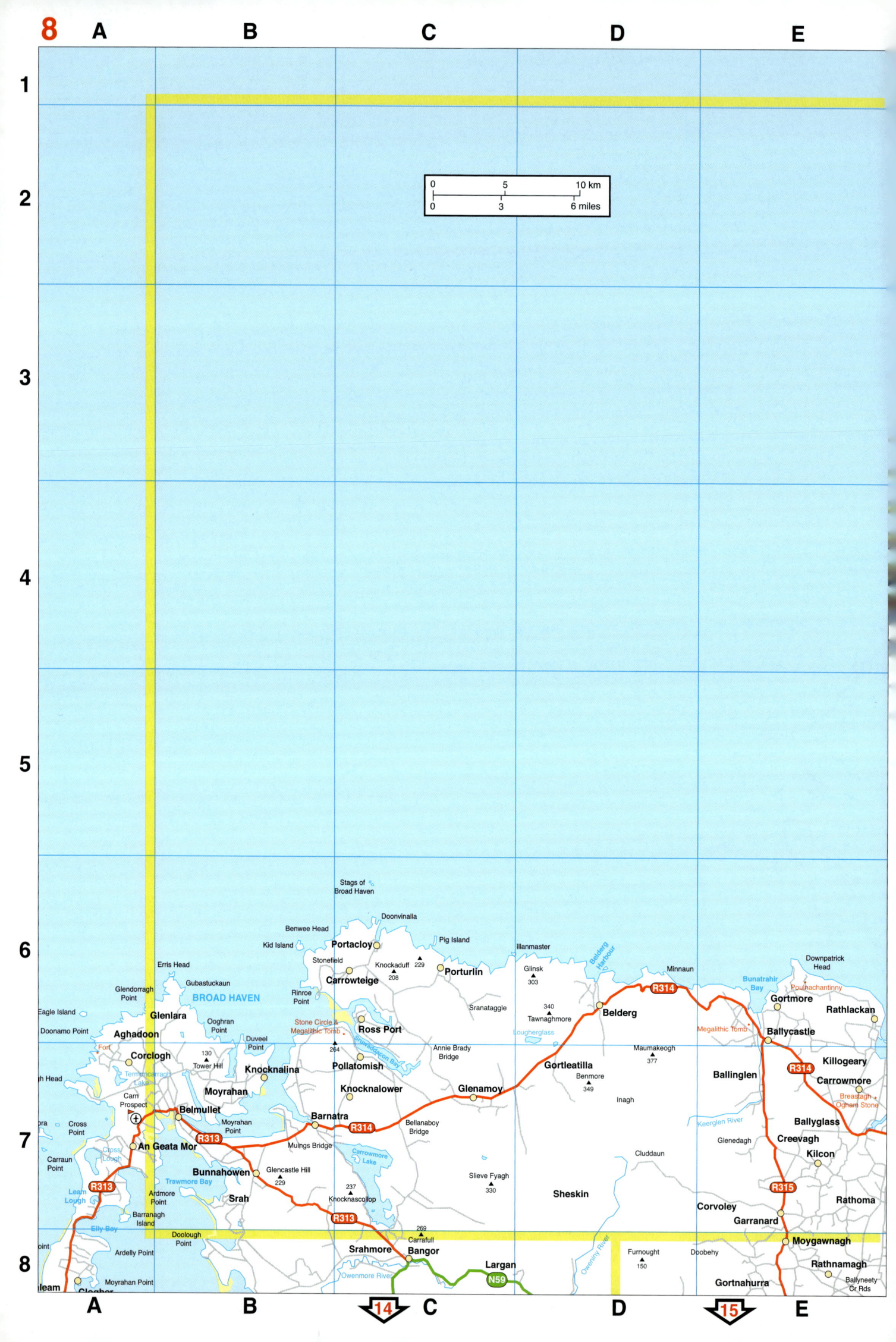

Grid References
A, B, C, D, E (columns)
1–8 (rows)

Scale: 0 — 5 — 10 km / 0 — 3 — 6 miles

Places (row 6)
- Stags of Broad Haven
- Benwee Head
- Kid Island
- Doonvinalla
- Portacloy
- Stonefield
- Pig Island
- Carrowteige
- Knockaduff 229
- Porturlin
- Illanmaster
- Glinsk 303
- Belderg Harbour
- Minnaun
- Downpatrick Head
- Bunatrahir Bay
- Gortmore
- Rathlackan
- Erris Head
- Gubastuckaun
- Glendorragh Point
- Eagle Island
- Doonamo Point
- Glenlara
- Aghadoon
- Broad Haven
- Ooghran Point
- Duveel Point
- Rinroe Point
- Stone Circle & Megalithic Tomb
- Ross Port
- Sranataggle
- Tawnaghmore 340
- Belderg
- R314
- Megalithic Tomb
- Ballycastle
- R314
- Killogeary
- Ballinglen
- Carrowmore
- Breastagh Ogham Stone

Places (row 7)
- Corclogh
- 130 Tower Hill
- Knocknalina
- Moyrahan
- Pollatomish
- 264
- Annie Brady Bridge
- Maumakeogh 377
- Benmore 349
- Inagh
- Keerglen River
- Ballyglass
- Glenedagh
- Creevagh
- Belmullet
- Moyrahan Point
- Barnatra
- R314
- Glenamoy
- Gortleatilla
- Cludduan
- Kilcon
- An Geata Mor
- R313
- Mulngs Bridge
- Bellanaboy Bridge
- Carrowmore Lake
- R315
- Rathoma

Places (row 7–8)
- Bunnahowen
- Glencastle Hill 229
- 237 Knocknascollop
- Slieve Fyagh 330
- Sheskin
- Corvoley
- Garranard
- Cross Point
- Crass Lough
- Trawmore Bay
- Srah
- Ardmore Point
- Barranagh Island
- Doolough Point
- R313
- 269 Carrafull
- Srahmore
- Bangor
- Largan
- N59
- Owenny River
- Furnought 150
- Doobehy
- Moygawnagh
- Rathnamagh
- Carraun Point
- Leam Lough
- R313
- Elly Bay
- Ardelly Point
- Owenmore River
- Gortnahurra
- Ballyneety Cr Rds
- Moyrahan Point
- Cloghor

↓14 ↓15

Roaninish
Gweebarra Bay
Dunmore Head
Inishkeel
Letterma
Portnoo
Clooney
Naran
Dawros Head
Stone Fort
Bonny Glen Wood
Maas
Inishbarnog
Lough Kiltooris
R261
Sheskinmore L.
Lough Aderry
Loughros More Bay
Loughros Point
Loughros Beg Bay
Crannogbay
Tormore Island
Slievetooey
Ardara
Port Hill
Lough Nalugraman
Glengesh Hill
Common Bridge
Glengesh Pass
Forest
Sturall
Crockuna
Meenacross
Croaghacullion
Glen Head
Glencolumbkille
Common Mountain
Mulmosog Mountain
Crocknamurrin
N56
Rossan Point
Crocknapeast
Malin More
Meenaneary
R263
Cloghanmore
Mulnanaff 473
Malin Bay
Lough Inna
Glen River
Malin Beg
Bungosteen Bridge
Carrick
Clonasillagh Forest
Rathlin O'Birne Island
Slieve League 595
494 Crownarad
Teelin
Killybegs
Kilcar
Largy
Bruc
Dunk
Carrigan Head
Muckros Head
Fintragh Bay
McSwayne's Bay
Carntullagh Head
Inishduff
Drumanoo Head
St John's Pt
Donegal Bay
Mullaghmore Head
Mullaghmore
Roskeeragh Pt
R279
N15
Castleg
Ballo
Inishmurray
Cliffony
Ballaghnatrillic
Streedagh Pt
Mount Temple
Grange
Benwiskin
Gleniff Forest
Truskm 647
Cullumore
Ballinfull
Lisadell Forest
Cashelgarran
Benbulbin
Ardboline
Cloghboley
Carney
King's Mountain
Glencar Lake
Raghly
High Cross & Round Tower
Drumcliff Bay
Drumcliff
Raghly Point
Croc
N16
Black Rock
Rathcormack
Creevagh Head
Coney Island
Rosses Point
R291
Lackan Bay
Benwee or Kilcummin Head
Lenadoon Point
Carrickadda Point
Sligo Bay
Calry
Killala Bay
Rathlee
R297
Easky
Carrownabinna Pt
SLIGO
Sligo Abbey
Colgagh Lough
Carrowpadeen
Donagh
Aughris
Strandhill
R292
Queen Maeve's Grave
Carns Forest
R286
Rathfran Bay
Belturlin
Rathcarrick Forest
Hazelwood Forest
Race Course
Ross Point
Castle
Cloonycarney
Dromore West
Templeboy
Knockaree
Megalithic Cemetery
Kilglass
Lugdoon
Skreen
Drumard
N4
Killerry Mtn
Bartragh Island
Drinaghan
Owenbeg
Beltra
Ballisadare Bay
Belladrihid
Slish Wood
Round Tower
Inishcrone
R284
R287
Killala
Culleens
Kingsmountain
Chapel Street
Ballysadare
Castledargan Forest
Abbey
R298
N59
Owenykeevan or Tawnanaddoo
Knockachree
Union Wood
Ballintogher
Mullafarry
545 Knockalongy
Glen Wood
R290
Correagh Forest
R314
Abbey
R297
Letterunshin
Slieve Gamph or The Ox Mountains
Collooney
Ballygawley
Castleconor
Corbally
Coolaney
Disused Railway
Carrownaskeagh Forest
Cloonkeelaun
Toberscanavan
Sooey
Rathroeen
Cloonagh Lough
Easky Lough
Coola Cr Rds
Beleek Demesne
Laughil
N4
Carroweden
SLIGO
Ballynacarrow
Loughanaboll

10

4

9

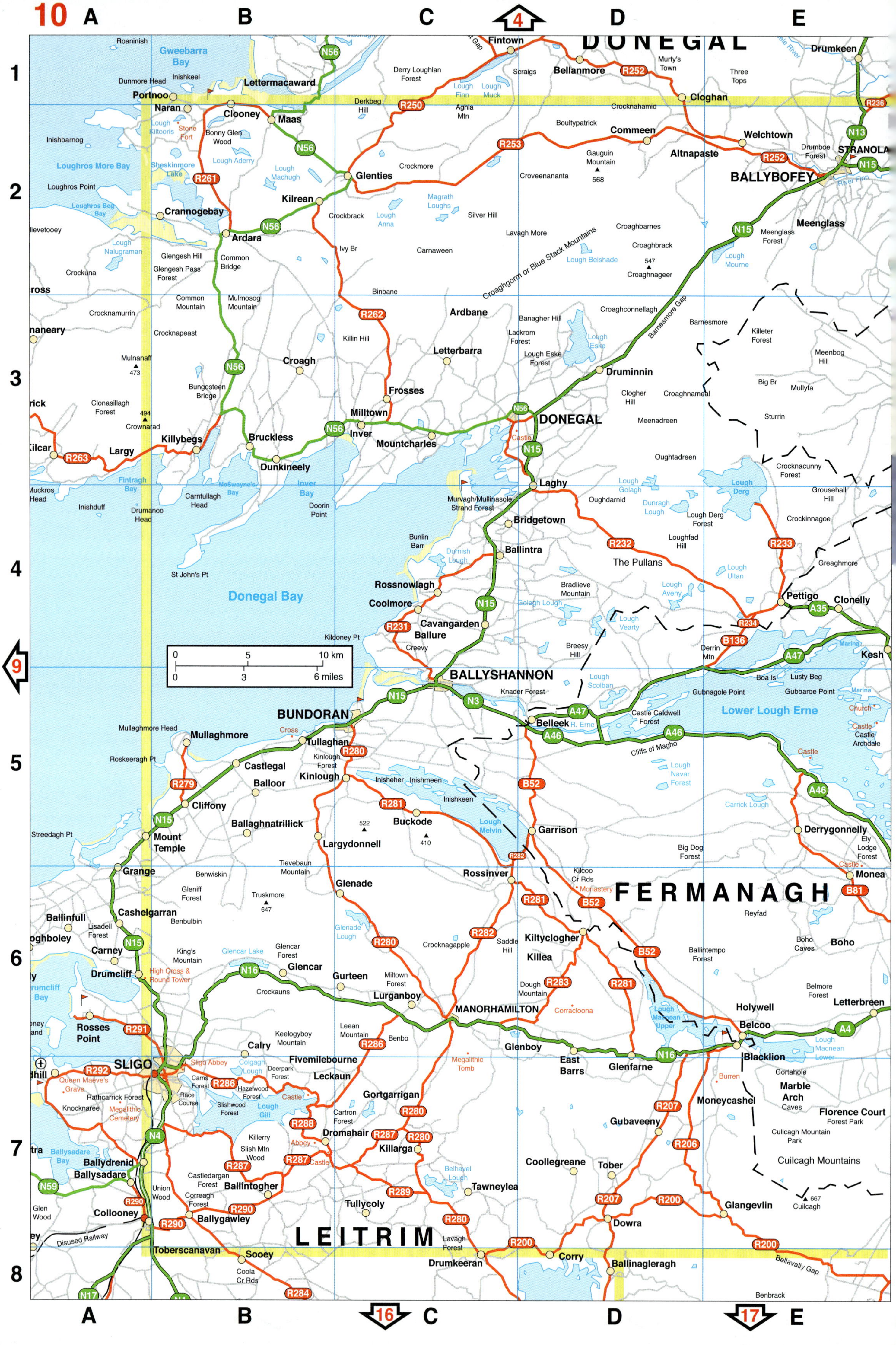

A
B
C
D
E
1
2
3
4
5
6
7
8
DONEGAL
FERMANAGH
LEITRIM
Roaninish
Gweebarra Bay
Dunmore Head
Inishkeel
Portnoo
Lettermacaward
Naran
Clooney
Maas
Inishbarnog
Lough Kiltooris
Stone Fort
Bonny Glen Wood
Lough Aderry
Loughros More Bay
Sheskinmore Lake
Loughros Point
Loughros Beg Bay
Crannogebay
Ardara
Lough Nalugraman
Glengesh Hill
Glengesh Pass Forest
Common Bridge
Crockuna
Common Mountain
Mulmosog Mountain
Crocknamurrin
Crocknapeast
Mulnanaff
473
Bungosteen Bridge
Clonasillagh Forest
494
Crownarad
Killybegs
Largy
Kilcar
Fintragh Bay
Muckros Head
Inishduff
Drumanoo Head
Carntullagh Head
McSwayne's Bay
Inver Bay
Doorin Point
St John's Pt
Donegal Bay
Lough Machugh
Kilrean
Glenties
Derry Loughlan Forest
Derkbeg Hill
Fintown
Lough Finn
Lough Muck
Aghla Mtn
Scraigs
Bellanmore
Murty's Town
Three Tops
Cloghan
Crocknahamid
Boultypatrick
Commeen
Welchtown
Altnapaste
Gauguin Mountain
568
Croveenananta
Crockmore
Magrath Loughs
Silver Hill
Crockbrack
Lough Anna
Ivy Br
Carnaween
Lavagh More
Croaghgorm or Blue Stack Mountains
Lough Belshade
Croaghbarnes
Croaghbrack
547
Croaghnageer
Binbane
Ardbane
Croaghconnellagh
Barnesmore Gap
Barnesmore
Killeter Forest
Banagher Hill
Lackrom Forest
Lough Eske
Lough Eske Forest
Killin Hill
Letterbarra
Druminnin
Croagh
Frosses
Milltown
Inver
Mountcharles
Bruckless
Dunkineely
DONEGAL
Castle
Clogher Hill
Croaghnameal
Meenadreen
Oughtadreen
Laghy
Drumkeen
STRANORLAR
BALLYBOFEY
River Finn
Drumboe Forest
Meenglass
Meenglass Forest
Lough Mourne
Meenbog Hill
Big Br
Mullyfa
Sturrin
Crocknacunny Forest
Grousehall Hill
Crockinnagoe
Greaghmore
Lough Derg
Lough Derg Forest
Lough Golagh
Dunragh Lough
Oughdarnid
Murvagh/Mullinasole Strand Forest
Bridgetown
Bunlin Barr
Durnish Lough
Ballintra
Loughfad Hill
The Pullans
Lough Ultan
Rossnowlagh
Coolmore
Bradlieve Mountain
Lough Avehy
Golagh Lough
Pettigo
Clonelly
Cavangarden
Ballure
Creevy
Kildoney Pt
Lough Vearty
Breesy Hill
Derrin Mtn
Kesh
Marina
Lough Scolban
BALLYSHANNON
Knader Forest
Boa Is
Lusty Beg
Gubnagole Point
Gubbaroe Point
BUNDORAN
Cross
Castle Caldwell Forest
Lower Lough Erne
Church
Castle
Castle Archdale
Belleek
R. Erne
Cliffs of Magho
Lough Navar Forest
Carrick Lough
Mullaghmore Head
Mullaghmore
Tullaghan
Kinlough Forest
Kinlough
Roskeeragh Pt
Castlegal
Balloor
Inisheher
Inishmeen
Inishkeen
Lough Melvin
Cliffony
Ballaghnatrillick
Buckode
522
410
Garrison
Big Dog Forest
Derrygonnelly
Ely Lodge Forest
Streedagh Pt
Mount Temple
Largydonnell
Tievebaun Mountain
Grange
Benwiskin
Glenade
Rossinver
Kilcoo Cr Rds
Monastery
Monea
Gleniff Forest
Truskmore
647
Ballinfull
Lisadell Forest
Cashelgarran
Benbulbin
Glenade Lough
Crocknagapple
Saddle Hill
Kiltyclogher
Killea
Reyfad
Boho Caves
Boho
Oghboley
Carney
King's Mountain
Glencar Lake
Glencar Forest
Ballintempo Forest
Drumcliff
High Cross & Round Tower
Glencar
Gurteen
Milltown Forest
Dough Mountain
Belmore Forest
Letterbreen
Drumcliff Bay
Crockauns
Lurganboy
MANORHAMILTON
Corracloona
Lough Macnean Upper
Holywell
Belcoo
Rosses Point
Leean Mountain
Benbo
Keelogboy Mountain
Glenboy
Lough Macnean Lower
Calry
Colgagh Lough
Fivemilebourne
Megalithic Tomb
East Barrs
Glenfarne
Blacklion
SLIGO
Sligo Abbey
Deerpark Forest
Carns Forest
Leckaun
Burren
Gortahole
Queen Maeve's Grave
Race Course
Hazelwood Forest
Castle
Marble Arch Caves
Rathcarrick Forest
Slishwood Forest
Lough Gill
Gortgarrigan
Moneycashel
Knocknaree
Megalithic Cemetery
Cartron Forest
Florence Court Forest Park
Killerry
Slish Mtn Wood
Dromahair
Abbey
Killarga
Gubaveeny
Cuilcagh Mountain Park
Ballysadare Bay
Ballydrenid
Ballysadare
Cuilcagh Mountains
Coollegreane
Tober
Castle
Castledargan Forest
Ballintogher
Belhavel Lough
Tawneylea
Union Wood
Corroagh Forest
Tullycoly
Glangevlin
667
Cuilcagh
Glen Wood
Collooney
Ballygawley
Dowra
Disused Railway
Lavagh Forest
Toberscanavan
Sooey
Corry
Ballinagleragh
Bellavally Gap
Coola Cr Rds
Drumkeeran
Benbrack
0
5
10 km
0
3
6 miles
N56
N15
N13
N16
N4
N59
N17
N3
A35
A47
A46
A4
B136
B52
B81
R236
R252
R250
R253
R261
R262
R263
R232
R233
R234
R231
R279
R280
R281
R282
R283
R286
R287
R288
R289
R290
R291
R292
R284
R207
R206
R200

16

17

F G 5 H J K

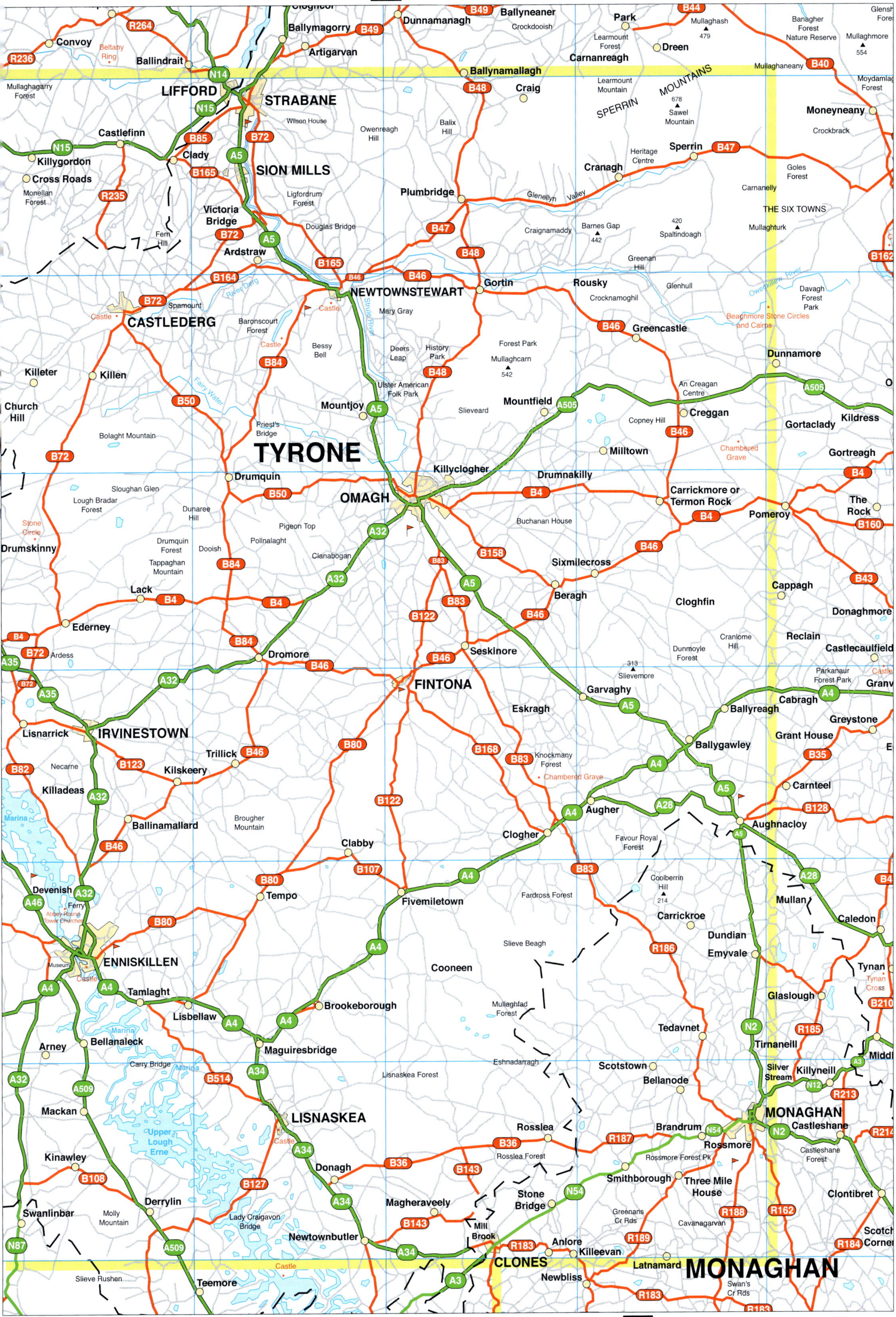

1 2 3 4 5 6 7 8

F 17 G H 18 J K

MAGHERA
MAGHERAFELT
RANDALSTOWN
BALLYMENA
ANTRIM
COOKSTOWN
CRUMLIN
COALISLAND
DUNGANNON
MOIRA
LURGAN
CRAIGAVON
WARINGSTOWN
PORTADOWN
RICHILL
TANDRAGEE
BANBRIDGE
ARMAGH
KEADY
MONAGHAN
BESSBROOK
NEWRY
ARMAGH
MONAGHAN
Lough Neagh
MOUNTAINS
Sperrin
Dreen
Mullaghash
Lisnamuck
Glen
Culnady
Gulladuff
Tobermore
Knockcloghrim
Curran
Bellaghy
Newferry
Chesney's Corner
Moneyglass
Castledawson
Toome
AHOGHILL
Gracehill
Killybegs
Whitesides Corner
Caddy
Kells
Connor
Tardree Forest
Peters Bridge
Mill Town
Shane's Castle Park
Muckamore
Randalstown Forest
Staffordstown
Cranfield Church
Mainwater Foot
Moneyneany
Crockbrack
Draperstown
Desertmartin
Goles Forest
Carnanelly
THE SIX TOWNS
Spaltindoagh
Mullaghturk
Chambered Grave
Slieve Gallion
Cranny
Traad Point
Ballyronan
The Loup
Marina
Moneymore
Glenhull
Davagh Forest Park
Stone Circles
Greencastle
Dunnamore
An Creagan Centre
Creggan
Orritor
Drum Manor Forest Park
Coagh
Kintyrk Flat
The Battery
Ardboe
Ardmore Point
The Diamond
Killead
Belfast International Airport
Aldergrove
Gortaclady
Kildress
Chambered Grave
Ardtrea
Kingsmill
The Diamond
Gortreagh
Tullyhogue
Fort
Carrickmore or Termon Roack
Pomeroy
The Rock
Sandholes
Brigh
Stewartstown
Blackers Rock
Gartree Point
Lennymore Bay
Rams Island
Sandy Bay
Glenavy
Lady Bay
Lough Beg
Mountjoy Castle
Newmills
Killeen
Hog Park Point
Gawleys Gate
Tolans Point
Ballinderry
Cappagh
Cloghfin
Carland
Washing Bay
Donaghmore
Reclain
Cranlome Hill
Dunmoyle Forest
Castlecaulfield
Maghery
Coney Island
Bannfoot
Ardmore Point
Oxford Island
Aghalee
Aghagallon
Maghaberry
Parkanaur Forest Park
Castle
Granville
Moygashel
Tamnamore
Laghey Corner
Peatlands Country Park
The Birches
Derryadd
Ski Centre
Magheralin
Dollingstown
Ballyreagh
Cabragh
Greystone
The Argory
Ballygawley
Grant House
Eglish
Tullyroar Corner
Scotch Street
Moy
Charlemont
Ardress
Carnteel
Bantry Lake
Bleary
Donaghcloney
Aughnacloy
Creeve Lake
Benburb
Castle
Blackwatertown
Loughgall
Kilmore
Allistragh
Ballyleny
Lawrencetown
Gilford
Seapatrick
Coolberrin Hill
Carrickroe
Mullan
Caledon
Laurelvale
Dundian
Emyvale
Killylea
Observatory
Museum
Hamiltonsbawn
Milltown
Scarva
Tynan
Friary
Milford
Clare
Gosford Castle Forest Park
Loughbrickland
Glaslough
Acton
Annaclone
Tedavnet
Markethill
Poyntz Pass
Middletown
Lisnadill
Tirnaneill
LC
Tassagh
Silver Stream
Killyneill
Cladymilltown
Corran Cr Rds
Mountnorris
Brandrum
Castleshane
Rossmore Forest Park
Rossmore
Castleshane Forest
Carrigatuke
Whitecross
Jerrettspass
Derrynoose
Darkley
Three Mile House
Clontibret
Carnagh
Camlough
Belleek
Newtownhamilton
Mullyash Mountain
Mayobridge
Cavangarvan
Scotch Corner
Creaghanroe
Camlough Mtn
Latnamard
Annayalla
Swan's Cr Rds
Burren
M1
M22
M12
A4
A5
A6
A26
A28
A29
A31
N2
N12
N54

11

F
G
7
H
J
K
1
2
3
4
5
6
7
8
19
Capanagh Wood
Agnews Hill
Kilwaughter
Millbrook
Ballylumford
Larne Lough
Isle of Muck
Dolmen
Portmuck
Mullaghboy
Glynn
Magheramorne
ISLAND MAGEE
The Gobbins
Moorfields
Battery Bridge
Gardiner's Corner
Ballyboley Forest
Big Collin
Glenoe
Beltoy
Ballycarry
Lough Mourne
Black Head
Tardree Mtn
Browndod
Ballyeaston
Ballynure
Five Corners
BALLYCLARE
Straid
Woodburn and North Carn Forest
WHITEHEAD
Doagh
Woodburn
312
Eden
CARRICKFERGUS
237
Parkgate
Knockagh
Castle
See Page 38
Dunadry
Templepatrick
Mossley
Monkstown
GREENISLAND
Light House Island
Mew Island
Lyle's Hill
Mallusk
Carnmoney
Whiteabbey
Belfast Lough
Grey Point
HELEN'S BAY
Coastguard Station
Groomsport
Copeland Island
Hyde Park
NEWTOWNABBEY
Craigavad
Marina
Coastguard Station
Loanends
Crawfordsburn
Foreland Point
Zoo
Cultra
BANGOR
DONAGHADEE
Cave Hill
Ulster Folk & Transport Museum
Clandeboye
Nutts Corner
Belfast City Airport
HOLYWOOD
Conlig
Six Road Ends
Ballycopeland Windmill
Legoniel
Cairn Wood
Millisle
Dundrod
BELFAST
NEWTOWNARDS
Stormont
DUNDONALD
Carrowdore
Ballyferis Point
Hannahstown
Ice Bowl
Scrabo Hill
Castlereagh
Stonyford
COMBER
Mount Stewart
Long Rock
Belvoir Park Forest
Ballywalter
DUNMURRY
Greyabbey
Skullmartin
Strangford Lough
Chapel Island
Abbey
Wallaces Rocks
Giant's Ring
White Mtn
Moneyreagh
Ballylesson
Drumbeg
Castle Espie
South Island
Lambeg
Lisbane
CARRYDUFF
Drumbo
Nendrum Monastic Site
Mahee Island
Ballyhalbert
LISBURN
Hillhall
BALLYGOWAN
Kircubbin
Skettrick Island
Mazetown Race Course
Castle
Glastry
Ravernet
The Temple
Killinchy
Rubane
Flatfield
Cuicavy
Boardmills
Balloo
Gransha Pt
Motor Racing Circuit
PORTAVOGIE
SAINTFIELD
Baileysmill
Raffrey
Islandmore
Kirkistown
HILLSBOROUGH
Pawle Island
Ardkeen
Ringboy Point
Derryboy
Ringburr Point
Annahilt
Cloghy
Island Taggart
Shrigley
Ballykeel
Listooder
BALLYNAHINCH
Kearney Point
DROMORE
KILLYLEAGH
Crossgar
Audley's Castle
Kilmore
Ferry
PORTAFERRY
Aquarium
Dromara
The Spa
Castleward Wood
Strangford
Annacloy
DOWN
Finnis
Drumaness
Balltculter
Saul
Raholp
Castle
532
Drumkeeragh Forest
Loughinisland
Slieve Croob
Inch Abbey
Kilclief
Ballyquintin Point
DOWNPATRICK
Dolmen
Drumaroad
Struell Wells
Bishops Court
Killard Point
Slievegarran
Seaforde
Race Course
Ballyhornan
Guns Island
Katesbridge
Lowtown
Stone Circle
Moneyslane
Leitrim
Clough
Chapeltown
Ballyward
Church
Ballyroney
Castlewellan Forest Park
Annsborough
Ballykinler
Killough
Ardglass
CASTLEWELLAN
Dundrum
Tyrella
Minerstown
Ringfad Point
Coastguard Station
RATHFRILAND
Lough Island Reavy
Bryansford
Maghera
Church
Dundrum Bay
Kilcoo
St John's Point
Tollymore Forest Park
0
5
10 km
0
3
6 miles
NEWCASTLE
Dolmen
Slieve Commedagh
Hilltown
Slieve Bearnagh
The Mourne Wall
850
Slieve Donard
Maggy's Leap
Spelga Dam
Slievelamagan
Bloody Bridge
Deers Meadow
Reservoir
MOURNE MOUNTAINS
Slieve Muck
Slieve Binnian
744
Annalong Wood
Slieve Roosley
Shanlieve
Reservoir
Crocknafeola
IRISH SEA
F
G
H
J
K

14

Grid 1
- Srah
- Glencastle Hill
- Knocknascallop 237
- Carrafull
- Sheskin 330
- R313
- Ardmore Point
- Barranagh Island
- Elly Bay
- Leam Lough
- Inishkea North
- Doolough Point

Grid 2
- Tiraun Point
- Ardelly Point
- Clogher
- Aghleam
- Moyrahan Point
- Blacksod
- Termon Hill 102
- Kanfinalta
- Blacksod Point
- Gweesalia
- Dooyork
- Tullaghanduff
- Rath Hill 61
- Tullaghan Bay
- Srahmore
- Bangor
- Largan
- Knocklettercuss 366
- Maumykelly 365
- Bellacorrick
- N59
- Inishkea South
- Duvillaun More
- Duvillaun Beg
- Blacksod Bay
- Doohooma
- Kinrovar
- Srahnamanragh Bridge
- Slieve Alp 328
- Corrslieve 541
- 719
- Nephin Beg 627

Grid 3
- Saddle Head
- Croaghaun 665
- Achill Head
- Dooagh
- Slievemore 671
- Megalithic Tomb
- Keel
- Keem Strand
- Trawmore
- Moyteoge Head
- Inishgalloon
- Doogort
- Ridge Point
- Sruhill Lough
- Inishbiggle
- Keel Lough
- R319
- Bunacurry
- Achill Island
- Cashel
- 464 Mweelin
- Doona
- Fahy Lough
- Ballycroy
- Bellagarvaun
- Castlehill
- Annagh Island
- Claggan
- N59
- Srahduggaun
- Owenduff River
- 627
- Glennamong
- 711 / 711
- Letterkeen Wood
- Bengorm 580
- Buckoogh 587
- Lough Feeagh

Grid 4
- Dooega Head
- Dooega
- Knockmore
- Sraheens
- Achill Sound
- Tonregee
- R319
- Claggan Mountain 380
- Mallaranny
- Rosturk
- Lettermaghera
- Furnace Lough
- Portnahally or Ashleam Bay
- Derreen
- Kildavnet Castle
- Corraun Hill 540
- Glassillaun
- Dooghbeg
- Gubbaun Point
- Castle
- Abbey
- Newport
- Bills Rocks
- Cloghmore
- Achillbeg Island
- Corraun
- Bolinglanna
- Gubacarrigan
- Newport Bay
- N59

Grid 5
- 0 5 10 km
- 0 3 6 miles
- Carrickfadda
- Ballytoohy
- Portlea
- Glassillangaraltagh
- Clare Island 461
- Kinnacorra
- Castle
- Ferry
- Clew Bay
- Westport Bay
- Carraholly
- Westport Quay
- Kinatevdilla
- Portnakilly
- Roonagh Quay
- Emlagh Point
- Cloghmoyle
- Old Head
- Kilsallagh
- R335
- Abbey
- Croagh Patrick 762
- Murrisk
- Knappagh
- N59
- Liscarney

Grid 6
- Inishturk
- Bunnashirra 189
- Dromore Head
- Caher Island
- Gubnagawny
- Ballybeg Island
- Carrickboorla
- Inishdalla
- Barnabaun Point
- Roonah Lough
- Killeen
- Killadoon
- Kinnadooh
- Cregganbaun 270
- Megalithic Tomb
- Formoyle
- Mullagh
- Louisburgh
- Lough Nacorra
- Mohor Lough
- Carrowkennedy
- Owenmore Bridge
- Drummin
- Glenkeen Br
- Sheeffry Hills 761
- Mweelrea Mountains
- Mweelrea 817
- Doo Lough
- Doo Lough Pass
- Ben Creggan
- Sheeffrey Wood
- Errif Br
- Lugacolliwee Lough
- N59

Grid 7
- Inishshark
- Inishbofin 86
- Davillaun
- Inishlyon
- Inishbroon
- Inishgort
- Ferry
- Cashleen
- Renvyle
- Tonakeera Point
- Inishdegil More
- Crump Island
- Castle
- Gowlaun
- Killary Harbour
- Delphi
- Ben Gorm
- Aasleagh Falls
- R335
- Tawnyard Lough
- Lough Glenawough
- 673 Buckaun
- Maumtrasna
- High Island
- Aughrusbeg Lough
- Cleggan
- Claddaghduff
- Ballynakill Harb
- Tully Cross
- 355 Tully Mountain
- Tully Lough
- Altnagaighera
- Garraun
- Lough Fee
- Kylemore Abbey
- N59
- Leenaun
- Cultural Centre
- 647
- Devilsmother
- Maumtrasna
- Rinavore
- 623
- Lough Nafooey
- Bunnacunneen
- Benbeg
- R336
- Joyces Country

Grid 8
- Errislannan Point
- Drinagh
- Ballinaboy
- Knock
- Mannin Bay
- R341
- Salt Lough
- Derryrea Lough
- Streamstown
- Moyard
- Letterfrack
- Diamond Hill
- Connemara National Park
- Kylemore Lough
- R344
- Maumturk Mountains
- R336
- Maum
- High Island
- Friar Island
- Cruagh
- Omey Island
- Iniskturk
- Eeshal Island
- Talbot Island
- Kill
- Lough Nahillion
- Cregg 633
- Benbaun 727
- CLIFDEN
- Clifden Bay
- Owenglin River
- The Twelve Pins or Benna Beola
- Derryclare
- Lehanagh Loughs
- Lough Innagh
- Derryvoreada
- Leckavrea Mountain 660
- Maumwee Lough
- Ballynahinch
- R341
- Recess
- Teernakill Br 700
- Maam Cross
- 666
- 577

F
G
H
J
K
8
9
16
21
1
2
3
4
5
6
7
8
SLIGO
MAYO
R315
Mullafarry
Abbey
R298
Owenykeevan or Tawnanadoo
Kingsmountain
Chapel Street
Knockachree 545
Knockalongy
Corvoley
Garranard
Rathoma
R297
N59
Letterunshin
Slieve Gamph or The Ox Mountains
R314
Castleconor
Corbally
Carrownaskeagh Forest
Moygawnagh
Cloonkeelaun
Furnought 150
Doobehy
Rathroeen
Easky Lough
Rathnamagh
Belleek Demesne
Laughil
Gortnahurra
Ballyneety Cross Rds
Cloonagh Lough
Carroweden
Knockanillaun
Loughanaboll
Kilcummin
Lough Dahybaun
Knockadangan Bridge
Crockets Town
Carrowmore
Esker agh Br
BALLINA
Bunnyconnellan
Disused Railway
Dooleeg
Crossmolina
Ardnaree Church
Behy Bridge
R294
414
Largan
Cloonacool
Megalithic Tomb
Lavagh
Garrycloonagh
Megalithic Tomb
R315
Lough Talt
Achonry
Corcullin
Rake Street
Newtown Cloghans
Lough Conn
N26
Mullany's Cross
Ballymore Lough
Attymass
368
Tobercurry
Chaffpool
R312
Castlehill
Abbey
Derrymanagh Lough
R294
Bunnanadden
Keenagh
R316
Brackwanshagh
R310
Carrowkerribly Lough
Aclare
Toorlestraun
Abbey
Banada
Glenagort
323 Tristia
Lahardaun
Moylough
386 Bullaunmore
Culkillew
Knockmore
Corlee
River Moy
N17
Doocastle
Nephin 806
R315
Owengarve River
Curry
Illannaglashy
Cullin
Roosky
Birreencorragh 697
Derreen
514 Knockaffertagh
R312
Bofeenaun
Drummin Wood
Pontoon Bridge
R310
R318
Foxford
Killasser
Cloonfinish
Levally Lough
Pontoon
Lough Cullin
Callow
Cloonmore Cross Rds
Glen Nephin
Gallow Loughs
Bellahy
Charlestown
N58
Disused Railway
Beltra
Kilmore
N5
Carracastle
Cloondaff
R310
SWINFORD
Mullaghanoe 234
Kilbride
R317
Derryhick Lough
Beltra Lough
428 Croaghmoyle
Ross West
Strade
Round Tower
Barnalyra
N17
Lurga
Knockmoyle Bridge
Levallinree Lough
Park
R321
Friary
Kilfaturty Lough
N5
R376
Johnsfort
Barnacahoge
Tawnyinah
Clydagh Bridge Forest
R320
Bohola
Disused Railway
R375
Ballaghaderreen
National Museum of Country Life
Bellavary
R325
Kilmovee
Midfield
Turlough
Round Tower
R311
R312
N5
R321
Kilkelly
Aghadiffin
Ballyglass
Lough Mallard
CASTLEBAR
Sraheens
Kiltamagh
R322
Urlaur
R311
Breaghwy
Cloonfallagh
Lough Roe
Castlebar Lough
Carrowmore Lough
258
Lough Nanoge
Cloonagh Lough
Cloonacolly Lough
Clogher
N60
R320
Bruff Cross Rds
Urlaur Lough
Ballin Lough
Clogher Lough
Islandeady
Manulla
Addergoole
Aghamore
Lough Naminna
R324
WESTPORT
N5
Cloonkeen
Athavallie
R323
Errit Lough
Round Tower
Balla
Cloonlee
R329
Bunnaglass Lough
Belcarra
Disused Railway
Mannin Lake
Ballyhean
R320
Knock
N83
Walshpool Lough
N60
Ballyfarnagh
Lough Caheer
R293
Island Lake
Mace
R330
R329
Aghagower
Killavally
Newtown
Mayo
N17
Derry Lough
R323
Lough Nageltia
Abbey
Clogher
Ballynastangford
Bekan
Bekan Lough
Ballyhaunis
Kiltarsaghaun
Ballintober
PLAINS OF MAYO
Barnycarroll
Coolnafarna
Tonlegee
Ballyglass
N60
N60
N84
154
Ballinlough
Cordarragh
Lough Nacorralea
Fort
Carrownacon
Knockanarra
Carrowbaun
Bohaun 392
Friary
CLAREMORRIS
Brickeens
Garranlahan
Moore Hall Forest
Cloon Lough
Mullingar Bridge
Cornanagh
N83
Croaghrimbeg
Srah
Partry
R327
Tulrohaun
Lough Carra
Ballygarries
Cloonfad
Partry Mountains
R331
Crossboyne
Robe River
R327
Williamstown
Dalgan River
Ballindine
Kilvine
Megalithic Tomb
Toormakeady
Scardaun
Irishtown
Hollymount
N17
Curragh West
Ellisland Lough
R328
145
Churchfield
Levally
Shanballymore
Roundfort
Garrafrauns
R360
Trean
Castle
R362
Killateeaun
BALLINROBE
Lough Mask
Castleville
Milltown
Dunmore
Dunmore Abbey
Ardkill
Sinking River
Fox Hill
R334
Carrowmore
Carrowkeel-anahglass
Killour
Altore Lough
Knocknamuck
Inishmaine Island
Carrowkeel
Rathgranagher
Cloghans Hill
Foxhall
N17
Ballagh
Cloonnacat
N84
Kilmaine
R332
Finny
Neale
Kilconly
N83
R328
Killavoher
Clonberne
Drumsheel
R345
Deerpark
Cloghbrack
Clonbur Wood
Castle
Castle
R334
Ballyhenry
Kilbenan Cross Rds
Beagh
Clonbur
Cong
Stone Circles
Cross
Crumlin
415
Coolin Lough
Market Cross
Cong Abbey
Tobernadarry
Ballyhear
Black River
Church & Round Tower
103
Levally
Levally Lough
Cornamona
R345
Ardnageeha Forest
Bunnafollistran
Shrule
TUAM
Inishdoorus
Inishmicatreer
69
R334
Caherlistrane
Turloughmore
Church of St Mary
Trasternagh
Ross Abbey
R333
Belclare
Glann Forest
Churches
167
R347
R332
Keeraunnageeragh
Lough Corrib
Owen
Knockmaa
Barnaderg
Inchiquin
Headford
River Clare
Grange River
N63

A
B
9
C
D
10
E
1
2
3
4
5
6
7
8
15
22
SLIGO
LEITRIM
ROSCOMMON
LOUGH ALLEN
LOUGH ARROW
LOUGH KEY
LOUGH GARA
BALLYMOTE
BOYLE
CARRICK-ON-SHANNON
ROSCOMMON
TUAM
Collooney
Ballygawley
Ballintogher
Tullycoly
Dowra
Drumkeeran
Corry
Ballinagleragh
Coolaney
Carroweden
Carrowmore
Lavagh
Ballynacarrow
Toberscanavan
Sooey
Riverstown
Drumfin
Drummacool
Geevagh
Cloonacool
Achonry
Graniamore
Ballindoon
Castlebaldwin
Arigna
Mountallen
Ballyfarnan
Kilmactranny
Tobercurry
Chaffpool
Bunnanaddan
Cloonkeevy
Kesh
Keadew
Drumshanbo
Toorlestraun
Banada
Moylough
Doocastle
Killavil
Culfadda
Ballinafad
Crossna
Curry
Roosky
Gorteen
Liskeagh
Mullaghroe
Knockvicar
Leitrim
Cootehall
Cloontia
Cloonloogh
Bellahy
Charlestown
Carracastle
Monasteraden
Barnalyra
Lurga
Tawnyinah
Kingsland
Killukin
Jamestown
Croghan
Callow
Flagford
Ballaghaderreen
Ballinameen
Clogher
Kilmovee
Ballyglass
Lurgan
Churchstreet
Hill Street
Kilmore
Aghadiffin
Tibohine
Frenchpark
Rodeen
Kilkelly
Urlaur
Moyne
Mullen
Drummullin
Elphin
Barnacawley
Fairymount
Bellanagare
Ballyroddy
Mantua
Aghamore
Clerragh
Loughglinn
Ballyglass West
Cloonsheever
Rathkineely
Brackloon
Largan
Lissananny
Cloonyquin
Cloonfower
Tulsk
Strokestown
Ballyhaunis
Bekan
Cloonkeen
Castlerea
Gortnasillagh
Rathkeva
Scramoge
Coolnafarna
Lissalway
Cloonyogan
Castleplunket
Cloonmurray
Ballinlough
Trien
Knockanarra
Brickeens
Carraghs
Garranlahan
Annagh
Knockalaghta
Caran
Lackan
Curraghroe
Ballintober
Carrowduff
Four Mile House
Tulrohaun
Newtown
Derrycanan
Cloontuskert
Ballymoe
Cloonfad
Ballymacurly
Rathconor
Ballagh
Williamstown
Derrywode
Kilroosky
Kilvine
Pollshask
Ballyleague
Coolshaghtena
Curragh West
Glinsk
Emmoo
Shanballymore
Kilsallagh
Gallagh
Cloonkeen
Kilteevan
Garrafrauns
Boyounagh
Cloonbrennaun
Dunamon
Dunmore
Keeloges
Kilbegnet
Carrowkeel-anahglass
Castlecoote
Milltown
Glennamaddy
Crosswell
Fuerty
Cloonagh
Ballymurray
Cloonnacat
Creegs
Gortnadeeve
Shanbally
Bracknagh
Passage
Killavoher
Clonbern
Scardaun
Knockcroghery
Athleague
Beagh
Kilkerrin
Kilglass
Milltown
Toomard
Lackan Cross
Churchboro Cross
Lecarrow
Levally
Ballygar
Mount Talbot
Rahara
Ballagh
Four Roads
Newbridge
Lismoyle
Trasternagh
Barnaderg
Moylough or Newtown Bellew
Mount Bellew Bridge
Ballyforan
Dysart
Curraghboy
Kiltoom
N4
N5
N17
N59
N60
N61
N63
N83
0
5
10 km
3
6 miles

R200
Glangevlin
667
Cuilcagh
Swanlinbar
Molly Mountain
Lady Craigavon Bridge
Derrylin
A34
Magheraveely
B143
Mill Brook
Stone Bridge
N54
High Cross & Round Tower
Anlore
Killeevan
CLONES
Newtownbutler
A34
R183
Newbliss
R200
Ballavally Gap
N87
A509
Slieve Rushen
B127
Teemore
Castle
A3
N54
MONAGHAN
Benbrack
Brackley Lough
A3
Corlough
Bawnboy
Doohat
R189
Bencroy or Gubnaveagh
R202
N87
Ballyconnell
Killywilly Lough
N3
Belturbet Marina
BELTURBET
Gannon's Cross
Redhills
Scotshouse
Drum
Slieve Anierin
Pottore
Derradda
Bunerky Lough
Templeport Lough
R197
R205
Ballyhugh
Fartrin Cross Rds
River Erne
Cloverhill
R212
Treehoo Cross Rds
Lisnageer
Cromlin
Aghacashel
Aughnasheelan
Shannon Erne Waterway
Ardlougher
Milltown
Lisboduff
Doocarrick
Cootehill
N54
R202
R199
Ballinamore
Derrycassan Lough
Newtown Gore
Drumlane Church & Round Tower
Inishmuck
Butlers Bridge
Inishmore
Ballyhaise
Annalee River
Bellanacargy
Drung
Tullyvin
R188
R208
Doogary
R199
Garfinny Lough
R208
Lough Scur
Foxfield
Garadice Lough
R201
N3
R188
Kill
R210
R209
Megalithic Tomb
Keshcarrigan
Fenagh
Drumlea
Killygar
Killashandra
Killykeen Forest Park
Clogh Oughter Castle
Stone Row
R165
Drumlaheen Lough
R204
Lough Oughter
CAVAN
Glasshouse Lough
N3
260
Kilnagross
R199
R201
Rockfield Lough
Stradone
Cannin
Garvagh
R201
Kilmore
Drumna
Carrigallen
Clifferna
R198
Slieve Glah
319
Cloone
R201
Aghavas
Gulladoo Lough
R198
Crossdoney
N55
R165
Cloone Grange
Garty Lough
258 Bruse Hill
Bellananagh
Carrickaboy
CAVAN
Cross Keys
Lough Acurry
Drumsna
R201
Mohill
Moyne
Arvagh
266
N3
Aghamore
R202
Leggah
188
River Erne
New Inn
Keeldra Lough
Lough Boderg
N55
Carrigan
R198
Gortletteragh
Loughduff
Crosserlough
R196
Loch Gowna
Rinn Lough
Corglass Lough
R154
Nadreegee Loughs
Ballyjamesduff
Lough Scannel
Ballinmuck
Kilnaleck
Farnaght
Megalithic Tomb
River Erne
R194
R194
Dromod
Clooneagh
Aghnacliff
Ballynarry
Lough Bofin
Megalithic Tomb
Lough Gowna
Cloonagh
232
Mullaghmacormick
Rinn River
LC
Ballyheelan
18
Castlerahan
Kilcogy
130
Ballymachugh
Roosky
Johnstownbridge
Derrycassin Forest
Drumlish
Dring
Clooneen
R394
R194
Mount Nugent
Eighter
Lough Acrick
LOUGH SHEELIN
191
276
Corn Hill
R195
Bunlahy
N4
R198
Esker South
Ross Wood
Ross
R154
109
Granard
R194
Finnea
Lough Kinale
Ballinalee
Browne's Cross Rds
Newtown Forbes
Aghaboy
R194
Motte
177
Ballynacree
Oldcastle
Lough Forbes
Cistercian Abbey
Castletown
258
Whitehall
Killoe
Abbeylara
Mullaghmeen Forest
Loughcrew Megalithic Cemetery
Clonbroney Cross Rds
Deeragh Lough
N55
Rahaghy
279
Termonbarry
R396
Lough Bane
241
Hill of Moat
Ballymanus
Moat Farrell
LONGFORD
Drinagh
Lisryan
R394
Drumone
Cloondara
N5
Erra
Kilmore Upper
R395
Lismacaffry
R195
N4
Corbey
River Shannon
Lisduff Cross Rds
Boherquill
Slieve Gullion 194
Coole
Lough Glore
LONGFORD
LC
Edgeworthstown
Coolnagun
Inny River
Cross Keys
Street
R395
Priory
215
Lough Bane
Lanesborough
Killashee
Danesfort
R393
LC
LC
Castlepollard
Fore
N55
Bawn Cross Rds
Bottomy
N63
Moydow
Ardagh
R397
Crossea
Kiltoom
The Cut
Lough Lene
Lough Arde
Archerstown
Lyneen Bridge
Rathowen
Lough Derravaragh
Whitehall
R392
Annaghmore
R398
Glen Lough
Black River
River Riffey
Collinstown
R395
Drumcree
Royal Canal
Abbeyderg
N4
Lackan
Yellow River
Rathaspick
Multyfarnham
Turreen
Derraghan Cross Rds
Abbeyderg Cross Rds
Carrickboy
Knockeyon
Legan or Lenamore
Ballinalack
214
R394
Formoyle
LC
River Gaine
Corlea
Keenagh
Inny River
Castle
Clawinch
Derrygowna
Corlea Trackway Visitor Centre
R393
Rathduff
Lough Iron
98
144
Crookedwood
Lough Analla
Bunbrosna
Barry
N55
Colehill
Ballynafid
St Munna's Church
R397
Kilpatrick Wood
Portnashangan
Fennor
Derry Lough
R399
Newtown Cashel
Forthill
Taghshinny
Ballynacarrigy
Scragh Bog
Turin
Monilea
Abbeyshrule
Derrymacar Lough
Carrowrory
Abbey
R392
R393
LOUGH OWEL
Knockdrin
Crazy Corner
Tevrin
N52
Brackl...
Lough Drin
Ballymahon
WESTMEATH
7
Saints Island
Rath River
Cloghan
Clonlost
151
Inchbofin
Castle
Pollagh Pt
Doons Lough
R392
Moyvore
Milltown
Clarks Cr Roads
N4
Lough Sheever
Warren Pt
Royal Canal
Tang
Rathconrath
MULLINGAR
Killucan
R156
Creggan Lough
Tang River
Skeagh
R390
LOUGH
Inchturk
Cloncullen
REE
The Pigeons
137
Mount Dalton Lough
The Downs
Rathwire
Auburn
Lough Sunderlin
Ballina
LC
Killucan
Inchmore
Ballynakill
Hill of Uisneach
R390
Disused Railway
LC
LC
Yew Pt
Kilkenny West
Ballymore
Gainstown
Coralstown
Hare Island
Drumraney
Killare
Loughanavally
LOUGH ENNELL
Gaybrook
116
N55
Glassan
N4
Killinure Point
135
Carn
Dysart

1 2 3 4 5 6 7 8

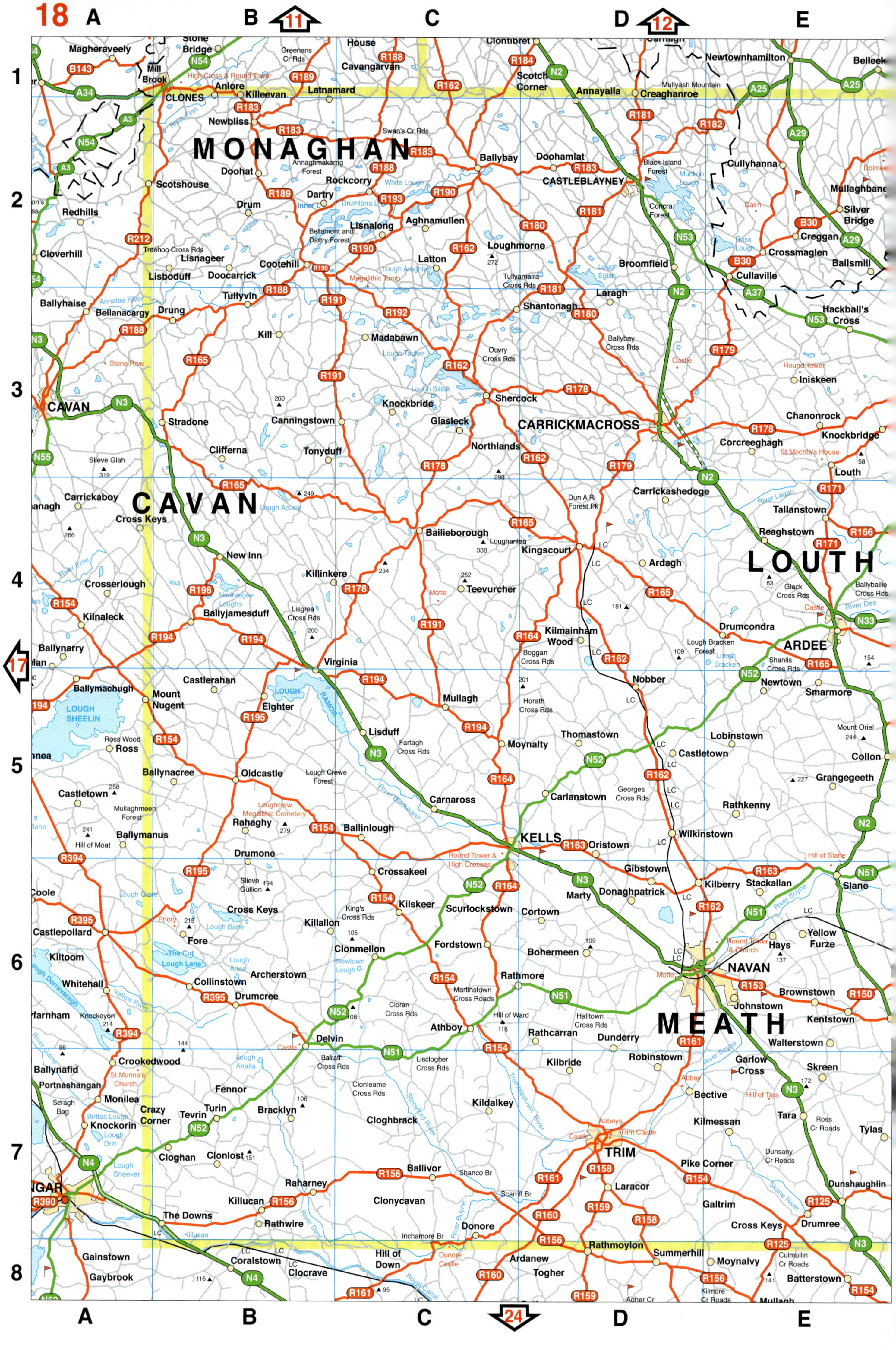
A
B
11
C
D
12
E
1
2
3
4
5
6
7
8
17
24
MONAGHAN
CAVAN
LOUTH
MEATH
Magheraveely
B143
Stone Bridge
Mill Brook
N54
High Cross & Round Tower
Greenans Cr Rds
House
R188
Cavangarvan
Clontibret
R184
Scotch Corner
N2
Carnagh
Newtownhamilton
Belleek
A34
CLONES
Anlore
Killeevan
R189
Latnamard
R162
Annayalla
Mullyash Mountain
Creaghanroe
A25
A3
River Finn
R183
Newbliss
R181
R182
Swan's Cr Rds
A29
Annaghmakerrig Forest
Ballybay
Doohamlat
Black Island Forest
Cullyhanna
Dolmen
Doohat
Rockcorry
White Lough
CASTLEBLAYNEY
Muckno Lough
Mullaghbane
Scotshouse
R193
R190
Silver Bridge
Dartry
Drumlona L
Inner L
Concra Forest
Cairn
Redhills
Drum
R180
B30
Lisnalong
Aghnamullen
Creggan
Bellamont and Dartry Forest
Ross Lough
Crossmaglen
R212
Treehoo Cross Rds
Loughmorne
N53
Cloverhill
Lisnageer
272
Latton
Lough Egish
Broomfield
Ballsmill
Cootehill
Lough Aphelin
Cullaville
Lisboduff
Doocarrick
Megalithic Tomb
Tullyamalra Cross Rds
A37
Annalee River
Tullyvin
R191
Laragh
Ballyhaise
Bellanacargy
Drung
R192
Shantonagh
Hackball's Cross
Kill
Madabawn
Ballybay Cross Rds
Stone Row
R165
Lough Tacker
Ouvry Cross Rds
R179
Castle
Round Tower
Iniskeen
260
Lough Sillan
R178
CAVAN
Knockbride
Shercock
Chanonrock
Stradone
Canningstown
Glasleck
CARRICKMACROSS
Knockbridge
Corcreeghagh
Northlands
N55
Slieve Glah
319
Clifferna
Tonyduff
St Mochta's House
58
Louth
298
249
Carrickaboy
Lough Acurry
Dun A Ri Forest Pk
Carrickashedoge
R171
anagh
Cross Keys
River Lagan
Tallanstown
266
Bailieborough
Loughanlea
338
Reaghstown
R166
New Inn
Kingscourt
LC
River Erne
234
Ardagh
Killinkere
252
Teevurcher
63
Glack Cross Rds
Ballybailie Cross Rds
Crosserlough
R196
Motte
Nadreegee Loughs
181
River Dee
Kilnaleck
Ballyjamesduff
Lisgrea Cross Rds
N33
R154
200
Drumcondra
Kilmainham Wood
Ballynarry
R194
R164
Lough Bracken Forest
ARDEE
Boggan Cross Rds
109
Lough Bracken
154
Virginia
Shanlis Cross Rds
Newtown
Castlerahan
201
Nobber
Smarmore
Ballymachugh
Mount Nugent
LOUGH RAMOR
Horath Cross Rds
LOUGH SHEELIN
Eighter
Mullagh
R195
Lisduff
Moynalty
Thomastown
Lobinstown
Mount Oriel
244
Ross Wood
Ross
Fartagh Cross Rds
N3
N52
Castletown
Collon
nnea
Ballynacree
Oldcastle
Lough Crewe Forest
227
Grangegeeth
Castletown
258
Carlanstown
Georges Cross Rds
River Blackwater
Loughcrew Megalithic Cemetery
Mullaghmeen Forest
Rathkenny
Rahaghy
279
Carnaross
Bane
241
Hill of Moat
Ballymanus
Ballinlough
KELLS
R163
Oristown
Wilkinstown
R394
Drumone
Round Tower & High Crosses
Hill of Slane
Gibstown
N51
Slane
Coole
Crossakeel
Kilberry
Stackallan
Slieve Gullion
194
Marty
Donaghpatrick
Lough Glore
Cross Keys
Kilskeer
Scurlockstown
River Boyne
R395
Priory
215
Lough Bane
King's Cross Rds
Cortown
Castlepollard
Killallon
Yellow Furze
Fore
105
Hays
Round Tower & Church
Kiltoom
The Cut
Lough Lene
Clonmellon
Fordstown
Bohermeen
137
Lough Adeel
Newtown Lough
Archerstown
NAVAN
Lough Derravaragh
Whitehall
Collinstown
Rathmore
Brownstown
R153
R150
Yellow River
Martinstown Cross Roads
Johnstown
rfarnham
Knockeyon
214
Drumcree
Cloran Cross Rds
106
Halltown Cross Rds
Kentstown
Hill of Ward
116
Athboy
Rathcarran
Dunderry
Walterstown
River Gaine
98
144
Delvin
Crookedwood
Lough Analla
Balrath Cross Rds
Lisclogher Cross Rds
Kilbride
Robinstown
Garlow Cross
Skreen
Ballynafid
St Munna's Church
Portnashangan
Fennor
Clonleame Cross Rds
Abbey
Bective
172
Scragh Bog
Monilea
106
Hill of Tara
Brittas Lough
Crazy Corner
Tevrin
Turin
Bracklyn
Stonyford River
Kildalkey
Tremblestown River
Knockorin
Lough Drin
Cloghbrack
Abbeys
Kilmessan
Tara
Ross Cr Roads
Tylas
Castle
Trim Castle
TRIM
Cloghan
Clonlost
151
Lough Sheever
Dunsany Cr Roads
Skane River
N4
R158
Pike Corner
Ballivor
R156
Shanco Br
R161
Laracor
Dunshaughlin
NGAR
R390
Raharney
Scarriff Br
Galtrim
R125
Killucan
Clonycavan
R159
R160
The Downs
Rathwire
River Deel
River Boyne
Inchamore Br
Donore
Cross Keys
Drumree
Killuean
Gainstown
Coralstown
Clocrave
Hill of Down
Dunore Castle
Ardanew
Rathmoylon
Summerhill
Moynalvy
Culmullin Cr Roads
Gaybrook
116
Togher
141
Batterstown
Royal Canal
95
Agher Cr
Kilmore Cr Roads
Mullagh
A
B
C
24
D
E

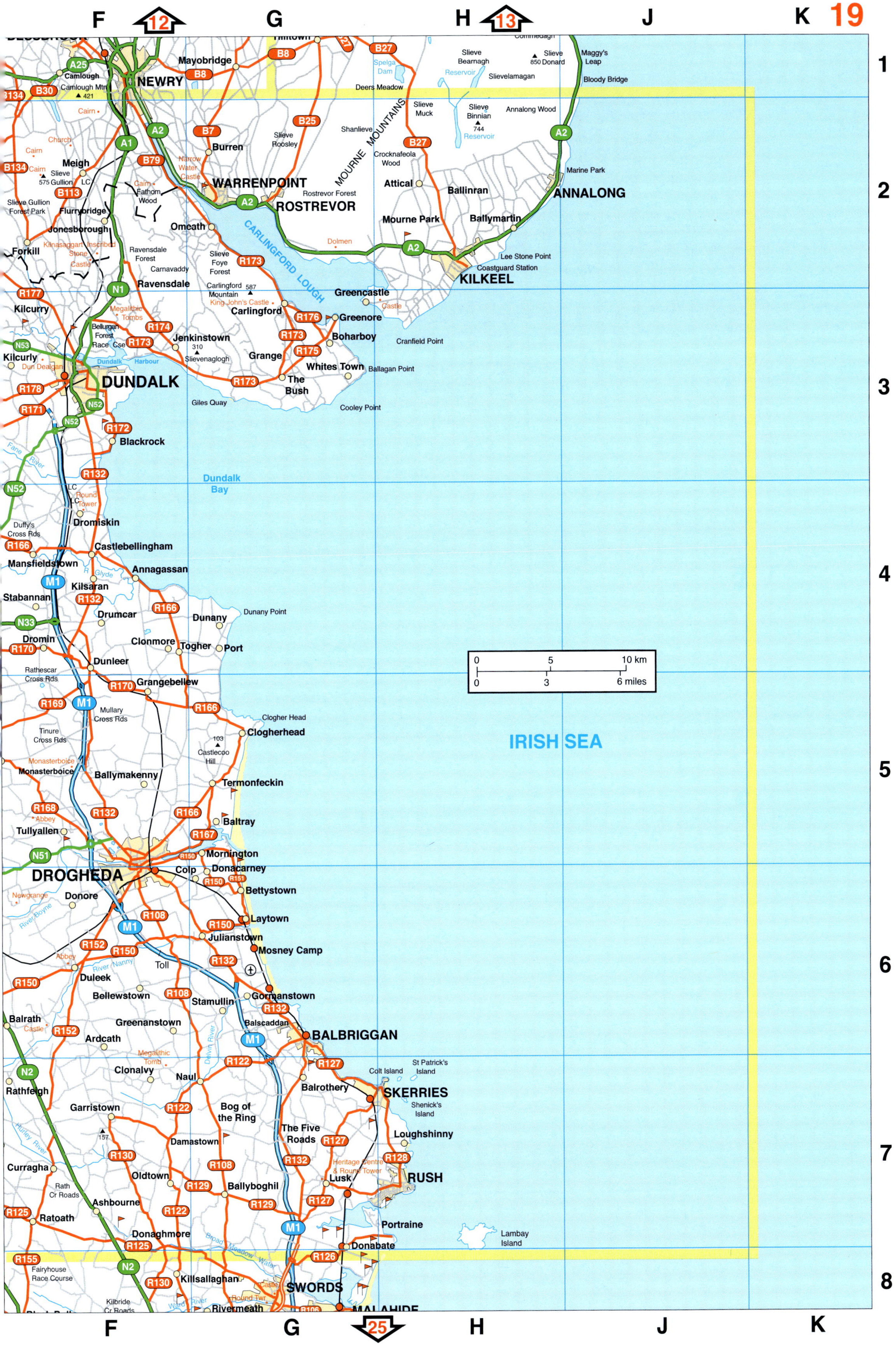
F
12
G
H
13
J
K
1
2
3
4
5
6
7
8
NEWRY
Camlough
Camlough Mtn
421
Mayobridge
Slieve Bearnagh
Slieve Donard
850
Maggy's Leap
Bloody Bridge
Spelga Dam
Reservoir
Slievelamagan
Deers Meadow
Slieve Muck
Slieve Binnian
744
Annalong Wood
Reservoir
Cairn
Church
Cairn
Meigh
Cairn
Slieve Gullion
575
LC
Slieve Gullion Forest Park
Flurrybridge
Jonesborough
Forkill
Kilnasaggart Inscribed Stone
Castle
Narrow Water Castle
Burren
Slieve Roosley
Shanlieve
MOURNE MOUNTAINS
Crocknafeola Wood
Cairn
Fathom Wood
WARRENPOINT
ROSTREVOR
Rostrevor Forest
Attical
Ballinran
Marine Park
ANNALONG
Omeath
Mourne Park
Ballymartin
Dolmen
Ravensdale Forest
Carnavaddy
Slieve Foye Forest
CARLINGFORD LOUGH
Lee Stone Point
Coastguard Station
KILKEEL
Ravensdale
Carlingford Mountain
587
King John's Castle
Carlingford
Greencastle
Castle
Greenore
Kilcurry
Megalithic Tombs
Bellurgan Forest
Race Cse
Jenkinstown
310
Slievenagloghy
Boharboy
Cranfield Point
Grange
Kilcurly
Dun Dealgan
Dundalk Harbour
DUNDALK
Whites Town
Ballagan Point
The Bush
Giles Quay
Cooley Point
Blackrock
Fane River
Dundalk Bay
LC
Round Tower
Dromiskin
Duffy's Cross Rds
Castlebellingham
Mansfieldstown
R Glyde
Annagassan
Kilsaran
Stabannan
Drumcar
Dunany
Dunany Point
Dromin
Clonmore
Togher
Port
Dunleer
Rathescar Cross Rds
Grangebellew
Mullary Cross Rds
Tinure Cross Rds
Clogher Head
Clogherhead
103
Castlecoo Hill
Monasterboice
Monasterboice
Ballymakenny
Termonfeckin
Abbey
Tullyallen
Baltray
Mornington
DROGHEDA
Colp
Donacarney
Bettystown
Newgrange
Donore
River Boyne
Laytown
Julianstown
Mosney Camp
Abbey
River Nanny
Toll
Duleek
Bellewstown
Stamullin
Gormanstown
Balrath
Castle
Greenanstown
Balscaddan
Ardcath
BALBRIGGAN
Megalithic Tomb
Delvin River
Clonalvy
Naul
Colt Island
St Patrick's Island
Rathfeigh
Balrothery
SKERRIES
Shenick's Island
Garristown
Bog of the Ring
The Five Roads
Hurley River
157
Damastown
Loughshinny
Curragha
Oldtown
Heritage Centre & Round Tower
Lusk
RUSH
Rath Cr Roads
Ballyboghil
Ashbourne
Ratoath
Portraine
Lambay Island
Donaghmore
Broad Meadow Water
Donabate
Fairyhouse Race Course
Killsallaghan
Castle
SWORDS
Kilbride Cr Roads
Ward River
Round Twr
Rivermeath
MALAHIDE
IRISH SEA
0
5
10 km
0
3
6 miles
A1
A2
A25
B7
B8
B25
B27
B30
B79
B113
B134
N1
N2
N33
N51
N52
N53
M1
R108
R122
R125
R126
R127
R128
R129
R130
R132
R150
R151
R152
R155
R166
R167
R168
R169
R170
R171
R172
R173
R174
R175
R176
R177
R178
F
G
25
H
J
K

20

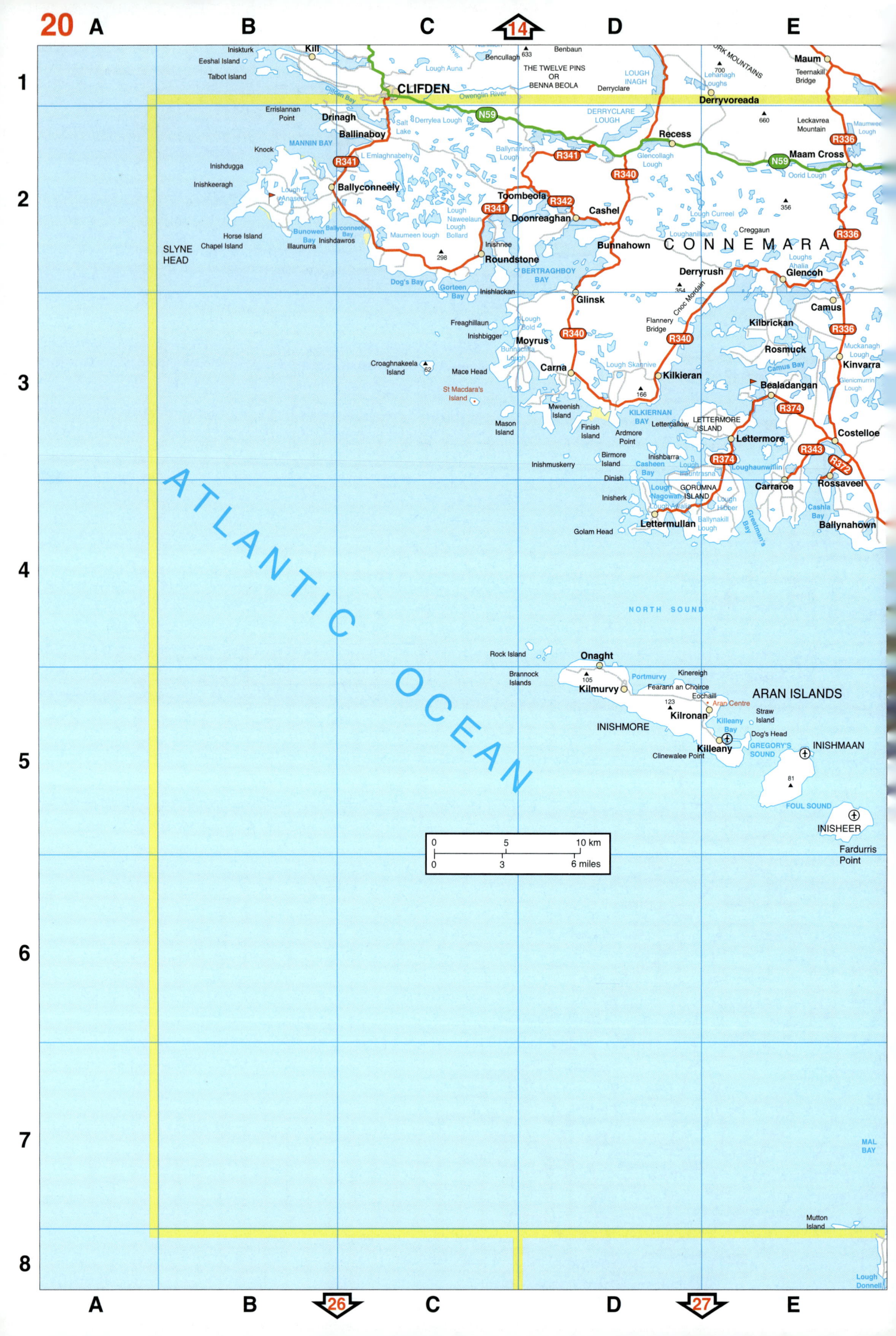

Map grid reference: A B C D E / 1–8

Grid C1 / D1 area (Connemara north):
- Iniskturk
- Eeshal Island
- Talbot Island
- Kill
- Lough Auna
- Benbaun 633
- Bencullagh
- THE TWELVE PINS OR BENNA BEOLA
- LOUGH INAGH
- Lehanagh Loughs 700
- ORK MOUNTAINS
- Maum
- Teernakill Bridge
- ↑ 14

Row 1–2:
- Errislannan Point
- Drinagh
- CLIFDEN
- Clifden Bay
- Owenglin River
- Derryclare
- Derryvoreada
- Ballinaboy
- Salt Lake
- Derrylea Lough
- N59
- DERRYCLARE LOUGH
- Recess
- Leckavrea Mountain 660
- Maumwee Lough
- R336
- Knock
- MANNIN BAY
- L Emlaghnabehy
- Ballynahinch Lough
- R341
- Glencoghlagh Lough
- Maam Cross
- N59
- Oorid Lough
- Inishdugga
- Inishkeeragh
- Ballyconneely
- Lough Anaserd
- Lough Naweelaun
- Toombeola
- R342
- R340
- Cashel
- Lough Curreel
- 356

Row 2–3:
- Horse Island
- Chapel Island
- SLYNE HEAD
- Bunowen Bay
- Ballyconneely Bay
- Inishdawros
- Maumeen Lough Bollard
- Illaunurra
- Doonreaghan
- Inishnee
- 298
- Roundstone
- Dog's Bay
- Gorteen Bay
- Inishlackan
- BERTRAGHBOY BAY
- Bunnahown
- Derryrush
- CONNEMARA
- Loughs Ahalia
- Glencoh
- Creggaun
- R336
- Freaghillaun
- Inishbigger
- Lough Bold
- Moyrus
- Bunnaclina Lough
- Glinsk
- Flannery Bridge
- Cnoc Mordan 354
- Kilbrickan
- Rosmuck
- Camus
- Muckanagh Lough
- Camus Bay
- Kinvarra
- R336
- Croaghnakeela Island 62
- Mace Head
- St Macdara's Island
- Carna
- R340
- Lough Skannive
- 166
- Kilkieran
- Bealadangan
- Glenicmurrin Lough
- R374
- Costelloe

Row 3–4:
- Mweenish Island
- Mason Island
- Finish Island
- Ardmore Point
- Lettercallow
- LETTERMORE ISLAND
- Lettermore
- R343
- R372
- Rossaveel
- Inishmuskerry
- Inishbarra
- Birmore Island
- Casheen Bay
- Lough Illaunirasna
- R374
- Loughaunwillin
- Dinish
- Inisherk
- Lough Nagowan
- GORUMNA ISLAND
- Lough Hibber
- Carraroe
- Cashla Bay
- Ballynakill Lough
- Lough Awalia
- Lettermullan
- Greatman's Bay
- Ballynahown
- Golam Head

ATLANTIC OCEAN

NORTH SOUND

Row 5 — Aran Islands:
- Rock Island
- Brannock Islands
- Onaght
- Kineragh
- Portmurvy
- Fearann an Choirce
- Eochaill
- ARAN ISLANDS
- Kilmurvy 105
- Aran Centre 123
- Kilronan
- Straw Island
- INISHMORE
- Killeany
- Killeany Bay
- Dog's Head
- Clinewalee Point
- GREGORY'S SOUND
- INISHMAAN
- 81
- FOUL SOUND
- INISHEER
- Fardurris Point

Scale: 0 — 5 — 10 km / 0 — 3 — 6 miles

Row 7–8:
- MAL BAY
- Mutton Island
- Lough Donnell

↓ 26   ↓ 27

15
F G H J K
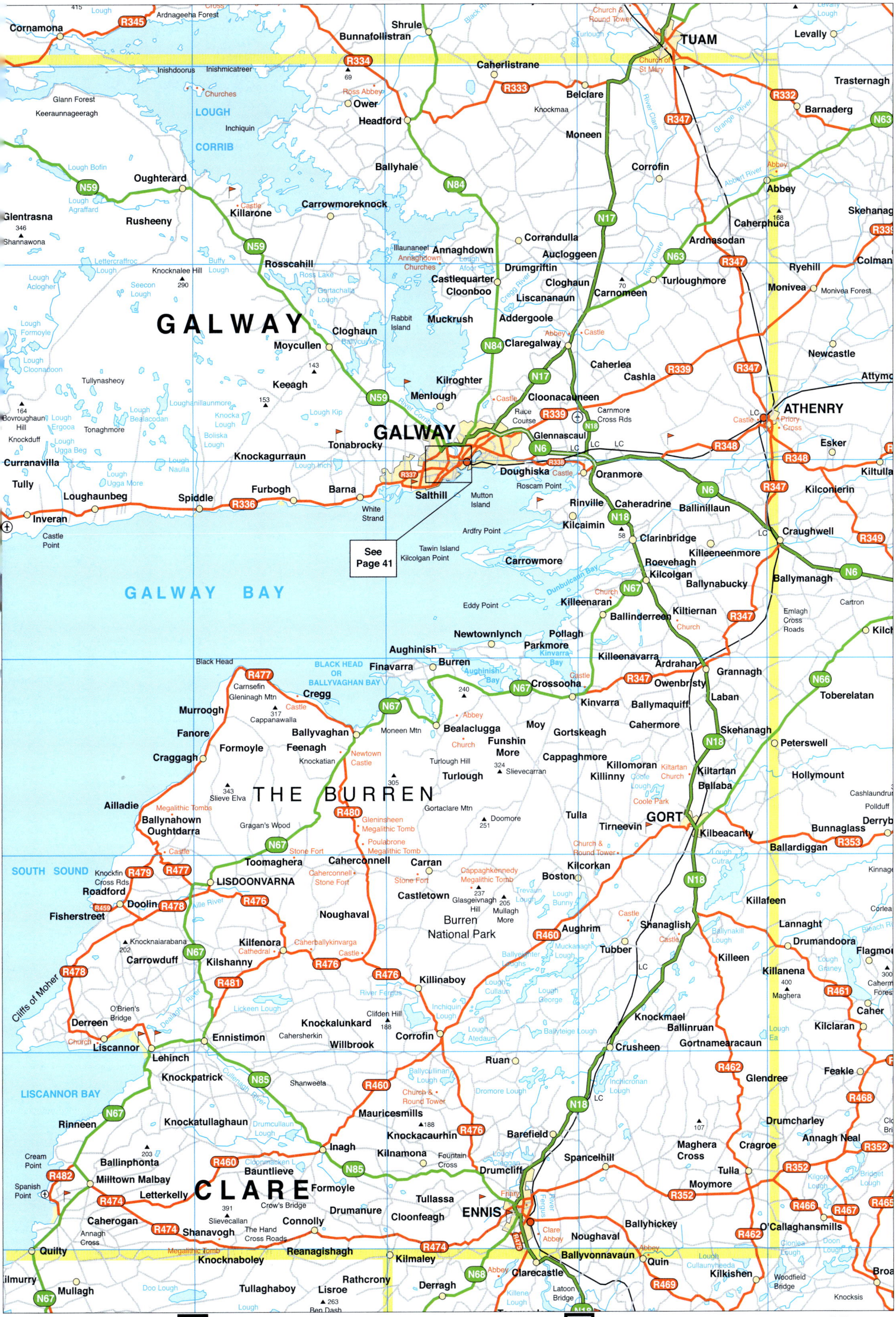

1 2 3 4 5 6 7 8
22
F G H J K
27 28

A B C D E

16

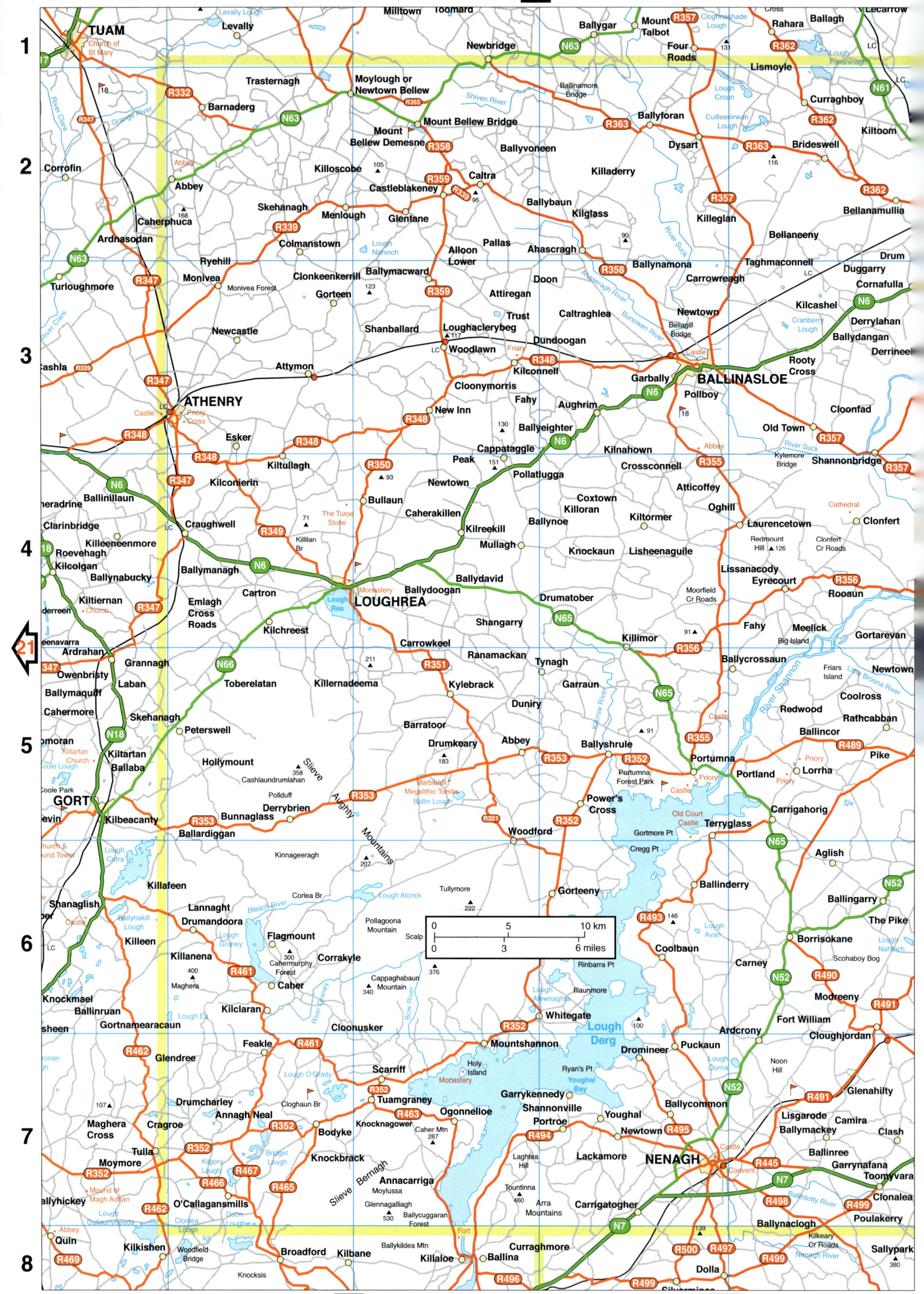

21

28

29

A B C D E

17

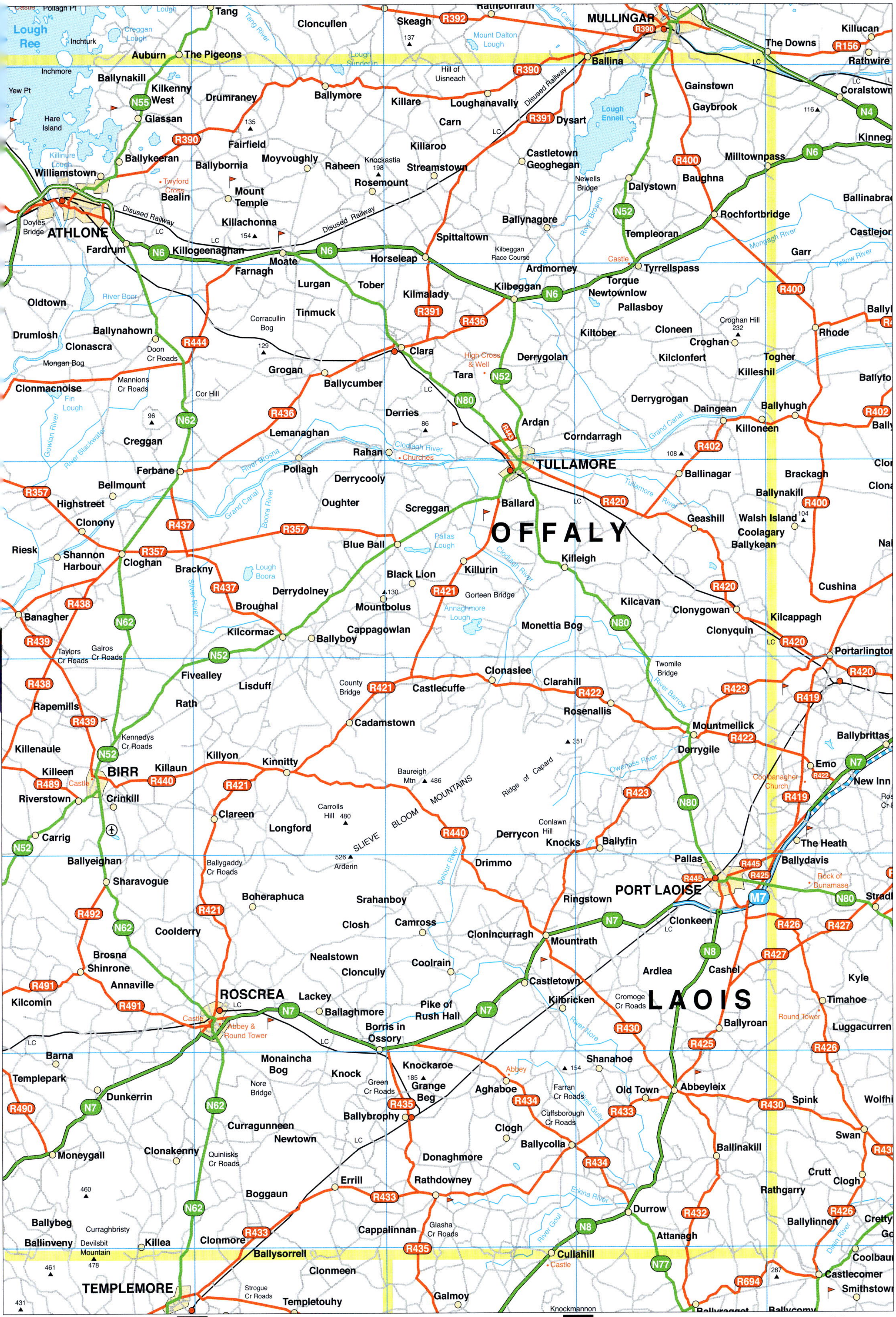
F
G
H
J
K
1
2
3
4
5
6
7
8
Lough Ree
Pollagh Pt
Lough
Tang
Cloncullen
Skeagh
R392
Rathconrath
MULLINGAR
R390
Killucan
Creggan Lough
Inchturk
Tang River
137
Mount Dalton Lough
The Downs
R156
Auburn
The Pigeons
Lough Sunderlin
Ballina
LC
Rathwire
Inchmore
Hill of Uisneach
R390
Gainstown
Coralstown
Ballynakill
Kilkenny West
Ballymore
Killare
Loughanavally
Disused Railway
Yew Pt
N55
Drumraney
Gaybrook
Hare Island
Glassan
135
Carn
R391
Dysart
Lough Ennell
116
N4
R390
Fairfield
Killaroo
Kinnegad
Killinure Lough
Ballykeeran
Moyvoughly
Knockastia 198
Raheen
Streamstown
Castletown Geoghegan
R400
Milltownpass
N6
Williamstown
Ballybornia
Rosemount
Twyford Cross
Newells Bridge
Dalystown
Baughna
Mount Temple
Bealin
Ballinabrack
Disused Railway
Doyles Bridge
ATHLONE
Killachonna
Ballynagore
River Brosna
N52
Rochfortbridge
154
Disused Railway
Castlejordan
LC
Fardrum
N6
Killogeenaghan
Spittaltown
Templeoran
Mongagh River
Moate
N6
Horseleap
Kilbeggan Race Course
Castle
Garr
Farnagh
Ardmorney
Tyrrellspass
Yellow River
Oldtown
River Boor
Lurgan
Tober
Kilbeggan
N6
Torque
R400
Kilmalady
Newtownlow
Tinmuck
R391
Pallasboy
Ballyboy
Ballynahown
Corracullin Bog
R436
Croghan Hill 232
Drumlosh
Kiltober
Cloneen
Rhode
Clonascra
Doon Cr Roads
R444
129
Clara
Croghan
Mongan Bog
High Cross & Well
Derrygolan
Kilclonfert
Togher
Grogan
Tara
N52
Killeshil
Clonmacnoise
Mannions Cr Roads
Ballycumber
Ballyfore
Fin Lough
Cor Hill
LC
N80
Derrygrogan
Ballyhugh
96
N62
R436
Derries
Ardan
Daingean
R402
Gowlan River
Lemanaghan
86
Corndarragh
Grand Canal
Killoneen
Bally
River Blackwater
Creggan
R443
R402
Rahan
Clodiagh River
Churches
108
Ferbane
River Brosna
Pollagh
TULLAMORE
Ballinagar
Brackagh
Clon
Bellmount
Derrycooly
Tullamore River
Clona
R357
Highstreet
Grand Canal
Boora River
Oughter
Screggan
Ballard
LC
R420
Ballynakill
R400
Clonony
R437
R357
Geashill
Walsh Island
104
Coolagary
Ballykean
Riesk
Shannon Harbour
R357
Cloghan
Blue Ball
Pallas Lough
OFFALY
Nal
Brackny
Lough Boora
Killeigh
Killurin
Clodiagh River
R438
R437
Derrydolney
Black Lion
R421
Gorteen Bridge
R420
Cushina
Banagher
Broughal
130
Silver River
Mountbolus
Annaghmore Lough
Kilcavan
Clonygowan
Kilcappagh
N62
Kilcormac
Cappagowlan
Monettia Bog
N80
Clonyquin
R439
Taylors Cr Roads
Galros Cr Roads
Ballyboy
LC
R420
Portarlington
N52
Fivealley
Clonaslee
Twomile Bridge
R420
R438
Lisduff
County Bridge
R421
Castlecuffe
Clarahill
R422
River Barrow
R423
R419
Rath
Rosenallis
Rapemills
R439
Cadamstown
Mountmellick
Ballybrittas
Kennedys Cr Roads
351
R422
Killenaule
Killyon
Derrygile
Owenass River
N52
Kinnitty
Emo
N7
Killeen
BIRR
Killaun
Ridge of Capard
R422
New Inn
R489
Castle
R440
Baureigh Mtn 486
Coolbanagher Church
Riverstown
Crinkill
R421
MOUNTAINS
R423
R419
Ros Cr R
Clareen
Carrolls Hill 480
BLOOM
N80
Carrig
Longford
SLIEVE
Conlawn Hill
The Heath
N52
R440
Derrycon
Knocks
Ballyfin
Ballyeighan
526
Arderin
Delour River
Drimmo
Pallas
Ballydavis
R445
Ballygaddy Cr Roads
R445
R425
Rock of Dunamase
Sharavogue
Boheraphuca
Srahanboy
Ringstown
PORT LAOISE
M7
N80
Stradbally
R492
R421
N7
Clonkeen
LC
Closh
Camross
Clonincurragh
R426
R427
N62
Coolderry
Mountrath
N8
Brosna
Nealstown
Coolrain
R427
Shinrone
Ardlea
Cashel
Kyle
Cloncully
Annaville
Castletown
R491
ROSCREA
Lackey
Pike of Rush Hall
Cromoge Cr Roads
LAOIS
Timahoe
Kilcomin
LC
Kilbricken
R491
Castle
N7
Ballaghmore
N7
River Nore
Round Tower
Abbey & Round Tower
Ballyroan
Borris in Ossory
R430
Luggacurren
LC
LC
R425
R426
Barna
Monaincha Bog
Knockaroe
Shanahoe
154
Abbey
Templepark
Knock
185
Nore Bridge
Green Cr Roads
Grange Beg
Aghaboe
Farran Cr Roads
Old Town
Abbeyleix
Dunkerrin
R434
River Gully
Spink
Wolfhill
R490
N7
N62
R435
R433
R430
Cuffsborough Cr Roads
Curragunneen
Ballybrophy
Clogh
Newtown
LC
Ballycolla
Swan
Moneygall
Clonakenny
Ballinakill
R430
Quinlisks Cr Roads
Donaghmore
R434
Crutt
460
Erkina River
Clogh
Erriill
Rathdowney
Rathgarry
N62
Boggaun
R433
R432
Durrow
R426
Ballybeg
Curraghbristy
Glasha Cr Roads
River Goul
Ballylinnen
Cretty
Ballinveny
Devilsbit Mountain 478
Killea
Clonmore
R433
Cappalinnan
N8
Attanagh
Dinin River
Go
R435
Cullahill
Coolbaun
461
Ballysorrell
Castle
N77
287
Clonmeen
R694
Castlecomer
TEMPLEMORE
Strogue Cr Roads
Smithstown
431
Templetouhy
Galmoy
Knockmannon
Ballyragget
Ballycomy

24
29
30

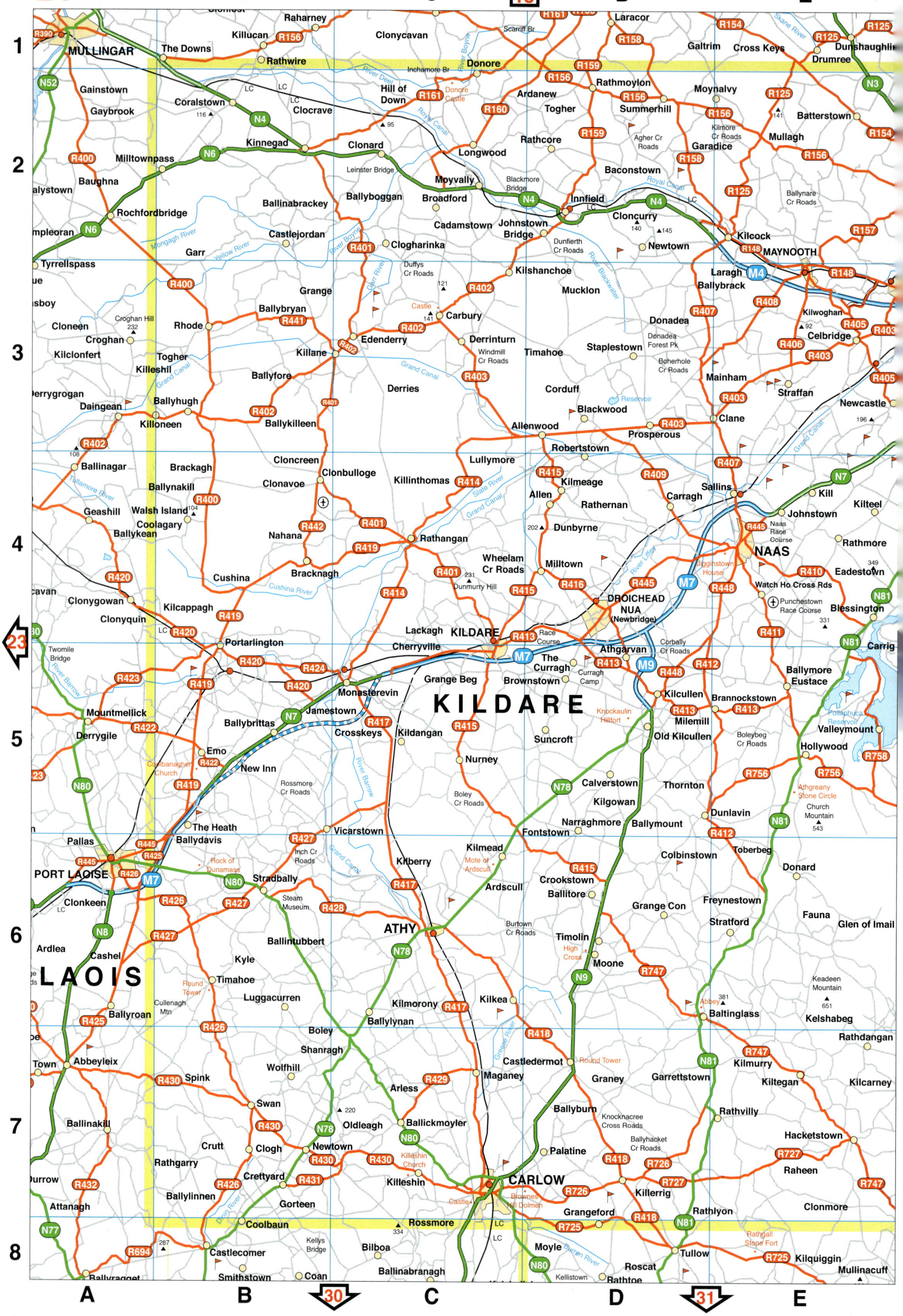
MULLINGAR
The Downs
Killucan
Raharney
Rathwire
Clonycavan
Donore
Laracor
Galtrim
Cross Keys
Dunshaughlin
Drumree
Gainstown
Gaybrook
Coralstown
Clocrave
Hill of Down
Ardanew
Togher
Rathmoylon
Summerhill
Moynalvy
Batterstown
Mullagh
Kinnegad
Clonard
Longwood
Rathcore
Garadice
Milltownpass
Baughna
Moyvally
Broadford
Baconstown
Innfield
Cloncurry
Kilcock
MAYNOOTH
Rochfordbridge
Ballinabrackey
Ballyboggan
Cadamstown
Johnstown Bridge
Newtown
Castlejordan
Clogharinka
Tyrrellspass
Garr
Kilshanchoe
Mucklon
Laragh
Ballybrack
Grange
Ballybryan
Carbury
Donadea
Celbridge
Cloneen
Croghan
Rhode
Kilclonfert
Togher
Killeshil
Killane
Edenderry
Derrinturn
Timahoe
Staplestown
Mainham
Straffan
Ballyfore
Derries
Corduff
Newcastle
Daingean
Ballyhugh
Killoneen
Ballykilleen
Allenwood
Blackwood
Prosperous
Clane
Ballinagar
Brackagh
Cloncreen
Clonbulloge
Lullymore
Robertstown
Clonavoe
Killinthomas
Kilmeage
Allen
Rathernan
Carragh
Sallins
Kill
Kilteel
Johnstown
Ballynakill
Geashill
Walsh Island
Coolagary
Ballykean
Nahana
Rathangan
Dunbyrne
NAAS
Rathmore
Cushina
Bracknagh
Wheelam Cr Roads
Milltown
Eadestown
Clonygowan
Clonyquin
Kilcappagh
DROICHEAD NUA (Newbridge)
Blessington
Portarlington
Lackagh
KILDARE
Cherryville
The Curragh
Athgarvan
Grange Beg
Brownstown
Kilcullen
Ballymore Eustace
Monasterevin
Jamestown
KILDARE
Brannockstown
Mountmellick
Derrygile
Ballybrittas
Crosskeys
Kildangan
Suncroft
Milemill
Old Kilcullen
Valleymount
Emo
Hollywood
New Inn
Nurney
Calverstown
Thornton
Kilgowan
The Heath
Ballydavis
Narraghmore
Ballymount
Dunlavin
Fontstown
Vicarstown
Pallas
Kilmead
Toberbeg
PORT LAOISE
Kilberry
Ardscull
Colbinstown
Donard
Clonkeen
Stradbally
Crookstown
Ballitore
Grange Con
Freynestown
Fauna
Stratford
Glen of Imail
ATHY
Ardlea
Cashel
Ballintubbert
Timolin
Moone
LAOIS
Kyle
Timahoe
Luggacurren
Kilmorony
Kilkea
Baltinglass
Ballyroan
Ballylynan
Kelshabeg
Boley
Rathdangan
Shanragh
Castledermot
Kilmurry
Abbeyleix
Spink
Wolfhill
Maganey
Graney
Garrettstown
Kiltegan
Kilcarney
Arless
Swan
Oldleagh
Ballickmoyler
Ballyburn
Rathvilly
Ballinakill
Crutt
Rathgarry
Clogh
Newtown
Palatine
Hacketstown
Crettyard
Killeshin
CARLOW
Killerrig
Raheen
Ballylinnen
Gorteen
Attanagh
Grangeford
Rathlyon
Clonmore
Coolbaun
Rossmore
Castlecomer
Bilboa
Moyle
Tullow
Kilquiggin
Mullinacuff
Ballinabranagh
Roscat
Rathtoe
Smithstown
Coan
Ballyragget
18
23
30
31

F
G
19
H
J
K
1
2
3
4
5
6
7
8
31
Ashbourne
Ratoath
Donaghmore
Fairyhouse Race Course
Killsallaghan
Black Bull
Kilbride Cr Roads
Nuttstown Cr Roads
Dunboyne
Clonee
Ward
St Margarets
Rivermeath
Dublin Airport
Portraine
Donabate
Lambay Island
SWORDS
MALAHIDE
PORTMARNOCK
Cloghran
Kinsaley
Carrigeen Bay
Ireland's Eye
Santry
Coolock
HOWTH
St Mary's Abbey
169
Drumleck Point
MULHUDDART
BLANCHARDSTOWN
Clonsilla
Observatory
Castleknock
LEIXLIP
Phoenix Park
Palmerstown
LUCAN
CLONDALKIN
Milltown
Casement Aerodrome
Round Tower
Rathcoole
Saggart
TALLAGHT
Clontarf
Dollymount
Car Ferry
Dublin Bay
See Pages 36 & 37
Isle of Man
Holyhead Liverpool
Holyhead
DUBLIN
Blackrock
DUN LAOGHAIRE
Car Ferry
Scotsmans Bay
DALKEY
Castles
Church
Dalkey Island
Dundrum
Stillorgan
Ballyboden
Sandyford
Leopardstown Race Course
Open 2005
Stepaside
Kilmashogue Wood
Carrickmines
Golden Ball
Killiney
Killiney Bay
Ballybrack Megalithic Tomb
Slieve Thoul Wood
395
Knockannavea
Brittas
Tibradden Forest
Ticknock Forest
Cruagh Wood
Kiltiernan
Shankill
The Scalp
Glencullen
647
Corrig Mountain
Kilbride
Glencree
Kilmalin
Enniskerry
BRAY
Lough Bray Lower
752
Kippure
Lough Bray Upper
Knockree
342
Megalithic Tomb
Glencree River
Dargle R
Reservoir
River Liffey
Source of the Liffey
Crone Forest
Kilmacanogue
Great Sugar Loaf
501
Kindlestown Forest
GREYSTONES
0
5
10 km
0
3
6 miles
Lackan
Sorrell Hill
600
Sally Gap
Djouce Woods
Djouce Mountain
724
Glen of the Downs
Delgany
Gravale
Duff Hill
Lough Tay
Ballinastoe Forest
Carriggower
Kilpedder
Kilcoole
Moanbane
847
847
Mullaghcleevaun
847
Ballyknockan
Glendarragh
Newtown Mt. Kennedy
Sraghmore
Vartry Reservoir
365
Leamore Strand
Togher
Wicklow Mountain National Park
Lough Dan
Roundwood
Newcastle
Lough Ouler
Granabeg
816
Tonelagee
Wicklow Gap
Ballyduff Cr Roads
Killiskey
Reservoir
Three Lakes
Lough Mananagan
699
Table Mountain
Annamoe
Vartry River
Brockagh
Glendalough Upper Lough
Round Tower
Laragh
Ballycullen
Ashford
Ballinalea
Broad Lough
Rathnew
WICKLOW
Carrick Mountain
380
Glenealy
Mullacor
Glenmalur
Wicklow Head
200
Lugnaquilla Mountain
924
Kellys Lough
457
WICKLOW
Kilbride
Ardmore Point
Rathdrum
392
Slieveboy Mtn
Aghavannagh
Croaghanmoira Mountain
662
Greenan
271
Rockstown
Ballinaclash
Avondale Forest Pk
Redcross
Kilcarney Cr Roads
Cushbawn
400
Meeting of the Waters
VALE
Jack Whites Cr Roads
Brittas Bay
Knockananna
Crafield
Three Wells
Askanagap
Moyne
Avoca
Mizen Head
Aughrim
Ballymoyle
AVOCA
Annacurragh
Johnstown
Ballinglen
Woodenbridge
Derry River
Avoca River
Bridgeland
Ferrybank
Tinahely
Curraghlawn
605
Croghan Mountain
ARKLOW
Johnstown
M1
M50
N1
N2
N3
N4
N7
N11
N31
N32
N81
N82
M11
R106
R107
R108
R115
R116
R117
R125
R750
R752
R755
R761

26

ATLANTIC OCEAN

Loop Head area (E4): Ross Bay, Moneen, Kilbaha, R487, LOOP HEAD, Dunmore Head

Kerry Head area (E5): Dreenagh, Tiduff, 216 Maulin Mountain, Glenderry, BALLYHEIGE BAY

Coastal features (E6): Black Rock, Banna Strand, Carrahane Strand, Barrow, Barrow Harb, Fenit, TRALEE BAY

Dingle Peninsula (C6–E8):
- Magharee Islands, Rough Point, Kilshannig, Fahamore
- BRANDON HEAD, BRANDON BAY, Brandon Point, Knockdeelea ▲310, Lisnakealwee, Masatiompan ▲762, Beennaman, Brandon, Caher Point, Teer, Ballyquin, Trench Bridge, Lough Gill, Castlegregory
- Pointagare, Cloonsharragh, Cloghane, Drom, Kilcummin, Stradbally, Killiney, Tullaree, Aughacasla, Carrigagharoe Point, R560
- Ballydavid Head 250, Ballyroe, Feohanagh, Brandon Mountain ▲950, Brandon Peak 840, Ballyduff, Stradbally Mountain ▲824, Carrigaday, Lough Acummeen, Camp
- Glashbeg, Kilquane, Ballinloghig, Lough Gal, Lough Crutta, Lough Adoon, Beenoskee ▲486, Lough Caum, Lough Slat, Cummeen 478, Knockbeg, Corrin 331, Gearhane, Baurtregaun
- Smerwick, Smerwick Harbour, Ballydavid, Ballysitteragh 622, Conair, Slievenagower ▲615, Araglen Forest, Lough Anscaul, Knocknakilton, N86 379, Knockbrack, Cahercontree, Moanlaur, ▲584 Caherbla 566
- Sybil Head, Murreagh, Ballinrannig, Gallarus Oratory, Kinnalkedar, Slievanea, Knockmoylemore, Flemingsown, Lougher, Aughils
- Sybil Point, Ballyferriter, Ballynana, Ballybowler, Lisdargan, Coumduff, Annagap, Brickany 374, Caheracruttera
- Clogher Head, R559, Teeravane, Ballineanig, R559, Knockavrogeen, Milltown, DINGLE, N86, Lispole, Anascaul, Inch, R561, CASTLEMAINE HARBOUR
- 172 Inishtooskert, Dunquin, Kildurrihy, Ventry, Dingle Harbour, Aglish
- The Blasket Centre, Mount Eagle ▲514, Ballymacadoyle Hill, Doonmanagh, 284 Red Cliff, Cromane Point
- Beginish, Beenacouma, Fahan, Ventry Harbour, Parkmore Point, Reenbeg Point, Bull's Head, Minard Head, Gubranna, Acres Point, Inch Point, Cromane, Tullig, Knockaunnaglashv
- Garraun Point, 290, SLEA HEAD, Cloghans, Dunbeg Fort
- GREAT BLASKET ISLAND, BLASKET SOUND

Scale: 0–10 km / 0–6 miles

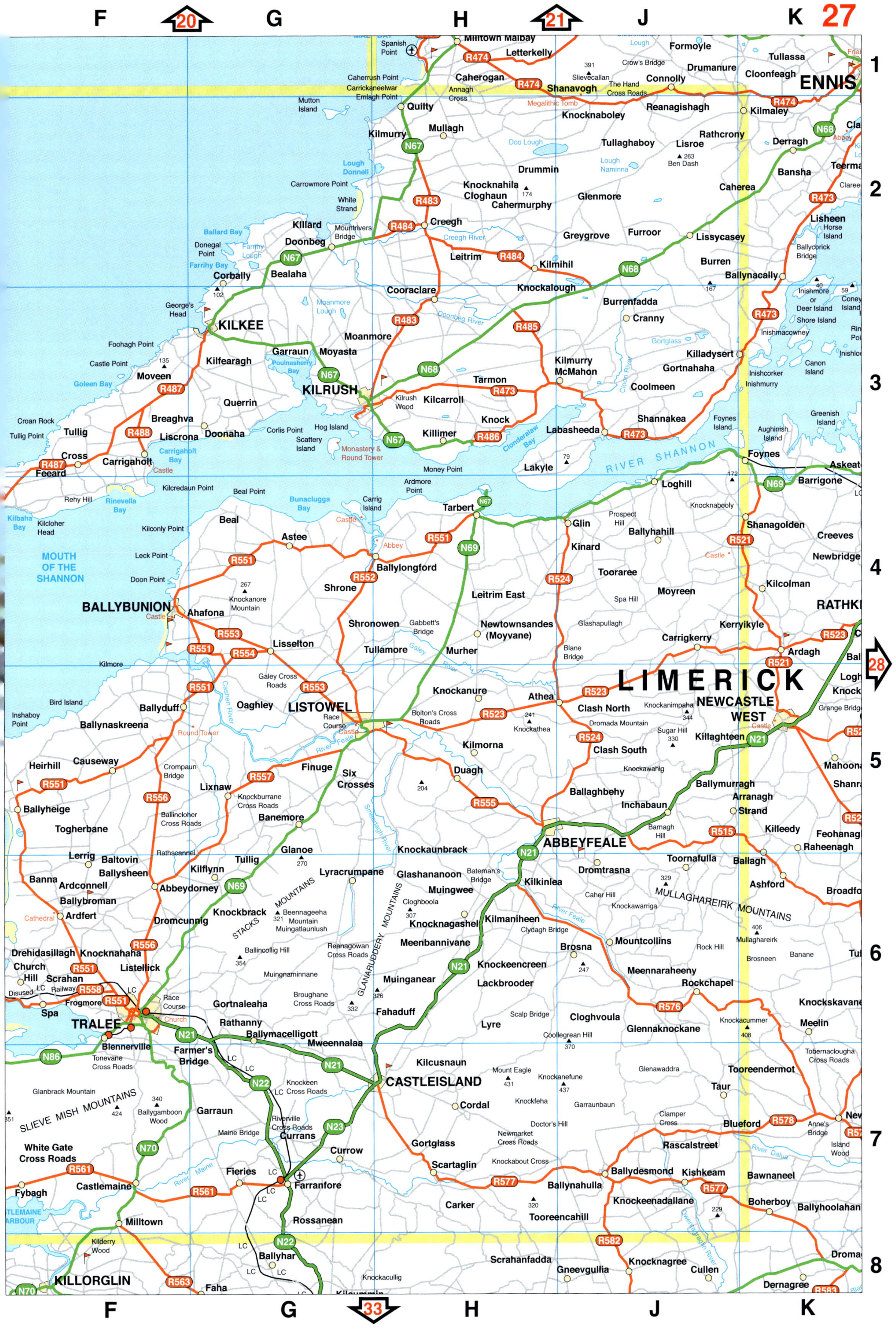
F
20
G
H
21
J
K
1
2
3
4
5
6
7
8
28
33
LIMERICK
Spanish Point
Milltown Malbay
R474
Letterkelly
Formoyle
Lough
Tullassa
Cahercrush Point
Carrickaneelwar
Emlagh Point
Caherogan
Annagh Cross
Shanavogh
Megalithic Tomb
391
Slievecallan
Crow's Bridge
The Hand Cross Roads
Connolly
Drumanure
Cloonfeagh
ENNIS
Mutton Island
Quilty
Knocknaboley
Reanagishagh
R474
Kilmaley
Kilmurry
Mullagh
N67
Doo Lough
Tullaghaboy
Lisroe
Rathcrony
263
Ben Dash
N68
Derragh
Abbey
Lough Donnell
Lough Naminna
Drummin
Bansha
Teerma
Carrowmore Point
Knocknahila
Cloghaun
174
Cahermurphy
Glenmore
Caherea
R473
White Strand
R483
Creegh
Creegh River
Greygrove
Furroor
Lissycasey
Lisheen
Horse Island
Ballard Bay
Killard
Mountrivers Bridge
R484
Donegal Point
Farrihy Lough
Doonbeg
Farrihy Bay
N67
Bealaha
Leitrim
R484
Kilmihil
Burren
Ballycorick Bridge
Corbally
102
Cooraclare
Knockalough
N68
Ballynacally
167
Inishmore or Deer Island
59
Coney Island
George's Head
Moanmore Lough
Doonbeg River
Burrenfadda
Cranny
R473
Shore Island
KILKEE
R483
R485
Inishmacowney
Foohagh Point
Moanmore
Gortglass
Killadysert
Inishloe
135
Castle Point
Kilfearagh
Garraun
Moyasta
Poulnasherry Bay
N68
Kilmurry McMahon
Gortnahaha
Canon Island
Moveen
Goleen Bay
R487
N67
KILRUSH
Tarmon
Cloon River
Coolmeen
Inishcorker
Inishmurry
Querrin
Kilrush Wood
Kilcarroll
R473
Breaghva
Knock
Shannakea
Greenish Island
Croan Rock
Doonaha
Hog Island
Labasheeda
Foynes Island
Aughinish Island
Tullig Point
Tullig
R488
Liscrona
Corlis Point
Scattery Island
Killimer
R486
Clonderalaw Bay
R473
Carrigaholt Bay
Monastery & Round Tower
N67
RIVER SHANNON
Foynes
Cross
Carrigaholt
79
Askeaton
R487
Feeard
Castle
Money Point
Lakyle
172
Kilcredaun Point
Ardmore Point
Loghill
N69
Barrigone
Beal Point
Rehy Hill
Rinevella Bay
Bunaclugga Bay
Carrig Island
N67
Tarbert
Knocknabooly
Kilbaha Bay
Kilcloher Head
Beal
Castle
Glin
Prospect Hill
Shanagolden
Kilconly Point
Ballyhahill
Astee
R551
N69
R521
Creeves
MOUTH OF THE SHANNON
Leck Point
Abbey
Kinard
Castle
Newbridge
R551
Ballylongford
Tooraree
Doon Point
R552
R524
Kilcolman
267
Knockanore Mountain
Shrone
Leitrim East
Spa Hill
Moyreen
BALLYBUNION
Castle
Ahafona
RATHK
Shronowen
Gabbett's Bridge
Newtownsandes (Moyvane)
Glashapullagh
Kerryikyle
R553
Lisselton
Tullamore
Galey River
Murher
Blane Bridge
Carrigkerry
R523
R551
R554
Ardagh
R521
Kilmore
Galey Cross Roads
Knockanure
Athea
Bird Island
R551
R553
R523
NEWCASTLE WEST
Grange Bridge
Inshaboy Point
Ballyduff
Oaghley
LISTOWEL
Race Course
Castle
Bolton's Cross Roads
R523
241
Knockathea
Clash North
Knockanimpaha
344
Ballynaskreena
Round Tower
Cashen River
River Feale
Kilmorna
Dromada Mountain
Sugar Hill
330
Castle
R524
Clash South
Killaghteen
N21
Heirhill
Causeway
Crompaun Bridge
R557
Finuge
Six Crosses
Duagh
Knockawahig
Mahoona
R551
Lixnaw
R556
Knockburrane Cross Roads
204
Ballaghbehy
Ballymurragh
Arranagh
Shanra
Ballyheige
Ballincloher Cross Roads
Banemore
R555
Inchabaun
Strand
Togherbane
Smearlagh River
Barnagh Hill
R515
Killeedy
Feohanagh
Raheenagh
Rathscannel
Glanoe
270
Knockaunbrack
ABBEYFEALE
Lerrig
Baltovin
Tullig
Kilflynn
Lyracrumpane
Glashanaoon
Bateman's Bridge
N21
Dromtrasna
Toornafulla
Ballagh
Banna
Ballysheen
MOUNTAINS
Muingwee
Kilkinlea
329
Ashford
Ardconnell
Abbeydorney
N69
Caher Hill
MULLAGHAREIRK MOUNTAINS
Broadfo
Ballybroman
Cloghboola
307
Knockawarriga
Cathedral
Ardfert
Knockbrack
STACKS
Beenageeha
321
Mountain
Muingatlaunlush
Knocknagashel
Kilmaniheen
River Feale
Clydagh Bridge
406
Mullaghareirk
Dromcunnig
GLANARUDDERY MOUNTAINS
Meenbannivane
Brosna
Mountcollins
Drehidasillagh
Knocknahaha
R556
Ballincollig Hill
354
Reanagowan Cross Roads
Rock Hill
Banane
Tul
Church Hill
R551
Listellick
Muingnaminnane
N21
Knockeencreen
247
Brosneen
Scrahan
Disused Railway
LC
R558
Lackbrooder
Meennaraheeny
Rockchapel
Knockskavane
Frogmore
R551
Race Course
Gortnaleaha
Broughane Cross Roads
326
Muinganear
Spa
Church
332
Fahaduff
R576
TRALEE
Rathanny
Lyre
Scalp Bridge
Cloghvoula
Glennaknockane
Knockacummer
408
Meelin
N21
Ballymacelligott
Blennerville
Mweenalaa
Coollegrean Hill
370
Farmer's Bridge
N86
Tonevane Cross Roads
LC
Kilcusnaun
Tobernaclougha Cross Roads
N21
Mount Eagle
Glenawaddra
Tooreendermot
CASTLEISLAND
Knockanefune
Glanbrack Mountain
N22
Knockeen Cross Roads
431
437
Taur
SLIEVE MISH MOUNTAINS
340
Ballygamboon Wood
Garraun
Cordal
Knockfeha
Garraunbaun
351
424
Riverville Cross Roads
Doctor's Hill
Clamper Cross
Blueford
R578
Anne's Bridge
New
Maine Bridge
Currans
N23
Newmarket Cross Roads
White Gate Cross Roads
N70
Gortglass
Rascalstreet
River Dalua
Island Wood
Currow
R561
Fieries
River Maine
Scartaglin
Knockabout Cross
Ballydesmond
Kishkeam
Bawnaneel
Castlemaine
Farranfore
R577
Ballynahulla
R577
Fybagh
R561
Knockeenadallane
Boherboy
Ballyhoolahan
CASTLEMAINE HARBOUR
Carker
320
229
Rossanean
Tooreencahill
Owentaraglin River
Milltown
N22
R582
Droma
Kilderry Wood
Ballyhar
Scrahanfadda
Gneevgullia
Knocknagree
Cullen
KILLORGLIN
R563
Knockacullig
Dernagree
N70
Faha
R583

21 22 27 34

A
B
C
D
E
1
2
3
4
5
6
7
8
Formoyle
Tullassa
Crow's Bridge
Drumanure
Connolly
Cloonfeagh
ENNIS
Friary
Clare Abbey
River Fergus
R352
Moymore
Mound
Ballyhickey
Kilgory Lough
R466
R465
Knockbrack
SLIEVE BERNAGH
Annacarriga
Moylussa
R494
Tountinna
460
ARRA MOUNTAINS
R462
O'Callaghansmills
Glennagalliagh
530
Ballycuggaran Forest
Kilmaley
R474
Reanagishagh
Noughaval
Ballyvonnavaun
Abbey
Quin
Lough Cullaunyheeda
Clonlea Lough
Doon Lough
Woodfield Bridge
Clarecastle
Rathcrony
Derragh
N68
Lisroe
Killene Lough
Latoon Bridge
R469
Kilkishen
Broadford
Kilbane
Ballykildea Mountain
Fort
Curraghmore
Killaloe
Ballina
263
Ben Dash
Teermaclane
Bansha
77
Knocksis
R496
Fort
Fin Lough
Kilmurry
307
Seefin
Knockaphunta
R463
R494
Caherea
Clareen Bridge
N18
Rosroe Lough
Annagore Bridge
Lough Castle
R466
Bridgetown
R473
Lisheen
Horse Island
Lough Gash
Newmarket on Fergus
R470
R471
Oatfield
Kilmore
Cloghera
R465
O'Briensbridge
R466
Birdhill
Furroor
Lissycasey
Ballycorick Bridge
Sixmilebridge
Kilnacreagh
Montpelier
R525
R504
R463
Culleen
Burren
Ballynacally
Clenagh
R472
Hurlers Cross
R471
Ballybroughan
Ballycar
Cloonlara
N68
167
40
Deenish Island
Inishmore or Deer Island
59
Coney Island
Inishmacnaghtan
N19
R462
310
Woodcock Hill
Cratloe Woods
R465
Ardnacrusha
R463
Castleconnell
Newport
Cranny
R473
Shore Island
Feenish
Shannon Airport
SHANNON
Castle
Bunratty
Cratloe
Parteen
See Page 40
Inishmacowney
Rineanna Point
Knockbeagh Point
R464
R463
RIVER SHANNON
N7
R503
Gortglass Lough
Killadysert
Gortnahaha
Inishloe
Carrigkeal
Mellon Point
N18
Battle Island
LIMERICK
Lisnagry
Annagh
Inishcorker
Inishmurry
Canon Island
Wallers Island
Creggaun
Coonagh
N18
Annacotty
Coolmeen
Ballysteen
Pallaskenry
Bleach Lough
Dromore Lough
Castle
N69
Mungret
Barringtonsbridge
Moroe
Shannakea
Foynes Island
Greenish Island
Aughinish Island
Hogan's Bridge
Clarina
Abbey
R510
R509
N7
Boherreen
R506
Abington
Mulkear River
R473
RIVER SHANNON
Foynes
Kilcornan
Oratory
New Kildimo
Routagh Bridge
N24
Ferry Bridge
Boher
172
Friary
N69
Old Kildimo
74
R526
N20
R505
Loghill
N69
Barrigone
Askeaton
Castle
Kilbreedy
Patrickswell
Friarstown
118
Ballyneety
Caherconlish
Currachase Forest Park
Race Course
Kilpeacon Cross Roads
Knocknabooly
R518
Stonepark
204
Kilmurry
R513
Shanagolden
Kilgrogan
Crecora
R511
R512
Ballyhahill
Creeves
Abbey
Adare
Friary
Castle
Cappagh
Priory
N20
R521
Castle
Newbridge
River Deel
Ballingarrane
Ballybrood
Boherroe
Clogh
N21
Croagh
Lough Nagirra
Fedamore
Longford Bridge
Kilcolman
R519
River Maigue
111
Moyreen
R523
RATHKEALE
R523
Round Tower
Croom
Monaster
Abbey
Camog River
R512
Lough Gur
R514
Kilteely
Ballyea
Kerryikyle
Kilfinny
Meanus
Herbertstown
Carrigkerry
R523
Courtmatrix
Holycross
Cromwell Hill
Enniskerry
Ardagh
R518
R519
New Bridge
146
Ballyallinan
R516
R516
R513
LIMERICK
R521
Loghill
Morenane
Knockainy
Knockaderry
213
Ballingarry
286
Bruff
R516
Hospital
R516
Knockanimpaha
344
NEWCASTLE WEST
Grange Bridge
Granagh
Athlacca
Mountain
Cloncagh
R519
R518
Castle
Bottomstown
R513
R515
Sugar Hill
330
Killaghteen
N21
R520
R520
Ballinleeny
Knockdarnan
Dromin
R512
Newtown
South
Mahoonagh
Ballynoe Bridge
Corronoher
R518
Knockawahig
273
Castletown
Rockhill
Bruree
Ballygubba
Elton
Knocklong
Kilmeedy
R518
R513
Ballymurragh
Shanrath
Garryfine
Bulgaden
R515
Arranagh
Ballyagran
Tankardstown
Abbey
Church
Garryspillane
Inchabaun
Strand
R519
Gorteen
Killacolla
Kilmallock
Foley's Cross Roads
Martinstown
R522
Fort Middle
Barnagh Hill
R515
Killeedy
Feohanagh
Broken Bridge
Feenagh
Kilbreedy
Glenbrohane
Raheenagh
Kilmurry
R512
Slievereagh
Toornafulla
Ballagh
R515
Blackpool
Earthworks
329
Charleville
CHARLEVILLE
LC
Kilfinnane
Griston
MULLAGHAREIRK MOUNTAINS
Ashford
Broadford
R515
Milford
Newtownshandrum
R515
Mote
Mortlestown
Thomastown
R515
Graigue Cross Roads
Ardpatrick
406
Mullaghareirk
Dromcolliher
258
R578
Milltown Cross Roads
Garrane Cross Roads
Ballyhaght
Greenwood Forest
528
R517
Glenroe
Rock Hill
Brosneen
Banane
Tullyease
Barrack Cross Roads
R522
Dromina
Carron Mountain
Seefin Mountain
Ballyorgan
Meenaraheeny
R579
R578
Tarrant's Cross Roads
0
5
10 km
0
3
6 miles
445
BALLYHOURA MOUNTAINS
R512
Coolfree Mountain
Knockanevin
Rockchapel
R576
Knockskavane
Glennaknockane
Knockacummer
408
Meelin
Freemount
Churchtown
Glenanaar Forest
Ballyvisteen
246
Castle
Liscarroll
Kilcolman Castle
R578
Tobernaclougha Cross Roads
R522
N20
Ballyguyroe North
Cullenagh
Glenawaddra
Tooreendermot
Bawn Cross Roads
Boherboy Cross Roads
Brough Cross Roads
Kildorrery
Taur
Lismire
Buttevant
Abbey
R522
Kilconnor
Farahy
Ballydeloughy
Clamper Cross
Newmarket
R579
Ballygrady
Turnpike Cross
R522
Rockmills
Blueford
R578
Anne's Bridge
R576
Kilbrin
R580
Shanballymore
Rascalstreet
River Dalua
Island Wood
River Allow
Doneraile
Awbeg River
N73
R512
Ballywalter
Castlecor
Kilmaclenine Cross Roads
R581
New Twopothouse Village
Ballydesmond
Kishkeam
Bawnaneel
Kanturk
Copstown Cross Roads
Old Twopothouse Cross Roads
Skenakilla Cross Roads
Ballydoyle
Scrarour
Knockeenadallane
R577
Boherboy
Ballyhoolahan
Castle
Cecilstown
Castletownroche
Parkacunna
229
Owenkeagh River
R576
Bannagh Cross Roads
Ballyclogh
N20
R579
N72
N72
Inchinapallas
MALLOW
Killavullen
Knocknagree
Dromagh
Banteer
N72
Castle
Glenagear Forest
Ballydague
Ballyhooly
Cullen
N72
Dernagree
R583
Blackwater
Mount Hillary
R621
Race Course
R619
R620
Castleblagh

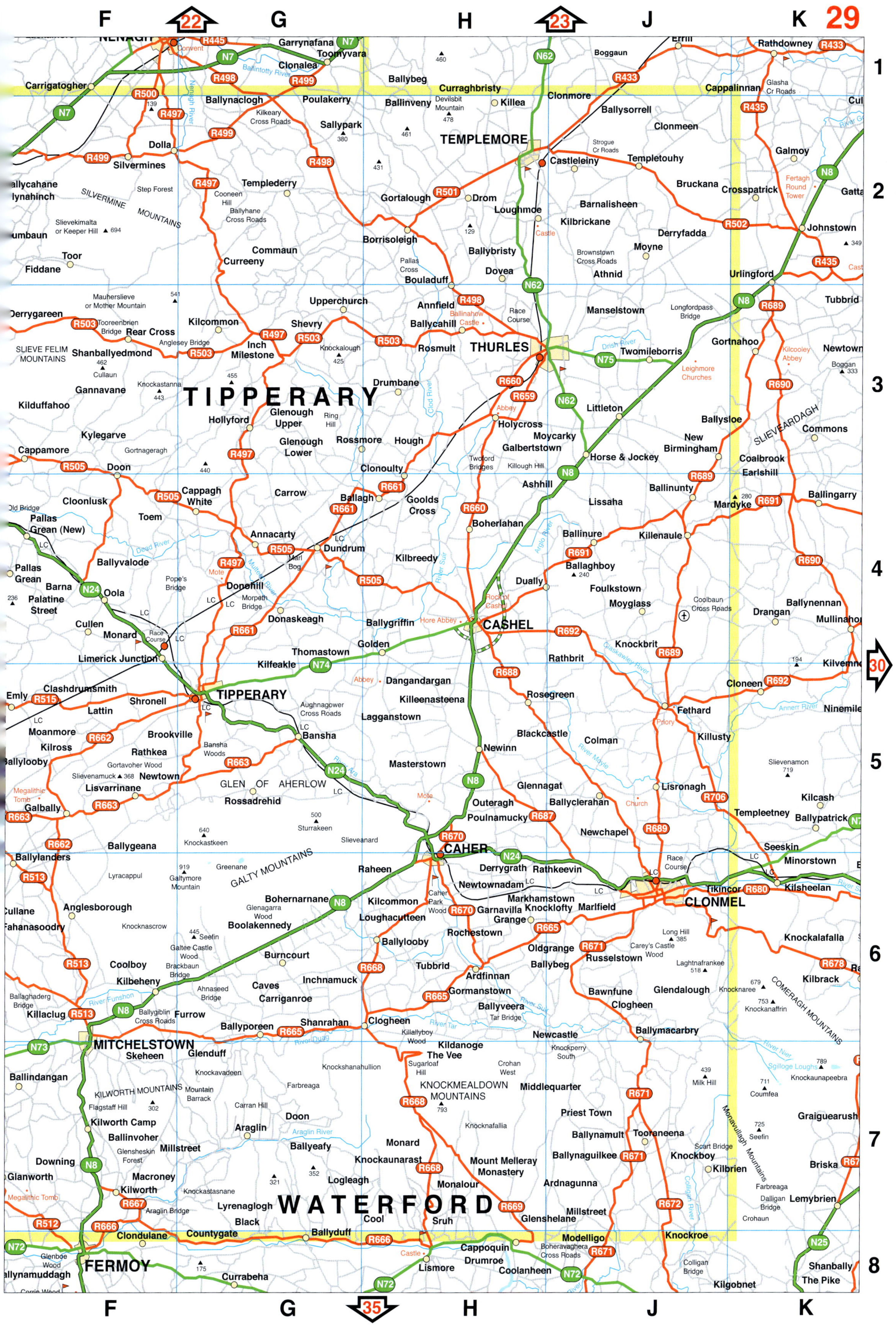

F
22
G
H
23
J
K
1
2
3
4
5
6
7
8
30
35
Garrynafana
Toomyvara
Clonalea
Ballintotty River
Convent
Carrigatogher
Ballynaclogh
Poulakerry
Kilkeary Cross Roads
Sallypark
380
Dolla
Silvermines
Ballybeg
Curraghbristy
Ballinveny
Devilsbit Mountain
478
Killea
Clonmore
Boggaun
Rathdowney
Glasha Cr Roads
Cappalinnan
Ballysorrell
Clonmeen
TEMPLEMORE
Strogue Cr Roads
Castleleiny
Templetouhy
Galmoy
Fertagh Round Tower
Gatta
Johnstown
Crosspatrick
Bruckana
Barnalisheen
Kilbrickane
Derryfadda
Moyne
Brownstown Cross Roads
Athnid
Urlingford
Castle
Loughmoe
Drom
Gortalough
Borrisoleigh
Ballybristy
Dovea
Pallas Cross
Bouladuff
Templederry
Cooneen Hill
Ballyhane Cross Roads
Commaun
Curreeny
SILVERMINE MOUNTAINS
Step Forest
Ballycahane
Glynahinch
Slievekimalta or Keeper Hill
694
Cumbaun
Toor
Fiddane
Mauherslieve or Mother Mountain
541
Derrygareen
Tooreenbrien Bridge
Rear Cross
Kilcommon
Upperchurch
Shevry
Inch
Milestone
Anglesey Bridge
Knockalough
425
Annfield
Ballinahow Castle
Ballycahill
Race Course
Rosmult
THURLES
Manselstown
Longfordpass Bridge
Drish River
Twomileborris
Gortnahoo
Kilcooley Abbey
Tubbrid
Newtown
Boggan
333
Leighmore Churches
SLIEVE FELIM MOUNTAINS
Shanballyedmond
462
Cullaun
Knockastanna
443
455
TIPPERARY
Gannavane
Kilduffahoo
Hollyford
Glenough Upper
Ring Hill
Drumbane
Clodiagh River
Abbey
Holycross
Littleton
Ballysloe
SLIEVEARDAGH
Commons
Kylegarve
Glenough Lower
Rossmore
Hough
Moycarky
Galbertstown
New Birmingham
Coalbrook
Earlshill
Cappamore
Gortnageragh
440
Doon
Clonoulty
Twoford Bridges
Killough Hill
Horse & Jockey
Ashhill
Ballinunty
Mardyke
280
Ballingarry
Old Bridge
Cloonlusk
Cappagh White
Carrow
Ballagh
Goolds Cross
Lissaha
Pallas Grean (New)
Toem
Dead River
Annacarty
Dundrum
Boherlahan
Ballinure
Killenaule
Marl Bog
Kilbreedy
Argid River
Ballaghboy
240
Pallas Grean
Ballyvalode
Mote
Pope's Bridge
Donohill
Morpeth Bridge
Multeen River
River Suir
Dually
Foulkstown
Moyglass
Coolbaun Cross Roads
Drangan
Ballynennan
Mullinahone
Barna
Oola
236
Palatine Street
Cullen
Monard
Race Course
Donaskeagh
Ballygriffin
Hore Abbey
Rock of Cashel
CASHEL
Rathbrit
Knockbrit
Glaskawley River
194
Kilvemnon
Limerick Junction
Thomastown
Golden
Kilfeakle
Emly
Clashdrumsmith
Shronell
Lattin
TIPPERARY
Aughnagower Cross Roads
Bansha
Abbey
Dangandargan
Killeenasteena
Lagganstown
Rosegreen
Cloneen
Fethard
Priory
Anner River
Ninemile
Moanmore
Kilross
Brookville
Rathkea
Bansha Woods
Blackcastle
Colman
River Moyle
Killusty
Ballylooby
Gortavoher Wood
Slievenamuck
368
Newtown
Newinn
Masterstown
River Ara
Slievenamon
719
Megalithic Tomb
Lisvarrinane
GLEN OF AHERLOW
Rossadrehid
Glennagat
Lisronagh
Kilcash
Galbally
Outeragh
Ballyclerahan
Church
Templeeney
Ballypatrick
Poulnamucky
500
Sturrakeen
640
Knockastkeen
Slieveanard
Newchapel
Seeskin
Ballygeana
Ballylanders
CAHER
Race Course
Minorstown
919
Galtymore Mountain
Greenane
GALTY MOUNTAINS
Raheen
Derrygrath
Rathkeevin
Lyracappul
Newtownadam
Kilsheelan
Tikincor
CLONMEL
River Suir
Cullane
Fahanasoodry
Anglesborough
Glenagarra Wood
Bohernarnane
Kilcommon
Caher Park Wood
Markhamstown
Garnavilla
Knocklofty
Marlfield
Grange
Knocknascrow
Boolakennedy
Loughacutteen
Rochestown
445
Seefin
Galtee Castle Wood
Burncourt
Ballylooby
Oldgrange
Russelstown
Carey's Castle Wood
Long Hill
385
Knockalafalla
Laghtnafrankee
518
Coolboy
Tubbrid
Ballybeg
Ardfinnan
Kilbrack
Kilbeheny
Brackbaun Bridge
Caves
Inchnamuck
Gormanstown
Bawnfune
Glendalough
Knocknaree
679
753
Knockanaffrin
COMERAGH MOUNTAINS
Ballaghaderg Bridge
River Funshion
Ahnaseed Bridge
Carriganroe
Ballyveera
River Suir
Tar Bridge
Clogheen
Killaclug
Ballygiblin Cross Roads
Furrow
Ballyporeen
Shanrahan
Clogheen
River Tar
Killallyboy Wood
Newcastle
Ballymacarbry
MITCHELSTOWN
Skeheen
Glenduff
River Duag
Kildanoge
The Vee
Knockperry South
River Nier
789
Sgilloge Loughs
Ballindangan
Knockavadeen
Knockshanahullion
Sugarloaf Hill
Crohan West
439
Milk Hill
711
Coumfea
Knockaunapeebra
KILWORTH MOUNTAINS
Mountain Barrack
Farbreaga
KNOCKMEALDOWN MOUNTAINS
Middlequarter
Monavullagh Mountains
Flagstaff Hill
302
Carran Hill
793
Knocknafallia
Priest Town
Kilworth Camp
Doon
725
Seefin
Graiguearush
Ballinvoher
Araglin
Araglin River
Ballynamult
Tooraneena
Scart Bridge
Glensheskin Forest
Millstreet
Ballyeafy
Monard
Knockboy
Downing
Knockaunarast
Mount Melleray Monastery
Ballynaguilkee
Kilbrien
Briska
Glanworth
352
321
Logleagh
Monalour
Ardnagunna
Colligan River
Farbreaga
Macroney
Knockastasnane
Dalligan Bridge
Lemybrien
Megalithic Tomb
Kilworth
Lyrenaglogh
WATERFORD
Glenshelane
Millstreet
Crohane
Aragin Bridge
Black
Cool
Sruh
Clondulane
Countygate
Ballyduff
Modelligo
Knockroe
Glenboe Wood
Castle
Cappoquin
Boheravaghera Cross Roads
Colligan Bridge
Shanbally
FERMOY
175
Lismore
Drumroe
Coolanheen
The Pike
Ballynamuddagh
Currabeha
Kilgobnet
Corrin Wood
N7
N62
N8
N75
N24
N74
N73
N72
N25
R445
R498
R499
R500
R497
R433
R435
R502
R501
R503
R498
R689
R690
R660
R659
R661
R505
R691
R692
R515
R662
R663
R688
R706
R670
R687
R513
R665
R668
R671
R678
R680
R512
R666
R667
R669
R672
LC

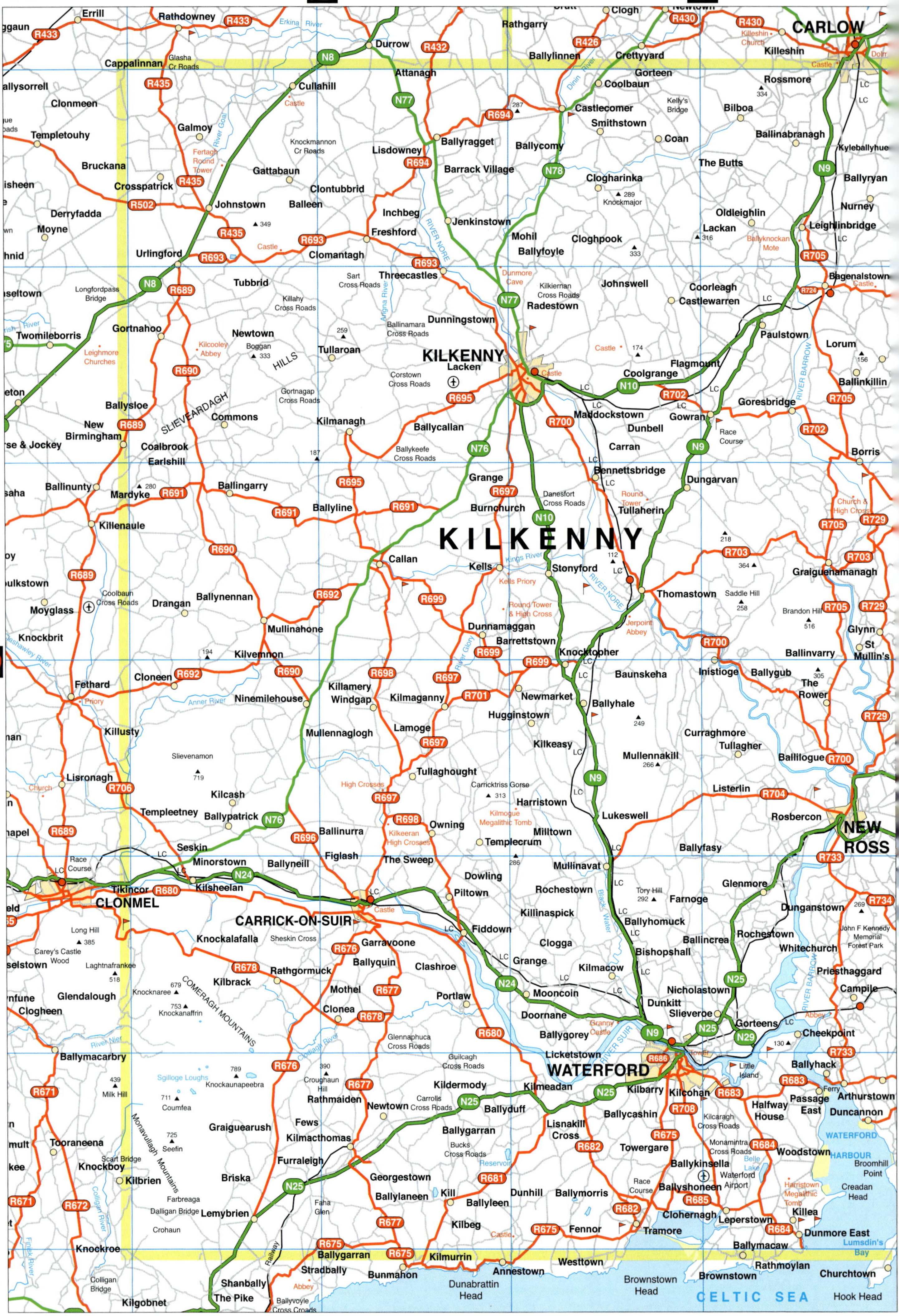

A
B
C
D
E
23
24
29
1
2
3
4
5
6
7
8
KILKENNY
CARLOW
KILKENNY
CLONMEL
CARRICK-ON-SUIR
WATERFORD
NEW ROSS
CELTIC SEA
WATERFORD HARBOUR
SLIEVEARDAGH HILLS
COMERAGH MOUNTAINS
Monavullagh Mountains
Errill
Rathdowney
Cappalinnan
Glasha Cr Roads
Durrow
Attanagh
Cullahill
Castle
Rathgarry
Clogh
Newtown
Ballylinnen
Crettyyard
Gorteen
Coolbaun
Killeshin Church
Killeshin
Rossmore
334
Galmoy
Fertagh Round Tower
Templetouhy
Clonmeen
Knockmannon Cr Roads
Lisdowney
Ballyragget
287
Castlecomer
Smithstown
Kelly's Bridge
Coan
Bilboa
Ballinabranagh
Kyleballyhue
Bruckana
Crosspatrick
Johnstown
349
Gattabaun
Clontubbrid
Balleen
Barrack Village
Ballycomy
Clogharinka
289
Knockmajor
The Butts
Ballyryan
Derryfadda
Moyne
Urlingford
Inchbeg
Freshford
Jenkinstown
Mohil
Ballyfoyle
Cloghpook
333
Oldleighlin
Lackan
316
Ballyknockan Mote
Nurney
Leighlinbridge
Clomantagh
Threecastles
Sart Cross Roads
Dunmore Cave
Kilkiernan Cross Roads
Radestown
Johnswell
Coorleagh
Castlewarren
Bagenalstown
Longfordpass Bridge
Tubbrid
Killahy Cross Roads
Ballinamara Cross Roads
Dunningstown
Twomileborris
Gortnahoo
Kilcooley Abbey
Leighmore Churches
Newtown
Boggan
333
259
Tullaroan
Lacken
Castle
174
Paulstown
Lorum
Flagmount
Coolgrange
156
Ballinkillin
Ballysloe
Corstown Cross Roads
Gortnagap Cross Roads
Commons
Kilmanagh
Ballycallan
Maddockstown
Gowran
Goresbridge
Race Course
New Birmingham
Coalbrook
Earlshill
Ballykeefe Cross Roads
187
Dunbell
Carran
Borris
Ballinunty
Mardyke
280
Ballingarry
Ballyline
Grange
Burnchurch
Danesfort Cross Roads
Bennettsbridge
Round Tower
Tullaherin
Dungarvan
Church & High Cross
Killenaule
Callan
Kells
Kings River
Kells Priory
Stonyford
River Nore
112
218
364
Graiguenamanagh
Coolbaun Cross Roads
Drangan
Ballynennan
Moyglass
Mullinahone
Round Tower & High Cross
Dunnamaggan
Barrettstown
Jerpoint Abbey
Thomastown
Saddle Hill
258
Brandon Hill
516
Glynn
Knockbrit
194
Kilvemnon
Knocktopher
Ballinvarry
St Mullin's
Fethard
Priory
Cloneen
Anner River
Ninemilehouse
Killamery
Windgap
Kilmaganny
Newmarket
Baunskeha
Inistioge
Ballygub
305
The Rower
Killusty
Mullennaglogh
Lamoge
Hugginstown
Ballyhale
249
Curraghmore
Tullagher
Kilkeasy
Mullennakill
266
Ballilogue
Slievenamon
719
Lisronagh
Church
High Crosses
Tullaghought
Carricktriss Gorse
313
Harristown
Listerlin
Kilcash
Templeetney
Ballypatrick
Kilmogue Megalithic Tomb
Lukeswell
Rosbercon
Milltown
Kilkeeran High Crosses
Owning
Templecrum
Ballinurra
Seskin
Race Course
Minorstown
Ballyneill
Figlash
The Sweep
286
Mullinavat
Ballyfasy
Tikincor
Kilsheelan
Dowling
Piltown
Rochestown
Tory Hill
292
Farnoge
Glenmore
Dunganstown
269
Castle
Long Hill
385
Carey's Castle Wood
Knockalafalla
Sheskin Cross
Garravoone
Fiddown
Killinaspick
Clogga
Ballyhomuck
Ballincrea
Rochestown
Whitechurch
John F Kennedy Memorial Forest Park
Laghtnafrankee
518
Ballyquin
Clashroe
Grange
Bishopshall
Kilmacow
Priesthaggard
Glendalough
Knocknaree
679
Kilbrack
Rathgormuck
Mothel
Mooncoin
Nicholastown
Campile
Clogheen
753
Knockanaffrin
Clonea
Portlaw
Doornane
Dunkitt
Slieveroe
Gorteens
Abbey
Checkpoint
River Nier
Glennaphuca Cross Roads
Ballygorey
Granny Castle
Licketstown
River Suir
130
Ballymacarbry
Guilcagh Cross Roads
Little Island
Ballyhack
Sgilloge Loughs
789
Knockaunapeebra
390
Croughaun Hill
Kildermody
Kilmeadan
Kilbarry
Kilcohan
Ferry
Arthurstown
439
Milk Hill
711
Coumfea
Rathmaiden
Newtown
Carrolls Cross Roads
Ballyduff
Lisnakill Cross
Ballycashin
Passage East
Halfway House
Duncannon
Graiguearush
Fews
Kilmacthomas
725
Seefin
Tooraneena
Ballygarran
Bucks Cross Roads
Towergare
Kilcaragh Cross Roads
Monamintra Cross Roads
Woodstown
Broomhill Point
Scart Bridge
Knockboy
Kilbrien
Furraleigh
Georgestown
Reservoir
Ballykinsella
Belle Lake
Waterford Airport
Race Course
Ballyshoneen
Harristown Megalithic Tomb
Creadan Head
Briska
Faha Glen
Ballylaneen
Kill
Ballyleen
Dunhill
Ballymorris
Farbreaga
Dalligan Bridge
Lemybrien
Clohernagh
Leperstown
Killea
Crohaun
Colligan River
Finisk River
Kilbeg
Castle
Fennor
Tramore
Dunmore East
Knockroe
Ballygarran
Kilmurrin
Ballymacaw
Lumsdin's Bay
Stradbally
Bunmahon
Annestown
Westtown
Rathmoylan
Churchtown
Colligan Bridge
Shanbally
Abbey
Dunabrattin Head
Brownstown Head
Brownstown
Hook Head
Kilgobnet
The Pike
Ballyvoyle Cross Roads
N8
N77
N78
N9
N10
N76
N24
N25
N29
R433
R435
R502
R693
R689
R690
R691
R692
R694
R695
R697
R698
R699
R700
R701
R702
R703
R704
R705
R706
R729
R733
R734
R426
R430
R432
R680
R671
R672
R675
R676
R677
R678
R681
R682
R683
R684
R685
R686
R708
R724
LC

F
24
G
H
25
J
K
1
2
3
4
5
6
7
8
CARLOW
WEXFORD
ST GEORGE'S CHANNEL
Browne's Hill Dolmen
Killerig
R726
R727
Raheen
Megalithic Tomb
R747
Annacurragh
R752
AVOCA
Johnstown
Bennekerry
Rathlyon
Clonmore
Ballinglen
Derry Water
Aughrim River
Woodenbridge
Avoca River
R750
R418
N81
R747
R772
Ferrybank
ARKLOW
R725
Grangeford
Bridgeland
Tinahely
Curraghlawn
605
Croghan Mountain
Moyle
Burren River
Tullow
Rathgall Stone Fort
R725
Kilquiggin
R749
Johnstown
Kellistown Cross Rds
Roscat
Rathtoe
Mullinacuff
356
Arklow Head
Boley
Church
Coolboy
Crosspatrick
Clonroe Cr Roads
Coolgreany
Scarnagh Cr Roads
Clogga
N80
Ardattin
419
Shillelagh
Ballard Cross Rds
R748
Coolattin
Pallis
Inch
N11
Kilmichael Point
Ballyveal
Moylisha
322
Killinierin
Ballon
Altamont Gardens
Park Bridge
River Slaney
Castletown
Monaseed
Derry River
R725
Hollyfort
Fennagh
Carnew
Tara Hill 251
N80
Craan
Clonegall
R746
R724
Watch House Village
Craanford
Ballymoney Cross Roads
Ballynakill
Garryhill
Myshall
Kildavin
312
Askamore
Church
GOREY
R725
R742
Courtown Beach
Corries Cross
Dumfea
454 Croughaun
Bunclody
Ballyroebuck
420
Clogh
Courtown
Clohamon
Ballyduff
Riverchapel
Mount Leinster 793
Black Roack Mountain
R746
Kilmyshall
Strahart
Kilthomas Cr Roads
Camolin
Ballyoughter
Ballycanew
Cashel
Killedmond
Clologe
Killenagh
Roney Point
MOUNTAINS
Ferns
Abbey Castle
232 Carrigroe Hill
Ballyfin
Mounthoward Cross Roads
Templeshanbo
Castledockrell
214
R745
Ballycarney
Ballygarrett
R702
R703
Ballymurphy
BLACKSTAIRS
R702
Kiltealy
R745
Ballindaggan
River Bann
The Harrow
R741
Monamolin
Clonevin Cross Roads
Cahore Point
Marshalstown
Tinnacross Cross Roads
Boleyvogue
R730
Gowlin
Old Town
Urrin River
Monagear
Raheenlusk
Wells
Ballygortin
Coolroe
Crane
Kilnamanagh
Kilmuckridge
494
Killann
R702
Milehouse
Ballybaun 512
Caim
Oulart
Rathnure
ENNISCORTHY
Killincooly
Rathfylane
R731
R744
Davidstown
Darby's Gap
Kilcotty
R742
Castleellis
Ballaghkeen
Ballyvaldon
Glenbrien
Donard
Ballywilliam
Clonroche
LC
R744
180
Ballymurn
Blackwater
Bree
Chapel
N30
R741
Blackwater Harbour
Oilgate
Ballylucas
Palace
R735
R730
Ballyhoge
Screen
R742
151
Redgate
WEXFORD or NORTH BAY
Ballagh
Lacken
189
Raheen
The Leap
Galbally
Tinnakilla
Curracloe
Old Ross
Adamstown
N11
R743
Courthoyle
Ballinclay
Crossabeg
Castlebridge
N25
Killurin
Glynn
126
180
R742
Carrickbyrne Hill Wood
Blackhall
R741
The Wexford Wildlife Reserve
Ballynabola
N25
WEXFORD HARBOUR
The Raven Point
N25
R736
R735
Newbawn
LC
WEXFORD
Cassagh
R735
Rosslare Point
Taghmon
Colestown
235 Forth Mountain
Kerloge
Ballynamona
Foulkesmill
Clonard
Aughfad
Great
N25
Drinagh
ROSSLARE or SOUTH BAY
Gusserane
R738
R733
Clongeen
Corock River
Murnstown
R736
Museum
LC
LC
Hilltown
R733
Cleristown
Piercetown
Rathmacknee Castle
LC
ROSSLARE
Cherbourg
Roscoff
Fishguard
Pembroke
Ballycullane
Tullycanna
Heavenstown
Killinick
R740
R734
LC
LC
Wellingtonbridge
R738
Horetown
N25
R736
Car Ferry
ROSSLARE HARBOUR
Ramsgrange
R733
Knocktown Cross Roads
Mayglass
LC
Ballycogly
Greenore Point
LC
Robinstown
Tagoat
Kilrane
Garrycullen
Abbey
Johnstown
LC
LC
R739
Hilltown
R736
Twelveacre Cross Roads
R737
Saltmills
Bannow Bay
Newtown
Carrick
R736
Bridgetown
Tenacre Cross Roads
Broadway
Cullenstown
Duncormick
Lady's Island
Ballare
R734
Park
Kilmore
R739
Tomhaggard
Tuskar Rock
Killag
Grange
Windmill
Tacumshane Lake
Lady's Island Lake
Clammers Point
Kerragh Islands
Ballyteige Bay
Newtown
Bastardstown
Ring
Churchtown
Fethard
Kilmore Quay
Carnsore Point
Baginbun Head
0
5
10 km
0
3
6 miles
Templetown
Crossfarnoge or Forlorn Point
Sandeel Bay
Slade
Saltee Islands
F
G
H
J
K

32

Map grid: A–E, 1–8

Row 1
- Inishtooskert (A1)
- 172 ▲ (A1)
- Clogher Head (B1)
- R559 (B1)
- Teeravane, Ballineanig, Ballyeightragh (B1)
- Croaghmarhin 403 ▲ (B1)
- Knockavrogeen, Ballybowler (C1)
- Milltown (C1)
- DINGLE (C1)
- Lisdargan (D1)
- Coumduff, Annagap (D1)
- Anascaul (D1)
- Lispole (C1/D1)
- N86 (C1)
- 26 (C1)
- Brickany 374 ▲ (E1)
- Caheracruttera (E1)
- Aughils (E1)
- 566 (E1)
- R561 (E1)
- CASTLEMAINE HARBOUR (E1)
- Dunquin (B1)
- Kildurrihy (B1)
- Ventry (B1)
- Dingle Harbour (C1)
- Aglish (C1)

Row 2
- Mount Eagle 514 ▲ (B2)
- Beginish (B2)
- GREAT BLASKET ISLAND (A2)
- BLASKET SOUND (B2)
- Beenacouma, Fahan (B2)
- Garraun Point (B2)
- SLEA HEAD (B2)
- Cloghans (B2)
- Dunbeg Fort (B2)
- Ventry Harbour (B2)
- Ballymacadoyle Hill (C2)
- Doonmanagh (C2)
- Parkmore Point (C2)
- Reenbeg Point (C2)
- Bull's Head (C2)
- Minard Head (C2/D2)
- 284 ▲ (D2)
- Acres Point (D2)
- Gubranna (D2)
- Red Cliff (D2)
- Inch (D2)
- Cromane Point (E2)
- Inch Point (E2)
- Cromane (E2)
- Tullig (E2)
- Knockaunnaglashy (E2)
- Illaunstookagh (E2)
- Lough Yganavan (E2)
- Muingaphuca (E2)
- Knockaunroe (E2)
- Caragh Bridge (E2)
- Tearaght Island (A2)
- Canduff 175 ▲ (A2)
- 290 ▲ (B2)
- Inishnabro (A2)
- 135 ▲ (A2)
- Inishvickillane (A2)
- DINGLE BAY (C2)

Row 3
- Rossbehy Creek (E3 area upper)
- Glenbeigh Wood (E3)
- Ross Behy (E3)
- R564 (E3)
- Glenbeigh (E3)
- 491 ▲ Seefin (E3)
- Feaklecally (D3)
- N70 (D3)
- Glanbehy Bridge (E3)
- King's Head (C3)
- Gleensk (D3)
- Darby's Bridge (C3)
- Wood Beenmore (D3)
- 668 (D3)
- Bunglasha (E3)
- Gortrelig (E3)
- Killurly Commons (C3)
- Kells (D3)
- King's Head (D3)
- Been Hill 662 ▲ (D3)
- Blackstones Bridge (E3)
- Canglass Point (B3)
- Slievagh (C3)
- Knocknadobar 688 ▲ (C3)
- Mullaghnarakill (D3)
- Coomaglaslaw Lake (D3)
- Lickeen Wood (E3)
- Glencar (E3)
- Coosfadda (B3)
- Castlequin (C3)
- Killelan Mountain (C3)
- Foilmore Bridge (C3)
- Teermoyle Mountain 772 ▲ (D3)
- Coomasaharn Lake (D3)
- 606 Macklaun (E3)
- Bealalaw Bridge (E3)
- DOULUS HEAD (B3)
- Stone Fort (C3)
- Coomduff (C3)
- Teeromoyle (D3)
- Meenteog 714 ▲ (D3)
- Colly 686 (E3)
- Dromalonhurst Bridge (E3)
- Boheeshil (E3)

Row 4
- Reenadrolaun Point (B4)
- Beginish Island (C4)
- Church (C4)
- Reenard Cross (C4)
- CAHERSIVEEN (C4)
- Knockaneden Cross (D4)
- Ballaghisheen Forest (D4)
- 547 (E4)
- Cloon Lough (E4)
- Mullaganattin 771 ▲ (E4)
- Fogher Cliff (B4)
- 268 ▲ (C4)
- Valencia Harb. (C4)
- Knights Town (C4)
- N70 (C4)
- Keelnagore (D4)
- Knockroe (D4)
- Owroe Bridge (D4)
- Knocknacusha (E4)
- Lough Reagh (E4)
- Beennakryraka Head (B4)
- VALENCIA ISLAND (B4)
- Chapeltown (B4)
- R565 (B4)
- PORTMAGEE CHANNEL (B4)
- Knockavohaun (D4)
- Lissatinnig Bridge (E4)
- BRAY HEAD (B4)
- Aghnagar Bridge (C4)
- Derreen (C4)
- Killeenleagh Bridge (D4)
- Knockmoyle 682 ▲ (D4)
- Lough Adoolig (D4)
- Finnararagh 663 ▲ (E4)
- Knockarig (E4)
- Eskine (E4)
- Portmagee (B4)
- Killoluaig (C4)
- Foilclogh 497 ▲ (D4)
- Dromaragh (D4)
- Toorenbog Lough (D4)
- Derriana Lough (D4)
- Knocknagantee (D4)
- Kealariddig (E4)
- Dromgour (B4)
- Teeranearagh (C4)
- 397 ▲ (C4)
- Emlaghmore (C4)
- R566 (C4)
- Mastergeehy (D4)
- River Inny (D4)
- Lough Namona (D4)
- Cloonaghlin Lough (D4)
- Tullakeel (E4)
- Knocknafreagha (E4)
- Ballyhahow (B4)
- Killurly (B4)
- R567 (C4)
- Muingydowda (C4)
- New Chapel Cross (D4)
- Caherbarnagh 673 ▲ (D4)
- Sallahig (D4)
- Lough Iskanamacteery (D4)
- Lomanagh (D4)
- Gortagowan (E4)
- Bracklöon (E4)
- Puffin Island (B4)
- Ballinskelligs (B4/C4)
- R566 (B4)
- 18 (C4)
- Waterville (C4)
- Ballybrack (C4)
- Church Island (D4)
- Isknagahiny Lough (D4)
- Esknaloughoge (D4)
- N70 (D4)
- Sneem (E4)
- Tahilla (E4)
- Derryloughlin (E4)

Row 5
- ST FINAN'S BAY (B5)
- Horse Island (C5)
- Mullaghbeg (D5)
- Eagles Hill 542 ▲ (D5)
- Stone Fort (D5)
- Derreenauliff (E5)
- Parknasilla (E5)
- Bolus 409 ▲ (B5)
- Ducalla Head (B5)
- Hog's Head (C5)
- Ardkearagh (C5)
- Coomakesta Pass (C5)
- Cahernageeha Mountain (C/D5)
- Castle Cove (D5)
- Nedanone (D5)
- Illaunleagh (E5)
- Bunnow Harbour (E5)
- Garinish (E5)
- Rossdohan Island (E5)
- Sherky Island (E5)
- BOLUS HEAD (B5)
- Beenarourke (C5)
- N70 (C5)
- Caherdaniel (C5/D5)
- Daniel's Island (D5)
- BALLINSKELLIGS BAY (B5/C5)
- Sheehan's Point (C5)
- Derrynane Nat. Park (C5)
- Abbey Island (C5)
- Derrynane Bay (C5)
- KENMARE RIVER (D5)
- Dog's Point (D5)
- Little Skellig (B5)
- Great Skellig (A5)
- Skellig Michael (B5)
- Deenish Island (C5)
- Scariff Island (B5/C5)
- Lamb's Head (C5)
- Collorus (E5)
- Ardgroom (E5)
- 598 ▲ (E5)
- Coomacloghane (E5)

Row 6
- Kilcatherine Point (D6)
- Lough Fadda (E6)
- Gortgarriff (E6)
- Glenbeg Lough (E6)
- Inishfarnard (D6)
- COULAGH BAY (D6)
- Ardacluggin Point (D6)
- Eyeries (E6)
- Crumpane (E6)
- Maulin 620 ▲ (E6)
- Cod's Head (C6)
- Urhin (D6)
- R575 (D6)
- Travara Bridge (D6)
- Kealincha Bridge (D6)
- R571 (E6)
- Curryglass (E6)
- Rossmackowen (E6)
- Knocknagallaun (D6)
- SLIEVE MISKISH MOUNTAINS (D6)
- 488 ▲ (D6)
- Knockgour (D6)
- CASTLETOWN BEARHAVEN (E6)
- R572 (E6)
- Allihies (D6)
- Gour Bridge (D6)
- Dinish Island (E6)
- BEAR HAVEN (E6)
- Ballynakilla (E6)
- Rerrin (E6)
- Ballydonegan (D6)
- Garnish Point (C6)
- Garnish Bay (D6)
- Dunboy Castle (D6)
- 9 (E6)
- BEAR ISLAND (E6)

Row 7
- ATLANTIC OCEAN (B7)
- DURSEY ISLAND (C7)
- Cable Car (C7)
- Ballynacallagh (C7)
- Lackacroghan (D7)
- Firkeel R572 (D7)
- Cahermore (D7)
- Fair Head (D/E7)
- Doonbeg Head (E7)
- Carricgbredia (E7)
- The Bull (B7)
- Kilmichael (C7)
- White Ball Head (D7)
- Black Ball Head (D7)
- DURSEY HEAD (C7)
- The Cow (C7)
- Crow Head (C7)
- Muntervary or Sheep's Head (E7)

Scale: 0 – 5 – 10 km / 0 – 3 – 6 miles

Row 8
- The Calf (B7/8)
- Three Castle Head (E8)
- Dunlough Bay (E8)
- MIZEN HEAD (E8)

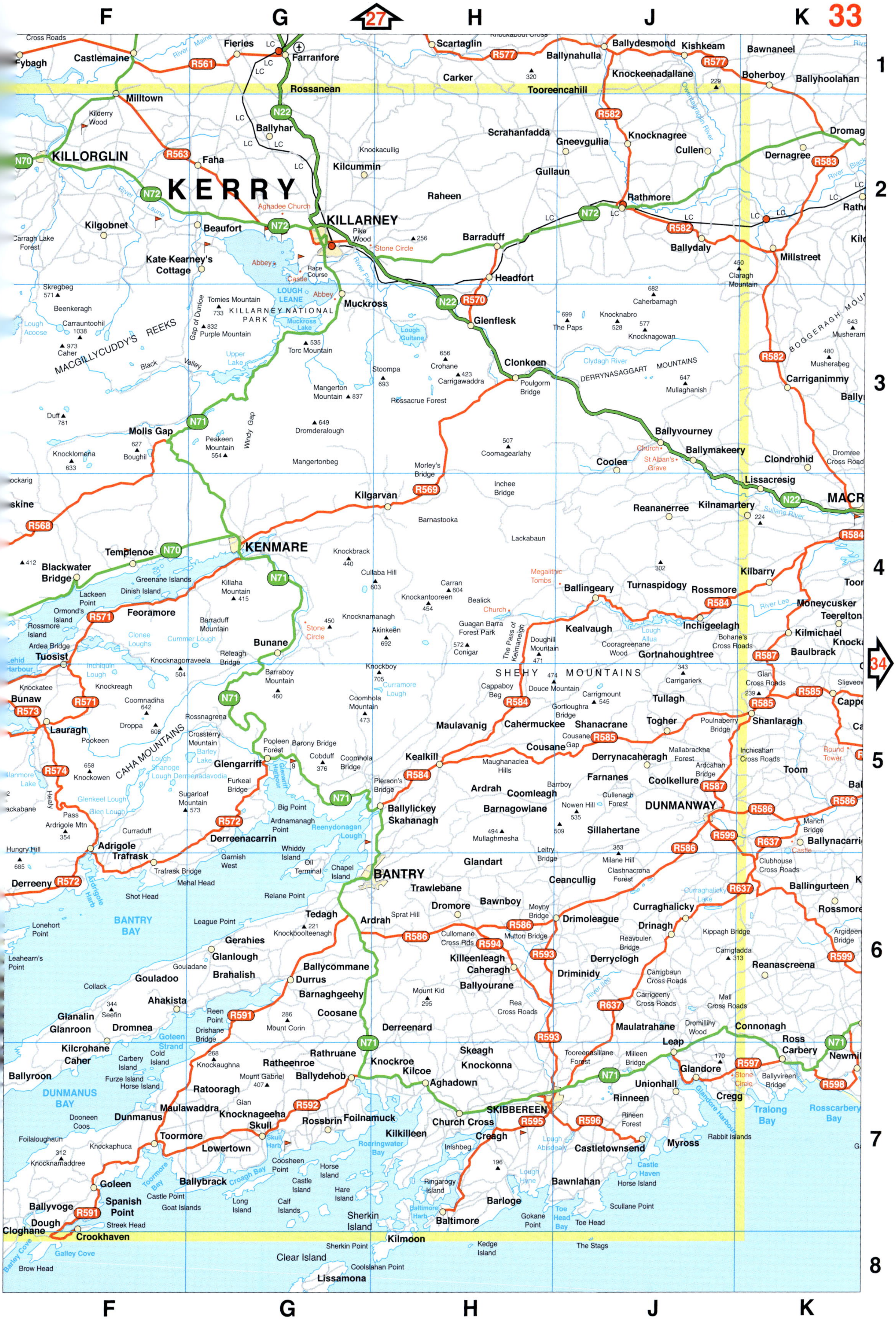

F
G
27
H
J
K
1
2
3
4
5
6
7
8
34
Cross Roads
Fybagh
Castlemaine
River Maine
Fieries
Farranfore
R561
Scartaglin
R577
Ballynahulla
Ballydesmond
Kishkeam
R577
Bawnaneel
Boherboy
Ballyhoolahan
Carker
320
Knockeenadallane
229
Rossanean
Tooreencahill
Milltown
N22
R582
Kilderry Wood
Ballyhar
Scrahanfadda
Gneevgullia
Knocknagree
Cullen
Owentaraglin River
Dromag
Dernagree
R583
N70
KILLORGLIN
R563
Faha
Knockacullig
Kilcummin
Gullaun
KERRY
N72
River Laune
Aghadee Church
Raheen
Rathmore
R582
Ballydaly
Millstreet
Rath
Kil
Blackwater River
Kilgobnet
Beaufort
N72
KILLARNEY
Pike Wood
256
Stone Circle
Barraduff
N72
Carragh Lake Forest
Kate Kearney's Cottage
Abbey
Castle
Race Course
River Flesk
Headfort
450
Claragh Mountain
Skregbeg
571
LOUGH LEANE
Abbey
Muckross
N22
R570
682
Caherbarnagh
Beenkeragh
Tomies Mountain
733
KILLARNEY NATIONAL PARK
Muckross Lake
Glenflesk
699
The Paps
Knocknabro
528
577
Knockagowan
BOGGERAGH MOUNTAINS
643
Musheram
Lough Acoose
Carrauntoohil
1038
Gap of Dunloe
832
Purple Mountain
Lough Guitane
973
Caher
MACGILLYCUDDY'S REEKS
Black Valley
Upper Lake
535
Torc Mountain
656
Crohane
Clonkeen
Clydagh River
DERRYNASAGGART MOUNTAINS
480
Musherabeg
R582
Stoompa
693
423
Carrigawaddra
Poulgorm Bridge
647
Mullaghanish
Carriganimmy
Ballyl
Mangerton Mountain
837
Rossacrue Forest
Duff
781
N71
649
Dromderalough
Windy Gap
Molls Gap
Peakeen Mountain
554
627
Boughil
Knocklomena
633
Mangertonbeg
507
Coomagearlahy
Morley's Bridge
Ballyvourney
Church
St Gobnet's Grave
Ballymakeery
Coolea
Clondrohid
Dromree Cross Roads
Lissacresig
ockarig
skine
R569
Kilgarvan
Inchee Bridge
Reananerree
Kilnamartery
N22
MACR
Sullane River
224
R568
Barnastooka
Lackabaun
R584
Templenoe
N70
KENMARE
Knockbrack
440
412
Blackwater Bridge
Greenane Islands
N71
Cullaba Hill
603
Megalithic Tombs
302
Kilbarry
Toor
Dinish Island
Lackeen Point
Killaha Mountain
415
Carran
604
Knockantooreen
454
Bealick
Church
Ballingeary
Turnaspidogy
Rossmore
R584
River Lee
Moneycusker
Teerelton
Ormond's Island
R571
Feoramore
Barraduff Mountain
450
Stone Circle
Knocknamanagh
Guagan Barra Forest Park
The Pass of Keimaneigh
Kealvaugh
Lough Allua
Inchigeelagh
Kilmichael
Rossmore Island
Clonee Loughs
Cummer Lough
Akinkeen
692
572
Conigar
Doughill Mountain
471
Cooragreenane Wood
Bohane's Cross Roads
Knocka
Ardea Bridge
Bunane
Gortnahoughtree
R587
Baulbrack
Tuosist
Inchiquin Lough
Releagh Bridge
Knockboy
705
SHEHY MOUNTAINS
343
Carrigarierk
Glan Cross Roads
Slievevo
ehid Harbour
Knockagorraveela
504
Barraboy Mountain
Curramore Lough
Cappaboy Beg
474
Douce Mountain
Carrigmount
545
239
R585
Cappe
Knockatee
Knockreagh
460
Coomhola Mountain
473
R584
Gortloughra Bridge
Tullagh
R585
Bunaw
R571
Coomnadiha
642
N71
Shanlaragh
R573
Rossnagrena
Maulavanig
Cahermuckee
Shanacrane
Togher
Poulnaberry Bridge
Ca
Lauragh
Droppa
608
Crossterry Mountain
Cousane
R585
Pookeen
CAHA MOUNTAINS
Barley Lake
Pooleen Forest
Barony Bridge
Cousane Gap
Mallabrackha Forest
Derrynacaheragh
Inchicahan Cross Roads
Round Tower
R574
658
Knockowen
Lough Shanoge
Lough Derreenadavodia
Glengarriff
Cobduff
376
Coomhola Bridge
Kealkill
Maughanaclea Hills
Ardcahan Bridge
Toom
lanmore Lake
Furkeal Bridge
Glengarriff Harbour
Pierson's Bridge
R584
Barrboy
Farnanes
Coolkellure
R587
Bal
Healy Pass
Glenkeel Lough
Glen Lough
Sugarloaf Mountain
573
N71
Ardrah
Coomleagh
Cullenagh Forest
Nowen Hill
535
DUNMANWAY
R586
ackabane
R572
Big Point
Ballylickey
Skahanagh
Barnagowlane
R586
Ardrigole Mtn
354
Curraduff
Derreenacarrin
Ardnamanagh Point
Reenydonagan Lough
494
Mullaghmesha
509
Sillahertane
R599
Manch Bridge
Hungry Hill
Adrigole
Whiddy Island
Leitry Bridge
353
Milane Hill
R637
Ballynacarri
Castle
685
Trafrask
Garnish West
Oil Terminal
Chapel Island
BANTRY
Glandart
Clashnacrona Forest
Clubhouse Cross Roads
Derreeny
R572
Trafrask Bridge
Mehal Head
Ceancullig
K
Adrigole Harbour
Shot Head
Relane Point
Trawlebane
Curraghalicky Lake
R637
Ballingurteen
Dromore
Bawnboy
Moyny Bridge
Curraghalicky
Rossmore
Lonehort Point
BANTRY BAY
League Point
Tedagh
221
Knockboolteenagh
Ardrah
Sprat Hill
Drimoleague
Drinagh
Kippagh Bridge
Argideen Bridge
Gerahies
Cullomane Cross Rds
R586
R586
R594
Mutton Bridge
Reavouler Bridge
Carrigfadda
313
Leahearn's Point
Glanlough
Gouladane
Killeenleagh
R593
Derryclogh
Reanascreena
R599
Gouladoo
Brahalish
Ballycommane
Caheragh
Driminidy
Carrigbaun Cross Roads
Collack
Durrus
Ballyourane
River Ilen
Barnaghgeehy
Mount Kid
295
Carrigeeny Cross Roads
Mall Cross Roads
344
Seefin
Ahakista
Glanalin
Reen Point
R591
286
Mount Corin
Coosane
Rea Cross Roads
R637
Glanroon
Dromnea
Goleen Strand
Drishane Bridge
Derreenard
Maulatrahane
Dromillihy Wood
Connonagh
R593
Leap
Ross Carbery
N71
Kilcrohane
Caher
Cold Island
268
Rathruane
Skeagh
Tooreenasillane Forest
Milleen Bridge
170
Newmil
Carbery Island
Knockaughna
Ratheenroe
Knockroe
Knockonna
R597
Glandore
Ballyroon
Furze Island
Horse Island
Mount Gabriel
407
Ballydehob
Kilcoe
N71
Stone Circle
Ballyvireen Bridge
R598
Aghadown
Unionhall
DUNMANUS BAY
Ratooragh
Rinneen
Cregg
Glan
Glandore Harbour
Tralong Bay
Rosscarbery Bay
Maulawaddra
R592
SKIBBEREEN
Dooneen Coos
Dunmanus
Knocknageeha
Rossbrin
Foilnamuck
Church Cross
R595
R596
Rineen Forest
Skull
Kilkilleen
Creagh
Foilaloughaun
Toormore
Skull Harbour
Roaringwater Bay
Inishbeg
Lough Abisdealy
Castletownsend
Myross
Rabbit Islands
Knockaphuca
Lowertown
312
Knocknamaddree
Coosheen Point
196
Ga
Castle Haven
Goleen
Toormore Bay
Croagh Bay
Horse Island
Castle Island
Lough Hyne
Horse Island
Ringarogy Island
Bawnlahan
Ballybrack
Hare Island
Castle Point
Goat Islands
Long Island
Calf Islands
Barloge
Sculiane Point
Ballyvoge
Spanish Point
Baltimore Harbour
Gokane Point
Toe Head Bay
Toe Head
R591
Dough
Streek Head
Sherkin Island
Baltimore
Cloghane
Crookhaven
Kilmoon
Sherkin Point
Kedge Island
The Stags
Barley Cove
Galley Cove
Clear Island
Brow Head
Coolsalahan Point
Lissamona

28

33

A
B
C
D
E
1
2
3
4
5
6
7
8
Kishkeam
Bawnaneel
River Dalua
Kanturk
Cecilstown
Copsetown Cross Roads
Old Twopothouse Cross Roads
N73
Castletownroche
Scrarour
Parkacunna
R577
Boherboy
Ballyhoolahan
Castle
R576
Ballyclogh
N20
Bannagh Cross Roads
R579
N72
Inchinapallas
MALLOW
Castle
Killavullen
Glenagear Forest
Ballyhooly
Ballydague
Knocknagree
Cullen
Dromagh
Banteer
Castleblagh
Dernagree
R583
River Blackwater
Mount Hillary
390
Lombardstown
Glantane
Drommahane
Race Course
R621
R619
R620
NAGLES MOUNTAINS
Gortroche Forest
Coolinny
Rathcool
Lyre
Monee Cross Roads
Ballynamona
Mourne Abbey
Tooreen
Seefin
Knocknaskagh
Powers Bridge
Lackendarragh North
R582
Ballydaly
Millstreet
Kilcorney
Nad
Laharan Cross Roads
Ballysimon Cross Roads
Knuttery
Mullenaboree
Toorgarriff
Coolea
Bweengduff Mountain
Knockdrislagh
Burnfort
Ardbrou Wood
Prap
Old Bride Bridge
Claragh Mountain
Bottlehill Forest
Caherbarnagh
BOGGERAGH MOUNTAINS
Bweeng
Glenville
Beheragh
Mountcatherine
Ahadallane Cross Roads
Glashaboy North
Glashaboy East
Ballynaglogh West
Knocknagowan
Musheramore
Carrigagulla
Lyradane
Grenagh
Dromboy South
R614
MOUNTAINS
Musherabeg
Barnard Cross Roads
Mullaghanish
Carriganimmy
Ballynagree
Rylane
Stuake
Fornaght
Ballyvaloon
Kilmona
Dromgariff
Carrignavar
Donoughmore
Whitechurch
Coolgreen
Crean's Cross Roads
Lisduff
Killavarrig
Templeusque
CORK
Burren
Ballyvourney
Aghabullogue
Matehy
Waterloo
Piercetown
R616
Church
Ballymakeery
St Alban's Grave
Rusheen
R579
See Page 39
Clondrohid
Dromree Cross Roads
Mullinhassig Wood
Model Village
Berrings
Blarney
White's Cross
Sallybrook
R639
Lissacresig
Bealnamorive
R619
Cloghroe
R617
Castle
Killeens Cross
Riverstown
Glanmire
MACROOM
Coachford
Dripsey
Reananerree
Kilnamartery
N22
Sullane River
Ummera Wood
R618
Model Village
R579
R615
R622
R618
CORK
R635
R639
N8
N25
Carrigadrohid
Killinardish
Larchill Cross Roads
R584
Farran Forest Park
Abbey
R618
N22
Tunnel
Blackrock
Lakelands
R619
R608
BALLINCOLLIG
R610
Kilbarry
Farran
Ovens
Tooms
Castle
Kilcrea Abbey
N28
Turnaspidogy
Rossmore
Warrenscourt Forest
Farnanes
R609
DOUGLAS
R584
River Lee
Moneycusker
Kilmurry
Cloughduv
Aherla
Knockburden
Waterfall
Johnstown
Monkstown
Teerelton
Poulanargid
R585
Knocknahilan
Inchigeelagh
Lough Allua
Bohane's Cross Roads
Kilmichael
Knockane
Knockacareigh
Crookstown
Ring Fort
Aghnamarroge Cross Roads
Knockhank
Cork Airport
Ballincreeshig
Ballygarvan
Gortnahoughtree
R587
Baulbrack
Lackareagh
Curraclogh
Bealnablath
Templemartin
Raheen
Warner's Cross Roads
Ballynagrumoolia
Shanbally
Carrigarierk
Garranereagh
Commons
Glan Cross Roads
Slieveowen
R585
Quarry
Moskeagh
Hill Fort
Cross Barry
Halfway
Ballinhassig
R613
Fivemilebridge
Tullagh
R585
Ballinvoher
Commons Cross Roads
R590
R589
Owenboy River
Sliggа Bridge
Carrigaline
Cappeen
Ballinaboy
Togher
Poulnaberry Bridge
Shanlaragh
Newcestown
Dukes Wood
Upton
R607
Ballymartle
R600
Coolsallagh
Doolieve
Castletown
Kilpatrick
Boardee
Mallabrackha Forest
Inchicahan Cross Roads
Round Tower
R588
Scrahane Cross Roads
Ballymarnane River
R589
N71
Inishannon
Ballynamaul Cross Roads
Riverstick
R611
Minane Bridge
Ardcahan Bridge
Toom
Heathfield
Ballynacourty
Coolkellure
R587
Ballineen
R586
Ballylangley
Ballady
Ballyfeard
Tracton
Bandon R.
BANDON
R605
Ballyregan
DUNMANWAY
R586
Enniskean
Kilcolman
Knocknacurra
Dunderrow
Belgooly
Ballyvorane
Manch Bridge
Breaghna
Cross Mahon
Lissaphooca cross Roads
Ballinadee
Nohaval
R586
R599
R637
Ballynacarriga
R602
R605
R600
Ballinclashet
Castle
Knoppage Bridge
KINSALE
Summer Cove
Clubhouse Cross Roads
Knockbrown
R606
Charles's Fort
Newfoundland Bay
Ballywilliam
Castle
Curraghalicky Lake
Knocks
R603
Kilbrittain Forest
Ballinvronig
R600
R637
Ballingurteen
R588
Kilkerran
Curraghalicky
Rossmore
Knockskagh
Ballinascarty
Kilshinahan
Kilbrittain
Ballinspittle
KINSALE HARBOUR
Drinagh
Kippagh Bridge
Argideen Bridge
R600
Hake Head
Reavouler Bridge
Stone Circle
N71
Ballinoroher
Abbey
Ballinspittle Forest
R604
Carrigfadda
Reanascreena
R599
Timoleague
Old Head
Carrigbaun Cross Roads
R600
R601
Lispatrick
Wood Point
Coolmain Point
Carrigeeny Cross Roads
Mall Cross Roads
CLONAKILTY
Courtmacsherry
COURTMACSHERRY BAY
Holeopen Bay East
Holeopen Bay West
North Ring
Tirnanean
Inchydoney Island
Lissavard
Butlerstown
Old Head of Kinsale
Connonagh
Dromillihy Wood
Ross Carbery
Ring Head
Seven Heads Bay
Milleen Bridge
Leap
N71
Lion's Cove
Glandore
R597
Newmills
Duneen Bay
Dunworly Bay
Castlefreke
Stone Circle
Ballyvireen Bridge
Castlefreke Wood
Ardfield
Seven Heads
R598
Dunnycove Bay
CLONAKILTY BAY
Unionhall
Cregg
Tralong Bay
Rosscarbery Bay
Ringlea Point
Rineen Forest
Rabbit Islands
Dunowen Head
Myross
Galley Head
Castle Haven
Horse Island
0 5 10 km
0 3 6 miles

F
G
29
H
J
K
1
2
3
4
5
6
7
8
WATERFORD
Glanworth
Macroney
Megalithic Tomb
Kilworth
R667
Araglin Bridge
Knockastasnane
321
352
Logleagh
Lyrenaglogh
Monalour
R669
Ardnagunna
Kilbrien
Farbreaga
Dalligan Bridge
Lemybrien
Crohaun
Colligan River
R672
Millstreet
Glenshelane
Black
Cool
Sruh
R512
R666
Clondulane
Countygate
Ballyduff
R666
Castle
Cappoquin
Modelligo
Boheravaghera Cross Roads
R671
Knockroe
N25
N72
Glenboe Wood
FERMOY
175
Currabeha
Lismore
Drumroe
Coolanheen
N72
Colligan Bridge
Shanbally
The Pike
Kilgobnet
Corrin Wood
Hill Fort
Cappagh
Coole Abbey
N72
N72
Ballinaspick
Tallowbridge
179
Killahaly
Kilnacarriga
Dromana Wood
Finisk River
Whitechurch
Ballymacmague
DUNGARVAN
N72
Old Pike Bridge
R675
Ballynacourty
Castlelyons
Knockmourne
Conna
River Bride
Blackwater
Villierstown
Keereen
Priory
Castle
Kilbrien
Aghern
Curraglass
Tallow
River Brickey
Ballynacourty
Rathcormack
Bridebridge
Killavarilly
Monagoun
Aglish
Ballycullane
Newtown
DUNGARVAN HARBOUR
Helvick
R628
Glengoura
Dromore
Kilcor
Garrycaheragh
Ballynoe
Kilwatermoy
R671
Drum Hills
R674
Ringville
Ballynagaul
Firmount
Britway
Kilcronat
Lyre
Dunmoon
Knockanore
Goish River
Bartlemy
Tourig River
The Pike
Gorteen
Desert
301
Carronadaverg
Monamraher
Skahanagh North
Hightown
Glentane
Glenacroghery
Brown's Cross Croads
N25
Muggort's B
N8
244
238
Murley's Crossroads
Breeda
202
Ballybrack
Cross
River
Ballycurrane
Licky River
Loskeran
Skahanagh South
Ardglass
Ballyknock Forest
Ballycolman
Boola
Kiely's Cross Roads
Watergrasshill
R626
Glendine Bridge
Ballyre
Clashmore
Newtown
R673
Reanaclogheen
Clonmult
R634
Riesk
Rathorgan
Inch
Grange
Kilcolman
Glenard
Mine Head
Ballincurrig
Walshtown
R627
Mount Uniacke
Tourig River
Kinsalebeg
N25
Rathfilode
197
Leamlara
202
Slievecorran
Lisgoold
Dangan
Glenbower Wood
Meeleen
Dungourney
YOUGHAL
R673
Curragh
Abbey
Moord
Knockraha
Crowbally
Ballykilty
Priory
Church & Round Tower
Ardmore
Ballynagaul
Curragh Wood
Ballynacole
Killeagh
58
Ardmore Head
Owennacurra River
Cabin Point
Ram Head
Mogeely
Railway
Gortaroo
MIDLETON
Disused
Knocknaskagh
Glounthaune
Disused Railway
Ballymadog
Clonard
Clonard Rock
N25
N25
Garrymore
Youghal Bay
Castlemartyr
R623
Carrigtohill
Ballynacorra
R632
Ballyhonock Lake
R633
Little Island
Foaty Island
Castlemartyr Wood
Ladysbridge
Ballymacoda
R624
Greenland
Lough Mahon
Belvelly
R632
Kilcredan
Knockadoon Head
PASSAGE WEST
43
Marlogue Wood
98
Great Island
R630
R629
Saleen
Cloyne
Garryvoe
Ballymore
89
Rostellan Wood
Cathedral
COBH
R631
Round Tower
R629
CORK HARBOUR
Killmacahill
Shanagarry
Ballycotton Bay
Spike Island
R630
Rostellan
Ballydavid
N28
Aghada
Churchtown
R629
Ringaskiddy
Whitegate
88
Ballycotton
R613
Lough Beg
Ardra
Currabinny Wood
Ballylanders
Church Bay
Crosshaven
Trabolgan
Inch
R612
Roche's Point
Gyleen
Ballinluska
Power Head
Myrtleville
Ringabella Bay
Robert's Cove
Robert's Head
Man of War Cove
Flat Head
CELTIC SEA

Dublin Street Plan
(For greater Dublin see page 25)

Dublin Street Index

D2	Abbey Street, Lower	D3	Kildare Street
C2	Abbey Street, Middle	B5	Kimmage Road, Lwr
C2	Abbey Street, Upper	B2	King Street, North
C4	Adelaide Road	C3	King Street, South
F5	Ailesbury Road	E4	Lansdowne Park
F1	Alexandra Road	E4	Lansdowne Road
E5	Anglesea Road	B5	Larkfield Park
C2	Anglesea Street	D4	Leeson Park
D2	Amiens Street	D3	Leeson Street, Lwr
C3	Anne Street, South	D4	Leeson Street, Upr
B2	Arbour Hill	C5	Leinster Road
B2	Arran Quay	D3	Leinster Street, Sth
C2	Aston Quay	E2	Liffey Street, Lower
C3	Aungier Street	C2	Liffey Street, Upper
C2	Bachelor's Walk	E2	Lime Street
D3	Baggot Street	D3	Lincoln Place
D3	Baggot Street, Lower	C2	Loftus Lane
D4	Baggot Street, Upper	D2	Lombard Street, East
E3	Bath Avenue	F3	Londonbridge Road
F3	Bath Street	C3	Lord Edward Street
D5	Beechwood Avenue	B2	Manor Street
C5	Belgrave Square	D5	Marlborough Road
B2	Benburb Street	D2	Marlborough Street
D2	Beresford Place	B3	Marrowbone Lane
B2	Blackhall Place	C2	Mary Street
A5	Blarney Park	C2	Mary's Lane
B2	Bow Street	B2	May Lane
C3	Bride Street	D2	Mayor Street, Lwr
F3	Bridge Street	B3	Meath Street
C3	Bridge Street	D2	Memorial Road
B2	Bridgefoot Street	B2	Merchant's Quay
B2	Brunswick Street, North	F4	Merrion Road
D2	Burgh Quay	D3	Merrion Row
D4	Burlington Road	D3	Merrion Square
F3	Cambridge Road	D3	Merrion Street, Upr
C4	Camden Street	D4	Mespil Road
C4	Canal Road	D3	Molesworth Street
C2	Capel Street	C2	Moore Street
E2	Cardiff Lane	E4	Morehampton Road
C3	Castlewood Avenue	D2	Moss Street
C2	Chancery Street	B5	Mount Argus Road
D4	Charlemont Place	E3	Mount Street, Lower
C4	Charlemont Street	C4	Mountpleasant Ave
D5	Charleston Road	D5	Moyne Road
C3	Chatham Street	D3	Nassau Street
D3	Chelmsford Road	C3	New Street, South
C3	Christchurch Place	C3	Nicholas Street
B2	Church Street	E2	North Wall Quay
D2	City Quay	D4	Northbrook Road
B4	Clanbrassil Street, Lower	E3	Northumberland Rd
D3	Clare Street	C2	O'Connell Street
C3	Clarendon Street	B3	Oliver Bond Street
B5	Clareville Road	C2	Ormond Quay, Lwr
A4	Clogher Road	C2	Ormond Quay, Upr
E4	Clyde Road	A2	Parkgate Street
C2	College Green	C2	Parliament Street
D2	College Street	B4	Parnell Road
C2	Commons Street	C2	Parnell Street
B2	Cook Street	C3	Patrick Street
C4	Cork Street	D2	Pearse Street
B3	Cornmarket	E4	Pembroke Road
C3	Cuffe Street	D3	Pembroke Street
D2	Custom House Quay	C4	Portobello Road
C2	Dame Street	B2	Queen Street
D4	Dartmouth Square	D5	Ranelagh
D3	Dawson Street	D4	Ranelagh Road
D2	D'Olier Street	B3	Ransford Street
A4	Dolphin's Barn	C5	Rathgar Road
A4	Dolphin's Barn Street	C5	Rathmines Road
E5	Donnybrook Road	B4	Raymond Street
B3	Donore Avenue	C4	Richmond Street, Sth
C3	Drury Street	E3	Ringsend Road
B4	Dufferin Avenue	A4	Rutland Avenue
C3	Duke Street	B5	Rutland Grove
D4	Earlsfort Terrace	D5	Sandford Road
F2	East Wall Road	D2	Sandwith Street
D2	Eden Quay	F4	Serpentine Avenue
E5	Eglinton Road	E2	Seville Place
B2	Ellis Quay	E3	Shelbourne Road
D3	Erne Street	D2	Sherriff Street
C3	Essex Quay	E2	Sherriff Street, Upr
C2	Essex Street, East	F4	Simmonscourt Road
C3	Eustace Street	E2	Sir John Rogerson's Qy
C3	Exchequer Street	B2	Smithfield
D3	Fenian Street	B4	South Circular Road
C2	Fishamble Street	C3	South Great Georges St
D4	Fitzwilliam Place	E3	South Lotts Road
D3	Fitzwilliam Square	B4	St Alban's Road
D3	Fitzwilliam Street	C3	St Andrew Street
D2	Fleet Street	D3	St Stephen's Green
D2	Foley Street	A5	Stannaway Road
B3	Francis Street	A2	Steven's Lane
D3	Frederick Street, South	F5	Stillorgan Road
D2	George's Quay	B2	Stoneybatter
D2	Gloucester Street, South	D2	Store Street
C3	Grafton Street	C3	Suffolk Street
E3	Grand Canal Quay	A5	Sundrive Road
E3	Grand Canal Street	D4	Sussex Road
D4	Grand Parade	D2	Talbot Place
C2	Green Street	D2	Talbot Street
B4	Greenville Terrace	D2	Tara Street
C5	Grosvenor Road	C2	Temple Bar
C5	Grove Road	D4	The Appian Way
E2	Guild Street	B3	The Coombe
E3	Haddington Road	B3	Thomas Court
D2	Hanover Street, East	B3	Thomas Street
E2	Hanover Quay	F1	Tolka Quay Road
C3	Harcourt Street	D2	Townsend Street
C3	Harcourt Road	C2	Trinity Street
B5	Harolds Cross Road	B2	Usher Street
C4	Harrington Street	B2	Usher's Island
D4	Hatch Street, Lower	B2	Usher's Quay
C4	Hatch Street, Upper	B2	Victoria Quay
C2	Henry Street	B4	Washington Street
F4	Herbert Park	D4	Waterloo Road
F4	Herbert Road	B2	Watling Street
C3	High Street	E4	Wellington Place
D3	Hogan Place	C2	Wellington Quay
D3	Holles Street	B5	Westfield Road
B2	Inns Quay	D3	Westland Row
F3	Irishtown Road	C2	Westmoreland St
D2	Island Street	C3	Wexford Street
D2	James Joyce Street	C3	Wicklow Street
A3	James's Street	C3	William Street, Sth
A3	James's Walk	D4	Wilton Terrace
C2	Jervis Street	A2	Winetavern Quay
C3	John Dillon Street	A2	Wolfe Tone Quay
B5	Kenilworth Square	C2	Wood Quay
C5	Kenilworth Road	F2	York Road
C5	Kevin Street	C3	York Street

Belfast Street Plan

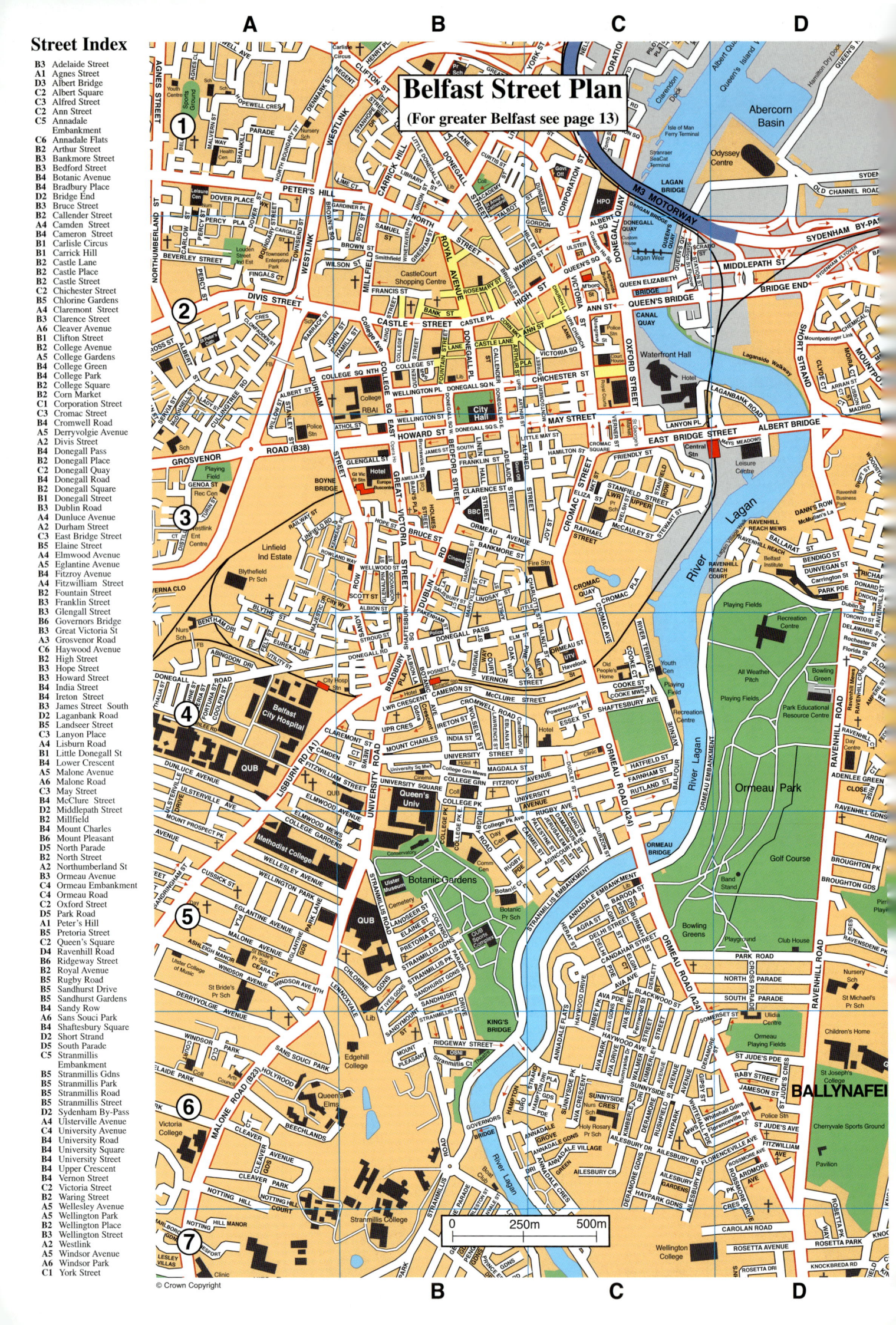

(For greater Belfast see page 13)

Street Index

B3	Adelaide Street
A1	Agnes Street
D3	Albert Bridge
C2	Albert Square
C3	Alfred Street
C2	Ann Street
C5	Annadale Embankment
C6	Annadale Flats
B2	Arthur Street
B3	Bankmore Street
B3	Bedford Street
B4	Botanic Avenue
B4	Bradbury Place
D2	Bridge End
B3	Bruce Street
B2	Callender Street
A4	Camden Street
B4	Cameron Street
B1	Carlisle Circus
B1	Carrick Hill
B2	Castle Lane
B2	Castle Place
B2	Castle Street
C2	Chichester Street
B5	Chlorine Gardens
A4	Claremont Street
B3	Clarence Street
A6	Cleaver Avenue
B1	Clifton Street
B2	College Avenue
A5	College Gardens
B2	College Green
B6	College Park
B2	College Square
B2	Corn Market
C1	Corporation Street
C3	Cromac Street
B4	Cromwell Road
A5	Derryvolgie Avenue
A2	Divis Street
B4	Donegall Pass
B4	Donegall Place
C2	Donegall Quay
B4	Donegall Road
B2	Donegall Square
B1	Donegall Street
B3	Dublin Road
A4	Dunluce Avenue
A2	Durham Street
C3	East Bridge Street
B5	Elaine Street
A4	Elmwood Avenue
A5	Eglantine Avenue
B4	Fitzroy Avenue
A4	Fitzwilliam Street
B2	Fountain Street
B3	Franklin Street
B3	Glengall Street
B6	Governors Bridge
B3	Great Victoria St
A3	Grosvenor Road
C6	Haywood Avenue
B2	High Street
B2	Hope Street
B3	Howard Street
B4	India Street
B4	Ireton Street
B4	James Street South
D2	Laganbank Road
B5	Landseer Street
C3	Lanyon Place
A4	Lisburn Road
B1	Little Donegall St
B4	Lower Crescent
A5	Malone Avenue
A6	Malone Road
C3	May Street
B4	McClure Street
D2	Middlepath Street
B2	Millfield
B4	Mount Charles
B6	Mount Pleasant
D5	North Parade
B2	North Street
A2	Northumberland St
B3	Ormeau Avenue
C4	Ormeau Embankment
C4	Ormeau Road
C2	Oxford Street
D5	Park Road
A1	Peter's Hill
B5	Pretoria Street
C2	Queen's Square
D4	Ravenhill Road
B6	Ridgeway Street
B2	Royal Avenue
B5	Rugby Road
B5	Sandhurst Drive
B5	Sandhurst Gardens
B4	Sandy Row
A6	Sans Souci Park
B4	Shaftesbury Square
D2	Short Strand
D5	South Parade
C5	Stranmillis Embankment
B5	Stranmillis Gdns
B5	Stranmillis Park
B5	Stranmillis Road
B5	Stranmillis Street
D2	Sydenham By-Pass
A4	Ulsterville Avenue
C4	University Avenue
B4	University Road
B4	University Square
B4	University Street
B4	Upper Crescent
B4	Vernon Street
C2	Victoria Street
B2	Waring Street
A5	Wellesley Avenue
A5	Wellington Park
B2	Wellington Place
B3	Wellington Street
A2	Westlink
A5	Windsor Avenue
A6	Windsor Park
C1	York Street

© Crown Copyright

Cork Street Plan
(For greater Cork see page 34)

Street Index

- C3 Academy Street
- C3 Albert Quay
- D3 Albert Street
- D3 Anglesea Street
- A2 Ardmore Avenue
- B4 Bachelor's Quay
- B2 Bakers Road
- C2 Bandon Road
- B3 Barrack Street
- B3 Bishop Street
- B4 Blackrock Road
- E4 Blarney Street
- A2 Camden Quay
- C2 Castle Street
- B2 Cathedral Road
- C2 Cathedral Street
- C2 Cathedral Walk
- B2 Coal Quay
- C2 College Road
- A4 Cork Street
- C2 Dean Street
- B3 Devonshire St
- C3 Dominick Street
- C2 Donovan's Road
- B3 Douglas Road
- C2 Dyke Parade
- B2 Eglinton Street
- C3 Evergreen Street
- B3 Frenche's Quay
- C4 Friar Street
- C3 George's Quay
- C2 Glasheen Road
- B2 Glanbey Street
- C3 Grattan Street
- C2 Horgan's Quay
- E3 Infirmary Road
- D4 John Redmond St
- B3 John Street
- C2 Lancaster Quay
- C2 Lavitt's Quay
- C3 Leitrim Street
- D4 Liberty Street
- C3 Lower Glanmire Rd
- D2 MacCurtain St
- C2 Magazine Road
- A4 Marlborough St
- C3 Maylor Street
- E2 Merchant's Quay
- C3 Military Hill
- D2 Morrison's Quay
- C3 North Main Street
- C3 North Mall Street
- C2 Oliver Plunkett St
- C3 Parliament Street
- C3 Paul Street
- C3 Penrose's Quay
- D3 Pope's Quay
- C2 Prince's Street
- C3 Proby's Quay
- D3 Richmond Hill
- D3 Roman Street
- C2 Shandon Street
- B3 Sharman Crawford St
- B2 Sheares Street
- C2 Sidney Park
- D2 South Mall
- C3 South Main Street
- C3 Southern Road
- D1 St Patrick's Hill
- C2 St Patrick's Quay
- C3 Saint Patrick's St
- C2 Sullivan's Quay
- D2 Summerhill
- D4 Summer Hill, Sth
- B2 Sunday's Well Ave
- B2 Sunday's Well Rd
- B1 Sunvalley Drive
- C3 Tuckey Street
- D3 Union Quay
- E3 Victoria Road
- E3 Washington Street
- B3 Wellington Road
- A3 Western Road
- B3 Winthrop Street
- D2 Youghal Old Rd

Limerick Street Plan
(For greater Limerick see page 28)

Street Index

- C2 Arthur's Quay
- C2 Athlunkard Street
- D3 Ballysimon Road
- B3 Bank Place
- B3 Barrington Street
- B2 Bedford Row
- D3 Blackboy Road
- C2 Broad Street
- C1 Carey's Road
- C1 Castle Street
- D1 Cathedral Place
- B3 Catherine Street
- D2 Cecil Street
- B3 Chapel Street
- D2 Charlotte's Quay
- C1 Clancy's Strand
- D2 Clare Street
- A3 Condell Road
- C1 Corbally Road
- B2 Cratloe Road
- C1 Cruise's Street
- B2 Davis Street
- A3 Dock Road
- B2 Denmark Street
- C2 Dominick Street
- D2 Dublin Road
- B2 Ellen Street
- D3 Ennis Road
- B2 Francis Street
- D3 Garryowen
- B2 George's Quay
- B2 Glentworth Street
- B2 Greenhill Road
- C2 Hartstonge Street
- B2 Harvey's Quay
- B2 Henry Street
- B1 High Road
- C2 High Street
- B2 Honan's Quay
- B2 Howley's Quay
- C3 Hyde Road
- C1 Island Road
- B3 John's Square
- C3 John's Street
- C3 Killeely Road
- B2 Lock Quay
- C2 Lwr Gerald Griffin St
- B2 Mallow Street
- B2 Mary Street
- B2 Michael Street
- B2 Mulgrave Place
- C2 Mungret Street
- D2 New Road
- B1 Nicholas Street
- A2 North Circular Road
- B2 O'Callaghan's Strand
- B2 O'Connell Avenue
- B2 O'Connell Street
- C2 O'Curry Street
- D2 Park Road
- C2 Patrick Street
- D2 Pennywell
- C2 Pery Square
- D2 Quinlan Street
- B3 Roche's Street
- C3 Roxborough Road
- B3 Rutland Street
- C2 Saint Lelia Street
- C2 Sarsfield Street
- B1 Sexton Street
- C3 Sexton Street North
- A1 Shannon Street
- B3 Shelbourne Road
- C2 Sir Harry's Mall
- B3 St Alphonsus St
- B3 St Gerard Street
- A3 South Circular Rd
- C2 Summerville Ave
- D2 Thomas Street
- C2 The Bishop's Quay
- B3 Wickham Street
- C2 William Street
- B3 Wolfe Tone Street

41

Galway Street Plan
(For greater Galway see page 21)

Street Index

Abbeygate St — E3
Bishop O'Donnell Rd — A3
Bohermore — F2
Bothar Irwin — F2
Bothar Ui Eithir — F2
Bothar Ui Eithir — F4
Bowling Green — E3
Brendan's Ave — F3
Bridge Street — E3
Canal Road — D3
Castle Street — E3
Circular Road — A2
Claddagh Quay — E3
College Road — G2
Costello Square — E2
Courthouse Square — E3
Cross Street — E3
Dalysport Road — B5
Dock Road — F3
Dock Street — F3
Dominick Street — E3
Dr Mannix Road — B5
Dyke Road — E4
Eglinton Street — E3
Eyre Square — F3
Eyre Street — F3
Fairhill — E3
Forster Street — F3
Fr Burke Road — E4
Fr Griffin Rd — D3
Gaol Street — E3
Grattan Road — D5
Guard Street — E3
Headford Road — F3
Henry Street — E3
High Street — E3
Lombard Street — E3
Lough Atalia Rd — F2
Market Street — E3
Mary Street — E3
Maunsells Street — C3
Merchants Street — E3
Middle Street — E3
Mill Street — D3
Munster Avenue — D4
New Road — D3
Newcastle Smith — D4
Nun's Island St — D3
Oaklands — D4
Presentation Road — D3
Prospect Hill — F3
Quay Street — E3
Queen Street — F3
Rahoon Road — B3
Raleigh row — D3
Rockbarton Road — A5
Rosary Lane — B4
Rosemary Ave — F3
Sea Road — D3
Salthill Road Lower — C5
Seamus Quirke Rd — C3
Shantalla Road — C3
Shop Street — E3
Siobhan McKenna Rd — B2
St Augustine St — E3
St Dominick's Rd — D4
St Francis Street — E3
St Helen's Street — E3
St Mary's Ave — C4
St Mary's Road — D3
St Patrick's Ave — F3
St Vincent's Ave — F3
Station Road — F3
Taylor's Hill Rd — C4
The Crescent — D4
The Long Walk — E3
Thomas Hynes Rd — C1
University Road — D3
Victoria Street — F3
Whitestrand Avenue — D5
Whitestrand Road — D5
Williamsgate St — E3
Wood Quay — E2

Londonderry Street Plan
(For greater Londonderry see page 5)

Street Index

D4	Abercorn Road
D3	Abbey Street
A4	Aranmore Avenue
A4	Artillery Street
E3	Bank Place
D4	Barrack Street
G4	Bann Drive
B2	Beechwood Avenue
D4	Bennett Street
D3	Bishop St Within
D3	Bishop St Without
B3	Bligh's Lane
D4	Brandywell Road
E4	Bridge Street
C3	Cable Road
E4	Carlisle Road
A3	Central Drive
D3	Chamberlain Street
F4	Chapel Road
D3	Clarendon Street
F3	Clooney Terrace
A3	Creggan Broadway
A3	Creggan Heights
C2	Creggan Road
D2	Creggan Street
A4	Cromore Gardens
D4	Duke Street
B3	Dungiven Road
E4	Eastway
D3	Fahan Street
A3	Fanad Drive
D4	Ferguson Street
F3	Ferryquay Street
F4	Fountain Hill
E3	Foyle Embankment
D5	Foyle Road
E3	Foyle Street
D3	Francis Street
F3	Frederick Street
D3	Glendermott Road
D2	Great James St
E3	Hawkin Street
B2	Infirmary Road
A4	Iniscarn Road
G5	Irish Street
E4	John Street
F3	King Street
G5	Knockwellan Park
C4	Lecky Road
B5	Letterkenny Road
G2	Limavady Road
E3	Linenhall Street
A4	Linsfort Drive
D3	Lisfannon Park
D3	Little Diamond
D3	London Street
C3	Lone Moor Road
D3	Magazine Street
E3	Market Street
C2	Marlborough Road
G5	Mourne Drive
E3	Orchard Street
D3	Palace Street
B5	Patrick Street
D3	Princes Street
D3	Pump Street
E2	Queen's Quay
D3	Rossville Street
D3	Shipquay Street
D3	Society Street
F4	Southway
D3	Spencer Road
D3	St Columb's Wells
E5	Strabane Old Road
D2	Strand Road
C6	The Diamond
D3	The Fountain
F6	Trench Road
D3	Victoria Road
D4	Wapping Lane
D4	Water Street
E3	Waterloo Street
F3	Waterside Link
D4	Westland Street
B2	Westway
D2	William Street

INDEX OF PLACE NAMES

A

- 22 B2 Abbey, Co Galway (An Mhainistir)
- 22 C5 Abbey, Co Galway (An Mhainistir)
- 27 F6 Abbeydorney (Mainistir Ó dTorna)
- 27 J5 Abbeyfeale (Mainistir na Feile)
- 17 H5 Abbeylara (Mainistir Leatghratha)
- 23 J7 Abbeyleix (Mainistir Laoise)
- 17 G7 Abbeyshrule (Mainistir Shruthla)
- 28 E3 Abington
- 14 C4 Achill Sound (Gob an Choire)
- 16 B2 Achonry (Achadh Conaire)
- 15 J3 Aclare (Áth An Cháir)
- 31 G5 Adamstown (Maigh Arnai)
- 28 C4 Adare (Áth Dara)
- 15 J4 Addergoole, Co Mayo
- 21 H3 Addergoole, Co Galway
- 33 F5 Adrigole
- 23 H7 Aghaboe (Achadh Bhó)
- 17 G5 Aghaboy
- 34 C3 Aghabullogue (Achadh Bolg)
- 17 F2 Aghacashel
- 35 F4 Aghada
- 16 B4 Aghadiffin
- 8 A6 Aghadoon
- 6 C6 Aghadowey (Achadh Dubhtaigh)
- 33 H7 Aghadown
- 12 E4 Aghagallon (Achadh Gallan)
- 15 F5 Aghagower (Achadh Ghobhair)
- 12 E4 Aghalee (Achadh Lí)
- 17 F4 Aghamore, Co Leitrim (Achadh Mór)
- 15 J5 Aghamore, Co Mayo (Achadh Mór)
- 25 F7 Aghavannagh
- 17 G3 Aghavas (Achadh an Mheasa)
- 35 G2 Aghern
- 14 B2 Aghleam
- 17 G4 Aghnacliff (Achadh na Cloiche)
- 18 C2 Aghnamullen (Achadh na Muileann)
- 6 C6 Agivey
- 32 D2 Aglish, Co Kerry (An Eaglais)
- 22 E6 Aglish, Co Tipperary (An Eaglais)
- 35 H2 Aglish, Co Waterford (An Eaglais)
- 27 G4 Ahafona
- 33 F6 Ahakista
- 22 D2 Ahascragh (Áth Eascrach)
- 34 D4 Aherla (An Eatharla)
- 6 D7 Ahoghill (Achadh Eochaille)
- 21 F5 Ailladie
- 12 E3 Aldergrove (An Garrán Fearnóigo)
- 24 D4 Allen
- 24 C3 Allenwood (Fiodh Alúine)
- 32 D6 Allihies (Na hAitchi)
- 12 C6 Allistragh (An tAilastrach)
- 22 C2 Alloon Lower
- 10 D2 Altnapaste
- 8 A7 An Geata Mór
- 26 D7 Anascaul (Abhainn an Scáil)
- 29 F6 Anglesborough
- 11 H7 Anlore
- 22 C7 Annacarriga
- 29 G4 Annacarty (Áth na Cairte)
- 12 E6 Annaclone (Eanach Cluana)
- 13 H6 Annacloy (Áth na Cloiche)
- 28 E3 Annacotty
- 25 F7 Annacurragh
- 26 D7 Annagap
- 4 B6 Annagary (Anagaire)
- 19 F4 Annagassan (Áth na gCasán)
- 28 E3 Annagh, Co Limerick
- 16 C6 Annagh, Co Roscommon
- 22 F7 Annagh Neal
- 21 H2 Annaghdown
- 17 F6 Annaghmore (Eanach Mór)
- 13 G5 Annahilt (Eanach Eiulte)
- 19 J2 Annalong (Áth na Long)
- 25 G6 Annamoe
- 23 F6 Annaville
- 18 D1 Annayalla (Eanaigh Gheala)
- 30 C8 Annestown (Bun Abha)
- 29 H3 Annfield
- 13 G7 Annsborough (Baile Anna)
- 12 E3 Antrim (Aontroim)
- 29 G7 Araglin (Airglinn)
- 18 B6 Archerstown (Baile an Airsirigh)
- 28 B4 Ardagh, Co Limerick (Ardach)
- 17 G6 Ardagh, Co Longford (Ardach)
- 18 D4 Ardagh, Co Meath (Ardach)
- 23 H3 Ardan
- 24 D2 Ardanew
- 10 B2 Ardara (Ard an Rátha)
- 31 F2 Ardattin (Ard Aitinn)
- 10 C3 Ardbane
- 12 D3 Ardboe
- 19 F6 Ardcath
- 27 F6 Ardconnell
- 22 E6 Ardcrony (Ard Cróine)
- 18 E4 Ardee (Baile Átha Fhirdhia)
- 27 F6 Ardfert (Ard Fhearta)
- 34 C7 Ardfield (Ard Ó bhFicheallaigh)
- 29 H6 Ardfinnan (Ard Fhionáin)
- 13 J7 Ardglass, Co Down (Ard Ghlais)
- 35 F3 Ardglass, Co Cork
- 32 E5 Ardgroom (Dhá Dhrom)
- 32 D4 Ardkearagh
- 13 J5 Ardkeen (Ard Caoin)
- 15 H6 Ardkill
- 23 J6 Ardlea
- 17 H2 Ardlougher (Ard Luachra)
- 36 J3 Ardmore (Aird Mhór)
- 23 H3 Ardmorney
- 28 D3 Ardnacrusha
- 29 J7 Ardnagunna
- 21 J2 Ardnasodan
- 28 E6 Ardpatrick (Ard Pádraig)
- 35 G4 Ardra
- 33 H5 Ardrah, Co Cork
- 33 G6 Ardrah, Co Cork
- 21 J5 Ardrahan (Ard Raithin)
- 12 C5 Ardress
- 24 C6 Ardscull
- 11 G2 Ardstraw (Ard Sratha)
- 12 C3 Ardtrea (Ard Tré)
- 16 E2 Arigna (An Airgnigh)
- 31 K2 Arklow (An tinbhear Mór)
- 24 C7 Arless
- 12 C6 Armagh (Ard Mhacha)
- 6 E5 Armoy (Oirthear Maí)
- 11 F6 Arney
- 28 B5 Arranagh
- 30 E7 Arthurstown (Colmán)
- 6 B5 Articlave (Ard an Chléibh)
- 5 G7 Artigarvan (Ard Tí Garbháin)
- 17 H4 Arvagh
- 19 F7 Ashbourne (Cill Dhéagláin)
- 28 B6 Ashford, Co Limerick
- 25 H6 Ashford, Co Wicklow (Áth na Fuinseoige)
- 29 H4 Ashhill
- 31 H3 Askamore (An Easca Mhór)
- 25 F7 Askanagap
- 28 B4 Askeaton (Eas Géitine)
- 27 G4 Astee (Eas Daoi)
- 15 H5 Athavallie
- 18 C6 Athboy (Baile Átha Buí)
- 27 H5 Athea (Ath an tSléibhe)
- 22 B3 Athenry (Baile Átha an Rí)
- 24 D5 Athgarvan (Áth Garbháin)
- 28 D5 Athlacca (An tÁth Leacach)
- 16 D7 Athleague (Áth Liag)
- 23 F2 Athlone (Baile Átha Luain)
- 29 J2 Athnid
- 24 C6 Athy (Baile Átha Í)
- 23 J7 Attanagh (Áth Tanaí)
- 19 H2 Attical (Áth Tí Chathail)
- 22 C4 Atticoffey
- 22 C3 Attiregan
- 15 H2 Attymass (Áth Tí an Mheasaigh)
- 22 B3 Attymon (Áth Tiomáin)
- 17 F7 Auburn
- 21 H2 Aucloggeen
- 26 E7 Aughacasla
- 11 J5 Augher (Eochair)
- 31 G6 Aughfad
- 26 E7 Aughils
- 21 H4 Aughinish (Eachinis)
- 11 J5 Aughnacloy (Achadh na Cloiche)
- 6 D7 Aughnacleagh
- 17 F2 Aughnasheelan
- 21 H6 Aughrim, Co Clare
- 22 D3 Aughrim, Co Galway (Eachroim)
- 25 F7 Aughrim, Co Wicklow (Eachroim)
- 25 G7 Avoca (Abhóca)

B

- 24 D2 Baconstown
- 30 E3 Bagenalstown (Muine Bheag)
- 13 G5 Baileysmill (Muileann Bhaile)
- 18 C4 Bailieborough (Colillan Chollaigh)
- 19 G6 Balbriggan (Baile Brigin)
- 15 H5 Balla (Balla)
- 21 J5 Ballaba
- 34 E5 Ballady
- 16 B7 Ballagh, Co Galway
- 28 B6 Ballagh, Co Limerick (An Bealach)
- 16 E6 Ballagh, Co Roscommon
- 16 E7 Ballagh, Co Roscommon
- 29 G4 Ballagh, Co Tpperary

INDEX OF PLACE NAMES

31 F5 Ballagh, Co Wexford	(Baile an Gharraí)	23 G4 Ballyboy
16 B4 Ballaghaderreen	28 C5 Ballingarry, Co Limerick	33 G7 Ballybrack, Co Cork
(Bealach An Doirín)	(Baile an Gharraí)	32 D4 Ballybrack, Co Kerry
27 J5 Ballaghbehy	33 J4 Ballingeary, Co Cork	24 D3 Ballybrack, Co Kildare
29 J4 Ballaghboy	(Béal Átha an Ghaorthaidh)	35 H3 Ballybrack, Co Waterford
31 H5 Ballaghkeen (An Bealach)	8 E7 Ballinglen, Co Mayo	29 H2 Ballybristy
23 G6 Ballaghmore	(Baile an Gleanna)	24 B5 Ballybrittas (Baile Briotais)
10 B5 Ballaghnatrillick	25 F7 Ballinglen, Co Wicklow	27 F6 Ballybroman
23 H4 Ballard	34 B6 Ballingurteen	28 E4 Ballybrood
22 B5 Ballardiggan	34 D4 Ballinhassig	23 G7 Ballybrophy (Baile Uí Bhróithe)
31 H7 Ballare	(Béal Átha an Cheasaigh)	28 C2 Ballybroughan
30 B2 Balleen	21 J4 Ballinillaun	24 B3 Ballybryan
24 C7 Ballickmoyler	30 E3 Ballinkillin	27 F4 Ballybunnion
(Baile Mhic Mhaoilir)	28 C5 Ballinleeny	(Baile an Bhuinneánaigh)
30 E5 Ballilogue	26 C7 Ballinloghig	24 D7 Ballyburn
15 H2 Ballina, Co Mayo	18 C5 Ballinlough, Co Meath	29 F2 Ballycahane
(Béal an Átha)	(Baile an Locha)	29 H3 Ballycahill (Bealach Achaille)
28 E2 Ballina, Co Tipperary	16 B5 Ballinlough, Co Roscommon	30 C3 Ballycallan
17 J7 Ballina, Co Westmeath	(Baile an Locha)	31 J3 Ballycanew
34 D5 Ballinaboy, Co Cork	35 F5 Ballinluska	(Baile Uí Chonnmhaí)
20 C2 Ballinaboy, Co Galway	17 G4 Ballinmuck	28 D2 Ballycar
24 B2 Ballinabrackey	34 C6 Ballinoroher	31 G4 Ballycarney
(Buaile na Bréachmhaí)	21 F7 Ballinphonta	(Baile Uí Chearnaigh)
30 E2 Ballinabranagh	19 H2 Ballinran (Baile an Raithin)	13 H2 Ballycarry (Baile Cora)
25 G7 Ballinaclash (An Chlais)	26 B7 Ballinrannig	30 D7 Ballycashin
34 D5 Ballinadee (Baile na Daibhche)	22 E7 Ballinree	6 E4 Ballycastle, Co Antrim
16 D3 Ballinafad (Béal an Átha Fada)	15 G6 Ballinrobe (Baile an Róba)	(Baile an Chaistil)
23 J4 Ballinagar (Béal na Glarr)	21 J6 Ballinruan (Baile an Ruaín)	8 E6 Ballycastle, Co Mayo
16 E2 Ballinagleragh	32 C4 Ballinskelligs (Baile an Sceilg)	13 F2 Ballyclare (Bealach Cláir)
(Baile na gCléireach)	34 D6 Ballinspittle	29 J5 Ballyclerahan
23 J7 Ballinakill	(Béal Átha an Spidéil)	28 C7 Ballyclogh (Baile Cloch)
17 H6 Ballinalack (Béal Átha na Leac)	15 G5 Ballintober, Co Mayo	31 H7 Ballycogly
25 G6 Ballinalea	(Baile an Tobair)	23 H7 Ballycolla (Baile Cholla)
17 G5 Ballinalee (Béal Átha na Lao)	16 C6 Ballintober, Co Roscommon	35 G3 Ballycolman
11 F5 Ballinamallard	(Baile an Tobair)	33 G6 Ballycommane
(Béal Átha na Mallacht)	10 B7 Ballintogher (Bailean Tóchair)	22 D7 Ballycommon
16 D4 Ballinameen (Béal an Átha Mín)	6 D4 Ballintoy (Baile an Tuaighe)	(Baile Uí Chomáin)
17 G3 Ballinamore	10 C4 Ballintra (Baile an tSratha)	30 D2 Ballycomy
(Béal an Átha Móir)	24 B6 Ballintubbert	20 C2 Ballyconneely (Baile Conaola)
34 C6 Ballinascarty (Béal na Scairte)	29 J4 Ballinunty (Baile an Fhantaigh)	17 H2 Ballyconnell (Béal Átha Conaill)
22 D3 Balinasloe	29 J4 Ballinure (Baile an Iúir)	35 G4 Ballycotton (Baile Choitín)
(Béal Átha na Sluaighe)	30 C5 Ballinurra	22 E5 Ballycrossaun (Baile Crosáin)
35 H2 Ballinaspick	30 84 Ballinvarry	14 D3 Ballycroy (Baile Chruaich)
30 E2 Ballinbranagh	23 F7 Ballinveny	35 J2 Ballycullane, Co Waterford
34 E5 Ballinclashet	29 F7 Ballinvoher, Co Cork	31 F6 Ballycullane, Co Wexford
31 G5 Ballinclay	34 B5 Ballinvoher, Co Cork	(Baile Uí Choiléain)
34 D4 Ballincollig (Baile an Chollaigh)	34 D6 Ballinvronig	25 G6 Ballycullen
22 E5 Ballincor	24 D6 Ballitore (Béal Átha an Tuair)	23 G3 Ballycumber
30 D6 Ballincrea	18 C7 Ballivor (Baile Íomhair)	(Beal Átha Chomair)
34 E4 Ballincreeshig	31 F2 Ballon (Balana)	35 J3 Ballycurrane
35 F3 Ballincurrig (Baile an Churraigh)	13 H5 Balloo	34 E2 Ballydague
31 G4 Ballindaggan (Baile an Daingin)	10 B5 Balloor	33 J2 Ballydaly
29 F7 Ballindangan	18 E2 Ballsmill (Baile an gCléireach)	22 E3 Ballydangan (Baile Daighean)
21 J4 Ballinderreen (Baile an Doirín)	13 J6 Balltculter	35 G4 Ballydavid, Co Cork
1 2 E4 Ballinderry, Co Antrim	10 C4 Ballure	22 C4 Ballydavid, Co Galway
(Baile an Doire)	28 C5 Ballyagran (Béal Átha Grean)	26 C7 Ballydavid, Co Kerry
22 D6 Ballinderry, Co Tipperary	28 B4 Ballyallinan	(Baile an oGall)
(Baile an Doire)	22 C2 Ballybaun	24 B6 Ballydavis
15 H6 Ballindine (Baile an Daighin)	18 C2 Ballybay (Béal Átha Beithe)	33 G7 Ballydehob (Béal an Dá Chab)
16 D2 Ballindoon	23 F7 Ballybeg, Co Tipperary	28 E7 Ballydeloughy
5 F7 Ballindrait (Baile an Droichid)	29 H6 Ballybeg, Co Tipperary	27 J7 Ballydesmond
26 B7 Ballineanig	(An Baile Beag)	(Baile Deasumhan)
34 B5 Ballineen (Béal Átha Fhínín)	25 G3 Ballyboden (Baile Baodáin)	32 D6 Ballydonegan
9 J6 Ballinfull	10 E2 Ballybofey (Bealach Feich)	22 C4 Ballydoogan
28 B4 Ballingarrane	24 C2 Ballyboggan	28 E7 Ballydoyle
(Baile an Gharraín)	19 G7 Ballyboghil	27 F5 Ballyduff, Co Kerry
22 E6 Ballingarry, Co Tipperary	6 C5 Ballybogy (Baile an Bhogaigh)	(An Baile Dubh)
(Baile an Gharraí)	23 G2 Ballybornia	26 D7 Ballyduff, Co Kerry
30 B4 Ballingarry, Co Tipperary	26 C7 Ballybowler	(An Baile Dubh)

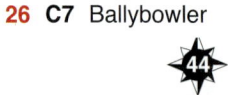

INDEX OF PLACE NAMES

30 C7	Ballyduff, Co Waterford (An Baile Dubh)	
35 G2	Ballyduff, Co Waterford (An Baile Dubh)	
31 H3	Ballyduff, Co Wexford (An Baile Dubh)	
28 C4	Ballyea	
29 G7	Ballyeafy	
13 F2	Ballyeaston (Baile Uistín)	
23 F6	Ballyeighan	
22 C3	Ballyeighter	
26 C7	Ballyeightragh	
15 H5	Ballyfarnagh (Bealach Fearna)	
16 E2	Ballyfarnan	
30 D5	Ballyfasy	
34 E5	Ballyfeard (Baile Feá Aird)	
26 B7	Ballyferriter (Baile an Fhairtéaraigh)	
23 J5	Ballyfin, Co Laois (An Bade Fionn)	
31 H3	Ballyfin, Co Wexford (An Baile Fionn)	
22 D2	Ballyforan (Béal Átha Feorainne)	
24 B3	Ballyfore	
30 D2	Ballyfoyle	
7 G7	Ballygalley (Baile Geithligh)	
16 D7	Ballygar (Béal Átha Ghártha)	
30 C7	Ballygarran, Co Waterford	
30 C8	Ballygarran, Co Waterford	
31 J4	Ballygarrett (Baile Ghearóid)	
15 G6	Ballygarries	
34 E4	Ballygarvan (Baile Garbháin)	
10 B7	Ballygawley, Co Sligo (Baile Uí Dhálaigh)	
11 J5	Ballygawley, Co Tyrone (Baile Uí Dhálaigh)	
29 F5	Ballygeana	
7 F7	Ballygelly	
8 E7	Ballyglass, Co Mayo (An Baile Glas)	
15 G5	Ballyglass, Co Mayo (An Baile Glas)	
16 B4	Ballyglass, Co Mayo (An Baile Glas)	
16 B5	Ballyglass West	
30 D6	Ballygorey	
5 H3	Ballygorman	
31 J4	Ballygortin	
13 H4	Ballygowan (Baile Mhic Gabhann)	
28 C7	Ballygrady	
29 H4	Ballygriffin	
30 E5	Ballygub	
28 D5	Ballygubba	
28 E7	Ballyguyroe North	
30 E7	Ballyhack	
28 D6	Ballyhaght	
27 J4	Ballyhahill (Baile Dhá Thuile)	
17 J3	Ballyhaise (Béal Átha hÉis)	
13 J4	Ballyhalbert (Baile Thalbóid)	
21 G2	Ballyhale, Co Galway (Baile Héil)	
30 D5	Ballyhale, Co Kilkenny (Baile Héil)	
34 D4	Ballyhank	
33 G2	Ballyhar (Baile Uí Aichir)	
16 B5	Ballyhaunis (Béal Átha hAmhnais)	
15 F5	Ballyhean (Béal Átha hÉin)	
15 H7	Ballyhear	
17 J4	Ballyheelan (Bealach an Chaoláin)	
27 F5	Ballyheige (Baile Uí Thaidhg)	
15 G7	Ballyhenry	
21 J7	Ballyhickey	
31 G5	Ballyhoge (Baile Uí Cheog)	
30 D6	Ballyhomuck	
28 B7	Ballyhoolahan	
34 E2	Ballyhooly (Baile Átha hUlla)	
13 J6	Ballyhornan (Baile Uí Chornáin)	
17 H2	Ballyhugh, Co Cavan	
24 B3	Ballyhugh, Co Offaly	
18 B4	Ballyjamesduff (Baile Shéamais Dhuibh)	
23 J4	Ballykean	
13 F5	Ballykeel (An Baile Caol)	
23 F2	Ballykeeran (Bealach Caorthainn)	
5 J6	Ballykelly (Baile Uí Cheallaigh)	
24 B3	Ballykilleen	
35 H3	Ballykilty	
13 G7	Ballykinler	
30 D7	Ballykinsella	
25 F5	Ballyknockan	
35 G5	Ballylanders, Co Cork (Baile an Londraigh)	
29 F6	Ballylanders, Co Limerick (Baile an Londraigh)	
30 C7	Ballylaneen	
34 D5	Ballylangley	
16 E6	Ballyleague	
30 C7	Ballyleen	
12 D6	Ballyleny	
13 G4	Ballylesson (Baile na Leasán)	
33 H5	Ballylickey	
5 G4	Ballyliffin (Baile Lifín)	
30 C4	Ballyline	
24 B7	Ballylinnen	
6 C5	Ballylintagh	
27 H4	Ballylongford (Baile Átha Longfoirt)	
29 H6	Ballylooby, Co Tipperary (Beala Átha Lúbaigh)	
29 F5	Ballylooby, Co Tipperary (Beala Átha Lúbaigh)	
31 H5	Ballylucas	
7 H7	Ballylumford	
24 C6	Ballylynan (Baile Uí Laigheanáin)	
29 J6	Ballymacarbry (Baile Mhac Cairbre)	
30 E7	Ballymacaw (Baile Mhac Dháith)	
27 G6	Ballymacelligot	
17 J5	Ballymachugh	
22 E7	Ballymackey (Baile Uí Mhacaí)	
35 J2	Ballymacmague	
35 H4	Ballymacoda (Baile Mhac Óda)	
16 D6	Ballymacurly (Baile Mhic Thorlaigh)	
22 C3	Ballymacward (Baile Mhic an Bhaird)	
35 H4	Ballymadog	
5 G5	Ballymagan (Baile Mhic Cionaoith)	
5 J4	Ballymagaraghy	
5 G7	Ballymagorry	
	(Baile Mhic Gofraidh)	
17 G7	Ballymahon (Baile Uí Mhatháin)	
33 J3	Ballymakeery (Baile Mhic Íre)	
19 F5	Ballymakenny	
22 B4	Ballymanagh	
17 J5	Ballymanus	
21 J5	Ballymaquiff	
19 H2	Ballymartin (Baile Mhic Grolla) Mhártain	
34 D5	Ballymartle	
6 E7	Ballymena (An Baile Meánach)	
16 C6	Ballymoe (Béal Átha Mó)	
6 D5	Ballymoney (Baile Muine)	
35 F4	Ballymore, Co Cork	
4 D5	Ballymore, Co Donegal (An Baile Mór)	
23 G2	Ballymore, Co Westmeath (An Baile Mór)	
24 E5	Ballymore Eustace	
30 D7	Ballymorris	
16 C2	Ballymote (Baile an Mhóta)	
24 D5	Ballymount	
31 H5	Ballymurn	
31 F4	Ballymurphy (Baile Uí Mhurchú)	
27 J5	Ballymurragh	
16 E7	Ballymurray (Baile Uí Mhuirigh)	
31 F6	Ballynabola	
21 J4	Ballynabucky	
28 B2	Ballynacally (Baile na Caillí)	
34 B5	Ballynacarriga (Béal na Carraige)	
17 H7	Ballynacarrigy (Baile na Carraige)	
16 B2	Ballynacarrow (Baile na Cora)	
22 E7	Ballynaclogh	
35 G3	Ballynacole	
35 G4	Ballynacorra	
35 K2	Ballynacourty, Co Waterford	
34 E5	Ballynacourty, Co Cork	
17 J5	Ballynacree	
17 J7	Ballynafid	
35 F3	Ballynagaul, Co Cork	
35 K2	Ballynagaul, Co Waterford	
34 E3	Ballynaglough West	
23 H2	Ballynagore (Béal Átha na nGabhar)	
34 B3	Ballynagree	
34 E4	Ballynagrumoolia	
29 J7	Ballynaguilkee	
13 G5	Ballynahinch, Co Down (Baile na hInse)	
29 F2	Ballynahinch, Co Tipperary (Baile na hInse)	
21 F5	Ballynahowan, Co Clare	
20 E4	Ballynahown, Co Galway (Baile na hAbhann)	
23 F3	Ballynahown, Co Westmeath (Baile na hAbhann)	
27 J7	Ballynahulla	
31 F3	Ballynakill, Co Carlow	
24 B4	Ballynakill, Co Offaly	
23 F2	Ballynakill, Co Westmeath	
32 E6	Ballynakilla	
5 H7	Ballynamallaght	
34 D2	Ballynamona, Co Cork (Baile an Móna)	
22 D3	Ballynamona, Co Galway	
31 F6	Ballynamona, Co Wexford	
34 E2	Ballynamuddagh	

INDEX OF PLACE NAMES

29 J7 Ballynamult *(Béal na Molt)*	19 G6 Balscaddan	15 G5 Belcarra
26 C7 Ballynana	33 H7 Baltimore *(Dún na Séad)*	21 J2 Belclare *(Béal Chláir)*
17 J4 Ballynarry	24 E6 Baltinglass *(Bealach Conglais)*	10 E6 Belcoo *(Béal Cú)*
27 F5 Ballynaskreena	27 F6 Baltovin	8 D6 Belderg *(Béal Deirg)*
15 H5 Ballynastangford *(Baile na Stanfard)*	19 G5 Baltray *(Baile Trá)*	13 F3 Belfast *(Béal Feiriste)*
5 H7 Ballyneaner *(Baile an Aonfhir)*	15 J3 Banada	34 E5 Belgooly *(Béal Guala)*
28 E4 Ballyneety *(Baile an Fhaoitigh)*	23 F4 Banagher *(Beannchar)*	14 E2 Bellacorick *(Béal Átha Chomhraic)*
30 B6 Ballyneill *(Baile Uí Néill)*	12 E5 Banbridge *(Droichead na Banna)*	9 J7 Belladrihid
30 B4 Ballynennan	34 D5 Bandon *(Droichead na Banda)*	14 D3 Bellagarvaun
35 G2 Ballynoe, Co Cork *(An Baile Nua)*	27 G5 Banemore	12 D2 Bellaghy *(Baile Eachaidh)*
22 C4 Ballynoe, Co Galway	13 H3 Bangor, Co Down *(Beannachar)*	15 J3 Bellahy
13 G2 Ballynure *(Baile an Iuir)*	14 D2 Bangor, Co Mayo *(Baingear)*	17 J3 Bellanacargy
28 E6 Ballyorgan *(Baile Uí Argáin)*	27 F6 Banna	16 D4 Bellanagare *(Béal Átha na gCarr)*
31 H3 Ballyoughter	12 D4 Bannfoot	11 F6 Bellanaleck *(Bealach na Leice)*
33 H6 Ballyourane	28 B2 Bansha, Co Clare	22 E2 Beallanamullia *(Béal Átha na Muille)*
30 B5 Ballypatrick *(Baile Phádraig)*	29 G5 Bansha, Co Tipperary *(An Bháinseach)*	17 J4 Bellananagh
29 G6 Ballyporeen *(Béal Átha Póirín)*	34 C2 Banteer *(Bántir)*	22 E2 Bellaneeny
26 D6 Ballyquin, Co Kerry	33 H6 Bantry *(Beanntraí)*	4 D7 Bellanmore
30 C6 Ballyquin, Co Waterford	5 J6 Baranailt	11 J7 Bellanode *(Béal Átha an Fhóid)*
30 C2 Ballyragget *(Béal Átha Ragad)*	21 H7 Barefield *(Gort Lomán)*	15 G4 Bellavary *(Béal Átha Bhearaigh)*
6 C5 Ballyrashane	33 H7 Barloge	12 D7 Belleek, Co Armagh *(Béal Leice)*
35 G3 Ballyre	21 G4 Barna, Co Galway *(Bearna)*	10 D5 Beleek, Co Fermanagh *(Béal Leice)*
11 J5 Ballyreagh	29 F4 Barna, Co Limerick	19 F6 Bellewstown *(Baile an Bheileogaigh)*
34 D5 Ballyregan	23 F7 Barna, Co Offaly	23 F4 Bellmount
23 J6 Ballyroan *(Baile Átha an Róine)*	15 J4 Barnacahoge	8 B7 Belmullet *(Béal an Mhuirthead)*
16 D4 Ballyroddy	16 C4 Barnacawley	13 G2 Beltoy
26 C7 Ballyroe	22 B2 Barnaderg *(Beara Dhearg)*	15 F3 Beltra, Co Mayo
31 G3 Ballyroebuck	33 G6 Barnaghgeehy	9 J7 Beltra, Co Sligo *(Béal Trá)*
12 D3 Ballyronan *(Baile Uí Rónáin)*	33 H5 Barnagowlane	17 H2 Belturbet *(Béal Tairbirt)*
13 F7 Ballyroney *(Baile Uí Ruanaí)*	29 J2 Barnalisheen	35 F4 Belvelly
33 F7 Ballyroon	15 J4 Barnalyra	12 B5 Benburb *(An Bhinn Bhorb)*
30 E2 Ballyryan	8 B7 Barnatra	6 D6 Bendooragh *(Bun Déurai)*
9 J7 Ballysadare *(Baile Easa Dara)*	15 H5 Barnycarroll *(Bearna Chearuill)*	30 D4 Bennettsbridge *(Droichead Binéid)*
10 C5 Ballyshannon *(Baile Átha Seanaidh)*	30 C2 Barrack Village	11 H4 Beragh *(Bearach)*
27 F6 Ballysheen	33 H2 Barraduff	34 D3 Berrings *(Biorainn)*
30 D7 Ballyshoneen	22 C5 Barratoor	12 D7 Bessbrook *(An Sruthán)*
22 D5 Ballyshrule	30 D4 Barrettstown	19 G6 Bettystown *(Baile an Bhiataigh)*
29 J3 Ballysloe	28 B4 Barrigone	30 E2 Bilboa *(Biolbó)*
29 J2 Ballysorrell	28 E3 Barringtonsbridge	28 E2 Birdhill *(Cnocánan Éin Fhinn)*
28 B3 Ballysteen	26 E6 Barrow	23 F5 Birr *(Biorra)*
21 G5 Ballyvaghan *(Baile Uí Bheachaín)*	17 G7 Barry *(Barraigh)*	13 H6 Bishops Court
31 J5 Ballyvaldon	35 F2 Bartlemy	30 D6 Bishopshall
29 F4 Ballyvalode	31 G7 Bastardstown	29 G7 Black
34 D3 Ballyvaloon	24 E2 Batterstown *(Baile an Bhóthair)*	25 F2 Black Bull
31 F2 Ballyveal	23 J2 Baughna	23 H4 Black Lion
29 H6 Ballyveera	34 B4 Baulbrack	29 H5 Blackcastle *(An Caisleán Dubh)*
28 E6 Ballyvisteen	30 D5 Baunskeha	31 G6 Blackhall
33 F7 Ballyvoge *(Baile Uí Bhuaigh)*	21 G7 Bauntlieve	10 E5 Blacklion *(An Blaic)*
22 C2 Ballyvoneen	28 B7 Bawnaneel	28 D6 Blackpool *(An Linn Dubh)*
28 B2 Ballyvonnavaun	17 G2 Bawnboy, Co Cavan *(An Bábhún Búi)*	34 E4 Blackrock, Co Cork *(An Dúcharraig)*
34 E5 Ballyvorane	33 H6 Bawnboy, Co Cork	25 G3 Blackrock, Co Dublin *(An Charraig Dhubh)*
33 J3 Ballyvourney *(Baile Bhuirne)*	29 J6 Bawnfune	19 F3 Blackrock, Co Louth *(Na Creagacha)*
6 E4 Ballyvoy *(Baile Bhóidh)*	33 J7 Bawnlahan	14 C2 Blacksod
28 E7 Ballywalter, Co Cork	15 J7 Beagh	31 J5 Blackwater *(An Abhainn Dubh)*
13 J4 Ballywalter, Co Down *(Baile Bháltair)*	27 G4 Beal	33 F4 Blackwater Bridge
13 F6 Ballyward *(Baile Mhic an Bhaird)*	21 H5 Bealaclugga *(Béal an Chloga)*	12 C5 Blackwatertown *(An Port Mór)*
6 B5 Ballywildrick	20 E3 Bealadangan *(Béal an Daingin)*	24 D3 Blackwood *(Coill Dubh)*
34 D6 Ballywilliam, Co Cork *(Baile Liam)*	27 G2 Bealaha	6 C5 Blagh
31 F5 Ballywilliam, Co Wexford	23 F2 Bealin *(Béal Linne)*	25 F2 Blanchardstown
6 C5 Balnamore *(Béal an Átha Móir)*	34 C4 Bealnablath	
19 F6 Balrath *(Baile na Ratha)*	34 C4 Bealnamorive	
19 G7 Balrothery	33 G2 Beaufort *(Lios an Phúea)*	
	18 E7 Bective	
	32 B2 Beenacouma	
	34 E2 Behernagh	
	15 J5 Bekan *(Béacán)*	

INDEX OF PLACE NAMES

(Baile Bhlainséir)
34 D3 Blarney (An Bhlarna)
12 E5 Bleary
27 F7 Blennerville
  (Cathair Uí Mhóráin)
24 E4 Blessington (Baile Coimín)
23 G4 Blue Ball (An Pháilís)
27 J7 Blueford
34 E5 Boardee
13 G5 Boardmills
  (An Muileann Adhmaid)
22 F7 Bodyke (Lúbán Díge)
15 F3 Bofeenaun
19 G7 Bog of the Ring
23 G7 Boggaun
19 G3 Boharboy
28 E3 Boher
23 G6 Boheraphuca
28 B7 Boherboy, Co Cork
  (An Bóthar Buí)
28 D3 Bohereen
29 H4 Boherlahan
  (An Bóthar Leathan)
18 D6 Bohermeen (An Bóthar Mín)
29 G6 Bohernarnane
17 H6 Boherquill
28 E4 Boherroe
10 E6 Boho (Botha)
15 H4 Bohola (Both Chomhla)
6 B5 Bolea (Both Liath)
6 C6 Boleran
24 B7 Boley, Co Laois
31 G2 Boley, Co Wicklow
31 H4 Boleyvogue
14 D4 Bolinglanna
35 H3 Boola
29 G6 Boolakennedy
30 E3 Borris (An Bhuiríos)
23 G6 Borris in Ossory
  (Buirios Mór Osraí)
22 E6 Borrisokane (Buiríos Uí Chéin)
29 H2 Borrisoleigh
  (Buiríos Ó Luigheach)
21 H6 Boston
28 E5 Bottomstown
17 H6 Bottomy
29 H2 Bouladuff (An Bhuaile Dhubh)
6 C7 Bovedy
5 J6 Bovevagh (Boith Mhéabha)
16 D3 Boyle (Mainistir na Búillle)
16 B6 Boyounagh
24 B4 Brackagh
16 C5 Brackloon
18 B7 Bracklyn
24 B4 Bracknagh, Co Offaly
  (Breacánach)
16 E7 Bracknagh, Co Roscommon
23 F4 Brackny
15 G3 Brackwanshagh
33 G6 Brahalish
26 D6 Brandon (Cé Bhréanainn)
11 J7 Brandrum
24 E5 Brannockstown
  (Baile na rnBreatnach)
25 H4 Bray (Bré)
5 G7 Bready (An Bhreadaigh)
34 B5 Breaghna
27 F3 Breaghva
15 G4 Breaghwy

31 G5 Bree (Brí)
35 H3 Breeda
15 J6 Brickeens (Na Broicíní)
35 F2 Bridebridge
22 E2 Brideswell (Tobar Bríde)
5 G6 Bridge End (Ceann an Droichid)
25 F7 Bridgeland
10 D4 Bridgetown, Co Donegal
28 E2 Bridgetown, Co Clare
  (Baile an Droichid)
31 G7 Bridgetown, Co Wexford
12 C4 Brigh
4 C5 Brinlack
30 B7 Briska
25 F4 Brittas (An Briotás)
35 G2 Britway
28 D2 Broadford, Co Clare
28 B6 Broadford, Co Limerick
  (Áth Leathan)
24 C2 Broadford, Co Kildare
31 H7 Broadway (Gráinseach lúir)
6 B6 Brockagh, Co Londonderry
25 F6 Brockagh, Co Wicklow
11 G6 Brookeborough (Achadh Lon)
29 F5 Brookville
18 D2 Broomfield (Achadh an Bhrúim)
27 J6 Brosna, Co Kerry (Brosnach)
23 F6 Brosna, Co Offaly
  (An Bhrosnach)
23 G4 Broughal
6 E7 Broughshane (Bruach)
24 C5 Brownstown, Co Kildare
30 E8 Brownstown, Co Waterford
18 E6 Brownstown, Co Meath
29 J2 Bruckana
10 B3 Bruckless
28 D5 Bruff (An Brú)
28 D5 Bruree (Brú Rí)
13 G7 Bryansford (Áth Bhriain)
7 F7 Buckna
10 C5 Buckode
28 E5 Bulgaden (Builgidin)
22 C4 Bullaun
14 C3 Bunacurry
33 G4 Bunane
33 F5 Bunaw
4 B6 Bunbeg (An Bun Beag)
17 H7 Bunbrosna (Bun Brosnaí)
31 G3 Bunclody (Bun Clóidi)
5 G5 Buncrana (Bun Cranncha)
10 B5 Bundoran (Bun Dobhráin)
32 E3 Bunglasha
17 H5 Bunlahy
30 C8 Bunmahon (Bun Machan)
15 G7 Bunnafollistran
22 V5 Bunnaglass
8 B7 Bunnahowen
20 D2 Bunnahown
16 B3 Bunnanaddan
  (Bun an Fheadáin)
15 H2 Bunnyconnellan
  (Muine Chonalláin)
28 C3 Bunratty
30 C4 Burnchurch
29 G6 Burncourt (An Chúirt Dóite)
5 G5 Burnfoot (Bun na hAbhann)
34 D2 Burnfort (Ráth an Tóiteáin)
21 H5 Burren, Co Clare (Boirinn)
27 J2 Burren, Co Clare (Boirinn)

19 G2 Burren, Co Down (Boirinn)
27 J3 Burrenfadda
4 B6 Burtonport (Ailt an Chorráin)
6 D4 Bushmills (Muileann na Buaise)
17 J3 Butler's Bridge
34 D6 Butlerstown
  (Baile an Bhuitléaraigh)
28 D7 Buttevant (Cill na Mallach)
34 D2 Bweeng

C

12 B5 Cabragh (An Chabrach)
24 C2 Cadamstown, Co Kildare
  (Baile Mhic Ádairn)
23 G5 Cadamstown, Co Offaly
  (Baile Mhic Ádaim)
12 E2 Caddy
6 C6 Caheny
22 B6 Caher, Co Clare (An Chathair)
33 F7 Caher, Co Cork
29 H5 Caher, Co Tipperary
26 E7 Caheracruttera
21 J4 Caheradrine
33 H6 Caheragh
22 C4 Caherakillen
32 D4 Caherbarnagh (An Chatair)
28 E4 Caherconlish
  (Cathair Chinn Lis)
21 G6 Caherconnell
32 D5 Caherdaniel (Cathair Dónall)
27 J2 Caherea
21 J3 Caherlea
15 H7 Caherlistrane
  (Cathair Loistréain)
32 D6 Cahermore, Co Cork
  (Cathair Mhór)
21 J5 Cahermore, Co Galway
33 H5 Cahermuckee
27 H2 Cahermurphy
21 F7 Caherogan
21 J2 Caherphuca
32 B3 Cahersiveen
  (Cathair Saidhbhín)
31 G4 Caim
12 B6 Caledon (Cionn Aird)
30 C4 Callan (Callain)
15 H3 Callow, Co Mayo (An Caladh)
16 C4 Callow, Co Roscommon
10 B6 Calry
22 C2 Caltra (An Cheatrach)
22 D3 Caltraghlea
24 D5 Calverstown
  (Baile an Chalbhaigh)
22 E7 Camira
12 D7 Camlough (Camloch)
31 H3 Camolin (Cam Eolaing)
26 E7 Camp (An Com)
30 E6 Campile (Ceann Poill)
23 H6 Camross (Camros)
20 E3 Camus
18 B3 Canningstown (Baile Chainín)
6 E5 Cape Castle
35 F2 Cappagh, Co Cork
28 C4 Cappagh, Co Limerick
12 B4 Cappagh, Co Tyrone
  (An Chapóg)
29 G4 Cappagh White (An Cheapach)
21 H5 Cappaghmore

INDEX OF PLACE NAMES

23 G4 Cappagowlan
23 G7 Cappalinnan
29 F3 Cappamore
        (An Cheapach Mhór)
22 C3 Cappataggle
        (Ceapaigh an tSeagail)
34 B5 Cappeen
35 H2 Cappoquin (Ceapach Choinn)
16 D5 Caran
24 C3 Carbury (Cairbre)
27 H7 Carker
12 B4 Carland (Domnach Carr)
18 D5 Carlanstown
        (Droichead Chearballáin)
19 G3 Carlingford (Cairlinn)
24 C7 Carlow (Ceatharlach)
6 B7 Carn, Co Londonderry
23 H2 Carn, Co Westmeath
20 D3 Carna (Carna)
12 C7 Carnagh (Carranach)
7 F7 Carnalbanagh
7 F7 Carnalbanagh Sheddings
5 J7 Carnanreagh
18 C5 Carnaross
7 G7 Carncastle
5 H4 Carndonagh (Carn Domhnach)
31 H3 Carnew (Carn an Bhua)
9 J6 Carney, Co Sligo
       (Fearann Uí Chearnaigh)
22 E6 Carney, Co Tipperary
       (Carnaigh)
7 F6 Carnlough (Carnlach)
13 G3 Carnmoney (Carn Monaidh)
21 J3 Carnoneen
12 B5 Carnteel (Carn tSiail)
16 B3 Carracastle
       (Ceathrú an Chaisil)
24 D4 Carragh (Céarach)
16 B5 Carraghs
14 E5 Carraholly (Ceathrú Chalaidh)
21 H6 Carran, Co Clare (An Carn)
30 D3 Carran, Co Kilkenny
20 E4 Carraroe (An Cheathrú Rua)
9 J3 Carrick, Co Donegal
       (An Charraig)
31 F7 Carrick, Co Wexford
       (An Charraig)
16 E3 Carrick-on-Shannon
       (Cora Droma Rúisc)
30 B6 Carrick-on'Suir
       (Carraig na Siúire)
17 J4 Carrickaboy (Carraigigh Bhuí)
4 E5 Carrickart (Carraig Airt)
18 D4 Carrickashedoge
17 G6 Carrickboy (An Charraig Bhuí)
13 H2 Carrickfergus
       (Carraig Fhearghais)
18 C3 Carrickmacross
       (Carraig Mhachaire)
25 G4 Carrickmines
       (Carraig Mhaighin)
11 J4 Carrickmore or Termon Rock
       (An Charraig Mhór)
11 J6 Carrickroe
23 F5 Carrig, Co Tipperary
24 E5 Carrig, Co Wicklow
26 D7 Carrigaday
34 C4 Carrigadrohid
34 C3 Carrigagulla

27 F3 Carrigaholt
       (Carraig an Chnabhaltaigh)
22 E5 Carrigahorig
       (Carraig an Chomhraic)
34 E5 Carrigaline (Carraig Uí Leighin)
17 G3 Carrigallen (Carraig Álainn)
17 J4 Carrigan (An Carraigín)
34 B3 Carriganimmy (Carraig an Irne)
29 G6 Carriganroe
5 G6 Carrigans (An Carraigin)
22 D7 Carrigatogher
       (Carraig an Tóchair)
25 G5 Carriggower
27 J4 Carrigkerry
34 E3 Carrignavar
       (Carraig na bhFear)
35 F4 Carrigtohill (Carraig Thuathail)
29 G4 Carrow
13 J4 Carrowdore (Ceathrú Dobhair)
21 F6 Carrowduff, Co Clare
16 D6 Carrowduff, Co Roscommon
16 B2 Carroweden
5 F5 Carrowkeel, Co Donegal
       (An Cheathrú Chaol)
22 C4 Carrowkeel, Co Galway
15 G7 Carrowkeel, Co Mayo
16 B6 Carrowkeelanahglass
14 E6 Carrowkennedy
5 J4 Carrowmenagh
21 H4 Carrowmore, Co Galway
8 E7 Carrowmore, Co Mayo
       (Ceathrú Mhór Leacan)
15 H7 Carrowmore, Co Mayo
16 B2 Carrowmore, Co Sligo
21 G2 Carrowmoreknock
15 G5 Carrownacon
9 G7 Carrowpadeen
22 D3 Carrowreagh
17 F7 Carrowrory
8 C6 Carrowteige
13 G4 Carryduff
       (Ceathrú Aedha Dhuibh)
22 B4 Cartron
31 F3 Cashel, Co Carlow
23 J6 Cashel, Co Laois
20 D2 Cashel, Co Galway
29 H4 Cashel, Co Tipperary (Caiseal)
5 F4 Cashel Glebe
9 J6 Cashelgarran
       (Caiseal an Ghearráin)
21 J3 Cashla
31 F6 Cassagh
16 C2 Castlebaldwin
       (Béal Átha an gCarraigíní)
15 G4 Castlebar
       (Caisleán an Bharraigh)
19 F4 Castlebellingham
       (Baile an Ghearlánaigh)
34 E2 Castleblagh
22 C2 Castleblakeney (Gallach)
18 D2 Castleblayney (Baile na Lorgan)
31 H5 Castlebridge
       (Droichead an Chaisleáin)
6 D4 Castlecat (Caiseal Cait)
12 B4 Castlecaulfield
       (Baile Uí Dhonnaile)
30 D2 Castlecomer
       (Caisleán an Chomair)
28 D3 Castleconnell

       (Caisleán Uí Chonaill)
15 H2 Castleconor
16 D6 Castlecoote
28 C7 Castlecor (Caisleán na Cora)
32 D5 Castle Cove
23 H5 Castlecuffe
12 D2 Castledawson
       (An Seanrnhullach)
11 F3 Castlederg
       (Caisleán na Deirge)
24 C7 Castledermot
       (Diseart Diarmada)
31 G4 Castledockrell
31 H5 Castleellis
11 F2 Castlefinn (Caisleán na Finne)
34 B7 Castlefreke
10 B5 Castlegal
26 E6 Castlegregory
       (Caisleán Ghriaire)
14 D3 Castlehill, Co Mayo
       (Caorthannán)
15 G3 Castlehill, Co Mayo
27 H7 Castleisland (Oilean Ciarrai)
24 B2 Castlejordan
       (Caisleán Shuirdáin)
25 F3 Castleknock (Caisleán Cnucha)
29 J2 Castleleiny
       (Caisleán Laighnigh)
35 F2 Castlelyons
       (Caisleán Ó Liatháin)
27 F7 Castlemaine
       (Caisleán na Mainge)
35 G4 Castlemartyr (Baile na Martra)
16 D5 Castleplunket (Lois Lachna)
17 J6 Castlepollard (Baile na gCros)
21 H3 Castlequarter
32 B3 Castlequin
18 B5 Castlerahan
16 C5 Castlerea
       (An Caisleán Riabhach)
13 G4 Castlereagh
6 B5 Castlerock (Carraig Ceasail)
12 B7 Castleshane
       (Caisleán an tSiáin)
21 H6 Castletown, Co Clare
34 B5 Castletown, Cork
       (Baile Chaisleáin Chinn Eich)
23 H6 Castletown, Co Laois
       (Baile an Chaisleáin)
28 C5 Castletown, Co Limerick
       (Baile an Chaisleáin)
18 D5 Castletown, Co Meath
       (Baile an Chaisleáin)
17 J5 Castletown, Co Westmeath
       (Baile an Chaisleáin)
31 J2 Castletown, Co Wexford
       (Baile an Chaisleáin)
32 E6 Castletown Bearhaven
23 H2 Castletown Geoghegan
28 E7 Castletownroche
       (Baile Chaisleáin an Róistigh)
33 J7 Castletownshend
       (Baile an Chaisleáin)
15 H6 Castleville
30 D3 Castlewarren
       (Caisleáin an Bhairinnigh)
13 G7 Castlewellan
       (Caisleáin Uidhilín)
27 F5 Causeway (An Tóchar)

INDEX OF PLACE NAMES

17 J3 Cavan *(An Cabhán)*	16 C5 Clerragh	24 B4 Clonbulloge *(Cluain Bolg)*
10 C4 Cavangarden	31 G6 Cleristown	15 F7 Clonbur *(An Fhairche)*
29 G6 Caves	14 C7 Clifden *(An Clochán)*	28 B5 Cloncagh *(Cluain Cath)*
33 J6 Ceancullig	18 B3 Clifferna *(An Chliaifearna)*	24 B4 Cloncreen
28 C7 Cecilstown *(Baile an Bhriotaigh)*	10 B5 Cliffony *(Cliafuine)*	17 G7 Cloncullen
24 E3 Celbridge *(Cill Droichid)*	24 B2 Clocrave	23 G6 Cloncully
16 B3 Chaffpool	30 D6 Clogga, Co Kilkenny	24 D2 Cloncurry
18 E3 Chanonrock	31 J2 Clogga, Co Wicklow	25 F3 Clondalkin *(Cluain Dolcáin)*
31 G5 Chapel	6 E6 Clogh, Co Antrim *(An Chloch)*	34 B3 Clondrohid
9 H7 Chapel Street	24 B7 Clogh, Co Kilkenny	35 F2 Clondulane
13 J6 Chapeltown, Co Down *(Baile an tSéipéil)*	23 H7 Clogh, Co Laois	30 C6 Clonea *(Cluain Fhia)*
32 B3 Chapeltown, Co Kerry *(An Caol)*	28 C4 Clogh, Co Limerick	25 F2 Clonee *(Cluain Aodha)*
12 C5 Charlemont	31 H3 Clogh, Co Wexford	23 J3 Cloneen, Co Offaly
15 J3 Charlestown *(Baile Chathail)*	6 E6 Clogh Mills *(Muileann na Cloiche)*	30 B5 Cloneen, Co Tipperary *(An Cluainin)*
28 C6 Charleville	10 D1 Cloghan, Co Donegal *(An Clochan)*	31 G3 Clonegall *(Cluain na nGall)*
30 E6 Cheekpoint *(Pointe na Síge)*	23 F4 Cloghan, Co Offaly	10 E4 Clonelly
24 C5 Cherryville	18 B7 Cloghan, Co Westmeath	18 B2 Clones *(Cluain Eois)*
12 D2 Chesney's Corner	33 F7 Cloghane, Co Cork	22 E4 Clonfert *(Cluain Fearta)*
35 F5 Church Bay	26 C7 Cloghane, Co Kerry *(An Chlochan)*	31 F6 Clongeen
33 H7 Church Cross *(Cnoc na Rátha)*	15 H7 Cloghans Hill	23 H6 Clonincurragh
4 E6 Church Hill, Co Donegal *(Min an Lábáin)*	24 C2 Clogharinka, Co Offaly	23 J6 Clonkeen, Co Laois
11 F3 Church Hill, Co Tyrone *(An Droim Meánach)*	30 D2 Clogharinka, Co Kilkenny	33 H3 Clonkeen, Co Kerry
27 F6 Church Hill, Co Kerry	27 H2 Cloghaun, Co Clare	22 B3 Clonkeenkerrill
5 G6 Church Town *(Tulaigh an Iúir)*	21 G3 Cloghaun, Co Galway	18 B7 Clonlost *(Cluain Loiste)*
16 E7 Churchboro Cross	21 H3 Cloghaun, Co Galway	23 F3 Clonmacnoise
15 F6 Churchfield	9 J6 Cloghboley *(Clochbhuile)*	5 G4 Clonmany *(Cluain Mainae)*
16 C4 Churchstreet	15 F7 Cloghbrack, Co Galway *(An Chloch Bhreac)*	29 J2 Clonmeen
28 C6 Churchtown, Co Cork *(Baile an Teampaill)*	18 C7 Cloghbrack, Co Meath	29 J6 Clonmel *(Cluain Meala)*
35 G4 Churchtown, Co Cork *(Baile an Teampaill Theas)*	5 G7 Cloghcor	18 C6 Clonmellon *(Ráistin)*
31 J7 Churchtown Co Wexford	29 H6 Clogheen, Co Tipperary *(An Chloichín)*	24 E7 Clonmore, Co Carlow *(Cluain Mhór)*
30 E8 Churchtown, Co Wexford	29 J6 Clogheen, Co Waterford	19 F4 Clonmore, Co Louth
11 G5 Clabby *(Clabaigh)*	15 F4 Clogher, Co Mayo	23 G7 Clonmore, Co Tipperary
14 B7 Claddaghduff *(An Cladach Dubh)*	15 G5 Clogher, Co Mayo *(An Clochar)*	35 G3 Clonmult
6 D7 Clady, Co Londonderry	14 C2 Clogher, Co Mayo	23 F4 Clonony
11 F2 Clady, Co Tyrone *(Clóidigh)*	16 E4 Clogher, Co Roscommon	29 H3 Clonoulty
12 C7 Cladymilltown *(Baile an Mhuillinn)*	11 H5 Clogher, Co Tyrone *(Clochar)*	31 F5 Clonroche *(Cluain an Róistigh)*
14 D3 Claggan	28 D2 Cloghera	25 F2 Clonsilla *(Cluain Saileach)*
24 E3 Clane *(Claonadh)*	19 G5 Clogherhead *(Ceann Chlochair)*	25 G3 Clontarf *(Cluain Tarbh)*
23 H3 Clara *(Clóirtheach)*	11 J4 Cloghfin	12 B7 Clontibret *(Cluain Tiobrad)*
23 H5 Clarahill	22 E7 Cloghjordan *(Cloch Shiurdáin)*	30 C2 Clontubbrid
12 D6 Clare *(An Clár)*	14 C4 Cloghmore *(An Chloich Mhóir)*	18 C7 Clonycavan
28 B2 Clarecastle *(Droichead an Chláir)*	30 D2 Cloghpook	23 J4 Clonygowan *(Cluain na nGamham)*
23 G5 Clareen *(An Cláirin)*	25 G2 Cloghran *(Clochrán)*	23 J4 Clonyquin
21 H3 Claregalway *(Baile Chláir)*	34 D4 Cloghroe	21 H3 Cloonacauneen
15 H5 Claremorris *(Clár Chlainne Mhuiris)*	27 J6 Cloghvoula	15 J2 Cloonacool *(Cluain na Cúile)*
28 C3 Clarina *(Clár Aidhne)*	13 J5 Cloghy *(Clochaigh)*	17 H4 Cloonagh
21 J4 Clarinbridge *(Droichead an Chláirín)*	31 G3 Clohamon *(Cloch Amainn)*	21 H3 Cloonboo
22 E7 Clash	30 D7 Clohernagh	16 C6 Cloonbrennaun
27 J5 Clash North	31 H3 Clologe	16 E7 Clooncah
27 J5 Clash South	30 C2 Clomantagh	15 F3 Cloondaff
29 F5 Clashdrumsmith	23 F7 Clonakenny *(Cluain Uí Chionaoith)*	17 F6 Cloondara *(Cluain Dá Ráth)*
35 H3 Clashmore *(Clais Mhór)*	34 C6 Clonakilty *(Cloich na Coillte)*	17 G3 Cloone *(An Chluain)*
30 C6 Clashroe	22 E7 Clonalea	17 F4 Cloone Grange
5 H7 Claudy *(Clóidigh)*	19 F7 Clonalvy *(Cluain Ailbhe)*	17 F4 Clooneagh
17 F6 Clawinch	35 H4 Clonard, Co Cork	17 H5 Clooneen
14 B7 Cleggan *(An Cloigeann)*	24 C2 Clonard, Co Meath *(Cluain Ioraird)*	10 B2 Clooney
28 B2 Clenagh	31 H6 Clonard Great	16 B6 Cloonfad, Co Roscommon
	23 F3 Clonascra	22 E3 Cloonfad, Co Roscommon *(Cluain Fada)*
	23 H5 Clonaslee *(Cluain na Slí)*	15 J4 Cloonfallagh *(Cluain Falach)*
	24 B4 Clonavoe	21 H7 Cloonfeagh
	16 B7 Clonbern *(Cluain Bheirn)*	15 J3 Cloonfinish
		16 B5 Cloonfower
		15 H2 Cloonkeelaun
		16 B6 Cloonkeen, Co Galway
		15 F5 Cloonkeen, Co Mayo

INDEX OF PLACE NAMES

16 C5 Cloonkeen, Co Roscommon	23 F6 Coolderry *(Cúl Doire)*	28 B4 Courtmatrix
16 C2 Cloonkeevy *(Cluain Ciabhaigh)*	17 J6 Coole *(An Chuil)*	31 J3 Courtown *(Baile na Cúirte)*
28 D2 Cloonlara *(Cluain Lára)*	35 F2 Coole Abbey	33 H5 Cousane
15 H5 Cloonlee	33 J3 Coolea, Co Cork *(Cúil Aodha)*	22 D4 Coxtown
16 C3 Cloonloogh *(Cluain Lua)*	34 E2 Coolea, Co Cork	31 H3 Craan
29 F4 Cloonlusk	10 D7 Coolegreane	31 H3 Craanford *(Áth an Chorráin)*
16 D5 Cloonmurray	30 D3 Coolgrange	25 F7 Crafield
16 B7 Cloonnacat	31 J2 Coolgreany *(Cúil Chréine)*	21 F5 Craggagh
16 C5 Cloonsheever	34 E3 Coolgreen	21 J7 Cragroe
16 B3 Cloontia *(Na Cluainte)*	34 E2 Coolinny	11 H2 Craig
16 E6 Cloontuskert	33 J5 Coolkellure	13 H3 Craigavad *(Creig an Bhada)*
22 F6 Cloonusker	27 J3 Coolmeen *(Cúil Mhín)*	6 C7 Craigavole
9 G7 Cloonycarney	10 C4 Coolmore	12 E5 Craigavon
22 C3 Cloonymorris	16 B5 Coolnafarna	6 D7 Craigs *(Na Creeaga)*
16 D5 Cloonyogan	17 H6 Coolnagun	11 J2 Cranagh *(An Chrannóg)*
16 D5 Cloonyquin *(Cluain Uí Choinn)*	25 G2 Coolock	31 H4 Crane
23 G6 Closh	23 H6 Coolrain *(Cúil Ruáin)*	4 E5 Cranford *(Craeamhghort)*
13 G6 Clough *(An Chloch)*	31 J4 Coolroe	10 B2 Crannogeboy
34 C4 Cloughduv	22 E5 Coolross	27 J3 Cranny, Co Clare
22 E7 Cloughjordan	34 E5 Coolsallagh	*(An Chrannaigh)*
17 J2 Cloverhill	16 E6 Coolshaghtena	12 C2 Cranny, Co Londonderry
35 G4 Cloyne *(Cluain)*	32 D3 Coomduff	28 C3 Cratloe *(An Chreatalach)*
34 C4 Coachford *(Áth an Chóiste)*	33 H5 Coomleagh	22 B4 Craughwell *(Creachrnhaoil)*
12 C3 Coagh *(An Cuach)*	28 D3 Coonagh	13 H3 Crawfordsburn *(Sruth Chráfard)*
30 B3 Coalbrook *(Glaise an Ghuail)*	11 H6 Cooneen *(An Cúinnín)*	17 J7 Crazy Corner
12 C4 Coalisland *(Oileán an Ghuail)*	27 H3 Cooraclare *(Cuar an Chláir)*	33 H7 Creagh, Co Cork
30 D2 Coan *(An Cuan)*	30 E3 Coorleagh	12 C7 Creaghanroe *(Crícheán Rua)*
35 F4 Cobh *(An Cóbh)*	33 G6 Coosane	28 D4 Crecora *(Craobh Chomhartha)*
24 D6 Colbinstown *(Baile Choilbín)*	16 E3 Cootehall *(Uachtar Thíre)*	27 H2 Creegh *(An Chríoch)*
17 G7 Colehill *(Cnoc na Góla)*	18 B2 Cootehill *(Muinchille)*	16 D7 Creegs
6 C5 Coleraine *(Cúil Raithin)*	24 B2 Coralstown	4 D5 Creeslough *(An Craoslach)*
31 G6 Colestown	*(Baile Mhic Cearúill)*	8 E7 Creevagh
18 B6 Collinstown	27 G2 Corbally, Co Clare	28 B4 Creeves
(Baile na gCailleach)	9 G7 Corbally, Co Sligo	21 G5 Cregg, Co Clare
18 E5 Collon *(Collan)*	*(An Corrbhaile)*	33 J7 Cregg, Co Cork
9 J7 Collooney *(Cúil Mhuine)*	17 G6 Corboy	18 E2 Creggan, Co Armagh
29 J5 Colman	8 A7 Corclogh	23 F3 Creggan, Co Offaly
22 B2 Colmanstown	18 E3 Corcreeghagh	11 J3 Creggan, Co Tyrone
(Baile Uí Chlúmháin)	15 F2 Corcullin	*(An Creagán)*
19 F6 Colp	27 H7 Cordal *(Cordal)*	14 D6 Cregganbaun
13 G4 Comber *(An Comar)*	15 F5 Cordarragh	*(An Creagán Bán)*
29 G2 Commaun	24 D3 Corduff *(An Chorr Dubh)*	24 B7 Crettyard
10 D2 Commeen	34 E4 Cork *(Corcaigh)*	5 J5 Crindle
34 C5 Commons, Co Cork	6 E6 Corkey *(Corcaigh)*	23 F5 Crinkill *(Crionchoill)*
30 B3 Commons, Co Tipperary	17 F6 Corlea	10 B3 Croagh, Co Donegal
(Na Coimíní)	15 H3 Corlee	28 C4 Croagh, Co Limerick
15 G7 Cong *(Conga)*	17 G2 Corlough	15 F6 Croaghrimbeg
13 H3 Conlig *(An Choinleic)*	22 E3 Cornafulla *(Corr na Fola)*	15 H2 Crockets Town
35 G2 Conna *(Conaithe)*	15 F7 Cornamona	23 J3 Croghan, Co Offaly *(Cruachán)*
20 E2 Connemara	15 H6 Cornanagh	16 D4 Croghan, Co Roscommon
21 G7 Connolly *(Fioch Rua)*	23 J3 Corndarragh	4 C6 Crolly
12 E2 Connor	22 B6 Corrakyle	32 E2 Cromane *(An Cromán)*
34 B6 Connonagh	21 H2 Corrandulla *(Cor an Dola)*	17 F2 Cromlin
5 F7 Convoy *(Conmhaigh)*	14 C4 Corraun	17 J7 Crookedwood *(Tigh Munna)*
12 C3 Cookstown	6 E7 Correen	33 F8 Crookhaven *(An Cruachán)*
(An Chorr Chríochach)	31 F3 Corries Cross	34 C4 Crookstown, Co Cork
29 H7 Cool	21 H6 Corrofin, Co Clare	*(An Baile Gallda)*
23 J4 Coolagary	*(Cora Finne)*	24 D6 Crookstown, Co Kildare
9 J7 Coolaney *(Cúil Áine)*	21 J2 Corrofin, Co Galway	28 D4 Croom *(Crornadh)*
35 H2 Coolanheen	28 C5 Corronoher	27 F3 Cross, Co Clare *(An Chrois)*
31 H2 Coolattin	16 E2 Corry	15 G7 Cross, Co Mayo
22 D6 Coolbaun, Co Tipperary	18 D6 Cortown *(An Baile Corr)*	35 J3 Cross, Co Waterford
(An Cúl Bán)	8 E7 Corvoley	34 D5 Cross Barry
30 D2 Coolbaun, Co Kilkenny	20 E3 Costelloe *(Casla)*	*(Croisan Bharraigh)*
(An Cúl Bán)	26 D7 Coumduff	17 J4 Cross Keys, Co Cavan
4 E6 Coolboy, Co Donegal	35 G2 Countygate	*(Carraig an Tobair)*
31 H2 Coolboy, Co Wicklow	31 F5 Courthoyle	18 B6 Cross Keys, Co Meath
(An Cúl Buí)	34 C6 Courtmacsherry	18 E7 Cross Keys, Co Meath
29 F6 Coolboy, Co Tipperary	*(Cúirt Mhic Shéafraidh)*	34 C5 Cross Mahon

INDEX OF PLACE NAMES

11 F2 Cross Roads (Na Croisbhealaí)	7 F5 Cushendun (Bun Abhann Duinne)	5 F4 Doagh Beg
31 H5 Crossabeg (Na Crosa Beaga)	24 B4 Cushina	29 F2 Dolla (An Doladh)
18 C6 Crossakeel (Crosa Caoil)		12 E5 Dollingstown
15 H6 Crossboyne		25 G3 Dollymount (Cnocán Doirinne)
22 D4 Crossconnell	## D	19 G7 Donabate (Domhnach Bat)
17 H4 Crossdoney (Cros Domhnaigh)	23 J3 Daingean (An Daingean)	19 G6 Donacarney
17 G6 Crossea	25 H3 Dalkey	24 D3 Donadea
17 J4 Crosserlough (Crois ar Loch)	23 J2 Dalystown	11 G7 Donagh
13 H5 Crossgar (An Chrois Ghearr)	19 F7 Damastown	13 J3 Donaghadee (Domhnach Daoi)
6 C5 Crossgare	6 C5 Damhead	12 E5 Donaghcloney (Domhnach Cluana)
35 F5 Crosshaven (Bun an Tábhairne)	17 G6 Danesfort (Dún Feart)	23 H7 Donaghmore, Co Laois (Domhnach Mór)
24 C5 Crosskeys (Na hEochracha)	35 G2 Dangan	19 F7 Donaghmore, Co Meath
18 E2 Crossmaglen (Crois Mhic Lionnáin)	29 H5 Dangandargan	12 B4 Donaghmore, Co Tyrone
15 F2 Crossmolina (Crois Mhaoilíona)	12 C7 Darkley (Dearclaigh)	12 D6 Donaghpatrick (Domhnach Phádraig)
16 D3 Crossna	18 B2 Dartry	31 F5 Donard, Co Wexford
21 H5 Crossooha	31 G4 Davidstown (Baile Dháith)	24 E6 Donard, Co Wicklow (Dún Ard)
30 B2 Crosspatrick, Co Kilkenny (Crois Phádraig)	15 H7 Deerpark (Páirc an bhFia)	29 G4 Donaskeagh
31 H2 Crosspatrick, Co Wicklow	25 H5 Delgany (Deilgne)	10 D3 Donegal (Dún na nGall)
16 C7 Crosswell	14 D6 Delphi	28 D7 Doneraile (Dún ar Aill)
35 G3 Crowbally	18 B6 Delvin (Dealbhna)	29 G4 Donohill (Dún Eochaille)
12 E3 Crumlin (Cromghlinn)	34 B2 Dernagree (Doire na Graí)	18 C7 Donore, Co Meath
32 E5 Crumpane	17 G2 Derradda (Doire Fhada)	19 F6 Donore, Co Meath (Dún Uabhair)
21 J6 Crusheen (Croisín)	28 B2 Derragh	34 C3 Donoughmore (Domhnach Mór)
24 B7 Crutt	21 F6 Derreen, Co Clare	14 B3 Dooagh (Dumha Acha)
15 G3 Cuilkillew	32 C4 Derreen, Co Kerry	15 F2 Doobehy
13 F5 Culcavy	14 C4 Derreen, Co Mayo (Dan Doirín)	18 B2 Doocarrick
5 H3 Culdaff (Cuil Dábhcha)	33 G5 Derreenacarrin	16 B3 Doocastle (Caisleán an Dumha)
16 C3 Culfadda	33 H6 Derreenard	4 C7 Doocharry (An Dúchoraidh)
5 H3 Culkeeny	32 E4 Derreenauliff	14 C4 Dooega (Dumha Éige)
30 B2 Cullahill (An Chúlchoill)	33 F6 Derreeny	17 G3 Doogary
29 F6 Cullane	23 H3 Derries, Co Offaly	14 D4 Dooghbeg
18 E2 Cullaville (Baile Mhic Cullach)	24 C3 Derries, Co Offaly	14 C3 Doogort
28 C2 Culleen	22 E3 Derrineel	18 D2 Doohamlat
9 G7 Culleens (Na Coillíní)	24 C3 Derrinturn	18 B2 Doohat (Dúháite)
33 J2 Cullen, Co Cork (Cuillin)	12 D5 Derryadd (Doire Fhada)	14 C2 Doohooma (Dumha Thuarna)
29 F4 Cullen, Co Tipperary (Cuilleann)	4 C5 Derrybeg (Doirí Beaga)	15 F2 Dooleeg
28 E7 Cullenagh	13 H5 Derryboy (Doire Buí)	34 E5 Doolieve
31 F7 Cullenstown	22 B5 Derrybrien (Daraidh Braoin)	21 F6 Doolin
15 H3 Cullin	16 E6 Derrycanan	22 D3 Doon, Co Galway
6 D7 Cullybackey (Coill na Baice)	33 J6 Derryclogh	29 F3 Doon, Co Limerick (Dún)
18 E2 Cullyhanna (Coilleach Eanach)	23 H5 Derrycon	29 G7 Doon, Co Tipperary
6 C7 Culnady (Cúil Chnáidí)	23 G4 Derrycooly	14 D2 Doona
13 G3 Cultra	23 G4 Derrydolney	27 G3 Doonaha (Dún Átha)
35 G2 Currabeha (An Chorr Bheithe)	29 J2 Derryfada	27 G2 Doonbeg (An Dún Beag)
31 H5 Curracloe (Currach Cló)	29 F3 Derrygareen	32 D2 Doonmanagh
34 B4 Curraclogh	23 J5 Derrygile	20 D2 Doonreaghan
35 J3 Curragh (An Currach)	23 H3 Derrygolan	30 D6 Doornane
16 B6 Curragh West (An Currach Thair)	10 D5 Derrygonnelly (Doire Ó gConaíle)	14 C2 Dooyork
19 F7 Curragha	17 F7 Derrygowna	33 F7 Dough
33 J6 Curraghalicky	29 H6 Derrygrath	21 H4 Doughiska
22 E2 Curraghboy (An Currach Buí)	23 J3 Derrygrogan	34 E4 Douglas (Dúglas)
31 H2 Curraghlawn	6 D5 Derrykeighan	29 H2 Dovea (Dubhfhéith)
30 E5 Curraghmore, Co Kilkenny	22 E3 Derrylahan	30 C6 Dowling
28 E2 Curraghmore, Co Tipperary	11 F7 Derrylin (Doire Loinn)	6 B5 Downhill (Dún Bó)
16 E6 Curraghroe (An Currach Rua)	32 E4 Derryloughlin	29 F7 Downing
35 G2 Curraglass (Cora Chlas)	26 E7 Derrymore	13 H6 Downpatrick (Dún Pádraig)
23 G7 Curragunneen (Currach Guinín)	33 J5 Derrynacaheragh	10 D7 Dowra (An Damhshraith)
12 C2 Curran (An Corrán)	12 B7 Derrynoose (Doire Núis)	30 B4 Drangan (Drongan)
21 F4 Curranavilla	20 D2 Derryrush	12 B2 Draperstown (Baile na Croise)
27 G7 Currans	16 C6 Derrywode	5 J7 Dreen
29 G2 Curreeny (Na Coirríní)	6 D5 Dervock (Dearbhóg)	26 E5 Dreenagh
27 G7 Currow (Corra)	14 E7 Derryvoreada	27 F6 Drehidasillagh
15 J3 Curry (An Choraidh)	35 F3 Desert	33 J6 Driminidy
32 E6 Curryglass	12 C2 Desertmartin (Díseart Mhártain)	23 H6 Drimmo
7 F5 Cushendall (Bun Abhann Dalla)	11 F6 Devenish (Daimhinis)	33 J6 Drimoleague (Drom Dhá Liag)
	26 C7 Dingle (An Daingean)	
	13 F2 Doagh (Dumhach)	

INDEX OF PLACE NAMES

23 J6 Drinagh, Co Cork (Draighneagh)
20 B2 Drinagh, Co Galway
17 F5 Drinagh, Co Roscommon
31 H6 Drinagh, Co Wexford
9 G7 Drinaghan
17 H5 Dring (Droing)
34 C4 Dripsey (An Druipseach)
19 F6 Drogheda (Droichead Átha)
24 D4 Droichead Nua (Newbridge)
26 D7 Drom, Co Kerry
29 H2 Drom, Co Tipperary (An Drom)
34 B2 Dromagh
10 B7 Dromahair (Droim dhá Thiar)
13 F6 Dromara (Droim Bearach)
32 D4 Dromaragh
34 E3 Dromboy South
28 B6 Dromcolliher (Drom Collachair)
27 G6 Dromcunnig
34 E3 Dromgariff
28 D5 Dromin, Co Limerick
19 F4 Dromin, Co Louth (Droim Ing)
28 C6 Dromina (Drom Aidhhne)
22 D7 Dromineer (Drom Inbhir)
19 F4 Dromiskin (Droim Ineasclainn)
34 C2 Drommahane (Droim Átháin)
33 F6 Dromnea
17 F4 Dromod (Dromad)
33 H6 Dromore, Co Cork
13 F5 Dromore, Co Down (Droim Mór)
11 G4 Dromore, Co Tyrone (An Droim Mór)
35 H2 Dromore, Co Waterford
9 G7 Dromore West (An Droim Mór Thiar)
27 J6 Dromtrasna
18 B2 Drum, Co Monaghan (An Droim)
22 E2 Drum, Co Roscommon
5 H6 Drumahoe
22 B6 Drumandoora
13 G6 Drumaness (Droim an Easda)
21 G7 Drumanure
9 J7 Drumard
13 G6 Drumaroad
22 D4 Drumatober
29 H3 Drumbane (An Drom Bán)
29 F2 Drumbaun
13 G4 Drumbeg
13 G4 Drumbo
19 F4 Drumcar (Droim Chora)
22 F7 Drumcharley
21 H7 Drumcliff, Co Clare
9 J6 Drumcliff, Co Sligo (Droim Chliabh)
18 E4 Drumcondra (Droim Conrach)
18 B6 Drumcree (Droim Cria)
16 C2 Drumfin (Droim Fionn)
5 G4 Drumfree (Droim Fraoigh)
21 H3 Drumgriftin
10 D3 Druminnin
22 C5 Drumkeary
4 E7 Drumkeen
16 E2 Drumkeeran (Droim Caoithainn)
17 G3 Drumlea (Droim Léith)
17 G5 Drumlish (Droim Lis)
23 F3 Drumlosh
16 D2 Drummacool

14 E6 Drummin, Co Mayo
27 H2 Drummin, Co Clare (An Dromainn)
16 E4 Drummullin (Droim Ailí)
17 G3 Drumna
7 G6 Drumnagreagh Port
11 H4 Drumnakilly (Droim na Coille)
5 F7 Drumoghill
18 B5 Drumone
11 G4 Drumquin (Droim Caoin)
23 G2 Drumraney (Droim Raithne)
18 E7 Drumree (Droim Rí)
35 H2 Drumroe
16 E3 Drumshanbo (Droim Seanbhó)
15 G7 Drumsheel
11 F4 Drumskinny (Droim Scine)
17 F4 Drumsna (Droim ar Snámh)
6 B6 Drumsurn (Droim Sorn)
17 J3 Drung
27 H5 Duagh (Dubháth)
29 H4 Dually
25 G3 Dublin (Baile Átha Cliath)
22 E3 Duggarry
19 F6 Duleek (Damhlaig)
31 F3 Dumfea
25 H3 Dún Laoghaire
13 F3 Dunadry (Dún Eadradh)
5 G4 Dunaff
16 D6 Dunamon
19 G4 Dunany (Dún Áina)
30 D3 Dunbell
25 F2 Dunboyne (Dún Búinne)
24 D4 Dunbyrne
30 E7 Duncannon (Dún Canann)
31 G7 Duncormick (Dún Chorrnaic)
19 F3 Dundalk (Dún Dealgan)
34 D5 Dunderrow (Dún Darú)
18 D6 Dunderry
11 J6 Dundian
13 H4 Dundonald (Dún Dónaill)
22 D3 Dundoogan
13 F3 Dundrod (Dún dTrod)
13 G7 Dundrum, Co Down (Dún Droma)
25 G3 Dundrum, Co Dublin
29 G4 Dundrum, Co Tipperary
4 D4 Dunfanaghy (Dún Fionnachaidh)
12 C4 Dungannon (Dún Geanainn)
30 E6 Dunganstown
30 D4 Dungarvan, Co Kilkenny (Dún Garbháin)
35 J2 Dungarvan, Co Waterford (Dún Garbháin)
6 B7 Dungivin (Dún Geimhin)
4 B7 Dunglow (An Clochán Liath)
35 G3 Dungourney (Dún Guairne)
30 D7 Dunhill
22 C5 Duniry
23 F7 Dunkerrin (Dún Cairin)
10 B3 Dunkineely (Dún Cionnaola)
30 D6 Dunkitt
24 E5 Dunlavin (Dún Luáin)
19 F4 Dunleer (Dún Léire)
4 D6 Dunlewy (Dún Lúiche)
6 D6 Dunloy (Dún Lathaí)
33 F7 Dunmanus
33 J5 Dunmanway (Dún Mánmhaí)
35 H2 Dunmoon

15 J6 Dunmore (Dún Mór)
30 E7 Dunmore East (Dún Mór)
13 F4 Dunmurry (Dún Muirigh)
30 C4 Dunnamaggan (Dún Iomagáin)
5 H7 Dunnamanagh (Dún na Manach)
12 B3 Dunnamore (Domhnach Mór)
30 C3 Dunningstown
26 B7 Dunquin (Dún Cbaoin)
6 D4 Dunseverick (Dún Sobhairce)
18 E7 Dunshaughlin (Dún Seachlainn)
23 J7 Durrow (Darú)
33 G6 Durrus (Dúras)
22 D2 Dysart, Co Roscommon (An Diseart)
23 H2 Dysart, Co Westmeath

E

24 E4 Eadestown
30 B3 Earlshill
9 G7 Easky (Iascaigh)
10 D7 East Barrs
13 G2 Eden (An tEadan)
24 C3 Edenderry (Éadan Doire)
11 F4 Ederney (Eadarnaidh)
17 H6 Edgeworthstown (Meathas Troin)
5 H6 Eglinton (An Mhagh)
12 B5 Eglish (An Eaglais)
18 B5 Eighter (Iochtar)
4 E6 Ellistrin (Eileastran)
16 E4 Elphin (Ail Finn)
28 E5 Elton (Eiltiún)
22 B4 Emlagh Cross Roads
32 C4 Emlaghmore
29 F5 Emly (Imleach)
16 E6 Emmoo
24 B5 Emo (Ioma)
11 J6 Emyvale (Scairbh an gCaorach)
21 H7 Ennis (Inis)
31 G4 Enniscorthy (Inis Córthaidh)
34 B5 Enniskean (Inis Céin)
25 G4 Enniskerry (Áth an Sceire)
11 F6 Enniskillen (Inis Ceithleann)
21 G6 Ennistimon (Inis Diomáin)
17 F6 Erra
23 G7 Errill (Eiréil)
22 B3 Esker (An Eiscir)
17 G5 Esker South
33 F4 Eskine
32 D4 Esknaloughoge
11 H5 Eskragh (Eiscreach)
32 E5 Eyeries (Na hAoraí)
22 E4 Eyrecourt (Dún an Uchta)

F

33 G2 Faha
27 H6 Fahaduff
26 D6 Fahamore
5 G5 Fahan, Co Donegal (Fathain)
32 B2 Fahan, Co Kerry
29 F6 Fahanasoodry
22 C3 Fahy, Co Galway
22 E4 Fahy, Co Galway
23 G2 Fairfield
16 C5 Fairymount (Mullach na Sí)
4 D5 Falcarragh (An Fál Carrach)

INDEX OF PLACE NAMES

21 F5 Fanore
28 E7 Farahy
23 F2 Fardrum *(Fardroim)*
27 F7 Farmer's Bridge
23 G3 Farnagh
17 F4 Farnaght
33 J5 Farnanes, Co Cork
  (Na Fearnáin)
34 C4 Farnanes, Co Cork
30 D6 Farnoge
34 C4 Farran *(An Fearann)*
27 G7 Farranfore *(An Fearann Fuar)*
24 E6 Fauna
22 F7 Feakle *(An Fhiacail)*
32 D1 Feaklecally
28 D4 Fedamore *(Feadamair)*
27 F3 Feeard
21 G5 Feenagh, Co Clare
28 C5 Feenagh, Co Limerick
  (Fionach)
5 J7 Feeny *(Na Fineadha)*
17 F3 Fenagh *(Fionnmhach)*
26 E6 Fenit *(An Fhianait)*
31 F2 Fennagh *(Fionnrmhach)*
30 D7 Fennor, Co Waterford
  (Fionnúir)
18 B7 Fennor, Co Westmeath
26 C7 Feohanagh, Co Kerry
28 B5 Feohanagh, Co Limerick
  (An Fheothanach)
33 F4 Feoramore
23 F4 Ferbane *(An Féar Bán)*
35 F2 Fermoy *(Mainistir Fhear Maí)*
31 H3 Ferns *(Fearna)*
28 C3 Ferry Bridge
31 J2 Ferrybank *(Portan Chalaidh)*
29 J5 Fethard, Co Tipperary
  (Fiodh Ard)
31 F7 Fethard, Co Wexford
30 B7 Fews
29 F2 Fiddane
30 C6 Fiddown *(Fiodh Dúin)*
27 G7 Fieries
30 C6 Figlash
21 G5 Finavarra
17 J5 Finnea *(Fiodh an Átha)*
13 F6 Finnis
15 F7 Finny *(Fionnaithe)*
11 H5 Fintona
4 D7 Fintown *(Baile na Finne)*
27 G5 Finuge *(Fionnúig)*
6 D6 Finvoy *(An Fhionnbhoith)*
32 D6 Firkeel
35 F2 Firmount
21 F6 Fisherstreet
13 F2 Five Corners
23 F5 Fiveally *(An Chúirt)*
10 B7 Fivemilebourne
  (Abhainn an Chartúin)
34 E5 Fivemilebridge
16 E4 Flagford
11 H6 Fivemiletown *(Baile na Lorgan)*
22 F6 Flagmount, Co Clare
  (Leacain an Éadain)
30 D3 Flagmount, Co Kilkenny
13 F5 Flatfield
26 D7 Flemingstown
10 E7 Florence Court
  (Mullach na Seangán)

19 F2 Flurrybridge
23 G7 Foilnamuck
24 D5 Fontstown
18 C6 Fordstown *(Baile Forda)*
18 B8 Fore *(Baile Ehobhair)*
19 F2 Forkhill (Foirceal)
21 G5 Formoyle, Co Clare
21 G7 Formoyle, Co Clare
14 D5 Formoyle, Co Mayo
17 F6 Formoyle, Co Longford
34 D3 Fornaght
28 C5 Fort Middle
22 E6 Fort William
17 F7 Forthill
31 F6 Foulkesmill *(Muileann Fúca)*
29 J4 Foulkstown
16 D6 Four Mile House
  (Teach na gCeithre Mhíle)
16 D7 Four Roads *(Tigh Sratha)*
15 F7 Fox Hill
17 F3 Foxfield
  (Cnocán an Mhada Rua)
15 H3 Foxford *(Béal Easa)*
15 H7 Foxhall
28 B3 Foynes *(Faing)*
28 C6 Freemount *(Cillín an Chrónáin)*
16 C4 Frenchpark *(Dún Gar)*
30 C2 Freshford *(Achadh Úr)*
24 E6 Freynestown
28 D4 Friarstown
27 F6 Frogmore
10 C3 Frosses *(Na Frosa)*
16 D7 Fuerty
21 H5 Funshin More
21 G4 Furbogh
30 B7 Furraleigh
27 J2 Furroor
29 G6 Furrow
27 F7 Fybagh

G

23 J2 Gainstown
29 F5 Galbally, Co Limerick
  (An Gallbhaile)
31 G5 Galbally, Co Wexford
29 H3 Galbertstown
6 E7 Galgorm *(Galgom)*
16 E6 Gallagh
32 B2 Galmoy *(Gabhalmhaigh)*
18 E7 Galtrim
21 H3 Galway *(Gaillimh)*
29 F3 Gannavane
24 D2 Garadice *(Garairis)*
22 D3 Garbally
18 E7 Garlow Cross *(Crois Chearla)*
29 H6 Garnavilla
24 B2 Garr
15 J6 Garrafrauns
8 E7 Garranard
34 B5 Garranereagh
16 B6 Garranlahan
  (An Garran Leathan)
27 G3 Garraun, Co Clare
22 D5 Garraun, Co Galway
27 G7 Garraun, Co Kerry
30 C6 Garravoone
24 D7 Garrettstown
10 D5 Garrison *(An Gasastún)*

19 F7 Garristown *(Baile Ghaire)*
35 G2 Garrycaheragh
15 G2 Garrycloonagh
31 F7 Garrycullen
6 D6 Garryduff
28 D5 Garryfine *(Garrai Phaghain)*
31 F3 Garryhill
21 C7 Garrykennedy
35 H4 Garrymore
22 E7 Garrynafana
28 E5 Garryspillane
35 G4 Garryvoe
17 F3 Garvagh, Co Leitrim
  (Garbhach)
6 C6 Garvagh, Co Londonderry
  (Garbhachadh)
11 J5 Garvaghy *(Garbhachadh)*
30 B2 Gattabaun *(An Geata Bán)*
12 E4 Gawleys Gate
  (Geata Mhic Amhlaí)
23 J2 Gaybrook *(Baile Réamainn)*
23 J4 Geashill *(Géisill)*
16 D2 Geevagh *(An Ghaobhach)*
30 C7 Georgestown
33 G6 Gerahies
18 D6 Gibstown
12 E6 Gilford *(Áth Mhic Giolla)*
33 F6 Glanalin
33 H6 Glandart
33 J7 Glandore *(Cuan Dor)*
10 E7 Glangevlin
33 G6 Glanlough
34 E4 Glanmire *(Gleann Maghair)*
27 G5 Glanoe
33 F6 Glanroon
34 C2 Glantane *(An Gleanntán)*
29 F7 Glanworth *(Gleannúir)*
6 D7 Glarryford *(An tÁth Glárach)*
26 B7 Glashabeg
34 E3 Glashaboy East
34 E3 Glashaboy North
27 H6 Glashananoon
18 C3 Glasleck *(Glasleic)*
12 B6 Glaslough *(Glasloch)*
23 F2 Glassan *(Glasán)*
14 C4 Glassillaun
13 J5 Glastry
5 J5 Glebe
24 E6 Glen Of Imail *(Gleann Ó Máil)*
25 G5 Glen Of The Downs
4 E5 Glen, Co Donegal *(An Gleann)*
6 C7 Glen, Co Londonderry
35 G3 Glenacroghery
10 C6 Glenade
15 F3 Glenagort
22 E7 Glenahilty
8 C7 Glenamoy
35 K3 Glenard *(Gleann Aird)*
7 F6 Glenariff or Waterfoot
  (Gleann Aireamh)
7 G6 Glenarm *(Gleann Arma)*
12 E4 Glenavy *(Lann Abhaidh)*
32 E2 Glenbeigh
10 D6 Glenboy *(Gleann Buí)*
31 H5 Glenbrien *(Gleann Bhriain)*
28 E5 Glenbrohane
32 E3 Glencar, Co Kerry
10 B6 Glencar, Co Leitrim
20 E2 Glencoh

INDEX OF PLACE NAMES

9 H3 Glencolumbkille
(Gleann Cholm Cille)
25 G4 Glencree
25 G3 Glencullen
29 J6 Glendalough, Co Waterford
26 E5 Glenderry
4 D6 Glendowan
21 J7 Glendree
29 G7 Glenduff
25 G6 Glenealy
5 H4 Gleneely (Gleann Daoile)
10 D7 Glenfarne (Gleann Fearna)
33 H3 Glenflesk
33 G5 Glengariff (An Gleann Garbh)
35 G2 Glengoura
5 J6 Glenhead
8 B6 Glenlara
5 F7 Glenmaquin
27 J2 Glenmore, Co Clare
30 E6 Glenmore, Co Kilkenny
(An Ghleann Mhór)
29 H5 Glennagat
27 J6 Glennaknockane
16 C7 Glennamaddy
(Gleann na Madadh)
21 H3 Glennascaul
13 G2 Glenoe
29 G3 Glenough Lower
29 G3 Glenough Upper
28 E6 Glenroe
29 H7 Glenshelane
35 G3 Glentane, Co Cork
22 C2 Glentane, Co Galway
10 C2 Glenties (Na Gleannta)
5 H4 Glentogher (Gleann Tóchair)
21 F2 Glentrasna
6 D6 Glenvale
5 F5 Glenvar (Gleann Bhairr)
34 E2 Glenville
(Gleann an Phréacháin)
27 J4 Glin (An Ghleann)
16 C6 Glinsk, Co Galway
20 D3 Glinsk, Connemara (Glinsce)
35 F4 Glounthaune
7 G7 Glynn, Co Antrim (An Gleann)
30 E4 Glynn, Co Wexford
31 G5 Glynn, Co Wexford
33 J2 Gneevgullia (Gníomh go Leith)
29 H4 Golden (An Gabhailin)
25 G4 Golden Ball
33 F7 Goleen (An Góilin)
29 H4 Goolds Cross
(Crois an Ghúlaigh)
30 E3 Goresbridge
(An Droichead Nua)
31 J3 Gorey (Guaire)
29 H6 Gormanstown, Co Tipperary
(Baile Mhic Gormáin)
19 G6 Gormanstown, Co Meath
21 J5 Gort (An Gort)
12 B3 Gortaclady
32 E4 Gortagowan
4 C5 Gortahork (Gort An Choirce)
29 H2 Gortalough
22 E4 Gortarevan
35 H3 Gortaroo
22 B3 Gorteen, Co Galway (Goirtín)
24 B7 Gorteen, Co Kilkenny
28 C5 Gorteen, Co Limerick

16 C3 Gorteen, Co Sligo
35 J2 Gorteen, Co Waterford
30 E6 Gorteens
22 D6 Gorteeny (Giortíní)
32 E5 Gortgarriff
10 C7 Gortgarrigan (Gort Geargáin)
27 H7 Gortglass
11 H3 Gortin (An Goirtín)
8 D7 Gortleatilla
17 F4 Gortletteragh
8 E6 Gortmore, Co Mayo
16 C7 Gortnadeeve
27 J3 Gortnahaha
5 J6 Gortnahey
30 B3 Gortnahoo (Gort na hUamha)
33 J4 Gortnahoughtee
15 F2 Gortnahurra
27 G6 Gortnaleaha
21 J6 Gortnamearacaun
16 C5 Gortnasillagh
12 B3 Gortreagh (An Gort Riabhach)
32 E3 Gortrelig
21 H5 Gortskeagh
33 F6 Gouladoo
14 C6 Gowlaun
31 F4 Gowlin
30 D3 Gowran (Gabhrán)
6 E7 Gracehill (Baile Uí Chinnéide)
30 B7 Graiguearush
30 E4 Graiguenamanagh
(Gráig na Manach)
25 F5 Granabeg
28 C5 Granagh
17 H5 Granard (Granard)
24 D7 Graney
30 B6 Grange, Co Kilkenny
(Gráinseach Chuffe)
30 C4 Grange, Co Kilkenny
19 G3 Grange, Co Louth
24 B3 Grange, Co Offaly
29 H6 Grange, Co Tipperary
9 J6 Grange, Co Sligo
(An Ghráinseach)
35 J3 Grange, Co Waterford
(An Greainsigh)
31 G7 Grange, Co Wexford
24 C5 Grange Beg, Co Kildare
23 H7 Grange Beg, Co Laois
24 D6 Grange Con
(Gráinseach Choinn)
19 F5 Grangebellew
(Greáinseach an Dísirt)
31 F2 Grangeford (An Ghráinseach)
18 E5 Grangegeeth
16 C2 Graniamore
21 J5 Grannagh
12 B5 Grant House
12 B5 Granville (An Doire Mhin)
25 G7 Greenan (An Grainán)
19 F6 Greenanstown
(Baile Uí Ghrianáin)
5 J4 Greencastle, Co Donegal
(An Caisleán Nua)
19 G3 Greencastle, Co Down
(Caisleán na hOireanaí)
11 J3 Greencastle, Co Tyrone
13 G3 Greenisland (Inis Glas)
35 H4 Greenland
19 G3 Greenore (Grianfort)

34 D3 Grenagh (Grenach)
13 J4 Greyabbey (An Mhainistir Liath)
27 J2 Greygrove
5 J6 Greysteel
12 B5 Greystone (An Chloch Liath)
25 H4 Greystones (Na Clocha Liath)
28 E6 Griston
23 G3 Grogan
13 J3 Groomsport
(Port an Ghialla Chruama)
10 D7 Gubaveeny
12 C2 Gulladuff
33 H2 Gullaun
10 C6 Gurteen
31 F6 Gusserane
(Ráth na gCosarean)
4 C6 Gweedore (Gaoth Dobhair)
14 C2 Gweesalia (Gaoth Sáile)
35 F5 Gyleen

H

18 E3 Hackball's Cross
24 E7 Hacketstown
34 D5 Halfway
30 E7 Halfway House (Tigh Leath Slí)
12 C6 Hamiltonsbawn
(Bábhún Hamaltún)
13 F4 Hannahstown (Baile Haine)
30 D5 Harristown
18 E6 Hays
21 G2 Headford (Áth Cinn)
33 H2 Headfort
34 E5 Heathfield
31 G6 Heavenstown
27 F5 Heirhill
13 H3 Helens Bay (Cuan Héilin)
28 E4 Herbertstown (Baile Hiobaird)
23 F4 Highstreet
35 F3 Hightown
24 C2 Hill of Down (Cnoc an Dúin)
16 E4 Hill Street
13 F4 Hillhall
13 F5 Hillsborough (Cromghlinn)
13 F7 Hilltown, Co Down (Baile Hill)
31 G6 Hilltown, Co Wexford
31 H7 Hilltown, Co Wexford
29 G3 Hollyford (Áth an Chuillin)
31 H2 Hollyfort (Ráth an Chuillin)
22 B5 Hollymount, Co Galway
15 H6 Hollymount, Co Mayo (Maolla)
24 E5 Hollywood (Cillín Chaoimhín)
28 E4 Holycross, Co Limerick
(Gaile na gCailleach)
29 H3 Holycross, Co Tipperary
(Mainstir na Croiche)
10 E6 Holywell
13 G3 Holywood (Ard Mhic Nasca)
31 H7 Horetown
29 J3 Horse and Jockey
(An Marcach)
23 G2 Horseleap
(Baile Átha an Urchair)
28 E5 Hospital (An tOspidéal)
29 H3 Hough
25 H2 Howth (Binn Éadair)
30 C5 Hugginstown
28 C2 Hurlers Cross
13 F3 Hyde Park

INDEX OF PLACE NAMES

I

32 E2 Illaunstookagh
21 G7 Inagh *(Eigneagh)*
35 G5 Inch, Co Cork
35 G3 Inch, Co Cork
5 G5 Inch, Co Donegal
26 E7 Inch, Co Kerry
29 G3 Inch, Co Tipperary
31 J2 Inch, Co Wexford *(An Inis)*
27 J5 Inchabaun
30 C2 Inchbeg
33 J4 Inchigeelagh *(Inse Geimleach)*
28 E7 Inchinapallas
29 G6 Inchnamuck
34 D5 Inishannon
9 F7 Inishcrone *(Inis Crabhann)*
6 C7 Inishrush
18 E3 Iniskeen *(Inis Caoin)*
30 E5 Inistioge *(Inis Tíog)*
24 D2 Innfield *(An Bóthar Buí)*
10 C3 Inver
21 F4 Inveran *(Indreabhan)*
15 J6 Irishtown *(An Baile Gaelach)*
11 F5 Irvinestown *(Baile an Irbhinigh)*

J

24 B5 Jamestown, Co Laois
16 E4 Jamestown, Co Leitrim
19 G3 Jenkinstown, Louth
30 C2 Jenkinstown, Co Kilkenny
12 E7 Jerrettspass *(Bealach Sheirit)*
15 H4 Johnsfort
34 E4 Johnstown, Co Cork *(Cill Sheanaigh)*
24 E4 Johnstown, Co Kildare
30 B2 Johnstown, Co Kilkenny *(Baile Sheáin)*
18 E6 Johnstown, Co Meath
31 G7 Johnstown, Co Wexford
31 J2 Johnstown, Co Wicklow
25 G7 Johnstown, Co Wicklow
24 C2 Johnstown Bridge
17 F5 Johnstownbridge
30 D3 Johnswell *(Tobar Eoin)*
19 F2 Jonesborough *(Baile an Chláir)*
19 G6 Julianstown *(Baile Iuiliáin)*

K

28 B7 Kanturk *(Ceann Toirc)*
33 F2 Kate Kearney's Cottage
13 F6 Katesbridge *(Droichead Cháit)*
16 E3 Keadew *(Céideadh)*
12 C7 Keady *(An Céide)*
33 H5 Kealkill *(An Chaolchoill)*
33 J4 Kealvaugh
21 G3 Keeagh
14 C3 Keel *(An Caol)*
32 D3 Keelnagore
16 C6 Keeloges
17 G6 Keenagh, Co Longford *(Caonagh)*
15 F3 Keenagh, Co Mayo
35 J2 Keereen
32 D3 Kells, Co Kerry
30 C4 Kells, Co Kilkenny
18 D5 Kells, Co Meath *(Ceananas)*
12 E2 Kells, Co Antrim *(Na Cealla)*
24 E6 Kelshabeg
33 G4 Kenmare *(Neidin)*
18 E6 Kentstown
31 H6 Kerloge
27 J4 Kerryikyle
10 E4 Kesh, Co Fermanagh *(An Cheis)*
16 C3 Kesh, Co Sligo
17 F3 Keshcarrigan *(Ceis Charraigin)*
26 E4 Kilbaha *(Cill Bheathach)*
28 E2 Kilbane *(An Choill Bhán)*
34 F4 Kilbarry, Co Cork
30 D7 Kilbarry, Co Waterford *(Cill Barra)*
21 J5 Kilbeacanty
30 C7 Kilbeg
23 H3 Kilbeggan *(Cill Bheagáin)*
16 D6 Kilbegnet
29 F6 Kilbeheny *(Coill Bheithne)*
15 J7 Kilbenan Cross Roads
24 C6 Kilberry, Co Kildare *(Cill Bhearaigh)*
18 E6 Kilberry, Co Meath
30 B6 Kilbrack
28 D5 Kilbreedy, Co Limerick
28 C4 Kilbreedy, Co Limerick
29 H4 Kilbreedy, Co Tipperary
20 E3 Kilbrickan
29 J2 Kilbrickane
23 H6 Kilbricken *(Cill Bhriocáin)*
15 J4 Kilbride, Co Mayo
18 D7 Kilbride, Co Meath
25 F4 Kilbride, Co Wicklow *(Cill Bhride)*
25 H6 Kilbride, Co Wicklow
35 F2 Kilbrien, Co Cork
29 J7 Kilbrien, Co Waterford
28 C7 Kilbrin
34 D6 Kilbrittain *(Cill Briotáin)*
21 H4 Kilcaimin
24 B4 Kilcappagh
9 J3 Kilcar *(Cinn Charthaigh)*
24 E7 Kilcarney
27 H3 Kilcarroll
30 B5 Kilcash
22 E3 Kilcashel
23 J4 Kilcavan
22 B4 Kilchreest *(Cill Chriost)*
22 F6 Kilclaran
13 J6 Kilclief
23 J3 Kilclonfert
24 E2 Kilcock *(Cill Choca)*
33 H7 Kilcoe
17 J5 Kilcogy *(Cill Chóige)*
30 D7 Kilcohan
21 J4 Kilcolgan *(Cill Cholgáin)*
34 C5 Kilcolman, Co Cork
28 B4 Kilcolman, Co Limerick *(Cill Cholmain)*
35 J3 Kilcolman, Co Waterford
23 F6 Kilcomin
29 H6 Kilcommon, Co Tipperary *(Cill Chuimín)*
29 G3 Kilcommon, Co Tipperary
8 E7 Kilcon
22 B4 Kilconierin
15 H7 Kilconly *(Cill Chonla)*
22 C3 Kilconnell *(Cill Chonaill)*
28 E7 Kilconnor
13 F7 Kilcoo *(Cill Chua)*
25 H5 Kilcoole *(Cill Chomhghaill)*
35 F2 Kilcor
21 J6 Kilcorkan
23 G4 Kilcormac (Frankford) *(Cill Chormaic)*
28 C3 Kilcornan
34 B2 Kilcorney *(Cill Coirne)*
31 H4 Kilcotty *(Cill Chota)*
35 H4 Kilcredan
33 F7 Kilcrohane *(Cill Chróchain)*
35 G2 Kilcronat
24 D5 Kilcullen *(Cill Chuillin)*
26 D7 Kilcummin, Co Kerry
33 G2 Kilcummin, Co Kerry *(Cill Chuimín)*
19 F3 Kilcurly *(Cill Choirle)*
19 F3 Kilcurry *(Cill an Churraigh)*
27 H7 Kilcusnaun
18 C7 Kildalkey *(Cill Dealga)*
24 C5 Kildangan *(Cill Daingin)*
29 H7 Kildanoge
24 C4 Kildare *(Cill Dara)*
31 F3 Kildavin *(Cill Damhain)*
30 C7 Kildermody
28 E7 Kildorrery *(Cill Dairbhre)*
12 B3 Kildress
29 F3 Kilduffahoo
26 B7 Kildurrihy
29 G5 Kilfeakle
27 G3 Kilfearagh
21 G3 Kilfenora *(Cill Fhionnúrach)*
28 E6 Kilfinnane *(Cill Fhíonáin)*
28 C4 Kilfinny
27 G6 Kilflynn *(Cill Flainn)*
33 G4 Kilgarvan *(Cill Gharbhain)*
22 D2 Kilglass, Co Galway
16 E7 Kilglass, Co Roscommon *(Cill Ghlais)*
9 G7 Kilglass, Co Sligo *(Cill Ghlas)*
33 F2 Kilgobnet, Co Kerry *(Cill Ghobnait)*
35 J2 Kilgobnet, Co Waterford
24 D5 Kilgowan
28 C4 Kilgrogan
24 C6 Kilkea
30 D5 Kilkeasy
27 G3 Kilkee *(Cill Chaoi)*
19 H2 Kilkeel *(Cill Chaoil)*
15 J4 Kilkelly *(Cill Cheallaigh)*
30 C3 Kilkenny *(Cill Chainnigh)*
23 F2 Kilkenny West
34 D6 Kilkerran
16 B7 Kilkerrin *(Cill Choirín)*
20 D3 Kilkieran *(Cill Chiaráin)*
33 H7 Kilkilleen
27 H6 Kilkinlea
28 C2 Kilkishen *(Cill Chisín)*
18 B3 Kill, Co Cavan *(An Chill)*
14 B7 Kill, Co Galway
24 E4 Kill, Co Kildare
30 C7 Kill, Co Waterford
23 G2 Killachonna
29 F6 Killaclug
28 C5 Killacolla
11 F5 Killadeas *(Cill Chéile Dé)*
22 D2 Killaderry

INDEX OF PLACE NAMES

Ref	Name
14 C6	Killadoon *(Coill an Dúin)*
27 J3	Killadysert *(Cill an Disirt)*
21 J6	Killafeen
31 G7	Killag
27 J5	Killaghteen
35 H2	Killahaly
9 F7	Killala *(Cill Ala)*
18 B6	Killallon
28 E2	Killaloe
5 H7	Killaloo
30 C5	Killamery
24 B3	Killane
15 F6	Killateeaun
22 F6	Killanena
31 F4	Killann *(Cill Anna)*
27 G2	Killard
23 H2	Killare
10 C7	Killarga *(Cill Fhearga)*
33 G2	Killarney *(Cill Airne)*
21 G2	Killarone
23 H2	Killaroo
17 H3	Killashandra *(Cill na Seanrátha)*
17 F6	Killashee *(Cill na Sí)*
15 H3	Killasser *(Cill Lasrach)*
23 F5	Killaun
15 F5	Killavally *(Coill an Bhaile)*
35 G2	Killavarilly
34 E3	Killavarrig
16 C3	Killavil *(Cill Fhábhail)*
16 B7	Killavoher
34 E2	Killavullen *(Cill an Mhuilinn)*
5 G6	Killea, Co Donegal
10 D6	Killea, Co Leitrim
23 F7	Killea, Co Tipperary *(Cill Sléibhe)*
30 E7	Killea, Co Waterford
12 E3	Killead *(Cill Éad)*
35 G3	Killeagh *(Cill Ia)*
20 D5	Killeany
31 F3	Killedmund
28 B5	Killeedy
21 J6	Killeen, Co Galway
14 D5	Killeen, Co Mayo
23 F5	Killeen, Co Tipperary
12 C4	Killeen, Co Tyrone
21 H4	Killeenaran
29 H5	Killeenasteena
21 J4	Killeenavarra
21 J4	Killeeneenmore
33 H6	Killeenleagh
34 E4	Killeens Cross
24 D7	Killerrig
11 J7	Killeevan
22 D2	Killeglan
23 H4	Killeigh *(Cill Aichidh)*
22 B5	Killernadeema
11 F3	Killen *(Cillín)*
31 J3	Killenagh
23 F5	Killenaule, Co Tipperary *(Cill Náile)*
29 J4	Killenaule, Co Tipperary
23 J3	Killeshil
24 C7	Killeshin
11 F3	Killeter *(Coill Iochtair)*
27 H3	Killimer
22 D4	Killimor *(Cill Iomair)*
21 H6	Killinaboy *(Cill Inine Baoith)*
34 C4	Killinardrish *(Cill an Ard-dorais)*
30 C6	Killinaspick
13 H5	Killinchy *(Cill Dhuinsí)*
31 J4	Killincooly
25 H4	Killiney, Co Dublin *(Cill Iníon Léinin)*
26 D7	Killiney, Co Kerry
31 H6	Killinick *(Cill Fhionnóg)*
31 J2	Killinierin *(Cill an Iarain)*
18 B4	Killinkere *(Cillín Chéir)*
21 J5	Killinny
24 C4	Killinthomas
25 G5	Killiskey
35 G4	Killmacahill
8 E7	Killogeary
23 F2	Killogeenaghan
17 G5	Killoe
32 C4	Killoluaig
21 J5	Killomoran
23 J3	Killoneen
22 D4	Killoran *(Cill Odhráin)*
33 F2	Killorglin *(Cill Orglan)*
22 B2	Killoscobe
13 H7	Killough *(Cill Locha)*
15 G7	Killour
25 F2	Killsallaghan
18 B7	Killucan *(Cill Liúcainne)*
16 E4	Killukin
23 H4	Killurin, Co Offaly
31 G5	Killurin, Co Wexford *(Cill Liúráin)*
32 C4	Killurly
29 J5	Killusty
12 E1	Killybegs, Co Antrim
10 B3	Killybegs, Co Donegal *(Na Cealla Beaga)*
11 H3	Killyclogher
17 G3	Killygar
11 F2	Killygordon *(Cúil na gCuiridín)*
6 C6	Killykergan *(Coill Uí Chiaragain)*
12 B6	Killylea *(Coillidh Léith)*
13 H5	Killyleagh *(Cill Ó Laoch)*
12 B7	Killyneill
23 G5	Killyon
25 H4	Kilmacanoge *(Cill Mocheanóg)*
30 D6	Kilmacow *(Cill Mhic Bhúith)*
4 E6	Kilmacrenan *(Cill Mhic Réanáin)*
30 B7	Kilmacthomas *(Coill Mhic Thomáisín)*
16 D2	Kilmactranny *(Cill Mhic Treana)*
30 C5	Kilmaganny *(Cill Mogeanna)*
15 G7	Kilmaine *(Cill Mheáin)*
18 D4	Kilmainham Wood *(Cill Maighneann)*
23 H3	Kilmalady
28 B2	Kilmaley *(Cill Mhaillie)*
25 G4	Kilmalin
28 D5	Kilmallock *(Cill Mocheallóg)*
30 C3	Kilmanagh *(Cill Mhanach)*
27 H6	Kilmaniheen
24 C6	Kilmead
30 D7	Kilmeadan *(Cill Mhíodháin)*
24 D4	Kilmeage *(Cill Maodbog)*
28 B5	Kilmeedy *(Cill Mide)*
18 E7	Kilmessan *(Cill Mheasáin)*
34 B4	Kilmicheal *(Cill Mhichíl)*
27 H2	Kilmihil *(Cill Mhichíl)*
34 D3	Kilmona
33 H8	Kilmoon
12 D5	Kilmore, Co Armagh *(An Chill Mhór)*
17 J3	Kilmore, Co Cavan
28 D2	Kilmore, Co Clare
13 H5	Kilmore, Co Down
15 H3	Kilmore, Co Mayo
16 E4	Kilmore, Co Roscommon *(Cill Mhór)*
31 G7	Kilmore, Co Wexford *(An Chill Mhór)*
31 G7	Kilmore Quay *(Cé na Cille Móire)*
17 F6	Kilmore Upper
27 H5	Kilmorna *(Cill Mhaonaigh)*
24 C6	Kilmorony
16 B4	Kilmovee
31 J4	Kilmuckridge *(Cill Mhucraise)*
30 C8	Kilmurrin
27 H2	Kilmurry, Co Clare
28 C2	Kilmurry, Co Clare *(Cill Mhuire)*
34 C4	Kilmurry, Co Cork *(Cill Mhuire)*
28 E4	Kilmurry, Co Limerick
28 C5	Kilmurry, Co Limerick
24 E7	Kilmurry, Co Wicklow
27 J3	Kilmurry McMahon *(Cill Mhuire Mhic Mhathúna)*
20 D5	Kilmurvy *(Cill Mhuirbhigh)*
31 G3	Kilmyshall
28 D2	Kilnacreagh
17 F3	Kilnagross *(Coill na gCros)*
22 D3	Kilnahown
17 J4	Kilnaleck *(Cill na Leice)*
31 H4	Kilnamanagh *(Cill na Manach)*
33 J4	Kilnamartery
21 G7	Kilnamona *(Cill na Móna)*
34 D5	Kilpatrick
25 G5	Kilpedder
26 C7	Kilquane
31 G2	Kilquiggin
6 D5	Kilraghts *(Cill Reachtais)*
31 H7	Kilrane *(Cill Ruáin)*
6 D6	Kilrea *(Cill Ria)*
10 B2	Kilrean *(Cill Riáin)*
22 C4	Kilreekill *(Cill Rícill)*
21 H3	Kilroghter
20 D5	Kilronan *(Cill Rónáin)*
16 E6	Kilroosky
29 F5	Kilross *(Cill Ros)*
27 G3	Kilrush *(Cill Rois)*
16 C6	Kilsallagh, Co Galway *(Coil Salach)*
14 D5	Kilsallagh, Co Mayo *(Coil Salach)*
19 F4	Kilsaran
24 C3	Kilshanchoe
26 E6	Kilshannig
21 G6	Kilshanny *(Cill Seanaigh)*
30 B6	Kilsheelan
34 C6	Kilshinahan
18 C6	Kilskeer *(Cill Scíre)*
11 F5	Kilskeery *(Cill Scíre)*
15 H4	Kiltamagh
15 F5	Kiltarsaghaun
21 J5	Kiltartan
31 F4	Kiltealy *(Cill Téile)*
24 E4	Kilteel
28 E4	Kilteely *(Cill Tíle)*
16 E6	Kilteevan
24 E7	Kiltegan
25 G4	Kiltiernan, Co Dublin

INDEX OF PLACE NAMES

21 J4 Kiltiernan, Co Galway *(Cill Tiarnáin)*
23 J3 Kiltober
22 E2 Kiltoom, Co Roscommon *(Cill Tuama)*
17 J6 Kiltoom, Co Westmeath
22 D4 Kiltormer *(Cill Tormóir)*
22 B4 Kiltullagh *(Cill Tulach)*
10 D6 Kiltyclogher *(Coilte Clochair)*
30 B4 Kilvemnon
15 J6 Kilvine
35 H2 Killwatermoy
7 G7 Kilwaughter *(Cill Uachtair)*
24 E3 Kilwoghan
29 F7 Kilworth *(Cill Uird)*
29 F7 Kilworth Camp
27 J4 Kinard
11 F7 Kinawley *(Cill Náile)*
4 B6 Kincaslough
4 D7 Kingarrow
18 D4 Kingscourt *(Dún an Rí)*
16 C4 Kingsland
12 C3 Kingsmill
10 B5 Kinlough *(Cionn Locha)*
24 B2 Kinnegad *(Cionn Átha Gad)*
23 G5 Kinnitty *(Cionn Eitigh)*
34 D5 Kinsale *(Cionn tSáile)*
35 J3 Kinsalebeg *(Baile an Phoill)*
25 G2 Kinsaley
20 E3 Kinvarra, Co Galway
21 J5 Kinvarra, Co Galway *(Cinn Mhara)*
13 J4 Kircubbin *(Cill Gbobáin)*
6 D5 Kirkhills
13 J5 Kirkistown
27 J7 Kishkeam *(Coiscím na Caillí)*
32 B3 Knights Town
27 H3 Knock, Co Clare *(An Cnoc)*
15 J5 Knock, Co Mayo
23 G7 Knock, Co Tipperary
21 H7 Knockacaurhin
28 B5 Knockaderry *(Cnoc an Doire)*
21 G3 Knockagurraun
28 E5 Knockainy *(Cnoc Áine)*
30 B6 Knockalafalla
16 C5 Knockalaghta
8 B7 Knockalina
27 H3 Knockalough *(Cnoc an Eanaigh)*
21 G6 Knockalunkard
25 F7 Knockananna *(Cnoc an Eanaigh)*
15 J5 Knockanarra
34 B4 Knockane
28 E6 Knockanevin *(Cnocan Aobhainn)*
35 H2 Knockanore
27 H5 Knockanure
23 H7 Knockaroe
21 F7 Knockatullaghaun
22 D4 Knockaun
29 H7 Knockaunarast
27 H5 Knockaunbrack
32 E2 Knockaunnaglashy
32 E2 Knockaunroe
26 C7 Knockavrogeen
29 J7 Knockboy *(An Cnoc Buí)*
22 F7 Knockbrack, Co Clare
5 F7 Knockbrack, Co Donegal *(An Cno Breac)*
27 G6 Knockbrack, Co Kerry
18 C3 Knockbride
18 E3 Knockbridge *(Droichead an Cnoic)*
29 J4 Knockbrit *(Cnoc an Bhriotaigh)*
34 C6 Knockbrown
34 D4 Knockburden
12 C2 Knockcloghhrim *(Cnoc Clocbhroma)*
16 E7 Knockcroghery *(Cnoc an Chrochaire)*
28 D5 Knockdarnan
17 J7 Knockdrin
34 D2 Knockdrislagh
27 J7 Knockeenadallane
27 H6 Knockeencreen
29 H6 Knocklofty
28 E5 Knocklong *(Cnoc Loinge)*
21 J6 Knockmael
15 G3 Knockmore *(An Cnoc Mór)*
35 G2 Knockmourne
27 J2 Knocknaboley
24 D5 Knocknacurra
27 H6 Knocknagashel *(Cnoc na gCaiseal)*
33 G7 Knocknageeha
22 C7 Knocknagower
33 J2 Knocknagree
27 F6 Knocknahaha
27 H2 Knocknahila
34 C4 Knocknahilan
8 B7 Knocknalina
8 C7 Knocknalower
35 G4 Knocknaskagh
33 H7 Knockonna
21 F7 Knockpatrick
35 F3 Knockraha *(Cnoc Rátha)*
33 H7 Knockroe, Co Cork
32 D3 Knockroe, Co Kerry
35 J2 Knockroe, Co Waterford
34 B6 Knocks, Co Cork
23 H5 Knocks, Co Laois
34 B6 Knockskagh
28 B6 Knockskavane
30 D4 Knocktopher *(Cnoc an Tóchair)*
16 E3 Knockvicar
34 E2 Knuttery
24 B6 Kyle
30 E2 Kyleballyhue
22 C5 Kylebrack *(An Choill Bhreac)*
29 F3 Kylegarve

L

27 J3 Labasheeda *(Leaba Shíoda)*
21 J5 Laban
11 F4 Lack *(An Leac)*
24 C4 Lackagh
22 D7 Lackamore *(An Leac Mhór)*
16 E7 Lackan Cross
30 E2 Lackan, Co Carlow
16 E5 Lackan, Co Roscommon
17 H6 Lackan, Co Westmeath
25 F5 Lackan, Co Wicklow *(An Leacain)*
34 B4 Lackareagh
27 H6 Lackbrooder
31 F5 Lacken, Co Kilkenny
34 E2 Lackendarragh North
23 G6 Lackey
31 H7 Lady's Island
35 G4 Ladysbridge *(Droichead na Scuab)*
6 D4 Lagavara
29 H5 Lagganstown
12 C5 Laghey Corner
10 D3 Laghy *(An Lathaigh)*
15 F3 Lahardaun
34 E4 Lakeland
27 H3 Lakyle
13 F4 Lambeg *(Lann Bheag)*
30 C5 Lamoge
17 F6 Lanesborough *(Beal Átha Liag)*
22 F6 Lannaght
18 D7 Laracor
24 E3 Laragh, Co Kildare
18 D3 Laragh, Co Monaghan
25 G6 Laragh, Co Wicklow
14 E2 Largan, Co Mayo
16 E5 Largan, Co Rosommon
15 J2 Largan, Co Sligo
9 J3 Largy
10 B5 Largydonnell
7 G7 Larne *(Latharna)*
18 B1 Latnamard
29 F5 Lattin *(Laitean)*
18 C2 Latton
33 F5 Lauragh
12 D6 Laurelvale *(Tamhnaigh Bhealtaine)*
22 E4 Laurencetown *(An Baile Mór)*
16 B2 Lavagh *(Leamhach)*
12 E6 Lawrencetown *(Baile Labhráis)*
19 G6 Laytown *(An Inse)*
4 A6 Leabgarrow
35 F3 Leamlara *(Léim Lára)*
33 J7 Leap *(An Léim)*
16 E7 Lecarrow *(An Leithcheathrú)*
10 B7 Leckaun
5 J4 Leckemy *(Leic Éime)*
14 D7 Leenaun *(An Líonán)*
17 G6 Legan or Lenamore
17 G4 Leggah
13 F3 Legoniel *(Lag an Aoil)*
21 F7 Lehinch *(An Leacht)*
30 E2 Leighlinbridge *(Leithghlinn an Droichid)*
27 H2 Leitrim, Co Clare
13 G6 Leitrim, Co Down
16 E3 Leitrim, Co Leitrim
27 H4 Leitrim East
25 F3 Leixlip *(Léim an Bhradáin)*
23 G3 Lemanaghan
30 B7 Lemybrien *(Léim Uí Bhriain)*
30 E7 Leperstown
27 F6 Lerrig
10 C3 Letterbarra
10 E5 Letterbreen *(Leitir Bhruín)*
14 C7 Letterfrack *(Leitir Fraic)*
21 F7 Letterkelly
4 E6 Letterkenny *(Leitir Ceanainn)*
6 B5 Letterloan
4 B7 Lettermacaward *(Leitir Mhic an Bhaird)*
20 D4 Lettermullan *(Leitir Mealláin)*
20 E3 Lettermore
16 B7 Levally, Co Galway

INDEX OF PLACE NAMES

	(An Leathbhaile)	
15 G6	Levally, Co Mayo	
30 D7	Licketstown	
11 F2	Lifford	
5 K6	Limavady (Léim an Mhadaidh)	
28 D3	Limerick (Luimneach)	
29 F4	Limerick Junction	
	(Gabhal Luimnigh)	
5 G4	Linsfort	
13 H4	Lisbane	
11 F6	Lisbellaw (Lios Béal Átha)	
17 J2	Lisboduff	
13 F4	Lisburn (Lios na gCearrbhach)	
21 H3	Liscananaun	
21 F6	Liscannor (Lios Ceannúir)	
14 E5	Liscarney (Lios Cearnaigh)	
28 C7	Liscarroll (Lios Cearuill)	
5 H7	Liscloon (Lios Claon)	
27 F3	Liscrona	
26 D7	Lisdargan	
21 G6	Lisdoonvarna	
	(Lios Dúin Bhearna)	
30 C2	Lisdowney	
18 C5	Lisduff, Co Cavan	
	(An Lios Dubh)	
34 E3	Lisduff, Co Cork	
23 G5	Lisduff, Co Offaly	
22 E7	Lisgarode	
35 F3	Lisgoold	
28 B2	Lisheen	
22 D4	Lisheenaguile	
16 C3	Liskeagh	
17 H6	Lismacaffry	
28 B7	Lismire	
35 H2	Lismore (Lios Mór)	
16 E7	Lismoyle	
12 C6	Lisnadill (Lios na Daille)	
18 B2	Lisnageer (Lios na gCaor)	
28 E3	Lisnagry (Lios na Graí)	
30 D7	Lisnakill Cross	
18 C2	Lisnalong	
12 B1	Lisnamuck (Lios na Muc)	
11 F5	Lisnarrick (Lios na nDaróg)	
11 G7	Lisnaskea (Lios na Scéithe)	
34 E6	Lispatrick	
26 D7	Lispole (Lios Póil)	
27 J2	Lisroe	
29 J5	Lisronagh (Lios Ruanach)	
17 H5	Lisryan	
34 B4	Lissacresig	
29 J4	Lissaha	
16 C5	Lissalway (Lios Sealbhaigh)	
22 E4	Lissanacody	
16 C5	Lissananny	
34 B6	Lissavard	
27 G4	Lisselton (Lios Eiltin)	
27 J2	Lissycasey	
	(Lios Uí Chathasaigh)	
27 F6	Listellick	
30 E5	Listerlin	
13 G5	Listooder	
27 G5	Listowel (Lios Tuathail)	
29 F5	Lisvarrinane (Lios Fearnáin)	
29 J3	Littleton (An Baile Beag)	
27 G5	Lixnaw (Leic Snámha)	
13 F3	Loanends (Carn Mhéabha)	
18 E5	Lobinstown (Baile Lóibín)	
17 H4	Loch Gowna	
27 J4	Loghill, Co Limerick	
	(Leamhchoill)	
28 B5	Loghill, Co Limerick	
29 G7	Logleagh	
34 C2	Lombardstown (Baile Limbaird)	
5 H6	Londonderry (Doire)	
17 G5	Longford, Co Longford	
	(An Longfort)	
23 G5	Longford, Co Offaly	
24 C2	Longwood (Maigh Dearmahaí)	
22 E5	Lorrha (Lothra)	
30 E3	Lorum	
35 K3	Loskeran	
22 C3	Loughaclerybeg	
29 H6	Loughacutteen	
15 J2	Loughanaboll	
23 H2	Loughanavally	
21 F4	Loughanbeg	
4 C6	Loughanure	
12 E6	Loughbrickland	
	(Loch Bricleann)	
17 H4	Loughduff	
26 E7	Lougher	
12 C5	Loughgall (Loch gCál)	
16 C5	Loughglinn (Loch Glinne)	
6 E5	Loughguile (Loch gCaol)	
13 G6	Loughinisland (Loch an 0ileáin)	
29 H2	Loughmoe (Luachma)	
18 C2	Loughmorne (Loch Morn)	
22 C4	Loughrea (Baile Loch Riach)	
19 H7	Loughshinny	
14 D5	Louisburgh (Cluain Cearbán)	
18 E3	Louth (Lú)	
33 G7	Lowertown	
13 F6	Lowtown	
25 F3	Lucan (Leamhcán)	
9 H7	Lugdoon	
24 B6	Luggacurren	
	(Log an Churraigh)	
30 D5	Lukeswell	
24 C4	Lullymore	
15 J4	Lurga	
12 E5	Lurgan, Co Armagh	
	(An Lorgain)	
23 G3	Lurgan, Co Offaly	
16 D4	Lurgan, Co Roscommon	
5 F5	Lurganboy, Co Donegal	
10 C6	Lurganboy, Co Leitrim	
19 G7	Lusk (Lusca)	
27 G6	Lyracrumpane	
	(Ladhar an Chrompáin)	
34 D3	Lyradane	
34 C2	Lyre, Co Cork	
	(Ladhar an Chrompáin or An Ladha)	
27 H6	Lyre, Co Kerry	
35 G2	Lyre, Co Waterford	
29 G7	Lyrenaglogh	

M

20 E2	Maam Cross	
10 B2	Maas	
15 F5	Mace	
11 F7	Mackan (Macan)	
6 B5	Macosquin (Maigh Choscáin)	
29 F7	Macroney	
34 B4	Macroom (Maigh Chromtha)	
18 C3	Madabawn	
30 D3	Maddockstown (Baile Mhadóg)	
24 C7	Maganey (Maigh Geine)	
12 E4	Maghaberry	
13 G7	Maghera, Co Down	
6 C7	Maghera, Co Londonderry	
	(Machaire Rátha)	
21 J7	Maghera Cross	
12 C2	Magherafelt (Machaire Fíolta)	
12 E5	Magheralin (Machaire Lainne)	
5 G7	Magheramason	
13 H2	Magheramorne	
	(Machaire Morna)	
11 H7	Magheraveely	
	(Machaire Mhílie)	
4 B7	Maghery, Co Donegal	
	(An Machaire)	
12 C4	Maghery, Co Armagh	
6 B5	Magilligan	
	(Aird Mhic Giollagain)	
11 G6	Maguiresbridge	
	(Droichead Mhig Uidir)	
28 B5	Mahoonagh	
24 E3	Mainham	
25 G2	Malahide (Mullach Íde)	
5 H3	Malin (Málainn)	
9 H3	Malin Beg (Málainn Bhig)	
9 H3	Malin More	
14 D4	Mallaranny (An Mhala Raiothní)	
34 D2	Mallow (Mala)	
13 F3	Mallusk (Maigh Bhloisce)	
5 F6	Manorcunningham	
	(Mainéar Uí Chuinneagáin)	
10 C6	Manorhamilton (Cluainín)	
29 J3	Manselstown	
19 F4	Mansfieldstown	
16 D5	Mantua (An Mointeach)	
15 G4	Manulla	
10 E7	Marble Arch	
30 B4	Mardyke	
5 J5	Margymonaghan	
12 D6	Markethill (Cnoc an Mhargaidh)	
29 H6	Markhamstown	
29 J6	Marlfield	
31 G4	Marshalstown	
	(Baile Mharascail)	
6 E6	Martinstown, Co Antrim	
	(Baile Uí Mháirtín)	
28 E5	Martinstown, Co Limerick	
18 D6	Marty	
32 D4	Mastergeehy	
29 H5	Masterstown	
34 D3	Matehy	
33 J6	Maultatrahane	
33 H5	Maulavanig	
33 F7	Maulawaddra	
14 E7	Maum (An Mám)	
21 G7	Mauricesmills (Muilte Mhuiris)	
31 H7	Mayglass	
24 E2	Maynooth (Maigh Naud)	
55 H5	Mayo (Maigh Eo)	
12 E7	Mayobridge	
	(Droichead Mhaigh Eo)	
13 F5	Mazetown	
6 E7	McGregor's Corner	
6 C6	McLaughlins Corner	
28 D4	Meanus (Méanas)	
22 E4	Meelick	
28 B6	Meelin (An Mhaoilinn)	
4 C5	Meenaclady	
4 B7	Meenacross, Co Donegal	

INDEX OF PLACE NAMES

9 J3 Meenacross, Co Donegal	12 E5 Moira *(Maigh Rath)*	11 G3 Mountjoy *(Muinseo)*
9 J3 Meenaneary	33 F3 Moll's Gap	23 J5 Mountmellick *(Mooínteach Milie)*
4 B6 Meenbannad	31 H4 Monagear	12 D7 Mountnorris *(Achadh na Cranncha)*
27 H6 Meenbannivane	12 B7 Monaghan *(Muineachán)*	23 H6 Mountrath *(Maigheán Rátha)*
10 E2 Meenglass	35 G2 Monagoun	22 C7 Mountshannon *(Baile Uí Bhealáin)*
4 C5 Meenlaragh	23 G7 Monaincha Bog	19 H2 Mourne Park
27 J6 Meennaraheeny	29 H7 Monalour	27 F3 Moveen
19 F2 Meigh	31 H4 Monamolin *(Muine Moling)*	5 J4 Moville *(Bun an Phobail)*
21 H3 Menlough, Co Galway	35 K3 Monamraher	21 H5 Moy, Co Galway
22 B2 Menlough, Co Galway *(Mionlach)*	29 F4 Monard, Co Tipperary	12 C5 Moy, Co Tyrone *(An Maigh)*
29 H7 Middlequarter	29 H7 Monard, Co Waterford	14 C7 Moyard *(Maigh Ard)*
12 B6 Middletown *(Coillidh Chanannain)*	31 H2 Monaseed *(Móin na Saighead)*	27 G3 Moyasta *(Maigh Sheasta)*
15 H4 Midfield *(An Trian Láir)*	28 E4 Monaster *(An Mhainistir)*	29 H3 Moycarky
35 G3 Midleton *(Mainistir na Corann)*	16 C4 Monasteraden *(Mainistir Réadáin)*	21 G3 Moycullen *(Maigh Cuilinn)*
31 G4 Milehouse *(Teach an Mhíle)*	19 F5 Monasterboice	17 G6 Moydow *(Maigh Dumha)*
24 D5 Milemill	24 C5 Monasterevin *(Mainistir Eimhín)*	12 B5 Moygashel *(Maigh gCaisil)*
29 G3 Milestone *(Cloch an Mhile)*	10 E6 Monea *(Maigh Niadh)*	15 G2 Moygawnagh
12 C6 Milford, Co Armagh *(Áth an Mhuilinn)*	26 E4 Moneen, Co Clare	29 J4 Moyglass *(Maigh Ghlas)*
28 C6 Milford, Co Cork *(Átha an Mhuilinn)*	21 J2 Moneen, Co Galway	31 F2 Moyle
11 H7 Mill Brook	23 H4 Monettia Bog	31 G2 Moylisha
12 E2 Mill Town *(Baile an Mhuilinn)*	4 C6 Money More, Co Donegal	22 C2 Moylough, Co Galway *(Maigh Locha)*
7 G7 Millbrook *(Sruthán an Mhuilinn)*	10 E7 Moneycashel	16 B3 Moylough, Co Sligo
5 F5 Millford *(Baile na oGallóglach)*	34 B4 Moneycusker	21 J7 Moymore
13 J3 Millisle *(Oilean an Mhuilinn)*	6 C6 Moneydig *(Muine Dige)*	18 C5 Moynalty *(Maigh Locha)*
29 F7 Millstreet, Co Cork *(Sráid an Mhuilinn)*	23 F7 Moneygall *(Muine Gall)*	24 D2 Moynalvy
34 B2 Millstreet, Co Cork	12 D2 Moneyglass *(An Muine Glas)*	25 F7 Moyne, Co Wicklow
29 J7 Millstreet, Co Waterford	12 C3 Moneymore *(Muine Mór)*	17 G4 Moyne, Co Longford
12 D6 Milltown, Co Armagh	12 B2 Moneyneany *(Món na nlonach)*	16 C4 Moyne, Co Roscommon *(An Mhaighean)*
17 H2 Milltown, Co Cavan *(Baile an Mhuilinn)*	13 G4 Moneyreagh *(Monadh Riabhach)*	29 J2 Moyne, Co Tipperary
4 E4 Milltown, Co Donegal	13 F6 Moneyslane	8 B7 Moyrahan
10 C3 Milltown, Co Donegal	17 J7 Monilea *(An Muine Liath)*	27 J4 Moyreen
25 F3 Milltown, Co Dublin	22 B3 Monivea *(Muine Mhéa)*	20 D3 Moyrus
16 C7 Milltown, Co Galway	13 G3 Monkstown, Co Antrim *(Baile na Manach)*	5 J6 Moys
15 J6 Milltown, Co Galway	34 E4 Monkstown, Co Cork *(Baile na Mhanach)*	24 C2 Moyvally *(Maigh Bhealaigh)*
27 F7 Milltown, Co Kerry	28 E2 Montpelier	27 H4 Moyvane/Newtownsandes *(Maigh Mheain)*
26 C7 Milltown, Co Kerry	30 D6 Mooncoin *(Móin Choinn)*	17 G7 Moyvore *(Maigh Mhórdha)*
24 D4 Milltown, Co Kildare	24 D6 Moone *(Maoin)*	23 G2 Moyvoughly *(Maigh Bhachla)*
30 D5 Milltown, Co Kilkenny	35 J3 Moord	29 H7 Mt. Melleray Monastery
6 B5 Milltown, Co Londonderry	7 F7 Moorfields *(Páirc an tSléibhe)*	12 E3 Muckamore *(Maigh Chomair)*
6 C6 Milltown, Co Londonderry	28 C5 Morenane	24 D3 Mucklon
11 J3 Milltown, Co Tyrone	19 G5 Mornington *(Baile Uí Mhornáin)*	33 G3 Muckross
17 H7 Milltown, Co Westmeath	28 E3 Moroe *(Maigh Rua)*	21 H3 Muckrush
21 F7 Milltown Malbay *(Sráid na Cathrach)*	28 E6 Mortlestown	5 H5 Muff *(Magh)*
23 J2 Milltownpass *(Belach Bhaile an Mhuilinn)*	34 C5 Moskeagh	27 H6 Muinganear
34 E5 Minane Bridge *(Droichead an Mhionnáin)*	19 G6 Mosney Camp	32 E2 Muingaphuca
13 H7 Minerstown *(Baile na Mianadóiri)*	6 D5 Moss-Side *(Mas Saíde)*	27 H6 Muingwee
30 B6 Minorstown	13 G3 Mossley *(Maslaí)*	32 C4 Muingydowda
29 F7 Mitchelstown *(Baile Mhistéala)*	30 C6 Mothel	25 F2 Mulhuddart *(Mullach Eadrad)*
27 G3 Moanmore, Co Clare	22 C2 Mount Bellew Bridge	9 F7 Mullafarry
29 F5 Moanmore, Co Tipperary	22 C2 Mount Bellew Demesne	18 C5 Mullagh, Co Cavan *(An Mullach)*
17 G5 Moat Farrell	17 J5 Mount Nugent *(Droichead Uí Dhálaigh)*	27 H2 Mullagh, Co Clare *(Mullach)*
23 G2 Moate *(An Móta)*	13 J4 Mount Stewart	22 C4 Mullagh, Co Galway
34 C3 Model Village, Co Cork	16 D7 Mount Talbot *(Mun Talbóid)*	14 D5 Mullagh, Co Mayo
34 D4 Model Village, Co Cork	23 G2 Mount Temple, Co Westmeath *(An Grianan)*	24 E2 Mullagh, Co Meath
35 J2 Modelligo	10 B5 Mount Temple, Co Sligo	18 E2 Mullaghbane
22 E6 Modreeny	35 G3 Mount Uniacke *(Cúil Ó gCorra)*	17 F4 Mullaghmacormick
35 G3 Mogeely *(Maigh Dhíle)*	16 E2 Mountallen	10 B5 Mullaghmore *(An Mullach Mór)*
30 D2 Mohil	23 G4 Mountbolus *(Cnocán Bhólais)*	16 C3 Mullaghroe
17 F4 Mohill *(Maothail)*	34 E3 Mountcatherine	6 D6 Mullan Head
	10 C3 Mountcharles *(Moin Searlas)*	6 C6 Mullan, Co Londonderry
	27 J6 Mountcollins *(Cnoc Uí Choileáin)*	12 B6 Mullan, Co Monaghan *(An Muileann)*
	11 H3 Mountfield *(Achadh Ard)*	

INDEX OF PLACE NAMES

15 J2 Mullany's Cross
16 C4 Mullen
34 E2 Mullenaboree
30 C5 Mullennaglogh
30 D5 Mullennakill
31 G2 Mullinacuff
  (Muileann Mhic Dhuibh)
30 B4 Mullinahone
  (Muileann na bUamhan)
30 D6 Mullinavat (Muileann an Bhata)
17 J7 Mullingar (An Muileann gCearr)
17 J6 Multyfarnham
  (Muilte Farannáin)
28 D3 Mungret (Mungairit)
27 H4 Murher
31 G6 Murntown (Baile Mhúráin)
26 B7 Murreagh (An Mhulríoch)
14 E5 Murrisk (Muraisc)
21 F5 Murroogh
27 G7 Mweennalaa
33 J7 Myross
35 F5 Myrtleville
31 F3 Myshall (Miseal)

N

34 E4 Naas (An Nás)
34 C2 Nad
24 B4 Nahana
10 B2 Naran
24 D5 Narraghmore
  (An Fhorrach Mhór)
19 F7 Naul (An Aill)
18 E6 Navan (An Uaimh)
15 G7 Neale (An Éill)
23 G6 Nealstown
32 D5 Nedanone
22 D7 Nenagh (An tAonach)
29 J3 New Birmingham
  (Gleann an Ghuail)
5 G6 New Buildings (An Baile Nua)
32 D4 New Chapel Cross
18 B4 New Inn, Co Cavan
  (An Dromainn)
22 C3 New Inn, Co Galway
  (An Cnoc Breac)
24 B5 New Inn, Co Laois
28 C3 New Kildimo
30 E5 New Ross (Ros Mhic Thriúin)
28 D7 New Twopothouse Village
  (Tigh Nua an Dá Phota)
31 F6 Newbawn (An Bábhún Nua)
18 B2 Newbliss (Cúil Darach)
16 C7 Newbridge, Co Galway
  (An Droichead Nua)
28 B4 Newbridge, Co Limerick
13 G7 Newcastle, Co Down
  (An Caisleán Nua)
24 E3 Newcastle, Co Dublin
22 B3 Newcastle, Co Galway
29 J6 Newcastle, Co Tipperary
25 H5 Newcastle, Co Wicklow
28 B5 Newcastle West
  (An Caisleán Nua)
34 C5 Newcestown (Baile Níos)
29 J5 Newchapel
12 D2 Newferry
29 H5 Newinn (Loch Ceann)
28 B7 Newmarket, Co Cork
  (Áth Trasna)
30 D5 Newmarket, Co Kilkenny
28 C2 Newmarket on Fergus
  (Cora Chaitlín)
34 B7 Newmills, Co Cork
4 E7 Newmills, Co Donegal
  (An Muileann Úr)
12 C4 Newmills, Co Tyrone
  (An Muileann Nua)
14 E4 Newport, Co Mayo
  (Baile Uí Fhiacháin)
28 E3 Newport, Co Tipperary
  (An Port Nua)
12 E7 Newry (An tIúr)
22 C4 Newtown, Co Galway
24 D2 Newtown, Co Kildare
30 B3 Newtown, Co Kilkenny
24 B7 Newtown, Co Laois
28 E5 Newtown, Co Limerick
15 G5 Newtown, Co Mayo
18 E5 Newtown, Co Meath
22 E5 Newtown, Co Offaly
16 D6 Newtown, Co Roscommon
22 D3 Newtown, Co Roscommon
22 D7 Newtown, Co Tipperary
29 F5 Newtown, Co Tipperary
30 C7 Newtown, Co Waterford
35 K2 Newtown, Co Waterford
35 J3 Newtown, Co Waterford
31 F7 Newtown, Co Wexford
31 G7 Newtown, Co Wexford
17 F7 Newtown Cashel
  (Baile Nua an Chaisil)
15 G2 Newtown Cloghans
  (An Baile Úr)
5 G6 Newtown Cunningham
  (An Baile Nua)
17 F5 Newtown Forbes
  (An Lois Breac)
17 G3 Newtown Gore (An Dúcharraig)
25 G5 Newtown Mt. Kennedy
  (Baile an Chinnéidigh)
6 E6 Newtown-Crommelin
  (Baile Nua Chromlain)
13 G3 Newtownabbey
  (Baile na Mainstreach)
29 H6 Newtownadam
13 H4 Newtownards
  (Baile Nua na hArda)
11 G7 Newtownbutler (An Baile Nua)
12 C7 Newtownhamilton (Baile Úr)
23 J3 Newtownlow
21 H4 Newtownlynch
27 H4 Newtownsandes
28 C6 Newtownshandrum
  (Baile Nua Sheandroma)
11 G3 Newtownstewart (An Baile Nua)
30 D6 Nicholastown
30 B5 Ninemilehouse
  (Tigh na Naoi Míle)
18 D5 Nobber (An Obair)
34 E5 Nohaval (Nuach a Bháil)
34 C6 North Ring
18 C3 Northlands
  (An Tácháirt Thuaidh)
21 G6 Noughaval, Co Clare
21 J7 Noughaval, Co Clare
30 E2 Nurney, Co Carlow (An Urnaí)
24 C5 Nurney, Co Kildare
13 F3 Nutts Corner (Coirnéal Nutt)

O

27 G5 Oaghley
28 D2 Oatfield
28 D2 O'Briensbridge
22 F7 O'Callaghansmills
22 D4 Oghill
22 C7 Ogonnelloe (Tuath Ó gConáile)
31 H5 Oilgate (Maolán na oGabhar)
34 E6 Old Head
24 D5 Old Kilcullen
28 C3 Old Kildimo
31 F5 Old Ross
23 J7 Old Town, Co Laois
22 E3 Old Town, Co Roscommon
  (An Seanbhaile)
31 F4 Old Town, Co Wexford
18 B5 Oldcastle (An Seanchaisleán)
29 H6 Oldgrange
24 C7 Oldleagh
30 E2 Oldleighlin (Seanleithghlinn)
19 F7 Oldtown, Co Dublin
23 F3 Oldtown, Co Roscommon
11 G4 Omagh (An Ómaigh)
19 F2 Omeath (Ó Méith)
20 D4 Onaght
29 F4 Oola (Úlla)
21 J4 Oranmore (Órán Mór)
18 D5 Oristown
12 B3 Orritor (Na Coracha Beaga)
21 F5 Oughtdarra
23 G4 Oughter
21 F2 Oughterard (Uachtar Ard)
31 H4 Oulart (An tAbhallort)
29 H5 Outeragh
34 D4 Ovens (Na hUamhanna)
9 G7 Owenbeg (An Abhainn Bheag)
21 J5 Owenbristy
21 G2 Ower
30 C5 Owning (Ónainn)

P

31 F5 Palace (An Phailís)
24 D7 Palatine
29 F4 Palatine Street
22 C2 Pallas, Co Galway
23 J6 Pallas, Co Laois
29 F4 Pallas Green (An tSeanphailís)
29 F4 Pallas Green (New)
  (Pailís Ghréine)
23 J3 Pallasboy
28 C3 Pallaskenry (Pailís Chaonraí)
31 J2 Pallis
25 F3 Palmerstown (Baile Phámar)
5 J7 Park, Co Londonderry
15 G4 Park, Co Mayo
31 G7 Park, Co Wexford
31 G2 Park Bridge
28 E7 Parkacunna
13 F2 Parkgate
21 H4 Parkmore (An Phairc Mhór)
32 E4 Parknasilla
28 D3 Parteen
15 G6 Partry (Partraí)
16 D7 Passage
30 E7 Passage East

INDEX OF PLACE NAMES

35 F4	Passage West (An Pasáiste)	
28 C4	Patrickswell (Tobar Phádraig)	
30 E3	Paulstown (Baile Phóil)	
22 C4	Peak	
22 B5	Peterswell (Tobar Pheadair)	
10 E4	Pettigo (Paiteagó)	
6 E5	Pharis (Fáras)	
34 E3	Piercetown, Co Cork	
31 H6	Piercetown, Co Wexford	
22 E5	Pike	
18 D7	Pike Corner	
23 H6	Pike of Rush Hall (An Paidhc)	
30 C6	Piltown (Baile an Phoill)	
5 F7	Pluck	
11 H2	Plumbridge (Droichead an Phlum)	
21 H4	Pollagh, Co Galway	
23 G4	Pollagh, Co Offaly (Pollach)	
22 C4	Pollatlugga	
8 C7	Pollatomish	
22 D3	Pollboy	
16 B6	Pollshask	
12 B4	Pomeroy (Pomeroy)	
15 G3	Pontoon	
19 G4	Port	
23 J6	Port Laoise	
8 C6	Portacloy	
12 D5	Portadown (Port an Dúnáin)	
13 J5	Portaferry (Port an Pheire)	
5 H3	Portaleen	
24 B5	Portarlington (Cúil an tSúdaire)	
13 J5	Portavogie (Port an Bhogaigh)	
6 C4	Portballintrae (Port Bhaile an Trá)	
6 D7	Portglenone (Port Chluain Eoghain)	
22 E5	Portland	
30 C6	Portlaw (Port Lách)	
32 B4	Portmagee (An Caladh)	
25 H2	Portmarnock (Port Mearnóg)	
7 H7	Portmuck	
4 D5	Portnablaghy (Port na Bláiche)	
17 J7	Portnashangan	
10 B1	Portnoo (Port Nua)	
19 H7	Portraine	
22 D7	Portroe (An Port Rua)	
6 C4	Portrush (Port Rois)	
5 F4	Portsalon (Port an tSalainn)	
6 B4	Portstewart (Port Stíobhaird)	
22 D5	Portumna (Port Omna)	
17 F2	Pottore	
8 C6	Porturlin	
22 E7	Poulakerry	
34 B4	Poulanargid	
29 H5	Poulnamucky	
22 D5	Power's Cross (Crois an Phaoraigh)	
12 D6	Poyntz Pass (Pas an Phointe)	
34 E2	Prap	
29 J7	Priest Town	
30 E6	Priesthaggard	
24 D3	Prosperous (An Chorrchoill)	
22 D7	Puckaun (Pocán)	

Q

6 E7	Quarrytown	
27 G3	Querrin (An Cuibhreann)	
5 H5	Quigley's Point	
	(Rinn Uí Choigligh)	
27 H2	Quilty (Coillte)	
28 C2	Quin (Cuinche)	

R

30 D3	Radestown	
13 H5	Raffrey (Rafraidh)	
9 J6	Raghly	
18 B5	Rahaghy	
16 E7	Rahara	
23 G3	Rahan (Raithean)	
18 B7	Raharney (Ráth Fhearna)	
24 E7	Raheen, Co Carlow	
34 D4	Raheen, Co Cork	
33 H2	Raheen, Co Kerry	
29 H6	Raheen, Co Tipperary	
23 G2	Raheen, Co Westmeath	
31 F5	Raheen, Co Wexford (An Ráithin)	
28 B5	Raheenagh	
31 J4	Raheenlusk	
13 H6	Raholp	
15 F2	Rake Street	
31 F7	Ramsgrange (An Ghráinseach)	
22 C5	Ranamackan	
12 D2	Randalstown (Baile Raghnaill)	
23 F5	Rapemills	
5 F7	Raphoe (Ráth Bhoth)	
27 J7	Rascalstreet	
6 D6	Rasharkin (Ros Earcáin)	
4 E7	Rashedoge	
23 F5	Rath	
24 C4	Rathangan (Rath Iomgháin)	
27 G6	Rathanny	
17 H6	Rathaspick	
29 J4	Rathbrit	
22 E5	Rathcabban (Ráth Cabáin)	
18 D6	Rathcarran	
16 D6	Rathconor	
17 H7	Rathconrath (Ráth Conarta)	
34 B2	Rathcool, Co Cork	
25 F3	Rathcoole, Co Dublin	
24 D2	Rathcore (Ráth Cuair)	
35 F2	Rathcormack, Co Cork	
9 J6	Rathcormack, Co Sligo	
27 J2	Rathcrony	
24 E7	Rathdangan (Ráth Daingin)	
23 H7	Rathdowney (Ráth Domhnaigh)	
25 G6	Rathdrum (Ráth Droma)	
17 H7	Rathduff	
33 G7	Ratheenroe	
24 D4	Rathernan	
19 F7	Rathfeigh (Ráth Faiche)	
35 F3	Rathfilode	
13 F7	Rathfriland (Ráth Fraoileann)	
31 F4	Rathfylane	
24 B7	Rathgarry	
30 B6	Rathgormack (Ráth Ó gCormaic)	
15 G7	Rathgranagher	
29 F5	Rathkea	
28 B4	Rathkeale (Ráth Caola)	
29 J6	Rathkeevin	
18 E5	Rathkenny (Ráth Cheannaigh)	
16 D5	Rathkeva	
16 C5	Rathkineely	
8 E6	Rathlackan	
9 G7	Rathlee (Ráth Lao)	
7 E3	Rathlin Island	
24 D7	Rathlyon	
30 C7	Rathmaiden	
5 F6	Rathmelton (Ráth Mealtain)	
33 J2	Rathmore, Co Kerry (An Ráth Mhór)	
24 E4	Rathmore, Co Kildare (An Ráth Mhór)	
18 C6	Rathmore, Co Meath	
30 E6	Rathmoylan, Co Waterford	
24 D2	Rathmoylon, Co Meath	
5 F5	Rathmullan (Ráth Maoláin)	
15 G2	Rathnamagh	
25 H6	Rathnew (Ráth Naoi)	
31 F4	Rathnure (Ráth an Iúir)	
8 E7	Rathoma	
35 G3	Rathorgan	
17 H6	Rathowen	
15 G2	Rathroeen	
33 G7	Rathruane	
31 F2	Rathtoe	
24 E7	Rathvilly (Ráth Bhile)	
18 B7	Rathwire	
19 F7	Ratoath (Ráth Tó)	
33 G7	Ratooragh	
19 F2	Ravensdale (Gleann na bhFiach)	
13 F5	Ravernet (Ráth Bhearnait)	
5 F5	Ray (An Ráith)	
18 E4	Reaghstown	
35 J3	Reanaclogheen	
27 J2	Reanagishagh	
33 J4	Reananerree	
34 B6	Reanascreena (Rae na Scríne)	
29 F3	Rear Cross (Crois na Rae)	
20 D2	Recess (Sraith Salach)	
12 B4	Reclain	
5 J5	Redcastle	
25 G7	Redcross (Chrois Dhearg)	
31 H5	Redgate	
17 J2	Redhills (An Croc Rua)	
22 E5	Redwood	
14 C6	Renvyle	
32 E6	Rerrin (Raerainn)	
6 C5	Revallagh	
24 B3	Rhode (Ród)	
12 D6	Richill (Log an Choire)	
35 F3	Riesk, Co Cork	
23 F4	Riesk, Co Offally	
31 H7	Ring (An Rinn)	
35 F4	Ringaskiddy (Rinn an Scidígh)	
6 B6	Ringsend (Droichead an Carraige)	
23 H6	Ringstown	
35 K2	Ringville (An Rinn)	
4 B6	Rinnafarset	
21 F7	Rinneen, Co Clare	
33 J7	Rinneen, Co Cork	
21 H4	Rinville	
31 J3	Riverchapel	
25 G2	Rivermeath	
34 E5	Riverstick (Áth an Mhaide)	
34 E4	Riverstown, Co Cork	
16 C2	Riverstown, Co Sligo (Baile Idir dhá Abhainn)	
23 F5	Riverstown, Co Tipperary (Baile Uí Lachnáin)	
21 F6	Roadford	
24 D3	Robertstown (Baile Riobaird)	

INDEX OF PLACE NAMES

18 D7 Robinstown, Co Meath *(Baile Roibín)*	21 F2 Rusheeny	29 G6 Shanrahan
31 G7 Robinstown, Co Wexford	29 J6 Russellstown	28 B5 Shanrath
30 D6 Rochestown, Co Kilkenny	22 B3 Ryehill	18 D3 Shantonagh *(Seantonnach)*
30 E6 Rochestown, Co Kilkenny	34 C3 Rylane	21 F7 Shanavogh
29 H6 Rochestown, Co Tipperary		23 F6 Sharavogue *(Searbhóg)*
23 J2 Rochfortbridge *(Droichead Chaisleán Loiste)*	**S**	18 C3 Shercock *(Searcóg)*
27 J6 Rockchapel *(Séipéal na Carraige)*	25 F3 Saggart	8 D7 Sheskin
18 C2 Rockcorry *(Buíochar)*	5 G7 Saint Johnstown	29 G3 Shevry
28 D5 Rockhill	30 E4 Saint Mullins	31 G2 Shillelagh *(Síol Ealaigh)*
28 E7 Rockmills	13 G5 Saintfield *(Tamhnaigh Naomh)*	23 F6 Shinrone *(Suí an Róin)*
25 G7 Rockstown	35 F4 Saleen	13 H5 Shrigley
16 E4 Rodeen	24 D4 Sallins *(Na Solláin)*	27 G4 Shrone
21 J4 Roevehagh	34 E3 Sallybrook	29 F5 Shronell
22 E4 Rooaun	29 G2 Sallypark	27 G4 Shronowen *(Srón Abhann)*
14 C5 Roonagh Quay	21 H4 Salthill	15 H7 Shrule *(Sruthair)*
16 B3 Roosky, Co Mayo	31 F7 Saltmills *(Muillean an tSáile)*	33 J5 Sillahertane
17 F5 Roosky, Co Roscommon *(Rúscaigh)*	12 B4 Sandholes *(Clais an Ghainimh)*	18 E2 Silver Bridge *(Beal Átha an Airgid)*
22 E3 Rooty Cross	25 G3 Sandyford *(Áth an Ghainimh)*	12 B7 Silver Stream
4 E4 Rosapenna	25 G2 Santry *(Seantrabh)*	29 F2 Silvermines *(Beal Átha Gabhann)*
30 E5 Rosbercon	13 H6 Saul	11 G2 Sion Mills *(Muileann an tSiáin)*
31 F2 Roscat	15 H6 Scardaun, Co Mayo	27 G5 Six Crosses
16 E6 Roscommon *(Ros Comáin)*	16 E7 Scradaun, Co Roscommon	13 H3 Six Road Ends
23 G6 Roscrea *(Ros Cré)*	22 C7 Scarriff *(An Scairbh)*	28 C2 Sixmilebridge *(Droichead Abhann)*
29 H5 Rosegreen *(Faiche Ró)*	27 H7 Scartaglin	
23 G2 Rosemount	12 E6 Scarva *(Scarbhach)*	11 H4 Sixmilecross *(Na Coracha Móra)*
23 J5 Rosenallis *(Ros Fhionnghlaise)*	12 B7 Scotch Corner	33 H5 Skahanagh
20 E3 Rosmuck *(Ros Muc)*	12 D5 Scotch Street *(Sráid na hAlbanach)*	35 F3 Skahanagh North
29 H3 Rosmult	17 J2 Scotshouse *(Teach an Scotaigh)*	35 F3 Skahanagh South
5 F4 Rosnakill *(Ros na Cille)*	11 J7 Scotstown *(Baile an Scotaigh)*	33 H7 Skeagh, Co Cork
17 J5 Ross, Co Meath *(An Ros)*	27 F6 Scrahan	17 H7 Skeagh, Co Westmeath
32 E2 Ross Behy	33 H2 Scrahanfadda	22 B2 Skehanagh, Co Galway
34 B6 Ross Carbery *(Ros Ó gCairbre)*	16 E5 Scramoge *(Scramóg)*	21 J5 Skehanagh, Co Galway
8 C6 Ross Port *(Ross Dumhach)*	28 E7 Scrarour	29 F7 Skeheen
15 G4 Ross West	31 H5 Screen *(An Scrín)*	19 H7 Skerries *(Na Sceirí)*
29 G5 Rossadrehid *(Ross an Droichead)*	23 H4 Screggan *(An Screagán)*	33 H7 Skibbereen *(An Sciobairín)*
27 G7 Rossanean	6 B6 Scriggan	18 E7 Skreen, Co Meath
20 E4 Rossaveel	18 C6 Scurlockstown	9 H7 Skreen, Co Sligo *(An Scrín)*
33 G7 Rossbrin	13 G6 Seaforde *(Baile Forda)*	33 G7 Skull *(An Scoil)*
21 G3 Rosscahill *(Ros Cathail)*	12 E6 Seapatrick	31 F8 Slade
9 J6 Rosses Point *(An Ros)*	30 B5 Seskin	18 E6 Slane *(Baile Shláine)*
10 C6 Rossinver *(Ros Inbhir)*	11 H4 Seskinore *(Seisceann Odhar)*	30 D6 Slieveroe *(Sliabh Rua)*
31 H6 Rosslare *(Ros Láir)*	33 J5 Shanacrane	9 J7 Sligo *(Sligeach)*
31 J7 Rosslare Harbour *(Calafort Ros Lair)*	35 G4 Shanagarry *(An Seangharraí)*	18 E5 Smarmore
11 H7 Rosslea *(Ros Liath)*	21 J6 Shanaglish	26 B7 Smerwick
32 E6 Rossmackowen	28 B4 Shanagolden *(Seanghualainn)*	11 J7 Smithborough *(Na Mullaí)*
33 J4 Rossmore, Co Cork	23 J7 Shanahoe *(Seanchua)*	30 D2 Smithstown
34 B6 Rossmore, Co Cork *(An Ros Mór)*	22 C3 Shanballard	32 E4 Sneem *(An tSnaidhm)*
30 E2 Rossmore, Co Laois	34 E4 Shanbally, Co Cork *(An Seanbhaile)*	16 D2 Sooey
11 J7 Rossmore, Co Monaghan	16 C7 Shanbally, Co Galway	27 F6 Spa *(An Spá)*
29 G3 Rossmore, Co Tipperary	35 K2 Shanbally, Co Waterford	21 H7 Spancelhill
10 C4 Rossnowlagh *(Ros Neamhlach)*	29 F3 Shanballyedmond	33 F7 Spanish Point *(Rinn na Spáinneach)*
35 G4 Rostellan *(Ros Tialláin)*	28 E7 Shanballymore, Co Cork	11 J2 Sperrin
19 G2 Rostrevor *(Ros Treabhair)*	15 J6 Shanballymore, Co Galway *(An Seanbhaile Mór)*	21 F4 Spiddle
14 D4 Rosturk	22 C4 Shangarry	24 B7 Spink
15 H6 Roundfort	25 G4 Shankill *(Seanchill)*	23 H2 Spittaltown
20 C2 Roundstone *(Cloch na Rón)*	34 B5 Shanlaragh *(Seanlárach)*	5 G6 Spring Town
25 G5 Roundwood *(An Tóchar)*	27 J3 Shannakea *(Seanachae)*	25 G5 Sraghmore
11 J3 Rousky	28 C3 Shannon	8 B7 Srah, Co Mayo
21 H7 Ruan *(An Ruán)*	23 F4 Shannon Harbour *(Caladh na Sionainne)*	15 F6 Srah, Co Mayo
13 J5 Rubane *(Rú Bán)*	22 E4 Shannonbridge *(Droichead na Sionainne)*	23 G6 Srahanboy
19 H7 Rush *(An Ros)*	22 C7 Shannonville	15 H4 Sraheens *(Na Sraithíní)*
34 B3 Rusheen	24 B7 Shanragh	14 D2 Srahmore *(An Strath Mór)*
		29 H7 Sruh
		25 G2 St Margaret's
		19 F4 Stabannan

INDEX OF PLACE NAMES

18 E6 Stackallan *(Stigh Colláin)*	27 H3 Tarmon *(An Tearmann)*	29 G4 Thomastown, Co Tipperary
12 D3 Staffordstown *(Baile Stafard)*	12 C7 Tassagh *(An Tasach)*	24 D5 Thornton
19 G6 Stamullin	27 J7 Taur	30 C3 Three Castles
24 D3 Staplestown	10 C7 Tawnylea	11 J7 Three Mile House
25 G4 Stepaside	5 F4 Tawny *(An Tamhnaigh)*	25 G7 Three Wells
12 C4 Stewartstown *(An Chraobh)*	15 J4 Tawnyinah	29 H3 Thurles *(Durlas)*
25 G3 Stillorgan	33 G6 Tedagh	16 C4 Tibohine *(Tigh Baoithán)*
11 H7 Stone Bridge	11 J6 Tedavnet *(Tigh Damhnata)*	26 E5 Tiduff
28 E2 Stonepark	9 J3 Teelin	29 J6 Tikincor
13 F4 Stonyford, Co Antrim	17 H2 Teemore	24 D3 Timahoe, Co Kildare
30 D4 Stonyford, Co Kilkenny *(Áth Stúin)*	26 D6 Teer	24 B6 Timahoe, Co Laois *(Tigh Mochua)*
13 G4 Stormont	26 B7 Teeravane	34 C6 Timoleague *(Tigh Molaige)*
11 G2 Strabane *(An Strath Bán)*	34 B4 Teerelton *(Tír Eiltín)*	24 D6 Timolin
30 B8 Stradbally, Co Waterford	28 B2 Teermaclane *(Tír Mhic Calláin)*	31 H2 Tinehaly *(Tigh na hÉille)*
26 D7 Stradbally, Co Kerry	18 C4 Teevurcher *(Taobh Urchair)*	23 G3 Tinmuck
24 B6 Stradbally, Co Laois *(An tSraidbhaile)*	9 H7 Templeboy *(Teampall Baoith)*	31 G5 Tinnakilla
15 G4 Strade	30 C5 Templecrum	29 G5 Tipperary *(Tiobraid Árann)*
18 B3 Stradone *(Sraith an Domhain)*	29 G2 Templederry *(Teampall Doire)*	6 C7 Tirkane *(Tír Chiana)*
24 E3 Straffan *(Teach Srafáin)*	30 B5 Templeetney	34 C6 Tirnanean
31 G3 Strahart *(Sraith Airt)*	34 C4 Templemartin *(Teampall Mártan)*	12 B6 Tirnaneill
13 G2 Straid *(An tSraid)*	29 H2 Templemore *(An Teampall Mór)*	21 J5 Tirneevin
28 B5 Strand *(An Trá)*	33 F4 Templenoe	10 D7 Tober, Co Cavan
9 J7 Strandhill *(An Leathros)*	23 J2 Templeoran	23 G3 Tober, Co Offaly
13 J6 Strangford *(Baile Loch Cuan)*	23 F7 Templepark	24 E6 Toberbeg
6 D5 Stranocum *(Sraith Nócam)*	13 F3 Templepatrick *(Teampall Phádraig)*	16 B3 Tobercurry *(Tobar an Choire)*
10 E2 Stranolar *(Srath an Urláir)*	31 G4 Templeshanbo *(Teampall Seanbhoth)*	22 B5 Toberelatan
24 E6 Stratford *(Áth na Sráide)*	29 J2 Templetouhy *(Teampall Tuaithe)*	12 C2 Tobermore *(An Tobar Mór)*
14 B7 Streamstown, Co Galway	31 F7 Templetown	15 G7 Tobernadarry
23 H2 Streamstown, Co Westmeath *(Baile an tSruthain)*	34 E3 Templeusque	16 C2 Toberscanavan
17 H6 Street *(An tSráid)*	11 G6 Tempo *(An tIompú Deiseal)*	29 F4 Toem *(Tuaim)*
16 E5 Strokestown *(Béal na mBuillí)*	4 E6 Termon	33 J5 Togher, Co Cork
5 J4 Stroove	14 F5 Termonbarry	19 G4 Togher, Co Louth
34 C3 Stuake	19 G5 Termonfeckin *(Tearmann Feichin)*	24 D2 Togher, Co Meath
34 E5 Summer Cove	22 D5 Terryglass *(Tír Dhá Ghlas)*	24 B3 Togher, Co Offaly
24 D2 Summerhill *(Cnoc an Linsigh)*	18 B7 Tevrin	25 F5 Togher, Co Wicklow
24 D5 Suncroft *(Crochta na Gréine)*	19 G3 The Bush	27 F5 Togherbane
24 B7 Swan	30 E2 The Butts	31 H7 Tomhaggard *(Teach Moshagard)*
11 F7 Swanlinbar *(An Muilcann Iarainn)*	5 H6 The Cross *(An Chrois)*	21 G3 Tonabrocky
6 C7 Swatragh *(An Suaitreach)*	24 D5 The Curragh *(An Currach)*	15 F5 Tonlegee
15 H4 Swinford *(Beal Átha na Muice)*	12 E3 The Diamond, Co Antrim	14 D3 Tonregee
25 G2 Swords *(Sord)*	12 C3 The Diamond, Co Tyrone	18 B3 Tonyduff *(An Tonnaigh Dhubh)*
	18 B7 The Downs *(Na Dúnta)*	34 B5 Toom *(Tuaim)*
T	6 E5 The Drones	34 B4 Tooms
22 E3 Taghmaconnell	6 D5 The Dry Arch	21 G6 Toomaghera
31 G6 Taghmon *(Teach Munna)*	19 G7 The Five Roads	16 C7 Toomard *(Tuaim Ard)*
17 G7 Taghshinny	31 H4 The Harrow	20 C2 Toombeola
31 H7 Tagoat *(Teach Gót)*	24 B5 The Heath	12 D2 Toome *(Droichead Thuama)*
32 E4 Tahilla	31 G5 The Leap	22 E7 Toomyvara *(Tuaim Uí Mheára)*
25 F3 Tallaght *(Tamhlacht)*	12 C3 The Loup *(An Lúb)*	29 F2 Toor *(An Tuar)*
18 E4 Tallanstown *(Baile an Tallúnaigh)*	17 G7 The Pigeons *(Na Colúir)*	29 J7 Tooraneena
35 H2 Tallow *(Tulach an Iarainn)*	22 E6 The Pike, Co Tipperary	27 J4 Tooraree
35 H2 Tallowbridge	35 H2 The Pike, Co Waterford	34 E2 Tooreen *(Tuairín)*
11 F6 Tamlaght, Co Fermanagh *(Tamhlacht)*	35 K2 The Pike, Co Waterford	27 H7 Tooreencahill
6 C7 Tamlaght O'Crilly	12 B4 The Rock *(An Charraig)*	28 B7 Tooreendermot
12 C4 Tamnamore *(An Tamhnach Mbór)*	4 B6 The Rosses	34 E2 Toorgarriff
12 D6 Tandragee *(Tóin re Gaoith)*	30 E5 The Rower *(An Robhar)*	15 J3 Toorlestraun
17 G7 Tang *(An Teanga)*	7 F7 The Sheddings	15 F6 Toormakeady *(Tuar Mhic Éadaigh)*
28 D5 Tankardstown	13 G6 The Spa *(An Spa)*	33 F7 Toormore *(An Tuar Mór)*
18 E7 Tara, Co Meath	30 C6 The Sweep	21 J6 Toornafulla
23 H3 Tara, Co Offaly	13 G5 The Temple *(An Teampall)*	23 J3 Torque
27 H4 Tarbert *(Tairbeart)*	29 H7 The Vee	30 D7 Towergare
	30 D4 Thomastown, Co Kilkenny *(Baile Mhic Andáin)*	35 F5 Trabolgan
	28 E6 Thomastown, Co Limerick	34 E5 Tracton
	18 D5 Thomastown, Co Meath	33 F6 Trafrask
		27 F6 Tralee *(Trá Lí)*
		30 D7 Tramore *(Trá Mór)*

INDEX OF PLACE NAMES

22 B2	Trasternagh	
33 H6	Trawlebane	
15 F6	Trean	
4 E6	Treantagh *(Na Treantachta)*	
16 C5	Trien *(An Trian)*	
11 G5	Trillick *(Trileac)*	
18 D6	Trim *(Baile Átha Troim)*	
22 C3	Trust	
15 J7	Tuam *(Tuaim)*	
22 C7	Tuamgraney *(Tuaim Gréine)*	
21 J6	Tubber *(An Tobar)*	
30 B3	Tubbrid, Co Kilkenny	
29 H6	Tubbrid, Co Tipperary	
21 J7	Tulla, Co Clare *(An Tulach)*	
21 H5	Tulla, Co Clare	
33 J5	Tullagh	
27 J2	Tullaghaboy	
10 B5	Tullaghan *(An Tulachán)*	
30 E5	Tullagher *(Tulachar)*	
30 C5	Tullaghought	
30 D4	Tullaherin	
27 H4	Tullamore, Co Kerry	
23 H4	Tullamore, Co Offaly *(Tulach Mhór)*	
26 E7	Tullaree	
30 C3	Tullaroan *(Tulach Ruáin)*	
21 H7	Tullassa	
27 F3	Tullig, Co Clare	
27 G6	Tullig, Co Kerry	
32 E2	Tullig Co Kerry	
31 F2	Tullow *(An Tulch)*	
21 F4	Tully	
14 C7	Tully Cross	
19 F5	Tullyallen *(Tulaigh Álainn)*	
31 G6	Tullycanna	
10 C7	Tullycoly	
12 C4	Tullyhogue *(Tulaigh Óg)*	
28 B6	Tullylease	
12 C5	Tullyroar Corner	
18 B3	Tullyvin *(Tulaigh Bhinn)*	
15 J6	Tulrohaun *(Tulach Shrutháin)*	
16 D5	Tulsk *(Tuilsce)*	
33 F4	Tuosist *(Tuath Ó Siosta)*	
18 B7	Turin	
21 H5	Turlough, Co Clare	
15 G4	Turlough, Co Mayo *(Turlach)*	
21 J3	Turloughmore *(An Turlach Mór)*	
33 J4	Turnaspidogy	
28 D7	Turnpike Cross	
17 F6	Turreen	
29 J3	Twomileborris *(Buiríos Léith)*	
18 E7	Tylas	
22 D7	Tynagh *(Tíne)*	
12 B6	Tynan *(Tuíneán)*	
13 H7	Tyrella	
23 J3	Tyrrellspass *(Belach an Tirialaigh)*	

U

33 J7	Unionhall *(Bréantrá)*
29 G3	Upperchurch *(An Teampall Uachtarach)*
6 C7	Upperlands *(Áth an Phortáin)*
34 D5	Upton *(Garraí Thancaird)*
32 D6	Urhin
16 B4	Urlaur *(Urlár)*
30 B2	Urlingford *(Áth na nUrlainn)*

V

24 E5	Valleymount *(An Chrois)*
26 C7	Ventry *(Ceann Trá)*
24 C5	Vicarstown *(Baile an Bhoicáire)*
11 G2	Victoria Bridge *(Droichead Victoria)*
35 H2	Villierstown *(An Baile Nua)*
18 B4	Virginia *(Achadh an Iúir)*

W

23 J4	Walsh Island
35 F3	Walshtown
18 E6	Walterstown
25 F2	Ward *(An Barda)*
12 E5	Waringstown *(Baile an Bhairínigh)*
19 G2	Warrenpoint *(An Pointe)*
24 E4	Watch House Cross Roads
31 G3	Watch House Village
34 D4	Waterfall *(Tobar an Iarla)*
30 D7	Waterford *(Port Láirge)*
35 F3	Watergrasshill *(Cnocán na Biolraí)*
34 D3	Waterloo
32 C4	Waterville *(An Coireán)*
10 E2	Welchtown
31 F6	Wellingtonbridge *(Droichead Eoin)*
31 J4	Wells
15 F5	Westport *(Cathair na Mart)*
14 E5	Westport Quay
30 D8	Westtown
31 H6	Wexford *(Loch Garman)*
24 C4	Wheelam Cross Roads
27 F7	White Gate Cross Roads
34 E3	White's Cross *(Crois an Fhaoitigh)*
13 G3	Whiteabbey *(An Mhainistir Fhionn)*
34 E3	Whitechurch, Co Cork *(An Teampall Geal)*
35 J2	Whitechurch, Co Waterford
30 E6	Whitechurch, Co Wexford
12 D7	Whitecross *(Corr Leacht)*
22 D6	Whitegate, Co Clare *(An Geata Bán)*
35 F4	Whitegate, Co Cork *(An Geata Bán)*
17 F5	Whitehall, Co Roscommon *(An Baile Nua)*
17 J6	Whitehall, Co Westmeath
13 H2	Whitehead *(An Cionn Bán)*
19 G3	Whites Town
12 E2	Whitesides Corner *(An Phrochlais)*
25 H6	Wicklow *(Cill Mhantáin)*
18 D5	Wilkinstown *(Baile Uilcín)*
21 G6	Willbrook
16 B6	Williamstown, Co Galway *(Baile Liam)*
23 F2	Williamstown, Co Westmeath *(Baile Liam)*
30 C5	Windgap *(Bearne na Gaoithe)*
24 B7	Wolfhill *(Cnocán na Mactíre)*
13 G2	Woodburn *(Sruth na Coille)*
25 G7	Woodenbridge
22 C5	Woodford *(An Ghráin)*
22 C3	Woodlawn
30 E7	Woodstown

Y

18 E6	Yellow Furze
35 H3	Youghal, Co Cork *(Eochaill)*
22 D7	Youghal, Co Tipperary

THE **MINI** ROUGH GUIDE TO
CARIBBEAN PORTS OF CALL

ROUGH GUIDES

YOUR TAILOR-MADE TRIP STARTS HERE

Tailor-made trips and unique adventures crafted by local experts

Rough Guides has been inspiring travellers for more than 35 years. Leave it to our local experts to create your perfect itinerary and book it at local rates.

Don't follow the crowd – find your own path.

HOW ROUGHGUIDES.COM/TRIPS WORKS

STEP 1 Pick your dream destination, tell us what you want and submit an enquiry.

STEP 2 Fill in a short form to tell your local expert about your dream trip and preferences.

STEP 3 Our local expert will craft your tailor-made itinerary. You'll be able to tweak and refine it until you're completely satisfied.

STEP 4 Book online with ease, pack your bags and enjoy the trip! Our local expert will be on hand 24/7 while you're on the road.

PLAN AND BOOK YOUR TRIP AT ROUGHGUIDES.COM/TRIPS

HOW TO DOWNLOAD YOUR FREE EBOOK

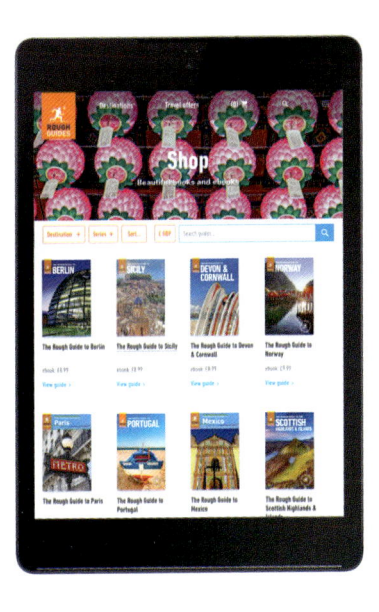

1. Visit **www.roughguides.com/free-ebook** or scan the **QR code** below

2. Enter the code **ports202**

3. Follow the simple step-by-step instructions

For troubleshooting contact: mail@roughguides.com

10 THINGS NOT TO MISS

1. **THE COCKSCOMB BASIN WILDLIFE SANCTUARY AND JAGUAR PRESERVE, BELIZE**
   You may be lucky enough to spot a jaguar here. See page 54.

2. **THE GRENADINES**
   Snorkelling and diving here is second to none. See page 151.

3. **PIRATES OF THE CARIBBEAN**
   The Caribbean's seafaring history is revealed at the Pirates of Nassau Museum in the Bahamas. See page 63.

4. **LES CHUTES DU CARBET, GUADELOUPE**
   Hike through lush forest and see the highest waterfall in the Caribbean. See page 119.

5. **CHICHÉN ITZÁ**
   Magical Maya ruins such as the Pyramid of Kukulcán (El Castillo) are the highlight of any visit to the Yucatán, Mexico. See page 48.

6. **COSTA RICA**
   Tropical rainforests, gushing rivers and rare wildlife make this a sublime destination. See page 57.

7. **SURFER'S PARADISE**
   Atlantic rollers at Bathsheba in Barbados. See page 148.

8. **THE PITONS**
   St Lucia's dramatic landmark peaks dominate the landscape at Soufrière. See page 137.

9. **RIVER RAFTING**
   A great way to travel in Jamaica. See page 78.

10. **EAGLE BEACH**
    On the northwest coast of Aruba, this idyllic beach is one of the Caribbean's best. See page 167.

A PERFECT CRUISE

Day 1

Barbados. Arrive a day before the cruise and take the time to explore Barbados. Take a jeep safari round the island, visiting the windswept beaches along the rugged Atlantic coast, or walk around Bridgetown, with its British influence and impressive Parliament building, and the nearby historic Garrison area.

Day 2

Mayreau, Grenadines. From the dock at tiny Mayreau, jump on a charter boat to the uninhabited Tobago Cays for some of the best snorkelling in the Caribbean. Exotic colourful fish dart in and out of the coral and the visibility thanks to the crystal clear waters is astonishing.

Day 3

St Lucia and Castries. Be on deck early as the ship approaches Soufrière, in the shadow of the dramatic Pitons, it is a stunning sight in the early morning light. Take a tour of St Lucia's wild side: the world's only drive-in volcano and the Diamond Waterfall, cascading over lush tropical foliage. In the afternoon, check out arty Castries – there are some great galleries selling batik, silk screens, sculpture, oils and watercolours, or try the Craft Market for local souvenirs.

Day 4

St-Barths. Step ashore amidst some of the most lavish private yachts to be found in the Caribbean. Stroll around Gustavia, the chic capital, or from the port, walk to pretty Shell Beach, which is overlooked by a cool Brazilian bar. On the way back to the dock, have a drink at Le Select (tel: 590-590 27 8687), a lively yachtie pub.

IN **THE CARIBBEAN**

Day 5

St-Martin. Wander around the little town of Marigot, capital of the French side of the island, complete with boulangerie. At lunchtime, take a taxi to Grand Case, a single street along the shore lined with some of the finest restaurants in the Caribbean. Grab a waterside table at La Cigale (www.lacigalerestaurantsxm.com), choose your lobster, order a glass of chilled rosé, and don't move until the sun goes down.

Day 6

Virgin Gorda (BVI). Spend the day splashing around at The Baths, one of the most beautiful beaches you'll come across in the Caribbean, a jumble of giant boulders are scattered on soft, white sand here, creating secluded pools and cool caves.

Day 7–8

All at sea. Two blissful days to bask by the pool with a book, or attend one of the onboard lectures. Or why not try out a class or indulge yourself in some serious pampering at the on-board spa. Keep an eye out for dolphins and whales off-shore too form the deck; they love racing the ship and it makes for a particularly great photo opportunity at sunrise and sunset.

Day 9

Miami. If you're on an evening flight, disembark from the ship, check in at the airport and then head to South Beach and the city's Art Deco district. A spot of lunch later, followed by a stroll on the beach and shopping, and you'll be in a relaxed mood for that flight home.

CONTENTS

OVERVIEW	10
OUT AND ABOUT	21

Sailing out of America
21

Miami 21, Fort Lauderdale 28, Port Canaveral 31, Orlando theme parks 32, Tampa 34, New Orleans 36, Galveston 37, Houston 38, Key West 39

Mexico and Central America
42

Cozumel 43, Beaches 44, Cancún 45, Playa del Carmen 45, Xcaret 46, Costa Maya 49, Belize 51, Honduras 55, Costa Rica 57

The Bahamas
60

New Providence Island 60, Paradise Island 63, Grand Bahama 64

The Western Caribbean
68

Cuba 68, Grand Cayman 71, Jamaica 75, Montego Bay 76, Falmouth 78, Martha Brae 78, Ocho Rios 79, Port Antonio 82, Dominican Republic 83, Samaná Peninsula 86, Puerto Rico 86

Eastern Caribbean
89

US Virgin Islands 90, St Thomas 92, St John 95, St Croix 95, British Virgin Islands 97, Tortola 97, Virgin Gorda 98, Sint Maarten 99

St-Martin
102

St-Barthélemy 103, St Kitts 105, Nevis 109, Antigua 110, Guadeloupe 114, Dominica 120, Roseau 123, Portsmouth 126, Martinique 127, St Lucia 134, Castries 135, Barbados 141, Bridgetown 145, The Platinum Coast 146, The wild east coast 148

The southern Caribbean
150

St Vincent and The Grenadines 151, Bequia and Mayreau 153, Grenada 154, Trinidad and Tobago 159, Trinidad 159, Scarborough 163, Aruba and Curaçao 165, A tropical Amsterdam 168

TRAVEL ESSENTIALS	**172**
INDEX	**190**

HIGHLIGHTS

How to be a savvy sailor	16
USA	22
US home ports	37
Hemingway's home	38
Mexico	40
The Maya legacy	50
Central America	53
San Blas Islands	57
The Bahamas	59
The Western Caribbean	69
Eastern Caribbean	91
Best beaches	101
Whale watching	127
Cricket, lovely cricket…	147
Southern Caribbean	156
Carnival in Trinidad	161
Cruising and the environment	169
Venezuelan ports of call	170

> ## A NOTE TO READERS
>
> At Rough Guides, we always strive to bring you the most up-to-date information. This book was produced during a period of continuing uncertainty caused by the Covid-19 pandemic, so please note that content is more subject to change than usual. We recommend checking the latest restrictions and official guidance.

OVERVIEW

The whole of the Caribbean region has had a turbulent and extremely varied history. You will notice on arrival at any island port that there is at least one fortress guarding the harbour mouth or perched up on a hillside with a panoramic view of the sea.

These scattered vestiges of military power, some ruined and others restored, remind us that the Caribbean has always been fought over. Its landscapes are marked not only by fortifications, but by reminders of battles, uprisings and massacres. The surrounding seas have witnessed countless naval engagements and they conceal a wealth of sunken warships, rusting cannons – and treasure.

Not only did competing European nations go to war over this rich and desirable region, fighting out their quibbles from home on this glorious sea, but pirates preyed on its ports, and African slaves rose up against their oppressors in bids for freedom. Only in more recent times have these islands discovered peace.

> **Privateers**
>
> Notorious pirates such as Henry Morgan and Edward 'Blackbeard' Teach were independent operators, attacking Spanish ships, smuggling and slave-trading, until they were sponsored by European rulers at home, and renamed privateers.

EARLY CONQUESTS

The first people to discover the Caribbean were Amerindians who, thousands of years ago, travelled here in dug-out canoes from the Orinoco Basin in Venezuela, peacefully settling the islands. Around AD1000, the Carib, also known as the Kalinago, paddled up in canoes from the same jungle

Sugar cane plantation, Montego, 1900

area of South America and ousted the inhabitants; the region was named after them.

The Carib invasion may have been violent, but it was mild in comparison to the horrors inflicted by the first European invaders. Backed by the Spanish monarchy, Christopher Columbus arrived 500 years later, thinking he had reached the East Indies, and heralded the start of the conquest by Europeans of the West Indies and the New World. He was closely followed by Spanish conquistadors in pursuit of gold. Greed for this precious metal drove the Spanish to colonise the larger islands of Hispaniola, Cuba and Puerto Rico, and they brutally forced the Amerindians to search for it. They in turn succumbed to European diseases or were killed in uprisings. From here, the Spanish went on to Mexico and Central America, where they discovered the treasures of the Maya civilizations. Lacking gold, the smaller Eastern Caribbean islands were not colonised until sugar was introduced.

EUROPEAN BATTLES

Other European nations watched the expansion of the Spanish Caribbean with keen interest. Protestant England was hostile towards Catholic Spain and Sir Francis Drake attacked and occupied Santo Domingo in Hispaniola, in 1585, destroying the pride of the Spanish Empire. At the same time pirates, such as Henry Morgan and Edward 'Blackbeard' Teach, began to prey on Spanish galleons and ports. In response, the Spanish fortified their towns and protected their fleets with warships.

Gradually, other European nations began to settle in the region. The English claimed St Kitts in 1624 and Barbados in 1627. The French took Martinique and Guadeloupe in 1635 and the Dutch took six Antillean islands between 1630 and 1640.

Throughout the 17th and 18th centuries, the European powers sent their fleets to battle for control of the West Indies and its rich sugar industry. The British took Jamaica from the Spanish in 1655 and did their utmost to weaken the Spaniards' dominance of the larger islands. At the same time, conflicts between the British, French and Dutch reflected wider hostilities in Europe. No sooner were peace treaties signed than a new outbreak of fighting shook the region. Between 1660 and 1814, the island of St Lucia changed hands between the British and French 14 times. During this period, millions of enslaved Africans were brought against their will to the islands to ensure the flow of sugar to Europe was not interrupted.

SUGAR AND SLAVERY

The sugar industry reached its zenith in the second half of the 18th century, the age of luxurious 'great houses' and fantastically rich West Indian planters. Tremendous fortunes were made, both by planters and manufacturers and traders in Europe.

The single event that changed the course of Caribbean history was the slave revolution of 1791–1804, which destroyed the French colony of Saint Domingue and created the independent republic of Haiti. The other Caribbean high societies watched with horror as the region's richest colony disintegrated. Another blow to 'King Sugar' came with the development of a rival beet sugar industry in Europe. European farmers and manufacturers began to compete with the vested interests of the old 'plantocracy'.

Statue acknowledging the country's past, Puerto Rico

Slavery was eventually abolished during the mid-19th century (it took longest to disappear in the Spanish colonies). Contract indentured labourers arrived from India and other countries to fill the gaps left by the departing slaves. But the industry went through hard times, and gradually the European powers lost interest in their Caribbean possessions.

ROADS TO INDEPENDENCE

As the 20th century dawned, what most of the Caribbean islands wanted was independence. Haiti proclaimed its independence in 1804, but had been plagued by instability and poverty. The Dominican Republic finally threw out the Spanish in 1864; Cuba and Puerto Rico followed suit in 1898.

But American influence had taken hold in the larger islands of the Western Caribbean, creating resentment among those who wanted to be free of outside interference. Afraid of communism, the US supported conservatives, including such unsavoury dictators as Rafael Leonidas Trujillo, who ran the Dominican Republic like a family business from 1930 to 1961. Washington's worst fears were realised when another dictator, Fulgencio Batista of Cuba, was ousted in 1959, and replaced by the revolutionary, later Communist, government of Fidel Castro.

Mostly, independence took a more peaceful form. The British colonies were given independence from the 1960s onwards, though some preferred to maintain their links with Europe. In 1946, Martinique and Guadeloupe voted to become *départements* of France, while the Dutch islands formed a federation with the Netherlands.

A few tiny territories, such as Montserrat, the Turks and Caicos and Anguilla, opted to remain British, rather than face the economic uncertainty of independence.

THE CARIBBEAN TODAY

In many respects, the modern Caribbean is something of a success story. With the exception of Cuba, the region mostly enjoys democratic government and a steadily growing standard of living. Barbados, for instance, has some of the best quality-of-life statistics outside Europe and North America. And the bitter chapter in USA–Cuba relations finally appears to be coming to an end; the two countries restored their diplomatic ties in 2014, ending over half a century of hostility. But there are still social and political flashpoints in the region. Cuba's future still remains pretty uncertain, Haiti's deep-seated problems seem no closer to a solution, and there is occasional trouble in the inner-city areas of Kingston, Jamaica.

However, the threats facing the Caribbean today are now more economic than political. As a cluster of small states, the islands are especially vulnerable to developments beyond their control. These range from the hurricanes that regularly ravage communities, to globalisation and the loss of export markets to cheaper producers around the world. But in the true Caribbean spirit, the islanders will

Cruise ships in St-Martin

not be beaten while the land and sea around them can still provide them with a livelihood in the form of tourism. The importance of this industry cannot be overstated: over 3 million jobs depend on tourism and it is estimated that some US$50 billion comes into the region through tourist spending. And they don't just work in hotels and restaurants; they include farmers, taxi drivers, entertainers and artisans.

CARIBBEAN CRUISING

The typical attractions of the Caribbean need no introduction and cruise ships offer a particularly inviting way to discover this rich and varied part of the world. In a week, for instance, it is possible to explore half a dozen entirely different islands, getting a tantalising taste of the Caribbean's diversity. In some cases, a day may be long enough to gain an impression of an island, especially if it's a small one; other islands will require a longer exploration. A brief visit may leave you wanting to see more, 85 percent of cruise passengers come back, and many people return for a longer stay in a place they first visited on a cruise ship.

The beauty of Caribbean cruising is that each day offers an entirely different cultural experience. At first sight, some of the islands may look similar, with wooded hills surrounding the harbour and mountains stretching into the interior. But on closer inspection, you will discover that each port, and each island, has its own distinctive flavour.

There is no mistaking the French feel of Pointe-à-Pitre in Guadeloupe, for instance, where ships moor next to the bustling Place de la Victoire, with its cafés, war memorial and colourful market. But just to the north, you'll find Antigua, where memories of Admiral Lord Nelson, an Anglican cathedral and a cricket ground give the island a resolutely British feel.

Whether you want to slap on the sun lotion, read a good book and bask in the sun, go diving in pristine coral reefs, hike through

HOW TO BE A SAVVY SAILOR

First time cruisers may find it bewildering at the start of a cruise, but those who have been before won't hang around discussing the size of their cabin (they are all small) but will get down to organising their leisure pursuits. Savvy sailors know to arrive at the harbour early and to embark as soon as possible. While others are waiting for their luggage to be taken to the stateroom (it takes hours), well-practised cruisers are moving from deck to deck, swiftly securing the best of everything. First, they book any exciting sounding shore excursions – they will often be snapped up before the ship has set sail – then they head for the spa and beauty salon to grab the limited appointments, such as spa and beauty treatments on 'at sea' days rather than 'in port' days. Seasoned cruisers also stake out prime positions around the pool, as loungers in the shade are like gold dust.

a rainforest, explore ancient Maya ruins or simply wander around the various ports of call, a Caribbean cruise can give you a taste of all of these things, and more. It is also possible to combine one cruise itinerary with another (on the same ship or two different ones) for two weeks' cruising.

BUILDING BIGGER

In recent years, most of the islands have experienced an enormous increase in cruise arrivals. The ships have also got larger. The two largest – Royal Caribbean International's 236,857-ton *Wonder of the Seas* and its sister, *Symphony of the Seas*, with a maximum capacity of 6,680 passengers – are intended to spend all year in the Caribbean because they are simply too big to be accommodated anywhere else.

Most Caribbean ports of call have done a great deal to upgrade and modernise their cruise terminal facilities as cruise numbers rise and larger ships appear. Visitors can normally expect an array of shops, bars and restaurants on shore. But it would be a mistake not to take a look at what is beyond and explore.

IN PORT

With a few exceptions, cruise ships moor close to the centre of the major Caribbean ports. In the smaller islands, it is normally only a brief walk or taxi ride from ship to town. Usually in the capital or main town, the port would have seen the height of the sugar trade. As a result, they are full of historic interest, revealing ancient

> **Forward planning**
>
> To get value for money from shore excursions offered on the ship, do your homework and research on the places you want to see beforehand. You may find it cheaper to explore an island or area on your own, or with just a few others by taxi. Take care not to overbook excursions, as a crowded schedule can be punishing on the pocket as well as physically exhausting.

warehouses, colonnaded arcades and imposing buildings as well as the traditional fortifications.

CRUISING THE CARIBBEAN

Douglas Ward, the world's leading authority on cruise ships, considers why many people choose to cruise the Caribbean

The tropical islands of the Caribbean – the West Indies – arc down from the southern Florida coast to Venezuela like a jewelled necklace, often within sight of one another. Each island has a character, atmosphere and flavour of its own, shaped by its history and its people. Embracing the vast Caribbean basin on its western shores are Mexico and the Central American countries and between them all they offer sandy beaches, turquoise and blue waters, coral reefs, bougainvillea, rainforests, exotic fruits, glowing sunshine, vibrant music, vivid history and friendly, laid-back people. So it's no wonder the countries of the Caribbean are among the most popular holiday destinations.

There was a time when just getting to the region was an adventure; now the adventure can start on a cruise, and travelling on a luxury floating hotel is a wonderful way to experience the atmosphere of the Caribbean, particularly for first-time visitors.

Nowhere in the world is there such a wide collection of exotic islands and countries to which ships, including the largest ones, can travel. With many cruises beginning in Florida, San Juan, Puerto Rico,

Island hibiscus

or in Barbados, much of the region is accessible on relatively short trips by sea, and the value for money is unbeatable. Today, cruising is not just for the older, wealthy few – passengers come from all age groups and walks of life, and cruises are designed to suit their different needs. The virtually crime-free environment is particularly attractive to families.

Cruising has come a long way since the 'booze cruises' of the 1930s, designed chiefly to escape Prohibition laws in the United States. The industry launched the revival of fortunes for many Caribbean islands, but World War II intervened and it was only in the 1960s that cruising was reborn, with passengers being flown to embarkation ports, and a working relationship emerging between cruise lines and airlines.

Most ships started in Miami and went no further than the Bahamas, the US Virgin Islands and maybe San Juan, on itineraries that lasted a week – still the favourite duration for most passengers, but the lines soon realised that they needed new ports and new islands to visit.

First, they sent their ships west to Mexico's Yucatán Peninsula, to Cozumel and Playa del Carmen (in reach of the Maya ruins), and then they turned south. But to get down south and see more than just one or two islands would take longer than a week if a ship started in Miami or another Florida port, so the cruise lines started to base ships at islands such as Barbados. One of the bonuses of starting and ending a cruise in a Caribbean port is that a holiday can be extended by staying an extra week on the island.

The worldwide cruise industry has grown enormously since then (despite taking a great hit due to the Covid-19 pandemic); the concept hasn't changed much but it has been vastly improved, refined, expanded and packaged. Ten companies operating large ships (loosely defined as ships carrying between 2,500 and 5,400 passengers) dominate the market, but smaller vessels (carrying fewer than 700 passengers) also have a place, able to enter the uncrowded harbours where their larger sisters cannot venture.

Small ship adventures with the Blount cruise line

OUT AND ABOUT

The Caribbean has it all: sheltered coves; cooling trade winds; lush rainforests and exotic wildlife – paradise. From the glitzy ships to islands as different as Barbados and St-Barthélemy, this guide aims to cover the popular ports of call, including places not considered part of the region, such as the Bahamas, Mexico and Central America, but which are often found on Caribbean cruise itineraries.

SAILING OUT OF AMERICA

The majority of cruises to the Caribbean begin at US ports and most of those are in Florida, particularly for the western and eastern cruise routes. Since the 11th September 2001 attacks, when many Americans were put off flying, cruises have been departing from a wider range of ports, notably New Orleans, in Louisiana, and Galveston and Houston in Texas. For southern Caribbean cruises, more routes start from Barbados and San Juan in Puerto Rico so that itineraries can take in more islands.

If you are going on a cruise and have extra time, you can have a land-based holiday first or stay on after disembarking.

MIAMI
The main gateway to the Caribbean and its islands, Miami has the largest cruise passenger port in the world, with about 5.5 million passengers passing through it every year. Major cruise lines such as Carnival Cruise Lines, Norwegian Cruise Line (NCL) and Royal Caribbean International (RCI) depart from the terminal here.

The city's intoxicating ambience is a draw, and many like to include a few days or a week here in their holiday plans.

USA

Location: **Miami** is on the southeastern Florida coast; **Fort Lauderdale** is about 35km (23 miles) north of Miami; **Port Canaveral** is at the northern end of Florida's Space Coast, 56km (35 miles) east of Orlando; **Tampa** is on Florida's east coast 120km (75 miles) southeast of Orlando; and **Key West** is at the very end of the Florida Keys, the islands off the tip of Florida, 260km (159 miles) from Miami. **New Orleans** is on the Mississippi Delta by the Gulf of Mexico. The two main ports for Texas are the city of **Houston** and the island of **Galveston** 80km (50 miles) to the south, also on the Gulf coast.

Time zones: UTC/GMT -4 (Florida); UTC/GMT -5 (New Orleans, Texas).

Population: 2.7 million (Miami-Dade); 470,000 (Miami City); 182,000 (Fort Lauderdale); 384,000 (Tampa); 26,400 (Key West); 383,00 (New Orleans); 2.3 million (Houston); 47,700 (Galveston).

Language: English (and Spanish in Miami).

Money matters: The US dollar ($) is divided into 100 cents (¢). Credit cards are accepted and there are plenty of ATMs (cashpoints).

Telephone & internet: Payphones are everywhere and take a quarter (25¢) coin. Buy a phone card (from visitor centres and shops) to call long distance. To call long distance within the US, dial 1+area code+local number; or to call overseas you must dial 011+country code+area code+local number.

Area codes: 305 and 786 (Miami and Key West); 954 (Fort Lauderdale); 321 (Port Canaveral); 813 (Tampa); 504 (New Orleans); 281, 346, 713 and 832 (Houston); 409 (Galveston).

Internet cafés are plentiful too; ask at the tourist office in the port.

Calendar highlights: Halloween: Miami, Tampa, New Orleans. Miami: Carnival (Feb/Mar), St Patrick's Day (Mar); Fort Lauderdale: Stone Crab & Seafood Festival (Jan); Las Olas Arts Festival (Mar); Cape Canaveral: Tico Warbird Air Show (Mar), Space Coast State Fair (Nov); New Orleans: Mardi Gras (Feb/Mar); Tampa: Gasparilla Pirate Festival (Feb).

Art Deco style in Miami's South Beach

In southeast Florida, Miami-Dade sprawls over 5,040 sq km (1,946 sq miles) in Dade County and is home to more than 2.6 million people, including immigrants from Latin America and the Caribbean, particularly from Cuba.

The **Port of Miami** ❶ (tel: 305-347 4800; www.miamidade.gov/portmiami), on Dodge Island, straddles Biscayne Bay between the city and Miami Beach. A top-class facility, the port has excellent security, plenty of car parking and check-in counters that can issue boarding passes for return flights home. **Miami International Airport** (www.miami-airport.com), only 13km (8 miles) away, has shuttle buses specifically for cruise passengers and a constant supply of taxis.

South Beach

Even if you just have a few hours to spare in Miami, a trip to **South Beach**, a few miles east of the port, should be a priority. The vibrant, flamboyant southern neighbourhood of **Miami Beach** is where everyone goes to see and be seen and, within 6.5 sq km (2.5 sq mile), it contains more than 800 well-preserved art deco buildings in the **Art Deco National Historic District**.

Start off on Ocean Drive, Florida's most famous street, at the **Art Deco Welcome Center** (daily 9am–5pm; tel: 305-672 2014; www.mdpl.org) and either sign up for a walking tour or pick up a free map along with any other information and souvenirs. The wonderful pastel 1930s' buildings are testament to the drive of the Miami Design Preservation League (MDPL), who fought off developers in the late 1970s.

Inside are murals of flamingos and etched glass windows. Even the lifeguard stations on the beach opposite are in pink art deco designs.

A cosmopolitan mix of colourful characters completes the scene at South Beach, and you can watch them go by from one of the many cafés and restaurants along the rather kitsch seafront, or join them in the nightclubs. Remember that to enter a bar or club you must have ID to prove you are 21 years old or over.

Away from the beach, the scene continues to buzz in the pedestrian-only **Lincoln Road Mall** (daily 10am-11pm; www.lincolnroadmall.com) between 16th and 17th streets. Here the art world flourishes, with the Oolite Arts (daily noon-5pm; free; tel: 305-674 8278; www.oolitearts.org) displaying the work of more than 100 artists, along with open studios where you can watch them at work.

For a different kind of architecture, and also under the auspices of the MDPL, go to **Espanola Way (www.visitespanolaway.com)**, just south of 15th Street. This eye-catching collection of bright pink Moorish arcades and hidden courtyards was built

> ### Retail therapy
>
> Shopaholics can have a field day in Florida, especially if kitsch is your bag, and there are plenty of shops selling designer clothes at factory prices too.

in Mediterranean Revival style in the 1920s and now houses a selection of galleries, cafés and shops. It was also the setting for many scenes of the latter-day TV series *Miami Vice*.

Downtown Miami

Driving west from South Beach, the view of downtown offers a big-city skyscraper skyline. Bilingual and multicultural but with an Hispanic heart, the centre of Miami is closer to the port and has a few interesting places to see. First on the horizon is the tiered **Bank of America Tower** on SE 2nd Street, built by architect I.M. Pei in 1983 as one of the tallest office skyscrapers south of New York. Another distinctive building is the Spanish-style, peach-coloured **Freedom Tower**, which was originally built as offices for the *Miami News* in 1925 and then became the reception centre for Cubans fleeing Fidel Castro's 1959 revolution.

Freedom Tower is a symbol of Cuban liberation

Opposite the edifice, on the waterfront, is **Bayside Marketplace**, the bustling outdoor shopping mall (Mon–Thu 10am–10pm, Fri–Sat 10am–11pm, Sun 11am–9pm; tel: 305-577 3344; www.baysidemarketplace.com). As well as shops in the waterside complex, there are bars and restaurants, and often live entertainment in the forecourt. You can also take a boat trip from here.

The **HistoryMiami Museum** (Wed–Sat 10am–5pm, Sun noon–4pm; tel: 305-375 1492; www.historymiami.org) on West Flagler Street provides a good background to the city's colourful history.

Another notable museum is the popular **Pérez Art Museum Miami** (Thurs 11am-9pm, Fri-Mon 11am-6pm; tel: 305-375 3000 www.pamm.org), with a cosmopolitan mix of permanent and visiting exhibits. It is located on the waterfront in the Museum Park, which is also home to the **Patricia and Phillip Frost Museum of Science** (daily 10am-7pm; tel: 305-434 9600; www.frostscience.org).

Little Havana

Travelling southward along the coast, you come to **Calle Ocho** (SW 8th Street), which takes you into the heart of **Little Havana**, the core of the Cuban community where the aroma of rich Cuban coffee fills the air. Calle Ocho is lined with interesting shops, Caribbean-style fruit stands and factories where specialists *(tabaqueros)* roll cigars by hand. The **Bay of Pigs Monument**, at the top of Cuban Memorial Boulevard, commemorates those who lost their lives in the failed invasion of Cuba in 1961. Elderly Cubans gather in Máximo Gómez Park (better known as **Domino Park**), to play dominoes and talk about the lives they left behind. **Woodlawn Park** Cemetery is where three former presidents of Cuba are buried.

A short distance southwest in the smart neighbourhood of **Coral Gables**, full of magnificent homes, you can take a tour of the lavish

Tabaqueros hard at work

historic **Biltmore Hotel** (tel: 305-445 1926; www.biltmorehotel.com) where the likes of Judy Garland and Al Capone stayed. Johnny Weissmuller, aka Tarzan, used to be a swimming instructor here and set a world swimming record in the hotel's pool in the 1930s.

Returning to the port via the one-time artists' colony of upmarket **Coconut Grove (tel: 305-461 5506; www.coconutgrove.com)**, make time to visit the **Vizcaya Museum and Gardens** (Wed–Mon 9.30am–4.30pm; tel: 305-250 9133; http://vizcaya.org), an Italian Renaissance-style palace with large formal gardens. Built in 1916, the villa is full of period furniture and valuable European antiques.

Everglades National Park

A trip to the Everglades

The **Everglades National Park** (tel: 305-242 7700; www.nps.gov/ever) is just an hour or two away from Miami. Many cruise lines offer an excursion here at the end of a cruise. Around 350 varieties of birds, 500 kinds of fish, 55 species of reptile, including crocodiles and alligators, and 40 mammal species live in the Everglades. It even has 45 indigenous species of plants that are found nowhere else on earth. You can spot some of them by walking along the numerous boardwalk trails or taking an airboat ride that skims over the swampland.

The **Ernest F. Coe Visitor Center** (daily 9am–5pm, mid-Dec–mid-Mar from 8am, tel: 305-242 7700) is at the park's main entrance on SR 9336, providing maps and brochures, as well as informative displays on various aspects of the park. A word of warning: beware the voracious mosquitoes; pack plenty of insect repellent.

FORT LAUDERDALE

Ships that sail from Fort Lauderdale dock at the ultra-modern **Port Everglades** ❷ (tel: 954-523 3404; www.portevergrades.net) in the southern part of the city. About 35km (23 miles) north of Miami, it is the second busiest cruise port in the world handling nearly 4 million passengers every year, but is far less congested than Port of Miami. Equipped with plenty of parking spaces, taxis, baggage handlers and comfortable waiting areas, it is just 3km (2 miles) from the **Fort Lauderdale-Hollywood International Airport (www.broward.org/airport)**.

Venice of America

It is hard to believe that less than a hundred years ago, Fort Lauderdale was a massive mangrove swamp stretching down to the coast. The wooden fort that gave the city its name, built in the Seminole Wars in the 1850s, had long since rotted away. The famous white sandy beaches still remain, stretching for 35km (23 miles) from Hollywood in the south to Deerfield Beach in the north.

> ### South Florida mall
> Make sure you visit the Sawgrass Mills Factory Outlet Mall (12801 W. Sunrise Boulevard; tel: 954-846 2350; Mon–Sat 10am–9.00pm, Sun 11am–8pm), the largest factory outlet mall in the US.

A 'wave wall' and walkway edge the 11km (7 miles) of beachfront in the city, making it a perfect place for a stroll, bike ride or a jog, with plenty of cafés, restaurants and shops to stop off at along the way.

The mangrove swamp was transformed into building

land by using the same technique that was applied to create Venice in Italy – dredging up a series of parallel canals and using the fill to create long peninsulas between them – hence its nickname, Venice of America. Today Fort Lauderdale has 560km (350 miles) of navigable waterways, flanked by beautiful homes; it is a mecca for water sports enthusiasts and yachties.

Fort Lauderdale's colourful coastline

Las Olas Boulevard

A free hop-on hop-off shuttle links the beach with downtown, and the city's cosmopolitan character, committed to the good life, can be witnessed along **Las Olas Boulevard** (tel: 954-258 8382; www.lasolasboulevard.com). A red-brick street, lined with old-fashioned gaslights, Las Olas offers visitors horse-drawn carriage rides, outdoor cafés, antiques shops and art galleries.

Towards the western end, a network of palm-lined footpaths and mini parks, called the **Riverwalk**, takes you past several historic sites on the banks of the New River. **Las Olas Riverfront** is a meandering outdoor complex filled with restaurants, art galleries, boutiques and bars; however, its best days seem to be behind it.

City museums

Not far from Las Olas Boulevard are several attractions. Housed in the New River Inn, a rustic 1905 inn, the **History Museum of**

the Fort Lauderale History Center (daily 10am–4pm; tel: 954-463 4431; www.historyfortlauderdale.org) contains exhibits on the area's history, including Indigenous American artefacts, historic photos and fine antiques.

Bonnet House (Tue–Fri 11am–3pm, Sat-Sun 11am–4pm; tel: 954-563 5393; www.bonnethouse.org) is the plantation-style winter home of the late art collector Frederick Bartlett and his wife Evelyn, who were both artists. It is a grand estate filled with unusual art and artefacts from around the world. The **Museum of Discovery and Science** (Mon–Sat 10am–5pm, Sun noon–5pm; tel: 954-467 6637; www.mods.org) is the largest science museum in South Florida and offers educational hands-on exhibits for children as well as an indoor citrus grove.

Closer to the port, if you have not had your fill of being waterborne, you may enjoy the intimate atmosphere of a 3-hour trip aboard the riverboat *Jungle Queen* (Mon 10am-5pm, Tues-Sun 10am-6:30pm; tel: 954-462 5596; www.junglequeen.com). This old-fashioned vessel will take you from the Bahia Mar Yacht Center along the New River so that you can see the riverside homes of some of the city's millionaires.

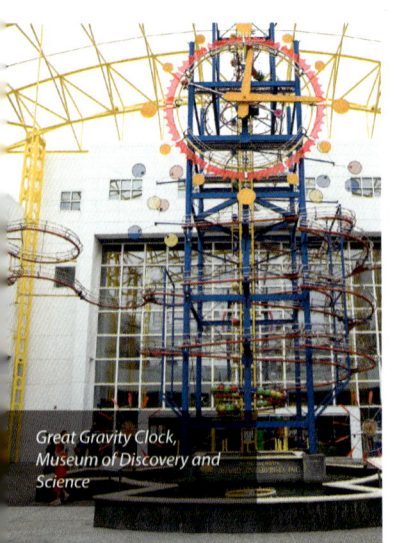

South of Fort Lauderdale is **Hollywood**, which has no connection with Tinseltown in California, but it does

Great Gravity Clock, Museum of Discovery and Science

All aboard the Jungle Queen for a New River tour

have a large entertainment complex of restaurants, bars and shops called **Oceanwalk** and a wonderful waterfront boardwalk.

If you have time, it is worth visiting the Arthur R. Marshall **Loxahatchee National Wildlife Refuge** (daily, daylight hours; tel: 561-732 3684; www.fws.gov/refuge/arm_loxahatchee), at the most northerly part of the Everglades. There are walking trails and you can see a variety of birds in their wetland habitat. To reach the refuge head north to Delray Beach and then travel 16km (10 miles) inland.

PORT CANAVERAL

Further north along the Atlantic coast of Florida, beyond Miami and Fort Lauderdale, **Port Canaveral** ❸ (tel: 321-783 7831; www.portcanaveral.org) used to be a smaller port catering mostly to the three-, four- and seven-day Caribbean cruise market, but 2014 saw the opening of a new terminal capable of accommodating the world's largest cruise vessels. It has long been the base for Disney Cruise Line, which has its own dedicated cruise terminal built to its *Disney Magic* specifications – a second-level 1,200-sq metres (13,000-sq ft) terrace is etched with a map of Florida and the Bahamas. Royal Caribbean and Carnival ships, among others, also depart from this port.

The port has quite a few attractions of its own, you can choose between its three parks or bike along the dedicated 2.5km (1.5-mile) trail. There are also deep-sea fishing facilities and several charter companies operate half-day or full-day trips for visitors from here. At the restaurants and cafés in **The Cove** leisure area on the waterfront (http://visitportcanaveral.com), you can sample the day's catch, cooked straight off the boats, and get some shopping done, too.

Port Canaveral is just 45 minutes away from both **Orlando International Airport** (tel: 407-825 2001; www.orlandoairports.net) 72km (45 miles) to the west and **Melbourne International Airport** (tel: 321-723 6227; www.mlbair.com) 40km (25 miles) to the south.

ORLANDO THEME PARKS

It's a straight road – the Beeline Expressway – west to **Orlando** and its plethora of theme parks and attractions. Four of the main ones are part of Walt Disney's empire with another two belonging to Universal Studios (including

Astronaut gear on display at the Kennedy Space Center

the immensely popular Wizarding World of Harry Potter), so if you like that sort of thing it's worth considering a cruise plus a week or so in Orlando. Cruises departing from here often offer pre- or post-cruise packages to Walt Disney World and other central Florida attractions.

Good buys

Main Street Titusville, Olde Cocoa Village and downtown Melbourne offer the best souvenir and knick-knack shops, while the beach shop, Ron Jon Surf Shop claims to sell 'everything under the sun'.

Kennedy Space Center

Stopping for a while at Port Canaveral gives you the opportunity to visit **Kennedy Space Center** (daily 9am–6pm; tel: 855-433 4210; www.kennedyspacecenter.com). You will need at least a day to tour NASA's launch and landing facilities, try out the rocket simulators, explore a life-size replica of a space shuttle and meet an astronaut – you can have lunch with one for an extra fee. The flagship centrepiece is the Space Shuttle Atlantis attraction, which opened in 2013. If you want to find out more, there are guided close-up tours available. Outside the centre is the **Astronaut Hall of Fame** (tickets: either separate or with the Kennedy Space Center Pass).

The nearby **Merritt Island National Wildlife Refuge** (daily, daylight hours; visitor centre: Tues-Sat 8am–4pm; tel: 321-861 0669; www.fws.gov/refuge/Merritt_Island), which sprawls over 57,000 hectares (140,000 acres), is also owned by NASA, as is the **Canaveral National Seashore** (daily 6am–6pm, extended summer hours). The salt marshes of the Refuge are home to hundreds of species of water birds, alligators, the threatened manatee and loggerhead turtles. The Seashore is a protected barrier island beach park with sand dunes and a network of marked canoe trails through a lagoon, where you can spot egrets, ibis, cranes, spoonbills, terns and herons.

TAMPA

Almost opposite Cape Canaveral on Florida's Gulf Coast lies **Tampa**, a small city by US standards. Its three cruise terminals at the **Port of Tampa** ④ (tel: 813-905 7678; www.tampaport.com) have car parking and baggage handling facilities, and are only 24km (15 miles) from Tampa International Airport (tel: 813-870 8700; www.tampaairport.com). The city is becoming popular as a turnaround port and most of the main cruise operators berth ships here, mainly sailing to Mexico and the islands of the Western Caribbean.

With a few hours to spare, you will find plenty to do in the terminal's massive **Sparkman Wharf** complex (www.sparkmanwharf.com), which has shops full of designer clothes and cigars, plus bars and cinemas, and you won't want to miss a visit to the state-of-the-art **Florida Aquarium** (daily 9.30am–5pm; tel: 813-273 4000; www.flaquarium.org), considered to be one of the best in the US. It features more than 4,000 varieties of fish including sharks and stingrays.

Theme park thrills

If you are staying in Tampa for a few days, you can experience an Orlando-style theme park at **Busch Gardens** (daily 9am–10pm, seasonal extended hours; tel: 813-884 4386; www.buschgardens.com). More akin to an African safari theme park, with a wide range of wild animals roaming free, it offers some world-class thrilling rides that are guaranteed to scramble your brains. Arrive prepared to get wet on some of the rides and allow a day to get the best out of a visit.

Orlando (see page 32), with its famous theme parks,

> **Amusement park**
>
> Busch Gardens has one of the best collections of rollercoasters in Florida. If you are visiting the park, be sure to collect a map at the entrance because the layout can be confusing.

The Tampa skyline is as vibrant as the city's nightlife

is only 120km (75 miles) away and worth a day trip, but make sure you plan carefully before you go, to make the most of it.

Downtown Tampa

The majestic minarets of the 19th-century Tampa Bay Hotel look out of place on the city's modern skyline. Today, the former hotel, built by a Florida railway magnate and now part of the University of Tampa campus, is home to the **Henry B. Plant Museum** (Tue–Sat 10am–5pm, Sun noon–5pm; tel: 813-254 1891; http://plant-museum.com), which contains some of its original furniture and valuable artefacts. Tours are available.

Established in 1886 by a Cuban cigar factory owner, **Ybor City** is an historic neighbourhood of old buildings, colourful Spanish-style tiles and wrought-iron gates. The **Ybor City State Museum** (1818 East 9th Avenue; Wed-Sun 9am–4pm; tel: 813-247 1434; www.ybormuseum.org) does a good job of explaining the history

Experience New Orleans' world-famous music scene

of the cigar-manufacturing community.

NEW ORLEANS

This throbbing city of jazz and gumbo, in Louisiana on the Mississippi River, is slowly being restored to its former glory after the devastation of Hurricane Katrina. The **Port of New Orleans** ❺ (tel: 1-800-776 6652; www.portno.com) operates **Julia Street Cruise Terminals** 1 and 2 and the newer **Erato Street Terminal** alongside with lots of car parking space.

New Orleans is a great place in which to spend a few extra days, offering world-famous nightlife and riverboat trips. Within walking distance of the terminal lies the atmospheric **French Quarter** (virtually untouched by the hurricane), here there is no shortage of walking or taxi tours to choose from. Royal Street and Bourbon Street are the most colourful, especially at Mardi Gras, which marks the last day before the beginning of Lent.

Jackson Square is the ideal place to start a tour, on foot or by horse-drawn carriage. Most tours take in the **New Orleans Historic Voodoo Museum** (724 Dumaine Street; daily 10am–6pm; tel:504-680 0128 www.voodoomuseum.com) and a typical Creole meal at **Brennan's Restaurant** (417 Royal Street, tel: 504-525 9711; www.brennansneworleans.com). Also worth a stop is the **New Orleans Pharmacy Museum (Wed-Sat 12pm-5pm; tel: 504-565 8027;** www.pharmacymuseum.org**)**. The home of America's first pharmacy displays dated medial remedies and fascinating artifacts, including voodoo potions and leeches.

GALVESTON

An island town in Texas, the **Port of Galveston** ❻ (tel: 409-765 9321; www.portofgalveston.com) is home port to Carnival Conquest, Carnival Conquest and Royal Caribbean's Voyager of the Seas, covering the Mexican coast to Belize, as well as Jamaica and the Cayman Islands.

Close to the terminal is **The Strand**, a renovated warehouse district full of shops and restaurants, and reminiscent of New Orleans' Bourbon Street, and like that colourful city, Galveston makes a big thing of Mardi Gras. If you can't be there for the pre-Lenten carnival, pop into the **Germain Wells Mardi Gras Museum** (813 Bienville St; free; Wed-Sat 5.30pm–9pm, Sun 10am-1.30pm; tel: 504-523 5433). This historical museum, located at Arnaud's Restaurant, showcases a magnificent collection of antique Mardi Gras costumes ranging from 1941 to 1968. At the **Texas Seaport**

> ## US HOME PORTS
>
> Since the 2001 terrorist attacks in the US, the ports of New Orleans, Galveston and Houston have grown in popularity as embarkation points for cruises to the Western Caribbean, Belize, Honduras, the Cayman Islands and Mexico's Yucatán Peninsula. This is because many Americans prefer not to fly and these ports along the Gulf Coast, all with good road and rail links to the rest of the country, serve a far-reaching area – a radius of 800km (500 miles) has a catchment of 47 million would-be cruise ship passengers. The major cruise lines – mainly Carnival, Royal Caribbean and NCL – have ships based at these ports.

Museum (daily 10am–5pm; tel: 409-763 1877) at Pier 21, you can explore a restored, 19th-century square-rigged tall ship, *Elissa*. Alongside is the **Pier 21 Theater (daily; showtimes vary; tel: 409-763 8808)**, which includes a powerful documentary with dramatic sound effects of the ferocious Great Storm in 1900, in which the town of Galveston was flattened by the sea and thousands of residents died.

HOUSTON

About 80km (50 miles) north of Galveston, the **Port of Houston** ❼ (tel: 713-670 2400; www.portofhouston.com) flourished at the expense of its hurricane-blown neighbour. A canal turned the city into an inland port, which is one of the busiest in the US. A veritable forest of skyscrapers knitted together by motorways, the city is home to NASA's **Space Center** (visitor centre: daily 10am–5pm;

HEMINGWAY'S HOME

The **Ernest Hemingway Home and Museum** (daily 9am–5pm; tel: 305-294 1136; www.hemingwayhome.com) on Whitehead Street, is where literary legend 'Papa' Hemingway lived with his second wife Pauline and their two sons from 1931 to 1939, when they divorced. He then moved to Cuba and she stayed on in the beautiful 19th-century Spanish colonial house until her death in 1951. Hemingway would use it as a stopover base until he died in 1961. He used to write in the cool of the mornings in his studio by the swimming pool – the first to be built in Key West – and he wove his many characterful local friends into his stories. His novel *To Have And Have Not* is a fine example of this. Perfectly preserved, the house is full of his antique furniture, art, old books and hunting trophies, giving the visitor a clear view into his life during his time there.

tel: 281-244 2100; http://spacecenter.org), and has a culture of eccentricity.

KEY WEST

Key West is literally at the end of the road – the US1, in fact, that connects the arc of islands called the Florida Keys with the mainland. The town is often the first port of call on a Western Caribbean cruise and has a flamboyant, offbeat personality of its own. As the Old Town is so small, you can wander around it easily and take in the gingerbread architecture, literary legacies and other historic landmarks.

The **Port of Key West** ❽ is perfectly positioned by **Mallory Square**, right in the middle of **Old Town**, and each year around 800,000 cruise passengers disembark here and at the Mole Pier a little further away. Every evening there's a **Sunset Celebration** (www.sunsetcelebration.org), when jugglers, mime artists, musicians, dancers and animal tamers come into the square and put on a free show.

Shipwrecks

For a classic tour of Key West visitors can either take the historic **Conch Tour Train** (daily 10.15am–4.15pm; tel: 888-916 8687; www.conchtourtrain.com), which has been giving narrated rides through the town since 1958, or the newer **Old Town Trolley** (daily 10am-4.30pm; tel: 305-296 6688; www.trolleytours.com/key-west); both depart from Mallory Square every 20 or 30 minutes. However, if you prefer to see the sights under your own steam, you can hire a bike from several outlets.

Key West's past is built on the bounty of the many ships that were wrecked off the island. The late diving pioneer Mel Fisher found heaps of treasure on the sea bed; you can see it at the **Mel Fisher Maritime Heritage Society and Museum** (200 Greene Street; daily 10am-4pm; tel: 305-294 2633; www.melfisher.org).

MEXICO

Cozumel, **Playa del Carmen** and **Costa Maya**

Location: The Yucatán is a huge, low-lying peninsula jutting out into the Gulf of Mexico in the Caribbean. Ports of entry include **Cozumel**, an island off the northeastern coast; **Playa del Carmen**, a purpose-built resort on the mainland, 19km (12 miles) across the sea from Cozumel; and **Puerto Costa** Maya about 225km (140 miles) further south along the coast of the Yucatán.

Time zone: UTC/GMT -5.

Pop: 129 million (all Mexico).

Language: Spanish and local dialects.

Money matters: Mexican peso. Travellers' cheques in US dollars are widely accepted, as are major credit cards (in tourist areas) but for public markets, restaurants and small shops carry cash. Banks are typically open Mon–Fri 9am–4pm.

Telephone & internet: The country code is +52, area code 987 (Cozumel); 984 (Playa del Carmen), 998 (Cancún). Payphones are available, for which you need a phone card (sold on newsstands). There are internet cafés in both Playa del Carmen and Cozumel, and many regular cafés and bars offer free Wi-Fi..

Beaches: On Cozumel, Playa del Sol or San Francisco Beach to the south or Playa Azul to the north have soft sand and facilities. Playa del Carmen is one long beach; the northern end is quieter. There is a good beach at Majahual next to Puerto Costa Maya.

Shopping: The best options are in Cancún, a 90-minute bus ride north of Playa del Carmen.

Outdoor activities: Watersports, snorkelling, boating, fishing, trips to the nearby antiquities.

Calendar highlights: Equinox Seasonal Event at Chichén Itzá (21 Mar/21 Sept) – a snake-shaped shadow appears on El Castillo pyramid; Cozumel: Carnival (Feb/Mar); San Miguel Arcangel Fiesta (Sept).

Duval Street, Key West

The **Little White House** (111 Front Street; daily 9.30am–4.30pm; tel: 305-615-4704; www.trumanlittlewhitehouse.com), which chronicles the many holidays that US President Harry S. Truman took here during the 1940s, is another popular attraction.

On Duval Street

Duval Street bisects the Old Town and is lined with shops and restaurants such as pop star Jimmy Buffet's Margaritaville Café (www.margaritavillekeywest.com). The **Oldest House Museum** in Key West at no.322 (daily 10am–4pm; free; tel: 305-294 9501; www.oldesthousekeywest.com) contains antiques and period artefacts that tell the story of old Key West, while at the **Key West Shipwreck Museum** (daily 9.30am–5pm, tel: 305-292 8990; www.keywestshipwreck.com) you will discover the town's era of wreckers. Escape to a tropical oasis at the Key West Butterfly and Nature Conservatory (daily 9am-5.30pm; tel: 305-296 2988;

> **Beautiful beaches**
>
> Playa San Francisco, in the southwest, is a beautiful 5km (3-mile) beach offering water sports and restaurants. Playa Bonita is one of the most secluded beaches on Cozumel.

www.keywestbutterfly.com) with their range of over 50 butterfly species and 20 exotic bird species. Sloppy Joe's (tel: 305-294 5717; www.sloppyjoes.com), one of Hemingway's favourite bars, is within staggering distance of his former home (see page 38). Another of his watering holes, Captain Tony's (tel: 305-294 1838; www.capttonyestore.com), is close by.

MEXICO AND CENTRAL AMERICA

Magical ancient Maya ruins, magnificent waterfalls, a spectacular barrier reef, stunning talcum powder beaches, majestic mountains, tropical rainforests, exotic gardens and people with strong national identities all add up to a fascinating and rich cruising experience along the far-reaching Caribbean coastline of Mexico and Central America.

Western Shores cruises vary, depending on the size of the ship, and change annually. Most companies offer three- to five-day itineraries, but often cruises to this region last for 10–14 days, either stopping at all the ports of call or a select few. The ports are all efficiently run, with modern amenities.

As a rule, after leaving the US, cruises generally set out for Mexico's **Yucatán Peninsula** just 800km (500 miles) from the Florida coast. Reaching out into the Gulf of Mexico and the Caribbean Sea, the peninsula's popularity stems from the wealth of archaeological treasures left by the ancient Maya civilization thousands of years ago.

COZUMEL

A favourite port of call is **Cozumel** ❾, Mexico's largest island at 48km (30 miles) long and 16km (10 miles) at its widest point. Until recently only a handful of ships a week called here, but it now draws so many that some have to tender passengers to land, usually into **San Miguel**. Those lucky enough to dock do so at the **International Pier (www.ssamexico.com)** or **Puerta Maya Pier (www.puertamaya.com)**. Just a few miles from town, both piers are modern facilities with information booths, international phone access and plenty of taxis and rental cars.

Across from the pier is the **Plaza del Sol**, the main town square where locals and tourists gather. The nearby seaside promenade, the **Malecón**, is jammed with craft and souvenir shops, as is the busy **Rafael Melgar Avenue**.

Also on Melgar is the **Museo de la Isla de Cozumel** (Cozumel Island Museum; Tues–Sun 9am–5pm; tel: 52-987-872 0833; ww.cozumelparks.com/cozumel-museum), a former 1930s luxury hotel that now contains exhibits on pre-Columbian and colonial history, maritime artefacts, coral-reef topography and displays on indigenous endangered animals. Guided tours of the museum are in English and Spanish.

For a wonderful insight into the magical world of

Cozumel's pristine beaches

Food stall in Cancún

the reefs offshore, without getting wet, you will find **Atlantis Submarine Tours** (several expeditions daily; tel: 52-987-872 5672; http://atlantissubmarines.travel) in front of the Casa del Mar Hotel, about 3km (2 miles) south of San Miguel.

A popular excursion from Cozumel is a long haul to the Maya site of Tulum on the mainland (see page 47). However, if you would rather not venture so far from San Miguel you can visit **El Cedral**, a small collection of Maya ruins where, every May, a colourful fiesta is held to commemorate the first Catholic Mass celebrated in Mexico in 1518.

Closer to the centre of the island, **San Gervasio** (daily 8am–4pm; www.cozumelparks.com/san_gervasio), hidden in the jungle, is another Maya site, which has a sanctuary to Ixchel, the goddess of fertility, medicine and midwifery. However, although both sites are well preserved, they do not come close in comparison with some of the other Maya settlements on the mainland.

BEACHES

At the southwestern end of the island is **Playa San Francisco**, a 3-mile (5km) beach dotted with restaurants and water sports operators.

Other good beaches are **Playa del Sol**, **Playa Plancar** and **Playa Bonita**, but the pride and joy of Cozumel is the popular beach at

Chankanaab Adventure Beach Park (Mon–Sat 8am–4pm; tel: 52-987-872 0093; www.cozumelparks.com/chankanaab). Along with a beautiful soft sand beach, the park contains a land-locked natural pool connected to the sea by an underground tunnel. It also features a lush botanical garden with over 800 species of plants, a small natural history museum, and a swim-with-dolphins programme.

CANCÚN

The resort city of Cancún has only come into being since 1970 when the first hotel was built along a 22km (14-mile) beach. Today high-rise hotels jostle with golf courses, marinas, restaurants and nightclubs to create a holiday mecca. The turquoise sea and fine beaches here are legendary. Although it's not a cruise ship stop you may visit on a shore excursion from Cozumel or Playa del Carmen, for the beach or shopping at the Orlando-style **La Isla Shopping Village** (tel: 52-998-883 5025; www.islacancun.mx) and **Plaza La Fiesta** (tel: 52-998-176 8138)

PLAYA DEL CARMEN

The Riviera Maya stretches from Cancún in the north of the Yucatán 160km (100 miles) down to Tulum in the south along a coastline of beautiful white sandy beaches. Although tourist development has increased since the 1980s, turning tiny fishing villages into towns, the beaches are mainly still unspoilt and the Mesoamerican reef provides some of the best diving in the world.

Halfway along the Riviera and opposite Cozumel is **Playa del Carmen** ❿, or Playa as it's commonly referred to, which 20 years ago was a small, peaceful fishing village without electricity. Today, it is one of the busiest ports of call in Mexico with a wealth of places to visit and things to do. Amazingly, the town has not developed into a forest of large resort-style hotels but rather retained a laid-back cosmopolitan atmosphere with a European influence. Old clapboard houses line the streets and a beach and café culture pervades.

The town revolves around **Avenida Cinco** (Fifth Avenue), a vibrant street, running parallel with the beach, full of inexpensive restaurants, bars offering margaritas, internet cafés, and jewellery shops selling silver and crafts.

Cruises stopping off at Playa either drop anchor off the coast and ferry passengers to shore; dock at Cozumel and ferry passengers back over; or they can dock at the **Puerto Calica Cruise Ship Pier**, about 13km (8 miles) south of the town. Excursions usually include a choice of trips to the Maya sites of Xcaret, Tulum, Xel-Há, Cobá and sometimes the big one to Chichén Itzá; or shopping and snorkelling in Cancún, a 90-minute bus ride away.

The Maya ruins at Tulum

XCARET

One of the more popular excursions from Playa is to **Xcaret** (Mon–Fri 7am–12am, Sat–Sun 7am–10pm; tel: 52-998-883 3143; www.xcaret.com), a uniquely designed ecological and archaeological theme park north of the cruise ship terminal. This is the Yucatán's answer to Disney World, Xcaret (pronounced *ish-car-et*) is a stunningly beautiful and thoroughly modern attraction with myriad diversions. While it is very commercialised, Xcaret can provide an entire day's worth of activities and is great fun for children.

Xel-Há

Another ecopark along similar lines is **Xel-Há** (daily 9am–6pm; tel: 52-998-883 3143; www.xelha.com), which is on the way to Tulum. Xel-Há (pronounced *shell-hah*) means 'the place where water

> ### Sinkhole snorkel
>
> The world's largest cavern diving and snorkelling complex can be found just south of Xel-Há at Hidden Worlds Cenotes (tours daily every half hour). Even novice snorkellers can enjoy this magical underground system of caves and *cenotes* (sinkholes).

was born' in Maya and its main attribute is a large natural inlet where the sea water mixes with fresh river water and is home to an amazing assortment of underwater life. The banks are covered in jungle laced with walking trails, you can hike to a Maya cave and some of the area's *cenotes* (see box above).

Tulum and Cobá

From Cozumel, as in other ports of call in the Yucatán, you can take an excursion over to the mainland to see the spectacular Maya ruins that stand on top of a cliff at **Tulum** (daily 8am–4pm). Expensive but worth it, this day-long trip, which involves a lot of travelling, gives you the opportunity to experience the only Maya site overlooking the sea at the Tulum National Park. The main building, the Castillo, which looks like a castle, is thought to have acted as a lighthouse.

Most of the site is flat and easy to walk around, but there are small buses operating from the main entrance, if you prefer. With miles of beautiful beaches, cafés and a turquoise sea at the bottom of the cliff, the ruins really do present a dramatic sight.

Pyramid of Kukulcán

Inland from Tulum lies the vast Maya city of **Cobá** (daily 8am–5pm). Set around a system of small lakes, there are supposed to be some 6,000 buildings here, although only a few have been excavated, including the **Templo de la Iglesia** (Church Pyramid), with unusual rounded corners, and a ball court. The Nohoch Mul (meaning large hill) pyramid, at 42 metres (138ft) high, is the tallest structure in the northern Yucatán and from here there are wonderful views.

Chichén Itzá

The most spectacular excursion in this area, however, is a full-day trip to the Maya ruins of **Chichén Itzá** (daily 8am–5pm; tel: 888-2340 557 www.chichenitza.com), about 150 miles (240km) inland from the coast. While it is costly (more than US$200), time consuming and tiring, a trip to Chichén Itzá is the highlight of any Yucatán holiday.

Among the best known ruins in Latin America, the fabled ancient city provides a fascinating picture of Maya life in the 10th century. Covering four sq miles (10 sq km), the site contains the towering **Pyramid of Kukulkán** which dominates the archaeological site. There are several temples, an observatory, ball courts, steam baths, a sacrificial well and a ceremonial house. Local guides offer excellent tours in English and there is an on-site restaurant for refreshments and an informative museum. In the evening, Chichén Itzá puts on an impressive, spectacular **sound-and-light show**.

The Maya dominated the people here and also the trade of the entire northern Yucatán, but by the end of the 13th century the city had more or less been abandoned due to revolt and inter-tribal battles breaking out.

COSTA MAYA

The coast stretching southward from Tulum to Belize is known as the **Costa Maya** ⓫ and in 2001 a port of call, **Puerto Costa Maya** (tel: 52-998-894 8597; www.costamaya.com), was opened about 280km (175 miles) south of Playa del Carmen. With a modern and efficiently run terminal, more akin to a holiday resort, the port quickly became a destination on most of the major cruise line itineraries.

Built next to the small coastal settlement of **Majahual** and a lovely palm-lined beach, the port) is laid out like a Maya city and has first-class amenities, swimming pool and bars, plus bazaars and folkloric shows in authentic-looking pavilions. The region is rich in ruins and has an untouched hinterland of tropical forests and mangrove swamps. Excursions include kayaking, snorkelling and diving trips and hikes in the jungle.

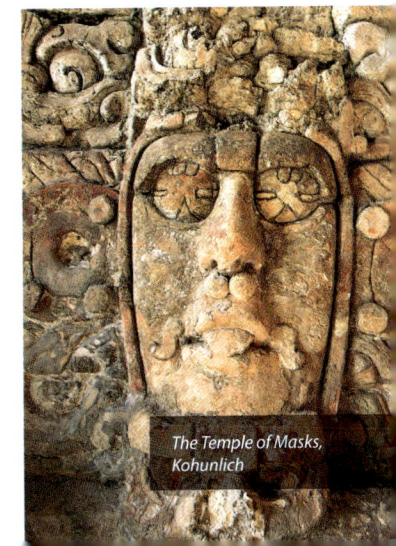

The Temple of Masks, Kohunlich

Kohunlich

A day trip to the early Classic ruins of **Kohunlich** (daily 8am–5pm), named after the large palm trees growing there, is a popular

THE MAYA LEGACY

The Maya people occupied the Yucatán, Belize, northern Honduras, Guatemala and El Salvador, and from around AD300–900 they developed dynasties forming a loosely connected network of city states and built impressive pyramids for temples. In the Yucatán, settlements grew up next to *cenotes*, sinkholes where fresh water collected. It was always something of a mystery as to how the Maya could have created such an advanced culture in a region where there was no surface water. Then it was discovered that the cenotes were linked and that water flowed between them; instead of the Nile or the Euphrates, the Maya had their underground rivers, which provided a constant supply of water. Life for the Maya came from below, a fact which might explain why the underworld featured so strongly in their beliefs. As at Chichén Itzá, the *cenotes* often doubled as sacred sites.

The Maya are considered by experts to have been the most advanced people of the Americas. They studied the stars and developed complicated calendar systems that rival even the technology of today for precision and complexity. They worshipped time and every aspect of their lives was driven by the calendar, from when to get married to the right time to sow a crop. They wrote in hieroglyphics, mathematically recording their sacred rituals, and were skilled artists and craftsmen, weaving and producing ceramics and jewellery.

No one really knows why the Maya civilization collapsed towards the end of the first millennium. However, the Maya people live on; some have integrated into the modern world, others retain their ancestral beliefs and are preserving their heritage for the world to see.

choice. Here you can see the spectacular Temple of Masks, a pyramid with a central stairway flanked by stucco god masks, built around AD500.

Some shore excursions may combine a trip to the ruins with a visit to the excellent **Museo de la Cultura Maya** (Tue–Sat 9am–6pm, Sun 9am-5pm; charge), in the border town of **Chetumal**, which showcases miniature reconstructed Maya cities under a glass floor.

Virgin Reef

The port is close to one of the last virgin reefs in the region offering world-class snorkelling and diving. The magnificent **Parque Nacional de Chinchorro Submarino** is about 48km (30 miles) long and 14km (9 miles) wide with depths dropping in places to 900 metres (3,000ft). It has more than 30 sunken ships to explore amid a forest of coral.

The **Reserva de la Biósfera Sian Ka'an** (tel: 52-984-145 6696; www.visitsiankaan.com) is a vast nature preserve, about 80km (50 miles) north of the port. The wetlands, savannah and jungle contain a variety of marine habitats and are havens for flamingos, colourful parrots and more than 300 other bird species, as well as crocodiles. On the water, the lucky few might spot a manatee coming up for air. Be warned: the mosquitoes can be fierce so cover up well and wear repellent.

BELIZE

Bordered by Mexico in the north and Guatemala to the west and south, the tiny, English-speaking country of Belize is a favourite port of call. It is a paradise for ecotourism, with the world's second largest barrier reef offshore, coral cays, rivers, mountains, vast swathes of rainforest and jungle, savannah and mangrove coasts, and a rich Maya legacy.

Ambergris Caye, Belize

While small vessels can drop anchor at Belize's offshore islands further south and at the smaller town of Dangriga, most large cruise ships call at **Belize City** ⓬.

For the time being they must anchor offshore, and use tenders to transport passengers for the 20-minute journey to the Tourism Village, which has been specially designed for day cruise-ship passengers. Here you can find plenty of shops, restaurants and taxis and access to land and marine tours. The centre of town is only a five-minute walk.

Belize City

Oozing rundown Caribbean atmosphere, Belize City, home to an ethnic mix of 60,000, has some interesting places to see that can be explored on a city tour excursion or by taxi. Towering over the harbour is the **Fort George Lighthouse and Park** with the **Baron Bliss Memorial** beneath it. Baron Bliss was a wealthy British yachtsman who lived here on his yacht for a year until his death in 1926. He left a legacy of US$2 million to the people of Belize from which its schools, health clinics, hospitals, museums and libraries still benefit.

CENTRAL AMERICA

Belize, **Honduras** and **Costa Rica**

Location: Belize (capital Belize City) lies south of Mexico and east of Guatemala. It shares the 300km (185-mile) long Mesoamerican Barrier Reef with the Bay Islands archipelago in Honduras to the south, where **Roatán** Island (main town Coxen Hole) is situated some 48km (30 miles) off the coast. **Costa Rica** (capital San José) lies further south between Nicaragua to the north and Panama.

Time Zone: UTC/GMT -6.

Pop: 57,000 (Belize City); 115,000 (Roatán); 5.1 million (Costa Rica).

Language: English; Spanish and local dialects (Roatán).

Money matters: The Belize dollar (BZ$) has a fixed rate of exchange of BZ$2 to US$1; check in shops or when taking a taxi; typical bank hours: Mon–Thu 8am–3pm, Fri 8am–4.30pm. Roatán uses the lempira, although the US dollar is widely accepted in Belize and Honduras. The currency in Costa Rica is the colón. Cash machines can be found in shopping centres. Private banks offer better exchange rates. Typical bank hours Mon–Fri 9am–3pm.

Telephone & internet: Country codes: 501 (Belize); 504 (Roatán); 506 (Costa Rica). There are internet centres in the Tourism Village, Belize City, in J.C. Commercial Center at Coxen Hole on Roatán, and at ATEC in Puerto Viejo de Limón in Costa Rica.

Calendar highlights: Belize: Carnival (Feb/Mar), Baron Bliss Day (Mar); Costa Rica: New Year's Day; Puerto Limón Columbus Day Carnival (Oct).

Resident at the Jaguar Preserve

Not far from the harbour is **Government House** (Mon–Thurs, Sat 9am–5pm; tel: 501-227 3050), a beautiful old colonial mansion. Opposite stands **St John's Cathedral** (Sun-Friy 9am–5pm), built in 1812 and the oldest Anglican Church in Central America. Just 47km (29 miles) west of the capital is the **Belize Zoo** (Mon-Sat 8.30am–5pm, Sun 8.30am-4pm; tel: 501-613 4966; www.belizezoo.org), where you can see indigenous Belizean animals in their natural surroundings.

Storks and jaguars

The wildlife reserves you'll get to visit in Belize are second to none. The **Crooked Tree Wildlife Sanctuary** (daily 8am–4.30pm; www.visitcrookedtree.com) is situated north of the city, and its wetlands, punctuated by rivers and lagoons, create the perfect habitat for kites, ospreys, and the rare jabiru stork, the largest bird in the Americas. Keep an eye out for the crocodiles and turtles who live here too.

Further south, and more accessible from Dangriga, is the **Cockscomb Basin Wildlife Sanctuary and Jaguar Preserve** (daily 8am–4.30pm; tel: 866-417 2377), set in over 415 sq km (160 sq miles) of dense tropical rainforest. There is plenty of bird- and wildlife here, but all you are likely to glimpse of the shy, nocturnal jaguar is a pawprint.

Ruins and reefs

Apart from the Maya requisite visits to the archaeological sites of **Xuanantunich**, near the Guatemalan border – known for its pyramid, El Castillo – and also **Altun Ha**, north of Belize City, you can take a boat trip along the New River to **Lamanai**, an ancient Maya ceremonial centre hidden in the jungle. Visitors can also go on a river ride through a series of caves on an inner tube; or snorkel, dive or kayak around the awe-inspiring coral reef at the **Hol Chan Marine Reserve** (tel: 501-226 2247; www.holchanmarinereserve.org) on **Ambergris Caye**, an island, just 56km (35 miles) north of the capital. Water taxis are another option for those who want to go off on their own explorations to Ambergris Caye and the **San Pedro Town**, at the southern tip of the island..

HONDURAS

The **Islas de la Bahía** (Bay Islands), are a chain of 70 coral islands off the coast of Honduras, that provide an idyllic port of call, with pristine beaches fringed with tall palm trees, lapped by a warm turquoise sea that conceals the magical world of the same coral reef that borders Belize. Swimming, snorkelling, diving and simply lazing on the beautiful fine white-sand beaches supping chilled drinks are the only activities required here.

Climb the ruins at Lamanai, an ancient Maya ceremonial site

A secluded beach in Roatán

Roatán

Ships dock at **Roatán** ⓭, the largest and most popular island at just 40km (25-miles) long. Its population has quadrupled since 2001 and now the island is home to 100,000 people, who tend to speak English rather than Spanish. With a jungle interior and houses on stilts, Roatán is a top dive destination, and at the port there is a wide choice of dive operators. For those not keen to don a tank, there are two glass-bottomed boats that offer a seabird's eye view of the underwater world.

The island has several small hotels and restaurants, and the 3km (2-mile) long, untouched **Camp Bay Beach** at the eastern end is a perfect place to spend a few hours. You can travel around by taxi or by bike, available for hire by the cruise ship pier, or hike along a trail once used by pirates such as Henry Morgan – it is widely believed that there is still buried treasure here waiting to be discovered. Look out for the indigenous red lored parrot, the Lala monkey and the Jesus lizard, which got its name because it can 'walk on water'.

Natural beauty

The islanders are keen to protect the unspoiled natural beauty of their environment and at **Anthony's Key Resort** (www.anthonyskey.com), in the Sandy Bay area, the conservationist museum, the **Roatán Institute for Marine Sciences** (504-2407 2244; www.roatanims.org), has environmentally aware tours and encounters with dolphins. Nearby, at the **Manawakie Eco Nature Park (www.manawakieecopark.com)**, you can tour through an interwoven tunnel of mangroves and meet their comprehensive collection of sloths, monkeys and macaws.

COSTA RICA

A dramatically beautiful country, Costa Rica is a peaceful and democratic oasis in a region known for its decades of unrest. With no armed forces to speak of, the Costa Ricans have benefitted from their resources being put into health, education and conservation rather than national defence. As a result, a quarter of the country's natural assets – its tropical rainforests, gushing rivers, active volcanoes, wonderful wildlife and glorious beaches – are protected, providing a popular destination for eco- and adventure tourists alike.

SAN BLAS ISLANDS

The smaller cruise ships often stop at the San Blas Islands that lie just off the northeast coast of Panama. Here, on these beautiful Caribbean islands without one brick of development, you can witness Kuna Amerindians living the simple Indian lifestyle, according to centuries-old traditions. The San Blas incorporate more than 60 islands supporting a population of about 30,000 Kuna.

They paddle out to the ships in dugout canoes to sell their wares, or tenders bring passengers ashore from the smaller ships. On land, you will experience a real time warp. Most of the Kuna speak only their native language and live in bamboo huts without electricity or running water. Fishing, farming and making *molas* – an intricate, patchwork-type of embroidery – are their livelihood.

Costa Rica's dense rainforest

Limón

Columbus landed here on his final voyage declaring the place a rich coast – *costa rica*. **Limón** ⑭ is a palm-fringed city with a mountain backdrop and an atmosphere that is more Afro-Caribbean than Latin American – many residents here speak English. It is a lively but slightly run-down city with a sprinkling of old wooden houses painted in bright pastel colours.

Parque Vargas, in the centre, is lined with dense with tropical trees and plants. Most Western Caribbean cruises stop here and passengers are ferried ashore.

Some cruises offer trips to the busy capital, **San José**, 112km (70 miles) inland. It's a long day but there are some excellent museums, such as the **Museo del Oro Precolombino** (Pre-Columbian Gold Museum; daily 9.30am–5pm; tel: 506-2243 4202; www.museosdelbancocentral.org), which documents the gold fever that consumed the conquistadors.

THE BAHAMAS

Location: The Bahamas is an archipelago of over 700 islands that start 97km (60 miles) off the eastern coast of Florida and stretch southeast for 900km (560 miles) to the Caribbean Sea. Just over 30 of the islands are inhabited. **New Providence Island** and **Grand Bahama** are the main ports of call.

Time zone: UTC/GMT -4

Pop: 393,000

Language: English; Creole

Money matters: The unit of currency is the Bahamian dollar (B$). US dollars and credit cards are widely accepted. Typical bank hours: Mon–Thu 9.30am–3pm, Fri 9.30am–5pm.

Telephone & internet: Country code: +242. The telephone system is sophisticated, with high-speed internet access and roaming agreements with many US cellular phone networks. Nassau, the capital, has several internet cafés and Wi-Fi hotspots, including a communications centre at Festival Place, the cruise ship terminal. Free Wi-Fi internet access is available in the Lucayan Harbour Cruise Facility on Grand Bahama Island.

Beaches: Cable Beach in Nassau (New Providence Island) and at the Atlantis Resort on Paradise Island; Paradise Cove and Fortune Beach (Grand Bahama).

Shopping: Bay Street in Nassau. Haggle for less expensive items at the Straw Market. Shopping hours: Mon–Sat 9am–5pm.

Outdoor activities: Water sports, submarine rides, golf, horse riding, dolphin encounters, caving and kayaking (Grand Bahama).

Calendar highlights: Bahamian Music and Heritage Festival (April); Junkanoo (Dec/Jan) Junkanoo in June (Nassau, June); Eleuthera Pineapple Festival (June); Emancipation Day (Aug); All Abaco Sailing Regatta (July); One Bahamas Music and Heritage Festival (Nov).

Taste of adventure

The diversity of the Costa Rican countryside provides visitors with a range of excursions: whitewater rafting trips; biking or kayaking through wildlife refuges, or bird- and turtle-watching, and eco-tours. Some operators offer a trip through the rainforest canopy of **Parque Nacional Braulio Carrillo**, 35 metres (120ft) above ground in the Rainforest Aerial Tram. At the **Parque Nacional Cahuita**, glass-bottomed boats will take you over the coral reef, and hiking trails wind through lush rainforest.

Nearer Limón, about 24km (15 miles) away, is the small and quirky town of **Puerto Viejo de Limón**. An eclectic mix of surfers, Rastafarians, expats and world-weary travellers gather here and the party atmosphere is contagious.

THE BAHAMAS

Despite the fact that the Bahamas are in the Atlantic, New Providence Island or Grand Bahama are often among the first ports of call, particularly if the cruise departs from any of the eastern Florida ports.. Only 20 of the islands are set up for tourism.

NEW PROVIDENCE ISLAND

Nassau ⓯, the national capital, on New Providence Island, has one of the biggest ports on most itineraries, with enough docking at Prince George Wharf to accommodate a dozen cruise ships at a time. **Festival Place** includes a communications centre, an internet café and authentic Bahamian arts and crafts. At the **Junkanoo Expo**, located on the wharf, visitors can see the brightly coloured costumes worn for the carnival-style celebrations on Boxing Day and New Year's Day.

Cruise ship passengers disembark virtually into the centre of this bustling one-time British colonial capital and there is usually

A costumed guide at Pirates of Nassau Museum

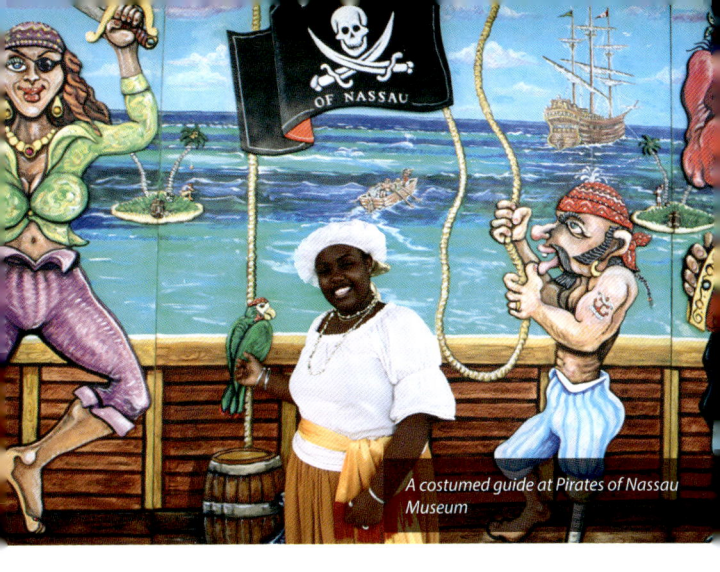

plenty of time for a guided walking tour around the historic parts or a ferry trip to nearby **Paradise Island** (www.nassauparadiseisland.com) or a flutter at the gambling table in the casinos of the luxurious Atlantis Resort. The dock is a pedestrian zone, so taxis, buses and tours are only available outside the terminal checkpoint.

Nassau

The city of Nassau is situated on the North Shore of New Providence Island, which is roughly 32km (20 miles) in circumference, and 13km (8 miles) wide. Around 180 nautical miles southeast of Miami, Florida, it is home to over a quarter of a million people. For many, the busy capital is the Bahamas.

There are plenty of ways to get to know Nassau with only a day in port. One of the most popular (and excellent value) is a professionally guided walking tour of the city with a Bahamahost. This is a local guide, trained by the Ministry of Tourism, who can take

Nassau Government offices

groups of up to 10 people on one-hour walks around two different areas of historic Nassau.

Either on the tour or exploring on your own, you will see the pretty, 19th-century, colonial buildings of **Parliament Square**, just off Bay Street, housing the government offices. The islands became an English colony in 1629, were briefly ruled by the Spanish in 1782 and eventually gained their independence from Britain in 1973 as the Commonwealth of the Bahamas. Continuing south, you will arrive at the **Supreme Court** building and the pink, octagonal **Nassau Public Library (Mon-Fri 9am-4.45pm, Sat 9am-3.45pm; tel: 242-322 4907)**, built in 1798. Once a prison, it contains a small collection of Amerindian artefacts.

Parliament Street has some more well preserved colonial buildings, most of them dating from the mid-19th century. Further west stand three houses of worship: **St Andrew's Presbyterian Church (www.standrewskirk.com)**, known as The Kirk; the **Trinity Methodist Church (www.tmcbahamas.com)**; and **Christ Church Cathedral (www.christchurchcathedralbahamas.com)**, which has a beautiful stained-glass window above the altar.

A horse-drawn surrey departs from Woodes Rogers Walk, at the port entrance, for a 20-minute clatter along Bay Street and around Old Nassau with a Bahamahost-trained guide. Rates are usually negotiable.

Pirates in the Bahamas

In the 17th and 18th centuries pirates and privateers – those with permission from the British Crown to attack ships for their treasure – terrorised the Caribbean and the waters around the Bahamas. And from 1700, they occupied Nassau, creating anarchy and frightening any law-abiding citizen, chasing them off to the smaller islands. The most notorious of them all was Blackbeard (Edward Teach) who made Nassau Fort his home. His story and others are told at the interactive **Pirates of Nassau Museum** (Mon–Fri 9am–5pm, Sat-Sun 10am–2pm; tel: 242-356 3759; www.piratesofnassau.com), opposite the cathedral.

On the 10-minute walk back to the ship you will pass the **Straw Market (daily 7.30am-5pm; tel: 242-363 2000)**, selling baskets, dolls, table mats and hats, all made from plaited thatch palm by crafts people living in the city and on the smaller out islands. The original straw market and neighbouring buildings burned down in 2001.

PARADISE ISLAND

At Prince George Wharf, you can take a taxi or ferry, either with an organised tour or on your own, to the smart resorts on **Paradise Island** (www.nassauparadiseisland.com) across Nassau Harbour. Once known less glamorously as Hog Island, its expensive pleasures

Bahamian straw baskets make lovely souvenirs

number the huge **Atlantis Resort** and casino (www.atlantisbahamas.com); the **Hurricane Hole** (www.hurricaneholemarina.com), a haven for luxury yachts; the **Yoga Retreat** (www.sivanandabahamas.org); a 14th-century **Gothic Cloister,** brought from France and reconstructed stone by stone; the **Versailles Gardens** surrounding the exclusive Ocean Club Hotel (www.fourseasons.com/oceanclub); and the 18-hole championship **Ocean Club Golf Course** (www.oneandonlyresorts.com/hotels-resorts). There is also a crescent-shaped white beach.

GRAND BAHAMA

Three times the size of New Providence, Grand Bahama sits at the northern end of the Bahamas chain. It lies 105km (65 miles) east of West Palm Beach and 128km (80 miles) northeast of Miami and has a population of just over 50,000. Freeport, the nation's northernmost island, is not as atmospheric as Nassau, having only come into being in the 1960s. However, it makes a good launching pad for an island that has plenty to offer, from limestone caves and exotic gardens to white sandy beaches, nature walks and eco-adventures – and casinos.

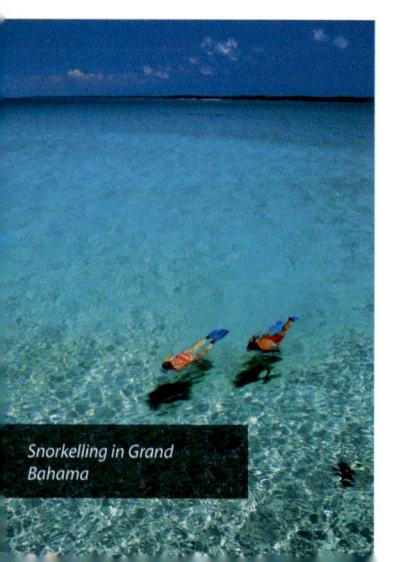

The **Lucayan Harbour Cruise Facility** ⓰ can accommodate the largest ships in the world and the

Snorkelling in Grand Bahama

huge multimillion dollar terminals have everything a cruise passenger could need. The port lies to the west of central Freeport and there are plenty of taxis available if you want to head off and explore the island alone.

Freeport

Although most of the attractions of Grand Bahama lie outside town a little way, there are some things to see and do in **Freeport**. Near the centre, you can visit the International Bazaar, a large shopping precinct with a few bargains. To the east of the Bazaar is a straw market, in case you haven't bought a basket yet, while, on the other side, the **Royal Oasis Golf Resort and Casino** has a spectacular freshwater beach pool (open to the public), with slides, a waterfall, swim-up bar and two golf courses.

As the International Bazaar is rather run-down now, it will certainly be more rewarding to shop in **Port Lucaya**, which is buzzing with life around the market place with straw craft shops, bijou boutiques, plentiful restaurants and live entertainment in Count Basie Square, plus a Colombian Emeralds outlet.

Dolphin show

Dolphins in Sanctuary Bay

The Dolphin Experience located at Sanctuary Bay, a 4-hectare (9-acre) lagoon, is just a short ferry ride from the UNEXSO (Underwater Explorers' Society, www.unexso.com) dock at Port

> **Grand developer**
>
> Wallace Groves, a Virginian financier, triggered the development of Grand Bahama when he established a timber business on the island in the 1940s. He founded Freeport in the late 1950s.

Lucaya. A visit to the bay includes a tour, during which visitors can enjoy various kinds of fun in-the-water and encounters up close with the dolphins.

Be aware, however, that even dolphins in captivity are still essentially wild mammals. While they may appear sweet looking, aggressive behaviour towards swimmers can occur from time to time, especially if encountered out at sea, and like any wild creature, they can be potentially dangerous.

Nature trails

At the 40-hectare (100-acre) **Rand Nature Centre** (Mon–Fri 9am–4.30pm, Sat 9am-1pm; tel: 242-352 5438; www.bnt.bs), to the north of Freeport, you can follow some interesting nature trails through natural coppice and pine forests, and see a flock of West Indian flamingos. You may also spot a hummingbird and the rare olive capped warbler. Run by the Bahamas National Trust, this National Park has well-informed guides who will enthusiastically enlighten you on the ecology of the Bahamian forest. A monthly bird walk is held on the first Saturday of each month. The peak bird-watching season is from October to May.

The **Garden of the Groves** (daily 9am–4pm; tel: 242-374 7778; www.thegardenofthegroves.com) to the east of Freeport and Port Lucaya, is a wondrous botanical garden with cascading waterfalls. The garden is named after Georgette and Wallace Groves, who created this lovely spot and Groves also founded the Grand Bahama Port authority. The garden has over 10,000 plants and native birds such as the Cuban emerald and the Greater Antillean bullfinch can be spotted amongst the lush vegetation.

Underwater caves

At the **Lucayan National Park** (daily 9am–4pm; tel 242-352 5438; www.bnt.bs), about 21km (13 miles) east of the Garden of the Groves, you can explore the caves that form one of the longest charted underwater cave systems in the world. Accompanied by knowledgeable guides, you can enter the caves by sea or by land and see where artefacts and bones relating to the island's first inhabitants have been discovered.

The 16-hectare (40-acre) park has trails through pine forests rich in tropical vegetation, including orchids. Mangrove lagoons brim with birdlife.

Smoking a cigar in Havana, Cuba

If you don't have much time in port, you can choose to join an organised snorkelling or kayaking trip; or just chill out at a beach party on the beautiful Lucayan Beach or Taino Beach, about 4km (2 miles) from the port.

THE WESTERN CARIBBEAN

For the purposes of this book, the Western Caribbean comprises the larger islands of Cuba, Jamaica, the Dominican Republic and Puerto Rico, with tiny Grand Cayman as one of the main ports of call on western itineraries and San Juan in Puerto Rico a homeport for ships heading south. Although these islands are all close to each other in geographical terms, culturally they are worlds apart and each has its own distinctive atmosphere, characteristics, cuisine and traditions. There is plenty to enthrall visitors on all of them..

CUBA

As Cuba, the largest of all the Caribbean islands, has grown in popularity as a holiday destination, more and more cruise lines have included a stop in Havana on their itineraries. There are still some restrictions in place for US citizens, due to the 1961 US embargo, although the Cuban thaw has reduced hostility. Ongoing efforts have been made since the Obama administration in 2014 to reduce barriers to travel for US citizens, though rules tend to vary with changing administrations. It is highly recommended to research before planning your trip. While some travellers prefer to travel via a third country, it has become increasingly easier to fly into Havana and airlines are expected to begin travel to other Cuban airports from the US. US citizens must obtain a license prior to travel under certain categories, are restricted to spending cash (unable to use ATMs, debit or credit cards) and are not allowed

THE WESTERN CARIBBEAN

Cuba, **Grand Cayman**, **Jamaica**, **Dominican Republic** and **Puerto Rico** (Greater Antilles)

Location: The Republic of **Cuba** (capital Havana) is more than 1,250km (775 miles) long and 190km (118 miles) wide, and 150km (93 miles) south of Miami. **Grand Cayman** (George Town), part of the Cayman Islands, lies south of Cuba and northwest of Jamaica. **Jamaica** (Kingston) lies 145km (90 miles) south of Cuba and 160km (100 miles) west of Haiti. The **Dominican Republic** (Santo Domingo) occupies the eastern part of the island of Hispaniola, shared with Haiti, 97km (60 miles) east of Cuba. **Puerto Rico** (San Juan) lies just 87km (54 miles) east of the Dominican Republic.

Time zones: UTC/GMT -4 (Puerto Rico); UTC/GMT -5 (Cuba, Dominican Republic, Grand Cayman, Jamaica).

Pop: 11.3 million (Cuba); 2.9 million (Jamaica); 10.8 million (Dominican Republic); 3.1 million (Puerto Rico); 69,000 (Grand Cayman).

Language: Spanish; English; Patois

Money matters: Cuba: the Cuban peso (CUP$); Grand Cayman: Cayman Islands dollar (CI$); Jamaica: Jamaican dollar (J$); Dominican Republic: the peso (RD$); Puerto Rico: United States dollar (US$). Main credit cards are accepted everywhere, except American ones in Cuba; US dollars are widely accepted (except in Cuba) – use small denominations. In shops, change is given in local currency.

Telephone & internet: Country codes: +53 (Cuba); +876 (Jamaica); +345 (Cayman Islands); +809 (Dominican Republic); +787 (Puerto Rico). In Cuba internet facilities are limited, although hotels usually have access. Internet access is available in larger hotels.

Calendar highlights: Carnivals: Havana (July), Jamaica (Mar/Apr) Grand Cayman (May); Jamaica: Reggae Sumfest (July); Grand Cayman: Pirates' Week (Nov); San Juan: Bautista Night (June).

to stay in government-run hotels. Following the Obama administration, many US-owned cruise lines included Cuba ports in their itineraries, including Havana and Santiago de Cuba. However, this drastically changed following the Trump administration's ban on travel to Cuba in 2019. At the time of writing, the Biden administration began to ease restrictions on travel to the island. While the fate of US-owned cruise lines in Cuba is uncertain, there are still numerous foreign-owned cruise lines that visit the island regularly.

Havana

Cubans are warm and welcoming and, as you can see by the well preserved vintage cars from the 1950s, they present a fine example of 'make do and mend'. Rich in colonial history and vibrating with Latin rhythms, the island is mountainous, rainforested and fringed with white beaches.

Sailing into the **Terminal Sierra Maestra** ⓱ at **Havana**, you see the 16th-century Spanish defences against the British and French, El Morro and La Cabaña fortresses on the left and La Punta and la Real Fuerza on the right. The terminal has modern facilities and passengers disembark directly onto the cobbled streets of **Habana Vieja** (Old Havana), where tour buses, taxis and horse-drawn carriages await.

Hemingway haunts

A walk around Habana Vieja will reveal the island's Spanish colonial heritage in all its architectural glory. The best squares to head for are **Plaza de Armas**, the oldest and noted for its second-hand book market as well as its palaces; **Plaza de la Catedral**, with its baroque

> **Restrictions**
>
> For more information on restrictions for US visitors to Cuba, visit www.treas.gov (the US Treasury website).

Architectural grandeur on Plaza Vieja

cathedral, colonial palaces and pavement café, El Patio; and **Plaza Vieja**, recently restored, also with mansions, cafés and a microbrewery. A walk down the main shopping street, **Calle Obispo**, will lead you to **El Floridita** (daily 12pm-1am; tel: 53-7-867 1300; www.barfloridita.com), one of novelist Ernest Hemingway's favourite bars when he lived in Cuba, and then on to the **Parque Central**, where you will find the theatre, fine art museum (tel: 53-7-863 3763), hotels and **El Capitolio**.

GRAND CAYMAN

The **Cayman Islands**, 160km (100 miles) or so south of Cuba, consist of three islands that offer some of the most spectacular diving in the world. **Grand Cayman**, the largest at 45km long and 11km wide (28 miles by 7 miles), is where 56,000 people live, as opposed to 1,600 on Cayman Brac and just a handful on Little Cayman. The smaller islands cater mainly for scuba divers.

A British Overseas Territory, Grand Cayman is not only a peaceful paradise but is also affluent and sophisticated, with the highest standard of living and the highest per capita income in the Caribbean. Just 750km (480 miles) south of Miami, it is the only one of the three islands that can accept large cruise ships. A few cruise lines start their itineraries here, especially if Cuba (see page 68) is one of the ports of call.

Grand Cayman is famed for its superlative diving

George Town

The port's two modern cruise ship terminals are located right in **George Town** ⑱, the Cayman Islands' capital. A small but busy commercial town, it has some colonial buildings and is easy to walk around. Taxis are available to take you further afield, or you can opt for an organised excursion.

On the waterfront are the remains of **Fort George**. Built in 1790 to ward off the Spanish, the original fort was made of solid coral rock with walls 1.5 metres (5ft) thick. It was used as a lookout during World War II to keep an eye out for German submarines. Across the street is the **Elmslie United Memorial Church** (tel: 345-949 7923; www.elmslieunitedchurch.ky). Its timber roof is shaped like an upturned schooner hull with stained-glass windows. Outside the church, some of the old stone grave markers resemble little houses.

National Museum

Further along is the popular **Cayman Islands National Museum** (Mon–Fri 9am–5pm, Sat 10am–2pm; tel: 345-949 8368; www.museum.ky) in the 19th-century Old Courts Building, white with green shutters and a bright red roof, which has served as a prison and courthouse. It is the second oldest building in Grand Cayman and a classic example of local architecture. One of the many excellent exhibits is a relief map of the underwaterscape surrounding the islands.

Opposite, you can see reef life for real, without getting wet, in the **Atlantis Submarine** *Seaworld Explorer* (daily tours; tel: 345-949 7700; www.atlantissubmarines.com). This is a submarine that takes visitors on an underwater tour 30 metres (100ft) deep.

Further along, the Craft Market (Mon–Fri 8.30am–3pm) is spilling over with local souvenirs. Look out for jewellery made from caymanite, a semi-precious stone that ranges in colour from beige to pink to brown, that is only found in the Caymans.

Going to Hell

Outside the capital, going north, the road hugs West Bay and Seven Mile Beach, a stretch of white sand attracting wall-to-wall hotels and condos to this bit of paradise, until you get to **Hell (tel: 345-949 3358)**. Yes, the village really is called

At the Devil's Hang Out in Hell

> **Island dives**
>
> The Cayman Islands have plenty of dramatic wall and drop off dives close to the shore, and accessible from a west coast beach. At sea, boats have a choice of more than 375 public moorings.

Hell, due to its surrounding acres of pockmarked limestone rocks that look like the charred remains of an inferno. Consisting only of a petrol station, a post office and a few shops and brightly-coloured houses, Hell is a touristy place with plenty of devilish touches, such as a gift shop called the **Devil's Hangout** (Mon-Sat 9am–5pm; tel: 345-945 2867), where the owner serves behind the counter dressed as the devil, and at the **Hell Post Office** (Mon–Fri 9am–5pm; tel: 345-949 1171), you can send postcards home from your holiday in Hell.

Turtles and stingrays

Not far from Hell, the **Turtle Farm** (daily 8am–5pm; tel: 345-949 3894; www.turtle.ky) has operated a breed-and-release programme since 1968 and has returned more than 31,000 tagged green turtles to the wild. Take the walkway around the tanks where over 16,000 of the endangered species live and breed and peer through the underwater viewing panels at a shark reef.

Off the northern coast and accessible only by tour boats, which leave from a pier near the port, **Stingray City** is considered to be one of the best 3.5-metre (12ft) dive spots in the world. Here stingrays are so used to humans that they will eat squid right out of your hands.

Great gardens

To the east of George Town, on top of a limestone cliff in Savannah, stands **Pedro St James Historic Site** (daily 8.30am–5pm; tel: 345-947 3329; www.pedrostjames.ky), a magnificently restored old stone manor house that's packed with antiques, and has formal English gardens. It was here, in 1835, that the Declaration of Emancipation was read, giving African slaves their freedom.

Inland, **Queen Elizabeth II Botanic Park** (daily 9am–5.30pm; tel: 345-947 9462; www.botanic-park.ky) is a 26-hectare (65-acre) nature preserve and one of the finest botanical gardens in the Caribbean. More than half of the islands' species of indigenous flora can be found growing naturally in the park.

JAMAICA

River trips, powdery beaches, the Blue Mountains, wildlife, gardens and colonial mansions, Jamaica has them all, backed by the irresistible rhythms of reggae and the irrepressible spirit of the people. Cruise ships have a choice of five ports of call at this island – the

Off Doctor's Cave Beach

one of largest in the Caribbean – Montego Bay, the main tourism centre, Falmouth, which receives the biggest ships, Ocho Rios, which attracts the majority of ships, smaller Port Antonio in the beautiful east or their newest port in Port Royal on the outskirts of Kingston, their capital city.

MONTEGO BAY

Cruise ships dock at the **Freeport** complex 2km (1 mile) or so to the west of **Montego Bay** ⓲, or MoBay as it's known, Jamaica's second largest city (after the capital Kingston). The island's hub of tourism, the city sprawls around the bay, with shops, bars and restaurants along the waterfront.

At the modern terminal, the **Freeport Shopping Centre** is a good source for gemstones, watches, cigars, rum and designer labels. Most ships run a shuttle service into town, or you can take an official taxi.

The town square, **Sam Sharpe Square**, is named after Sam 'Daddy' Sharpe, who led slave rebellions in 1831–32 and was hanged by the British. In the square you can still see the stone cell, called the Cage, used to imprison runaway slaves and disorderly sailors.

The Hip Strip

MoBay is dedicated to shopping and partying, and along the seafront

Enjoying the water at Buccaneer Beach

on Gloucester Avenue you will find the **Montego Bay Shopping Centre**, the **Craft Market** and a long line of bars and restaurants. Known as the **Hip Strip**, it ends at the busy **Doctor's Cave Beach** (daily 8.30am-5.30pm; tel: 876-952 2566; www.doctorscavebathingclub.com) to

> ### Common sense
>
> Although Jamaica has had some incidents of tourists being robbed at gunpoint, serious incidents are rare. Use common sense and don't go off the beaten track on your own.

the north. The beach was made famous in the early 1900s by Dr Alexander McCatty, who claimed that the water had curative powers, attracting lots of rich Americans. Visitors still flock to the beach, which has good facilities and coral gardens close to the shore that are perfect for snorkelling. At the cyber café there, you can check your email at cheaper rates than on the ship.

Back on the Strip, **Margaritaville (www.margaritavillecaribbean.com)**, a noisy, action-packed beach bar, offers Jamaican food and fajitas that you can wash down with any of 52 varieties of margarita. Alternatively, try the sizzling, peppery jerk pork and chicken at the outdoor **Pork Pit (tel: 876-940 3008)**. If you are in port in July you can soak up the atmosphere and island rhythms at **Reggae Sumfest** (http://reggaesumfest.com), a huge six day music festival.

Great houses

Not far from Montego Bay several plantation houses still stand at the centre of huge estates. The beautifully restored 18th-century **Rose Hall** (day tours Mon-Sat 9am-5pm; night tours Wed-Sat 6pm-9pm; tel: 876-953 2341; https://rosehall.com) was once the home of the alleged 'white witch', Annie Palmer, who is supposed to have murdered three of her husbands.

Nearby, heading eastwards, is **Greenwood Great House** (daily tours 9am–4pm; tel: 876-631 3456; www.greenwoodgreathouse.com), which was built by relatives of the poet Elizabeth Barrett Browning in 1800. Greenwood contains a great many antiques and the largest collection of rare musical instruments.

FALMOUTH

35km (22 miles) east of Montego Bay is the Georgian town of **Falmouth** [20], home of the cruise ship port in Jamaica opened in 2011, which can receive the huge Oasis class ships. The pier is triangular and has been developed as an 18th-century concept town with cobbled streets, shops, boutiques and restaurants

The old town, from where sugar and rum were shipped, has a fine colonial court house, St Peter's Anglican church and pretty 18th century houses with wrought iron balconies. The Jamaica National Heritage Trust has declared the whole town a National Monument. Tram cars and horse-drawn carriages take visitors on tours around town.

Methodist manse

The pretty gingerbread-style Harmony Hall, in St Ann, was a Methodist manse built in the mid-1800s. It is now houses a restaurant, Summerhouse (Wed-Sat 11am-9.30pm; Sun 11am-6pm; tel: 876- 210 2141; www.summerhouseja.com), and boutique showcasing products by local artisans.

MARTHA BRAE

Excursions from Falmouth include rafting on the beautiful **Martha Brae** river (daily tel: 876-952 0889; www.jamaicarafting.com). Guides will punt you gently downstream on a 30-foot long bamboo raft for two. It takes about an hour to travel the three miles to Martha's Rest at the mouth of the river, about 2 miles (5km) from Falmouth.

Overlooking the Martha Brae is the **Good Hope Great House** a fine example of a Georgian plantation house with a commanding view over the surrounding countryside. The estate features an old water wheel, kiln and sugar mill ruins, and guests are able to stay overnight in their villas, cottages and rooms (www.goodhopejamaica.com). Tours, ziplining and river tubing is available on the estate via Chukka (www.chukka.com).

OCHO RIOS

Known locally as Ochi, **Ocho Rios** ㉑ is backed by hills of coconut palms and fruit plantations, while its soft, white beaches are protected by colourful coral reefs. The well-equipped cruise ship terminal is within easy walking distance of the town centre, but in the heat, you might prefer to take one of the taxis that line up at port.

In the town centre, a shopping mall, the **Taj Mahal** (daily 9am–5pm; tel: 876-837 7007), has outlets for gemstones, jewellery, designer watches, coffee and cigars. At the **Olde Craft Market** on Main Street, you can find wood carvings, batik and T-shirts. Everything is overpriced, but friendly haggling is expected.

Fern Gully

Just outside Ochi is **Fern Gully**, a lush, hardwood rainforest where giant ferns

Olde Craft Market artwork

and lianas hang over the narrow road. More than 60 species of fern have been recorded here, but they have dwindled a little due to hurricane damage, as well as pollution from traffic.

Ocho Rios is one of the best areas on the island for plant life and has two excellent botanical gardens. **Shaw Park Botanical Gardens** (daily tours 8am–4pm; tel: 876-893 5899) is within walking distance of the port, but on a hill so take a taxi. Its 10 hectares (25 acres) of tropical trees and shrubs surround a lovely waterfall. Nearby, further up the road is the **Konoko Falls** (daily 8am–4.30pm; tel: 622 1712; www.konokofalls.com), a lush, tranquil water garden around an interesting small Taíno Amerindian museum.

Dunn's River Falls

Just a 5-minute drive from the terminal, a visit to **Dunn's River Falls** (daily 8.30am–4pm; tel: 876-656 8446; www.dunnsriverfallsja.com) will be a cooling experience. In the middle of a rainforest, Dunn's River cascades 180 metres (600ft) down a series of limestone shelves. With an official guide (who will expect a tip), you can join a group to climb up the slippery rocks, stopping for photos by the freshwater pools. You don't have to climb with a guide, but the water is powerful enough in places to make you lose your footing. Wear rubber-soled shoes or hire shoes at the falls.

For a different perspective of the island, you can go on a three-hour excursion on horseback at **Chukka Cove** (daily 9am-4pm; tel: 876-979 8500; www.chukka.com), 11km (7 miles) west of Ocho Rios. You will ride along a beautiful beach and through two of the island's oldest sugar estates before stopping at Chukka Cove's private beach for a swim.

A short drive east of Ocho Rios stands a fine example of a working plantation. **Prospect Estate** (www.prospect-villas.com) grows bananas, sugar cane, cocoa, coconuts, pineapples and cassava on

Dunn's River Falls

its 800 hectares (2,000 acres) of land. An estate tour includes the White River Gorge, Sir Harold's Viewpoint, and a grove of memorial trees.

Writers' retreats

James Bond fans will not want to miss a visit to Oracabessa Bay and **Goldeneye**, the one-time home of the suave hero's creator, novelist and former British Naval Intelligence officer, Ian Fleming (1908–64). The house is now part of a small villa and cottage resort (www.goldeneye.com) and incorporates the predictably named **James Bond Beach Club**, which has three beaches with good snorkelling, a Jamaican restaurant, water sports and changing rooms. A little further along the coast is **Firefly** (www.firefly-jamaica.com), the former holiday retreat of another writer, Noël Coward (1899–1973). The house has fantastic views and offers a fascinating insight into the life of the actor, composer and playwright.

The rugged coastline of Port Antonio

PORT ANTONIO

Backed by the Blue Mountains, the twin harbours of the tranquil, secluded town of **Port Antonio** ㉒ greet the boats as they approach the tropical green rugged coastline of Portland. Cruise ships started docking here when the **Errol Flynn Marina** (tel: 876-715 6044) was built in the West Harbour and the **Ken Wright Cruise Ship Pier** was opened on property in 2002.

In front of the harbour lies the enchanting **Navy Island**, once used by the British Navy but more famously the playground of film star Errol Flynn, who bought it in 1946. Guests attending his wild parties here included Clara Bow, Ginger Rogers and Bette Davis. The dilapidated island is awaiting redevelopment.

Banana Gold

In the late 18th century, Port Antonio became the banana capital of the world and triggered an exclusive tourist industry when bananas, grown on the foothills of the Blue Mountains, were exported to America by boat from here. The returning banana boats then brought wealthy American visitors back to the island. This was where Harry Belafonte's *Banana Boat Song* originated.

The marina is close to the centre of town, where there is a busy food market (Thu and Sat) in West Street and a shopping mall tucked behind a façade of what looks like a row of Amsterdam canal houses in Fort George Street. From **Christ Church**, built in 1840, in Harbour Street, there is a fine view of the East Harbour. On a peninsular bluff that juts out between the two harbours is **Fort George**, built by the British in 1729 to protect against Spanish invasions. Across the harbour lies the Folly Ruins, a dilapidated mansion built in the early 1900s which collapsed due to the use of seawater in its construction.

On the Rio Grande

The **Rio Grande** cuts its way down through dense rainforest to the sea just west of Port Antonio. Bananas from the hillsides were once transported to the port on long bamboo rafts, but the actor Errol Flynn started the craze of riding down the river on them. Today, you can do just the same with a two- to three-hour ride from Berridale to Rafter's Rest (tel: 876-993 5778).

DOMINICAN REPUBLIC

The beautiful southeastern region of the Dominican Republic has a split personality. The coastline is edged with endless white beaches that have become a magnet for large scale, exclusive, all-inclusive tourist development, but venture inland and you find rural simplicity – peasant farmers on horseback tending their cattle and fields of waving sugar cane.

Money does grow on trees

The Spanish-speaking Dominican Republic shares the island, called Hispaniola, with the poverty-stricken and disaster prone French-speaking Haiti. It was the first Caribbean island to be visited by Christopher Columbus in 1492 and **Santo Domingo**, the capital of the Dominican Republic was the first city to be built. Whether your cruise ship docks in Santo Domingo or east of the city at La Romana, a visit to the historic quarter of the capital is worth putting on the agenda. The old town, known as the Zona Colonial, is packed with architectural gems, cobbled streets and historic museums, churches and palaces within what is left of its fortified walls.

La Romana

The port of **La Romana** ㉓, established in 1502, is 97km (60 miles) east of the capital. Port facilities are limited and most people opt for a ship excursion, although taxis are available at the terminal for those who want to explore independently. The town is dominated by the country's largest sugar factory, and is just 10km (6 miles) from **Casa de Campo** (House in the Country; tel: 809-523 3333; www.casadecampo.com.do), one of the most sumptuous holiday resorts in the Caribbean.

This haunt of the rich and famous has three golf courses, a marina, polo club, 15 pools, 17 tennis courts, large riding stables and a beach. Cruise passengers are welcomed on an organised ship excursion, but individuals will find themselves turned away at the big electric iron gates at the entrance.

Above the resort, on the edge of the Chavón Gorge, is the pretty artists' enclave of **Altos de Chavón**, a mock 15th-century Italian village created in the 1980s. The village has a large amphitheatre, seating up to 4,000 people and drawing top performers. The **Museo Arqueológico Regional** (Tues-Sun 9am–5pm; call to arrange a visit: tel: 809-523 8554) exhibits a large collection of Amerindian artefacts.

Eastern Islas

A 20-minute boat trip from La Romana is **Isla Catalina**, also called **Serena Cay** by some cruise ships. There are no developments on this tropical island, which is dry and flat, but visitors come in their thousands during the cruise ship season. The beach here is protected by a reef, which provides interest for divers and passengers in glass-bottomed boats, and there are plenty of watersports on offer.

A 30-minute drive away, heading south, is the fishing village of **Bayahibe**, its beaches now developed with several all-inclusive hotels as well as hostels for dedicated divers. It sits on the edge of the **Parque Nacional del Este**, where archaeological discoveries have been made dating human habitation of the area to 2000BC. Offshore, but still part of the National Park, is **Isla Saona**. A feature of this trip is the *piscina natural*, a natural swimming pool of waist-deep water formed by a sand bar where boats stop for you to have a swim.

Northern coast

The country's northern coast, which hasn't been on cruise ships' itineraries since the 1980s, has started hosting super-sized vessels as a brand-new harbour facility called **Amber Cove** (www.ambercove.com), which opened in October 2015 just outside the town of Puerto

Scuba diving at Serena Cay

> **Price check**
>
> San Juan used to be known as a cheap, duty-free port, especially for gold jewellery, but if your cruise is going to St Thomas, it's better to wait as prices are generally better there.

Plata. It is the Caribbean's newest cruise destination and offers beaches and water sports as well as culture and adventure options, such as the Ocean World Adventure Park (tel: 809-291 1000; www.oceanworld.net).

SAMANÁ PENINSULA

Cruise ships coming in to the Samaná peninsula on the northeast coast offer a beach excursion to the little island of **Cayo Levantado**. The centre of the island is taken up by an all-inclusive hotel, but at one end there is a broad sweep of sand and palm trees. From January to March, the highlight of any trip to Samaná is **whale watching**. At that time, some 3,000 humpback whales migrate from the north to mate and calve in Samaná Bay, a National Marine mammal sanctuary, and one of the best places in the world for whale watching.

PUERTO RICO

At 160km (100 miles) long and 51km (32 miles) wide, Puerto Rico, a US territory, is one of the larger islands in the Caribbean. Its capital **San Juan** ㉔ is well positioned as a homeport for cruise ships heading south to the islands of the Lesser Antilles in the Eastern Caribbean. With a varied landscape of tropical beaches and densely forested mountains, most of the 3.6 million inhabitants live in the main towns.

San Juan is the busiest cruise port outside the US mainland. The majority of ships dock at **Calle Marina**, just to the south of **El Viejo San Juan** (Old San Juan), and from here it's an easy walk from the terminal into the most interesting part of the capital city. At the busiest times, some ships have to dock at the Pan American Dock some distance away from the centre, but then a shuttle to Old San Juan is usually provided.

San Juan

To get right to the heart of **Old San Juan**, walk up Calle San Justo. Weatherwise, the town is one of the hottest places in the Caribbean, but you'll find plenty of shade and small, unpretentious cafés serving authentic Puerto Rican cuisine – a variation on traditional Spanish food, with rice and beans, the staple dish. The traffic can get so bad that it's not worth taking an air-conditioned coach, you'll see much more on your own. If you get tired you can hop on one of the free trolley buses.

Puerto Rico may have been a US territory for over a century, but not much has changed since the days of Spanish rule in the old town, which dates back to 1521. The narrow, cobbled streets are lined with pretty 16th- and 17th-century Spanish colonial houses with wrought-iron balconies.

Castles and fortresses

Calle Fortaleza, a busy shopping street full of souvenirs, crosses San Justo; if you turn right you reach **Plaza Colón** (Columbus Square), with a monument commemorating the explorer. Behind the square stands the 17th-century **El Castillo de San**

Juan Ponce de Leon statue in Old San Juan

Cristóbal (daily 9am–6pm; guided tours), which has a fascinating history, a network of tunnels and fabulous views of the city. At the other end of the street is the white castellated mansion of **La Fortaleza (tel: 787-721 7000)**, built in 1540 and now the residence of the Governor of Puerto Rico. Soon after the fort was built, the Spanish realised that it didn't give enough protection to the town and set about constructing El Castillo San Felipe del Morro, known as El Morro, on the tip of the peninsula. **El Morro** (daily 9.30am–4.30pm; tel: 787-729 6960) is a hugely atmospheric place – the walls are 6 metres (20ft) thick in places and inside there is a maze of medieval nooks and crannies, as well as a small museum.

Old town sights

Back in the old town, down Calle del Cristo you come to the classy **Gran Hotel El Convento** (tel: 787-723 9020; www.elconvento.com), a former Carmelite convent built in the 17th century, but long used as a hotel. Opposite stands the magnificent **San Juan Cathedral** (Mon-Fri 9am–4pm, Sun 8am-1pm; tel: 787-722 0861; www.catedralsanjuanbautista.org), built in 1540 and site of Juan Ponce de León's tomb. He founded the first settlement in 1508 and became the first governor of Puerto Rico. Nearby is **Plaza de Armas**, a replica of Madrid's main square. Trolley buses pass through here and stop right at the cruise pier.

El Yunque

You don't have to go far to find yourself in the rainforest. Designated a National Forest with a network of well-marked trails, **El Yunque** (daily 7.30am–6pm; tel: 787-888 1880; www.fs.usda.gov/elyunque), a 11,000-hectare (27,000-acre) area of rainforest, is home to about 250 species of trees and plants, plus hundreds of frogs and the brilliant Puerto Rican parrot. En route is the palm-fringed **El Luquillo Beach**, the prettiest on the island, where you can snorkel on the reef.

The thick walls of El Morro

Ponce

If time allows, it is worth visiting **Ponce**, a Spanish colonial town on the south coast, about 90 minutes away. A detour takes you to the massive cave network at **Río Camuy Cave Park** (Wed–Sun 8am–3pm; tel: 787-898 3136). The best golf courses are about an hour from San Juan; pre-book before your trip.

EASTERN CARIBBEAN

Whichever combination of ports and islands makes up your eastern Caribbean itinerary, there will always be a cosmopolitan flavour to the cruise. From the homeports of San Juan, in Puerto Rico, and Barbados, ships can reach many of the small island ports of the Lesser Antilles in a week.

A visit to a number of islands in this region delivers a heady cultural mix of European, African and indigenous influences. The larger, more developed islands that have become major tourist destinations in their own right, contrast with the smaller islands, which are still off the main tourist track.

It is also in this region that the classic Caribbean islands of our dreams are to be found. The white sandy beaches, fishing boats in hidden coves, and scenic yacht-filled harbours, combine with modern towns and historic neighbourhoods to ensure cruises with a genuinely romantic appeal.

US VIRGIN ISLANDS

The US Virgin Islands comprise 68 islands, although only four are inhabited: St Thomas, St John, St Croix and Water Island. They are included on both western and eastern Caribbean cruise itineraries and offer the best of both worlds. **St Thomas** ㉕ is a shopping mecca with the best duty-free goods in the region and **St John**, just a short boat ride away, is mostly one large national park of unspoiled beauty and remains the least developed of the US islands.

Some ships call at St John instead of St Thomas, but experienced cruise visitors to the latter know that they should do their shopping in the morning in Charlotte Amalie, the capital, and then take a short ferry ride to St John for an afternoon on one of its glorious beaches.

Snorkelling in the USVI

EASTERN CARIBBEAN

USVI, BVI, Sint Maarten/St-Martin, St-Barths, St Kitts, Antigua, Guadeloupe, Dominica, Martinique, St Lucia, Barbados

Location: The Lesser Antilles extend from the Virgin islands to Aruba, divided into the Leeward Islands in the north and Windward Islands to the south. The USVI (capital Charlotte Amalie) comprise 60+ islands about 64km (40 miles) east of Puerto Rico; The BVI (Road Town) comprise 50+ islands. **Sint Maarten/St-Martin** (Philipsburg/Marigot) lies eastwards, north of **St Kitts** (Basseterre); Antigua (St John's) is centrally located between St-**Barths** (Gustavia), St Kitts and **Guadeloupe** (Point-à-Pitre) to the south. Then comes **Dominica** (Roseau), first of the Windward Islands, followed by **Martinique** (Fort-de-France), south of the Tropic of Cancer. **St Lucia** (Castries) lies 35km (21 miles) further south and **Barbados** (Bridgetown) 160km (100 miles) to the southeast, outside the Antillean curve.

Time zone: utc/gmt -4 (all islands)

Pop: 106,000 (USVI); 30,000 (BVI); 81,650 (Sint Maarten/St Martin); 9,900 (St-Barths); 53,000 (St Kitts); 97,000 (Antigua); 4384,000 (Guadeloupe); 71,900 (Dominica); 364,500 (Martinique); 183,600 (St Lucia); 287,300 (Barbados).

Language: English (USVI, Antigua, Barbados); English/Creole (BVI, St Kitts, Dominica, St Lucia); French/Creole (Guadeloupe, Martinique, St-Martin), Dutch (Sint Maarten); English is also spoken in Sint Maarten/St-Martin.

Money matters: USVI, BVI: US$; Sint Maarten/St-Martin, St-Barths, Martinique, Guadeloupe: Euro; St Kitts, Antigua, Dominica, St Lucia: EC$; Barbados: BDS$. US dollars are accepted in all islands.

Telephone & internet: Country codes: +340 (USVI); +284 (BVI); +7 (Sint Maarten); +590 (St-Martin, St-Barths, Guadeloupe); +869 (St Kitts); +268 (Antigua); +767 (Dominica); +596 (Martinique); +758 (St Lucia); +246 (Barbados). Internet is widely available.

Sunrise on Morning Star beach, St Thomas

St Croix, out on a limb to the south, is a complete contrast to St Thomas, quieter and less developed with a marine national park and a varied landscape, from grassy hills to lush rainforest.

ST THOMAS

Although a few ships anchor in the bay when stopping off at **St Thomas**, and tender passengers into the heart of the capital, **Charlotte Amalie**, most berth at **Havensight Dock**, just over 2km (1 mile) east of town. Barely off the ship, you can start intensive retail therapy in **Havensight Mall** (Mon-Sat 10am-5pm; tel: 340-777 5313) at the dock, for every major duty-free retailer has an outlet here as well as in the capital's shopping centre.

Crown Bay, on the other side of the harbour, about twice as far from the capital as Havensight, is also used on busy days. The port area has a replica sugar mill and other facilities but the shops at Crown Bay Center (tel: 340-774 2132; www.crownbaycentervi.com)

are not as extensive as at Havensight. The ferry to **Water Island**, the fourth US Virgin Island, leaves from Crown Bay Marina.

Charlotte Amalie

Scores of taxis wait by the dockside – not all official, but all operating on a shared basis. Progress will be slow driving into **Charlotte Amalie**, so if you can, you might as well walk. Just follow the road along the seafront.

The capital has one of the most attractive harbours in the region, especially when the sun sets behind the sails of the yachts filling the bay. Behind the wharf, where ferries depart for St John, stands **Fort Christian** (Mon-Fri 9am-3pm; 340-714 3678), which houses the **Virgin Islands Museum**. Built by the Danes in 1680, it is the oldest building in continuous use on the island. Behind the museum, **Emancipation Gardens** marks the start of shop-filled **Dronningens Gade** (Main Street), which has endless alleyways running down to the waterfront, each with a mini-shopping mall. At No. 14 stands the house where Impressionist artist Camille Pissarro was born in 1830, which is now a small **art gallery** selling paintings and prints by local and regional artists.

Castle on the hill

Although richer in shops than historical sights, Charlotte Amalie does have a legacy of piracy, and what is left of **Blackbeard's Castle** is at the top of several long flights of steps cut into the hillside. Built by the Danes in 1679, it was supposed to have

Take the tram

For a good view of Charlotte Amalie, take the Paradise Point Tramway – a seven-minute cable car ride to a viewing platform 210 metres (700ft) up. The tramway station is just across the road from Havensight Mall. For more information contact 340-774 9809 or visit www.paradisepointvi.com.

been used by the notorious English pirate, Edward Teach, aka Blackbeard. Now it's home to a hotel, and self-guided tours are available (tel: 340-776 1234; www.blackbeardscastle.com).

On Kongens Gade (Government Hill), 99 Steps can lead you to and from the castle. Built in the 18th century, these historic steps were constructed with repurposed ships' ballasts. The climb itself is relatively easy, leading you through colourful, historic houses surrounded by tropical plants and flowers to one of the most spectacular views overlooking the harbour.

The Danes were the first Europeans to settle in St Thomas and St John in the 17th century and eventually sold the islands to the US in 1917 for US$25 million.

Across the island

The majority of excursions are on the water, involving sailing or kayaking, swimming, snorkelling and scuba diving in beautifully clear waters awash with colourful marine life. It's cheaper to hire a taxi independently rather than through the ship, or hire a car if you want to go further afield. The rates are fixed so you don't need to haggle.

To the north of the capital is the **St Peter Greathouse and Botanical Gardens** (tel: 340-774-4999;) where you can walk through the

Lorikeet arboreal parrot

4 hectares (11 acres) of landscaped gardens. At about 305 metres (1,000ft) above sea level, you can see up to 24 islands.

At **Coral World Ocean Park** (daily 9am–4pm; tel; 340-775 1555; http://coralworldvi.com), 15 minutes from Havensight on the northeast coast, a three-level underwater observatory gives a fish's eye view of an enormous range of marine life, and it's fun to watch the divers at feeding time.

> **Underwater trails**
>
> Boats travel from Christiansted to Buck Island Reef National Monument, which has its own marked underwater trails around the coral reef for divers and snorkellers. You can either join your ship's excursion or one run by the dive shops.

ST JOHN

A visit to the neighbouring island of **St John** is one of the most popular excursions, either as part of a tour or on your own. Two-thirds of St John is an unspoilt national park (gifted to the US by the Rockefellers) with 110 different types of tree and many species of birds and butterflies. It also has more than 40 beaches and coves with an eco-resort at **Caneel Bay**. The best, though, is **Trunk Bay**, which has an underwater snorkelling trail, giving you a chance to snorkel round the coral reef.

Regular ferries cross from Charlotte Amalie (45 minutes) and from Red Hook (about 25 minutes from Havensight) on the east coast. These are cheaper and more frequent.

ST CROIX

Large cruise ships arrive at **St Croix** (pronounced Croy, as in boy) on the west coast at the modern 450-metre (1,500ft) pier in **Frederiksted** ㉖, where you'll find a handful of shops, the renovated 18th century **Fort Frederik** (Mon–Sat 9am–4pm, tel: 340-772 2021), with its museum and art gallery, and the **Caribbean Museum Center for the Arts** (Tues–Sat 9am–4pm; tel: 340-772 2622; www.cmcarts.org) promoting regional art. The capital, **Christiansted**, a shuttle bus ride away, on the north coast, has more shops, bars and restaurants in **King's Alley Walk**, but only the smaller ships can dock here.

At 212 sq km (82 sq miles), St Croix is larger than St Thomas, but it is less developed, and far less crowded. It is also well known for its magnificent beaches at **Sandy Point**, **Cane Bay** and **Davis Bay**, which are just a short coach or taxi ride from Frederiksted. **Salt River Bay National Historic Park (tel: 340-773 1460)**, on the north coast, is the site of a Columbus landing – the only one on US territory. It has a huge mangrove forest and an underwater canyon which is ideal for scuba diving.

Some of the best places to visit include the **Cruzan Rum Distillery** (Mon-Sat 10am-4pm; tel: 340-692 2280; http://cruzanrum.com), the **St George Village Botanical Garden** (daily 9am–3pm; tel: 340-692 2874; www.sgvbg.org), set among the ruins of a plantation village, and the restored **Whim Great House** (Wed–Sat 10am–4pm; 340-772 0598), which portrays plantation life during Danish rule.

A store in Road Town, Tortola

BRITISH VIRGIN ISLANDS

However you choose to spend your time ashore in the British Virgin Islands, it won't be hurried. These volcanic outcrops are Robinson Crusoe-style havens rich in banana trees, palms and mangoes, garlanded with white sandy beaches and secret coves set in a perfect sea, and all you can do here is revel in it.

> ### US currency
>
> When other British islands gained independence in the 1960s and 1970s, the BVI remained a self-governing British Overseas Territory, along with Montserrat and Anguilla. To maintain economic ties with the USVI, the US dollar is used as currency.

There is very little development to spoil it all. Most of the 50 or so British Virgin Islands are uninhabited, the 30,000-strong population being concentrated on the three biggest – Tortola, Virgin Gorda and Jost Van Dyke. The topography of Tortola and Virgin Gorda is very rugged and mountainous: Tortola's Mount Sage is 536 metres (1,709ft) and Gorda Peak 414 metres (1,369ft), not good terrain for building high-rise hotels, casinos and shopping malls.

These islands have become a haven for 'yachties', who sail among them and know what it's like to have a beach that's inaccessible by land to themselves.

TORTOLA

Most cruise lines visit **Tortola** but only the small-ship cruise companies tend to stop at Virgin Gorda and Jost Van Dyke. Ships usually tender passengers ashore in the harbour of the pretty capital of Road Town. A road around the 54-sq km (21-sq mile) island was completed in the early 1980s and, with a line of taxis offering round-trip tours, it's relatively easy to explore.

Road Town

Road Town ㉗ is the island's quaint and colourful capital city. Along **Main Street** – five minutes' walk from the pier and yachting marina at Wickhams Cay – many of the traditional, Caribbean wooden houses have been restored and house several shops. There is a lively crafts market, where you'll find brightly coloured mobiles, driftwood napkin rings and other fun items. On the waterfront, the landmark **Pusser's Road Town Pub (daily 11am-9.30pm; 284-494 3897; www.pussers.com)**, an attractive gingerbread-style building, offers English food and the Pusser's Painkiller, a notorious rum cocktail.

Island tours and beaches

If you're not after isolation, for a whole beach experience go to **Cane Garden Bay**, where the restaurant at **Rhymers'** Beach Hotel serves tasty seafood, makes great barbecues and provides showers, and some water sports facilities, including windsurfing, especially in November's perfect conditions. Some ships offer excursions on open-air safari buses, which include a stop at the beach. Local companies organise boat and snorkelling tours and sailing trips from the pier in Road Town.

For a walk with the island's most wonderful vistas, visit the **Mount Sage National Park** (www.bvinpt.org/sage-mountain), where you can hike along a rainforest trail towards the highest point across both the US and British Virgin Islands.

VIRGIN GORDA

The tiny but beautiful island of **Virgin Gorda** lies 20km (12 miles) from Tortola and plenty of boats go there from Road Town's pier, docking at **Spanish Town**. On the other side of the small shopping plaza is the **Virgin Gorda Yacht Harbour** (tel: 284-499 5500), where you can eat and admire the view at the **Bath and Turtle and Rendezvous Bar (daily 7am-9pm; tel: 284-495 5239)**.

Snorkelling at The Baths, Tortola

The most popular attraction here is **The Baths**, in the **Devil's Bay National Park**, a magical beach where gigantic boulders have formed grottoes and salt-water pools. An easy trail runs through it all. Ships often offer excursions to The Baths, or you could negotiate with one of the taxi drivers at Spanish Town for a round-trip fare there. Alternatively, you can take a taxi to the island's best beach, **Spring Bay**, a good place for some excellent snorkelling.

Arriving at **Jost Van Dyke** is like stepping into a time warp: a clutch of houses in a bay surrounded by green hills, and goats grazing in the cemetery. A water taxi will take you round to the blissful beach at White Bay.

SINT MAARTEN

The Netherlands are in bed with France on the tiny island of **Sint Maarten/St-Martin** and have been peacefully so for more than 200 years. The border divides the smallest land mass – 96 sq km (37

Soaking up the sun

sq miles) – in the world shared by two countries, and they couldn't be more different. The smaller Dutch Sint Maarten is brash with large resorts, casinos and fast food joints, whereas the French St-Martin is prettier, quieter and more sophisticated, with Parisian-style shops and cafés.

Philipsburg

Most of the major cruise lines include **Philipsburg** ㉘, the capital of Sint Maarten, as a port of call. Some people may recognise it from the film *Speed 2: Cruise Control*, in which a ship (*Seabourn Legend* in real life) crashes dramatically into the harbour front. The **Pointe Blanche cruise terminal** (www.portstmaarten.com) is just 2km (1 mile) away from the town centre and is well furnished with shops, facilities and taxis – opt for a multi-passenger minibus for a cheaper ride into the centre. Sometimes ships anchor in the bay and tender passengers right to the pier in town.

It's easy to find your way around Philipsburg. The town curves around Great Bay Beach and a board walk makes this a pleasant stroll. There are only two streets, running parallel to the waterfront and one is called **Voorstraat** (Front Street), the other **Achterstraat** (Back Street). These are the main shopping areas and tend to get very crowded when cruise ship passengers descend on the duty-free port, which has designer boutiques and traditional architecture. **Old Street** is one of many lanes *(steegjes)* connecting the two, and here you will find pretty, alfresco restaurants and the **Old Street Shopping Centre**, a small mall with more than 20 shops as well as restaurants.

Shopping treats

In **Wathey Square** (De Ruyterplein), which faces the pier, there's a late 18th-century courthouse, and some beautiful old buildings decorated with traditional West Indian gingerbread fretwork. A lively market, a selection of restaurants and plenty more shops

---

BEST BEACHES

The most convenient beaches are Great Bay – just along from Philipsburg's Front Street – and Little Bay, slightly further west, but they may both be crowded. For more privacy, take a taxi further afield to Simpson Bay Beach (good for water sports and for gambling, as the nearby Pelican Resort has a big casino); Dawn Beach (great for snorkelling); or Maho Bay Beach, where you can sunbathe in style or play the tables at the Sonesta Maho Bay Hotel and Casino.

On the French side, Baie Orientale is gorgeous, with good beachside cafés and a classic French Riviera atmosphere. Baie Rouge is best for snorkellers, while Baie Longue is uncrowded. Clothing is optional on most beaches on the French side.

Eat at l'Escargot, St Maarten

make this a place to head for, along with the little lanes, lined with more boutiques, cafés and the occasional courtyard, spilling over with tropical plants.

Among the best buys is jewellery, which is reasonably priced (as it is throughout the Caribbean). Posh shops sell Gucci and other designer goods as well as alcohol and leather products at duty-free prices – although not as low as they are in St Thomas. But for a real taste of the West Indies, look in at a local store crammed with spices, cane sugar, batik clothing, handwoven hammocks, local crafts and guavaberry liqueur, the local rum-based firewater made from wild red berries, which can spike up a cocktail.

ST-MARTIN

The smaller cruise ships sometimes anchor outside Marigot, the capital of the prettier French side of the island, and tender passengers in to the harbour. Otherwise, unless your time in Sint Maarten is very short, try to get over here and experience the difference between the two parts. Big cruise ships usually offer a tour to Marigot from Philipsburg with a detour through the district of Orléans to visit **La Ferme des Papillons** (daily 9am–3.30pm; www.thebutterflyfarm.com) a butterfly farm featuring a fascinating collection of species from around the world. Another option from

Philipsburg is a drive to the lovely French **Baie Orientale** for a swim, sunbathing (chairs provided) and a leisurely lunch.

Marigot
Much less commercialised than Philipsburg, **Marigot** ㉙ really feels like a French seaside resort. It has colourful markets and a broad, beautiful harbour overlooked by restaurants and cafés featuring the best of Caribbean and French cuisine. Several offer a good lunchtime Créole set menu. Then walk off the meal with a 15-minute stroll up to the ruins and views from **Fort St Louis**.

The stylish shops can be found in rue de la République, rue de la Liberté and the **Marina Port La Royale** (tel: 590-590 77 31 26; www.marinaportlaroyale.com), where there are more smart cafés looking out at the yachts.

If you have a full day ashore, you could take a taxi tour of the island or a cab from Philipsburg to Marigot. Negotiate the fare in advance (US dollars are accepted) and ask the driver to build in waiting time, or come back at a specified hour if you want to stop at a beach or a restaurant.

ST-BARTHÉLEMY
The essence of France in a paradise on earth is how St-Barthélemy has often been described and its reputation as a quintessential hideaway for the rich and famous has meant that its 26 sq km (10 sq miles) of land provides some of the most sought after property in the world.

With 22 beaches and coves to choose from, many of them

> ### Spoilt for choice
>
> Foodies should schedule a trip to Grand Case in the north of St-Martin. This little town offers more than its fair share of places to eat, and is reputed to have more restaurants than inhabitants.

Fort Louis, overlooking Marigot Bay

empty, windy cliffside walks, nature reserves and salt marshes, it's easy to get away from it all in St-Barths, as it is affectionately called. Chic, stylish and sophisticated in the way that only the French know how, it remains unpretentious with simple architecture – no big hotels here – reflecting the island's casual atmosphere.

Gustavia

Only the smaller cruise ships can call at St-Barths, dropping anchor in the outer harbour at **Gustavia** ㉚, the island's capital. Tenders take passengers to **L'Espace Gambier**, a small welcome centre at the entrance to the port where you can find a taxi, book an excursion or pick up a walking tour.

Picturesque, red-roofed buildings climb up the steep hill behind, harbouring duty-free shops with the latest Paris fashions all available in the exclusive boutiques, and funky bars and pavement cafés full of people chilling and spilling out on to the streets.

From the late 18th to 19th century, the island was occupied by the Swedes, hence the name Gustavia. In 1784 Louis XVI gave the island to Sweden in exchange for trading rights in the port of Gothenburg. This was a stroke of good luck for the islanders as it meant they were spared the terrors of the French Revolution a few years later, which spread to the other islands of the French West Indies. The Swedes left the island the forts: Oscar, Karl and Gustav, and beneath Fort Oscar is the **Wall House Museum** (Le musée territorial Wall House; Mon and Fri 9.30am–1pm and 3pm-7pm, Wed 2pm-7pm, Sat 9.30am–1pm; tel: 590-590 27 71 83), which provides a history of the island.

Eating at the beach

There are few things better than having a long relaxed lunch on a beautiful beach, and this is possible at **Shell Beach**, which, as its name suggests, is a shell-covered stretch of gleaming sand within walking distance of Gustavia, near the ruins of Fort Karl.

The most popular beach at **St Jean**, on the north coast, is backed by shops, hotels and bistros, but is rarely crowded. The luxury **Eden Rock Hotel** (www.edenrockhotel.com) stands on a spit of rock dividing the beach at St Jean in two.

Another good beach, and one of the most secluded, is **Colombier** at the tip of the northwest peninsula, where turtles nest every year. It can only be reached by boat from Gustavia or a half-hour walk from Colombier village.

ST KITTS

Travellers in search of the 'real' West Indies won't be disappointed with St Kitts, which crams an astonishing range of terrain – from cane fields to rainforest and mountains – into its 170 sq km (65 sq miles). With a laid-back atmosphere and a varied history, the slow rhythm of this miniature nation has to be infectious.

Arriving at the **Port Zante Cruise Terminal**, with its duty-free shops, restaurants and casino in the heart of the graceful capital, **Basseterre** ㉛, you can walk right off the ship and into the town.

Dependent on tourism, the astute islanders have restored many of Basseterre's gingerbread-trimmed public buildings and homes to their former glory, giving the palm-filled town an olde worlde charm. **Independence Square**, a former slave market now transformed into an attractive park surrounded by 18th-century houses,

The harbour in Gustavia

is particularly worth a look; as is the **Circus** traffic intersection on Fort Street, with a clock-tower of elaborately-worked cast iron in the centre.

Wander through the back streets off Bay Road and you'll find goats and chickens wandering free and roadside stalls selling fish, fruit and flowers. The town has a few galleries stocked with good-quality art, crafts and antiques.

The best local buys are leather and cotton goods, spices, pottery and sea opal jewellery; Fort Street and Liverpool Row are good places for unusual finds. Those who prefer brand name shopping may find something in the Pelican Shopping Mall.

St Kitts Scenic Railway

A 49km (30-mile) narrow gauge railway encircles St Kitts, which mostly basks in a sleepy haze, with fields of sugar cane rising up to the edge of the rainforest around Mount Liamuiga (1,156 metres/3,792ft). Built between 1912 and 1926 to transport sugar cane to the sugar mill in Basseterre, the sugar mill has closed but the railway line is back in action with a comfortable double decker train equipped to take visitors on a circular tour around the island in just four hours with a better view than you get from the road. The **St Kitts Scenic Railway** (Mon-Fri 7.30am-4pm; tel: 869-465 7263; www.stkittsscenicrailway.com) links up to the cruise lines' timetables and is a wonderful way to see the island. For those wanting to see more, taxi drivers offer tours of the island too, and can include a stop for lunch. Check the rates listed in the cruise terminal, as they are not displayed in cabs, and establish the fare with the driver first.

Driving westward from Basseterre, you come to **Romney Manor** (Old Road Town; tel: 869-465 6253; www.caribellebatikstkitts.com), 2.4 hectares (6 acres) of glorious gardens containing a saman tree believed to be more than 350 years old, so big it covers half an acre. In the grounds of the plantation is the **Caribelle Batik** factory where you can see hand-printed fabrics being made, using a traditional Indonesian process. A three-minute walk from Romney Manor is **Wingfield Estate**, with the ruins of a sugar mill and rum distillery. Wingfield is the place to come for **Sky Rides** zip line tour (tel: 869-466 4259; www.skysafaristkitts.com), where cables allow you to fly over Wingfield River through the rainforest.

Further along the road is **Brimstone Hill National Park** (daily 9.30am–5.30pm; tel: 869-465 2609; www.brimstonehillfortress.org), a huge fortress, with a small

Music event

The St Kitts Music Festival is a well-organised spectacular four-night event held every June, and features top Caribbean artists from every musical genre (tel: 869-465 1999; www.stkittsmusicfestival.net).

Sugar cane fields surround a church on St Kitts

museum, deemed a UNSECO World Heritage Site. From here you can see the two volcanic cones of St Eustatius and Saba to the northwest. The British called this 'the Gibraltar of the West Indies' until it was captured for nearly a year by the French in 1782. For lunch, you can stop at **Ottley's Plantation Inn** (tel: 869-465 7234), on the island's Atlantic side, which has a spring-fed pool and rainforest trails.

Contrasting beaches

For a day on the beach, head for the southeastern peninsula. **Frigate Bay**, a long stretch of soft white sand, is a complete contrast to the black sand beaches further north. There is an 18-hole championship golf course here and lots of hotels. Beyond it is **Friar's Bay**, a narrow strip of land divided by the road where you can enjoy a unique experience of swimming in the Atlantic Ocean on one side and the Caribbean Sea on the other. Towards the end of the peninsula is **Turtle Beach**, a paradise for bird-watchers and nature lovers and where visitors can snorkel, go kayaking or windsurf. Power boats are available to take you further around the coast or to the neighbouring island of Nevis.

NEVIS

Ferries regularly leave Basseterre for the 45-minute, 20km (12-mile) journey to the tiny island of **Nevis**, where Horatio Nelson married Fanny Nisbet in 1787. The trip is an experience in itself – you can travel in style or share the cargo boat with livestock and sacks of vegetables.

The ferry docks in **Charlestown**, which has beautifully restored, pastel-tinted, gingerbread-trimmed houses with tropical gardens. Here, street vendors will tempt you with fruit wines made from gooseberry, sorrel and pawpaw (papaya) – but beware the island's speciality hot pepper sauce if you don't have an asbestos tongue. You can also buy colourful batik, pottery and unusual handicrafts at the **Cotton Ginnery** on the waterfront. For a lovely beach and a good lunch, take a taxi to **Pinney's Beach**, a short hop from Charlestown.

Some cruise lines offer excursions to Nevis, which may include a rainforest hike to **Nevis Peak**. If you prefer to go independently,

Fishing boats, Nevis

Fishing in the shadow of Nevis Peak

do check the return ferry schedules to allow plenty of time to get back to the ship.

ANTIGUA

Since the demise of the sugar industry, the 270-sq-km (108-sq-mile) heart-shaped island of Antigua has come to depend on tourism. With the ever increasing sizes of cruise liners, the island has built three quays in **St John's** ㉜: **Redcliffe** and **Heritage** quays and **Nevis Street Pier**. Ever conscious of the desire to give visitors a variety of things to do, Antigua offers much beyond beach, boat or shopping trips. It also boasts a new major state-of-the-art airport for the whole Caribbean region, which opened in 2015.

St John's

Ships dock in the centre of the island's pretty capital, set around a large natural harbour. Historic Redcliffe's picturesque quay offers a range of shops and restaurants in a pleasantly shaded setting of restored wooden buildings, with lattice-work balconies. By the other two quays is a breezy, pastel-coloured mall, with an air-conditioned casino and duty-free shops. Between them, local traders selling sarongs, T-shirts and sunhats are gathered under the roof of the **Vendors' Mall** (Mon-Sat 8am-6pm), once a

Alongside the shops and restaurants, the port-side area provides banking and telecommunication facilities, which are located on High and Long streets. Island cash tills readily swallow US dollars, although paying with local currency (Eastern Caribbean dollars) normally means slightly lower prices, once the exchange rates have been calculated.

With its single-storey wooden houses in muted hues, flanking the narrow lanes, St John's offers the perfect chance to explore the urban Caribbean. Take an early morning start, and grab a coffee and cake from one of the excellent local bakeries or cafés in lower St Mary's Street or Redcliffe Quay. You will catch the cool of the day and obtain an insight into the intriguing events of a small Caribbean island.

Island heritage

A few minutes from the quayside, the former courthouse on Long Street, solidly built in 1747 from local stone, is now the **Museum of Antigua and Barbuda** (Tue–Sat 8.30am–4.30pm; donations; tel: 268-462 1469; www.antiguamuseums.net). The renovated building is packed with local heritage. Exhibits in the airy main hall highlight island life and history, while next door houses a database of monument inscriptions from around Antigua and the associated isle of Barbuda.

The Anglican **Cathedral of St John the Divine** (tel: 268-462 0820), a few minutes further up Long Street, originally dates from 1683 but, like so many buildings, it was damaged and restored

A game of beach cricket in Antigua

after a severe earthquake in 1834. The landmark towers of this striking baroque edifice have long proclaimed St John's presence to new arrivals.

Across the road, the **Antigua Recreation Ground** is the hallowed home of Antiguan cricket, and the spot where local sporting hero Sir Vivian Richards – the 'Master Blaster' – knocked off the fastest century in cricket. His bat is on display at the Museum of Antigua and Barbuda. However, a new ground with higher specifications, named after Sir Viv Richards, was built for the 2007 World Cup further out towards the airport, and Test Matches are now held there.

Return down Redcliffe and St Mary's streets, the **Ebenezer Methodist Church** (268-462 9794) was completed in 1839, but twice restored after earthquakes rattled its foundations. On Market Street, opposite the West Bus Station, you can buy tropical fruits in the covered **Heritage Market** and craftwork souvenirs in the building next door.

Out of town

Nowhere is far away in Antigua, but the full range of stunning beaches and historic sites lies out of walking distance. Cycling will get you a bit further under your own steam, and the best biking destination is **Fort Bay**, a leisurely 20-minute ride northeast of the town centre. Continue along Popeshead Street and turn left at the sign for Miller's-by-the-Sea to reach this popular locals' beach. At the southern end of the promontory, **Fort James** dates from 1739 and guards perfect views out to sea.

English Harbour

Further afield, at English Harbour to the southeast, lies one of Antigua's most historic attractions and UNSECO World Heritage Site, **Nelson's Dockyard** (tel: 268-481 5021). It's about 30 minutes away from St John's by local bus from the West Bus Station or by taxi (check the fixed rates). A series of beautifully restored mid-18th century buildings give this harbour an historic atmosphere. It was once a key command post for the British Navy, and where Admiral Horatio Nelson was based while he commanded HMS *Boreas*.

The stunning bay is overlooked by the impressive fortifications of **Fort Shirley**, where there is a lookout spot known as **Shirley Heights**. It comes alive with the music of reggae and steel pan bands, and barbecues on Sunday evening.

Sugar Museum

Taxi drivers offer a tour of the whole island, but if time is limited, it's worth slowing down to savour one or two sites. **Betty's Hope** (Pares Village), on the loop back from English Harbour, was built in the 1650s as the first sugar plantation on the island. Remnants of sugar mills are scattered across the island, but here the sugar mill has been restored and

Sail away

English Harbour is the focal point of Antigua Sailing Week held each April, when yachting enthusiasts from all over the world converge on the island for some top-class sailing – and partying (tel: 268-725 6651; www.sailingweek.com).

The colourful waterfront in St John's

occasionally grinds the cane in full sail. Other plantation buildings remain in ruins for lack of finance, but there is a small visitor's centre.

To the east, the natural limestone arch of **Devil's Bridge** offers an interesting stop en route to the sands of **Half Moon Bay**.

Every Antiguan promotes a favourite beach, and with a beach for every day of the year around the island, competition is tough. Darkwood Beach, Hawksbill Bay and Ffryes Bay on the west coast are all strong contenders.

If you have the time and feel energetic enough, **Boggy Peak** (402 metres/1,319ft), Antigua's highest point, is a rewarding 2-hour hike in the southwest of the island. Ask to be dropped off at the start of the track just beyond Urlings.

GUADELOUPE

A piece of the Republic of France, Guadeloupe is a butterfly-shaped island that is a French *département* and, although you will breathe in the unmistakable tropical air as you leave the ship, you will undeniably be entering a part of the European Union, where the currency is the euro and the lingo is French.

Divided in two by the slender Rivière Salée, the eastern region, Grande-Terre, is a lush land rich in banana plantations, cane fields and gentle hills, but with a stormy, wind-battered Atlantic coastline. It is also reasonably well developed with hotels and beach resorts. Basse-Terre to the west is a dramatically mountainous region, with a live volcano, La Soufrière, and dense forests holding more attractions for hikers and nature lovers. The seas are calm and the beaches are white and glorious. You cross from one region to the other via a drawbridge across the strait.

None of these wonderful attributes will be apparent, however, when you first emerge from the cruise terminal in the capital, **Pointe-à-Pitre** ❸. Although you'll find some nice facilities at the port – including landscaped gardens and duty-free stores, with more shops and small markets close by, it is not a friendly place and you will need to negotiate heavy traffic to explore the main town. Opinions vary as to whether it's worth the effort. If you like your towns neat and pretty, you won't want to waste much time here. But if you enjoy seedy grandeur and a down-to-earth, hard-working atmosphere, you could let the town work its charm.

Pointe-à-Pitre

In the **Place de la Victoire**, a short stroll along the waterfront, are some elaborate French colonial houses, complete with balconies and

Taxi fares

You'll have to negotiate hard over taxi fares in Pointe-à-Pitre if you want to explore on your own. Fares are regulated and should be listed at taxi stands, but it's always best to agree a firm price before you begin your tour, or ask the tourist bureau at the port to find you a cooperative driver.

shutters, and the pretty harbour of **La Darse**, which lies off the square. Here is the main tourist information office, which is worth popping into since Guadeloupe is not the easiest island to explore on your own. There is also a small but helpful information bureau in the cruise terminal, where you can pick up local maps, find a scrupulous taxi guide, perhaps, and get useful advice on getting about.

If your ship docks early, go to the rue St-John Perse to find the town's covered market, **Le Marché Couvert**. It is at its colourful best in the morning. Here you can find stylish cotton clothing and fabric, straw bags and local crafts and feast your senses at stalls piled high with fragrant spices and exotic fruits and vegetables, then head off for a coffee, a pastry and a chance to watch the world go by from a café. Just as you would in France, you must expect to pay for everything in euros, not US dollars, so either take a good supply with you or get some from an ATM onshore.

For more serious shopping, the rues Schoelcher, Nozières and Frébault have the best boutiques, while the **Distillerie Bellevue** on rue Bellevue Damoiseau is the best place to sample and buy Rhum Agricole, the island's distinctive falling-down water, which locals claim will not give you a hangover because it's made from pure cane sugar juice – but don't take that too seriously.

Nelson's Dockyard

Clothes shops in Le Moule on Grande Terre

As it's part of France, Guadeloupe offers the best bargains for perfume, crystal-ware, cosmetics and fashion accessories from French design houses; should you choose, you can stock up on Lalique, Hermès, Dior, Chanel, and French lingerie.

Créole specialities

With its French Créole heritage, Guadeloupe is a great place to eat; you can sample crayfish, stuffed crab and even sea oyster omelettes, and the local specialities of goat curry and black pudding, or *boudin*. The best places to enjoy lunch with a view, are at Grande Anse, in northwest Basse-Terre, and La Marina at **Bas-du-Fort**, just outside Pointe-à-Pitre.

Two museums worth visiting are the **Musée de St-John Perse** (9 rue Nozières; Mon–Fri 9am–5pm, Sat 8.30pm–12.30pm; tel: 590- 590 90 01 92), a beautiful, and pristinely restored colonial building commemorating the work of the island's Nobel Prize-winning poet; while the **Musée Schoelcher** (24 rue Peynier; Mon–Fri 9am–5pm; tel: 820 804) celebrates the life and anti-slavery campaigns of Victor Schoelcher, a leading 19th-century abolitionist. Afterwards, head northeast to the Place de l'Eglise to see the exquisite stained-glass (and apparently hurricane-proof) windows of the **Cathédrale de St-Pierre et St-Paul** (tel: 590-590 82 02 17), which has a flower market near its entrance.

Grande-Terre

The advantage of arriving at Pointe-à-Pitre is that it lies in the middle of the island near to the bridge over the Rivière Salée in the south, and is well-placed for exploring both Grande-Terre and Basse-Terre. A 10-minute taxi ride will take you to **La Marina** at **Bas-du-Fort**, where you'll find an attractive marina surrounded by shops, restaurants and cafés. Here, you can hire a motorboat or join an excursion to tour Guadeloupe's mangrove swamps, or visit a giant aquarium (daily 9am–7pm; tel:590-590 90 92 38; www.aquariumdelaguadeloupe.com) which houses more than 900 types of Caribbean sea creatures.

Further east from Pointe-à-Pitre, on Grande-Terre's south coast, lies **Le Gosier**, which has 8km (5 miles) of beach bordered by some of the region's best resorts. A spectacular 18th-century fortress, **Fort Fleur-d'Epée** (daily 9am–5pm, Mon from 10am; free), commands fine views from here. Continue on to **Pointe des Chateaux** at the easternmost tip of the island, and you'll discover breathtaking, craggy coastal scenery beaten into castle-like formations by the fierce Atlantic waves.

Basse-Terre

The best beach in Basse-Terre – and, indeed, on the whole island – is **Grande Anse** on the northwest coast, though **Deshaies** (slightly to the south) is good for snorkelling.

Further inland nature lovers will be captivated by Basse-Terre's huge **Parc National de la Guadeloupe** (tel: 590-590 41 55 55; www.guadeloupe-parcnational.fr), where you can enjoy a hike and a swim beneath a crystal clear waterfall, **Cascade de l'Ecrevisse**. Just driving along the winding coast road bordering the park is a delight in itself. Many cruise ships organise short jungle hikes through rainforest as part of an excursion.

The focal point of the park is **La Soufrière** volcano, soaring 1,467 metres (4,812ft) above sea level. To reach its peak (if you dare) you'll have to drive up twisting roads past banana trees and exotic vegetation, stopping en route to view the lovely tropical gardens at **St-Claude**. The road ends at 1,000 metres (3,300ft), but hikers can walk the rest of the way and have the rather scary experience of feeling the ground beneath their feet grow hotter, and the rotten-egg smell of sulphur grow more intense, as they climb.

East of Soufrière are **Les Chutes du Carbet**, with three cascades at 115 metres (380ft), 110 metres (360ft) and 20 metres (65ft) it is believed to be the highest waterfall in the Caribbean. To reach the falls requires a forest hike, so you'd be advised to join a guided tour.

Before heading back to the port along the east coast you can stop at **Trois Rivières** to see the **Parc Archéologique des Roches**

Wearing colourful Antillean Creole dress

Gravées (tel: 590-590 92 91 88)– ancient rocks etched with images of men and animals, which were carved by the Amerindians who originally inhabited Guadeloupe.

Trips to the islands

From Trois Rivières, two ferries a day make the 25-minute trip to Les Saintes, where in 1872 Britain's Admiral Rodney defeated the French in the Battle of the Saints. Only two of the eight islands are inhabited, and they are sparsely populated by the descendants of Breton pirates who took refuge there. Boats from Point-à-Pitre also go to Les Saintes as well as the circular Marie-Galante, named after Columbus's ship and bordered by white sandy beaches (for more information, visit www.valferry.fr).

Réserve Cousteau

Most cruise lines offer three- to four-hour tours around one or both parts of the island, and to Soufrière, often including lunch. But one of the most eye-opening trips is to the **Réserve Cousteau** off Malendure on the west coast, a marine park set up by the French underwater explorer Jacques Cousteau in 1955. Here, a spectacular underwater world has been created by the hot volcanic springs which occur in the area, which can be savoured by both scuba divers and snorkellers – and, for those who want to stay dry, from a glass-bottomed boat.

DOMINICA

The volcanic, rainforested island of Dominica thrusts out of the Caribbean Sea from a deep magical underwater seascape of submerged pinnacles and corals.

On land, Dominica offers nature in the raw, divided by a cloud-covered spine of forested peaks, narrow ridges, bubbling waterfalls, sulphurous springs and a boiling lake. Wild and untamed,

Suspended walkways in the Parc National

this 'Nature Island' is the only Caribbean island that Christopher Columbus would still be able to recognise some 500 years later.

Located in the Windward Islands, between French Guadeloupe and Martinique, Dominica has been settled by Britain and France. English is the official language, but a French Creole patois is widely spoken. The island remains the last outpost of the Carib Indians (Kalinago), Amerindians who were calling the Caribbean home centuries before the Europeans arrived. The blending of the Carib, African, French and English cultures is celebrated on Creole Day at the end of October or in the beginning of November, when everyone wears national costume to go to work or school.

Cocoa and coffee-growing under the French gave way to the cultivation of sugar and limes under the British. Bananas became the byword for economic success in the 1930s, but with plantation economies in decline, Dominica turned to eco-tourism. The **Waitukubuli National Trail** (tel: 767-266 5864; www.

Carib craftsman

waitukubulitrail.dm) runs 115 miles (184km) from the far north to the far south, touching both the east and west coasts, and meanders up and down mountains, across rivers and through forest reserves – it's stunning scenery and a hiker's dream.

Natural wonders

Dominica has two cruise ship terminals: Portsmouth, the northern port, is the perfect starting point for a boat ride along Indian River, for scenic wanderings in the Cabrits National Park, or for a trip into Carib Territory. Roseau, the island's capital, in the south, offers an even wider range of options, from a Jeep safari into the tropical interior to a trek to the Valley of Desolation and Boiling Lake.

Most cruise lines focus on trips (by minibus or Jeep) to the Emerald Pool, Titou Gorge or Trafalgar Falls, but you can go independently by taxi, too. You can also go on kayak, canyoning, scuba-diving and snorkelling trips, as well as whale-watching safaris off the west coast.

Under the sea

Part of Dominica's appeal is the sharpness with which the ocean floor drops off from the shore, reaching depths of several hundred metres. Most shore excursions include the option of exploring the reefs or snorkelling in the shallows.

Scuba-diving is mostly around Soufrière Bay and Scotts Head, where hot and cold water springs bubble under the surface. But diving is also feasible in the north, around the Cabrits Peninsula – and at night, when octopuses, turtles, stingrays and the black-tipped reef sharks reveal themselves.

ROSEAU

Tatty tin-roofed houses and old French colonial buildings with hanging verandas give **Roseau** ❹ (pronounced Ro-zo) a ramshackle air. Dominicans are dedicated to the land and most have their own vegetable 'gardens' either up in the forest or next to their home. Saturday is market day when the bounty of the countryside is brought into town.

A T-shaped cruise ship pier allows you to disembark on Bayfront in the middle of town for some sightseeing followed by a meal at the historic Fort Young, now a waterfront hotel. The engaging **Dominica Museum** (Mon–Fri 8am–4pm; tel: 767-448 2401), is housed in the old post office, and covers everything from island geology and economy to the history of the slave trade. Behind it is the Old Market Plaza, still used by vendors of crafts and souvenirs, containing the old, red market cross. A walk up King George V Street will lead you to the

The forest and mangroves are a haven for birdlife

> **Carib ancestors**
>
> South American Indians from the Orinoco River region are likely to be the ancestors of the 3,000 Caribs/Kalinago who continue to survive in Dominica on fishing, weaving, carving, and basket-making.

Botanical Gardens (daily 6am–7pm; tel: 767-503 4630), the main recreational park, used for cultural events. In 1979, Hurricane David devastated the vegetation, leaving uprooted trees still visible, including an African baobab tree. There is still a varied collection of tropical trees, however, proof that everything in Dominica grows at a rapid rate.

Trafalgar Falls

Most cruise lines offer a Jeep safari into the rainforest and to **Trafalgar Falls** (daily 7.30am–7pm), or you can take a taxi. From the capital you cross a valley that was once a productive lime and cocoa plantation. Kalabash trees, bananas, avocados and mangoes line the winding roads. Beyond are orchids, heliconia and the red-flowering ginger lily, as well as the cinnamon tree.

The short trail to the waterfalls is signalled by a handy bar and restaurant and craft vendors round the car park. An invigorating but comfortable climb through dense vegetation ends in a viewing platform overlooking two waterfalls. Keen swimmers can clamber over slippery rocks to bathe in the pool, but swimming is better at the **Titou Gorge**, where hot and cold streams intermingle in a natural plunge pool.

The Boiling Lake

One of the toughest trails in the Caribbean, the hike to the **Boiling Lake** is used as a fitness test by the Dominican army, and is offered only by cruise lines with a fair proportion of active passengers.

This full-day hike from the Titou Gorge up into the **Morne Trois Pitons National Park**, a UNESCO World Heritage Site, takes up to four hours in each direction. Rewards include the pleasures of passing under canopies of greenery formed by giant tree ferns, of fording mineral-rich streams, relishing rare views of Martinique and Guadeloupe, and climbing knife-edged ridges into a primeval landscape.

The track passes through the **Valley of Desolation**, a lunar landscape in a long, jagged volcanic fissure, with boiling pools of mud and vents and geysers belching out stinking clouds of sulphurous gases.

Suddenly the Boiling Lake comes into view, it is usually shrouded in clouds of steam. When the mists clear, the magma-heated cauldron reveals a surface heaving with bubbles – the second largest

Trafalgar Falls

Valley of Desolation

pot of boiling water in the world.

PORTSMOUTH

Smaller cruise ships sometimes dock in **Portsmouth** ㉟, within easy reach of **Cabrits National Park** (daily 8am-6pm), a spectacular dry tropical forest full of bay, mahogany, sandbox, white cedar and logwood. Among the trees are the lovingly restored 18th-century British fortifications of **Fort Shirley**, complete with gun batteries, storehouses and officers' quarters. It is a moving sight to see small cruise ships under sail come into Prince Rupert Bay and anchor just under the fortress, much as ships must have done since the 18th century when it was built. The seascape around the headland is a protected marine park providing excellent diving and snorkelling.

South of town, a popular excursion is to travel by wooden boat along the **Indian River**, festooned with foliage, and the boatmen will point out the wildlife as you go. There's no need to book in advance as enterprising boatmen will be vying to take you.

From Portsmouth you can also take a trip to the **Carib Territory** along the northeastern wild Atlantic coast, where Dominica's Carib/Kalinago Indians grow cassava (manioc), live in houses built on stilts and sell colourful basketwork from stalls by the roadside. In the Carib Territory is a model village, **Kalinago Barana Auté** (daily 9am-4pm; tours; 767-445 7979), where guides explain the culture and history of the people and you can watch women weaving their intricate and beautiful baskets, before a singing and dancing folklore troupe bids visitors a traditional farewell.

MARTINIQUE

As with Guadeloupe, arriving in Martinique is like taking a big step into France spiked with a large dose of Caribbean flavour. Strange as it may seem, disembarking here means that you are entering the French Republic and visiting a far-flung corner of the European Union, where the local currency is the euro, and the people speak French.

It may not feel much like it to begin with, but this Caribbean island is politically and constitutionally a part of France. Since 1946, when its people voted to become an overseas *département*, Martinique, like Guadeloupe, has been a little tropical

WHALE WATCHING

Dominica is the ideal place to spot pilot whales, false-killer whales, sperm whales and spotted whales, as well as bottle-nosed dolphins. Between November and March, a classic whale and dolphin trip offers a 90 percent success rate in spotting both creatures. The catamarans are equipped with sonar, backed up by a look-out scanning the surface for tell-tale signs. The boats head along the west coast, stopping regularly to take soundings. The humpback whale is more often heard than seen, and you may see one just basking at the surface, like a huge rock, until after about 40 minutes or so it flips its great black fin tail and dives back down into the depths. The pilot whale prefers to travel in pods of 60, while a sperm whale might be accompanied by a 6-metre (20ft) calf. As for dolphins, they love to surf the wake of a boat.

piece of Europe. Its people are French citizens, enjoying the same rights as any other *citoyens*, and in many ways act just like their European compatriots, but with one major exception – they are also Caribbean.

As you travel about the island you will notice how French it is, compared with other islands – the well-maintained roads, signs and industrial zones and the villages and towns with their churches, squares and town halls. But the difference is that they are located around a bay, edged with black beaches the further north you go, and white beaches to the south. The church and square lead on to a promenade and jetty jutting out into the bay, where each fishing community hauls in their catch and sells it in the beachside pavilions. Here you can hear the locals discussing the state of the world in Créole, a French-based patois.

The coastline of Martinique

Fort-de-France

Cruise ships arrive in **Fort-de-France ㊱**, the island's main port and capital, a city of some 100,000 inhabitants. Some dock at Quai des Tourelles, to the east of the old city, by the naval dockyard. From here, it is a short taxi ride into the centre, or a long, hot walk. If you are lucky your ship will berth at the purpose-built **Pointe Simon Terminal** (www.martiniquecruise.com/pointe-simon), close to the heart of the city. In a matter of minutes you can be in the bustling and unmistakably French-flavoured shopping streets of the capital. There is little to keep you at the cruise terminal and it is better to head straight out on to boulevard Alfassa, the road running parallel to the waterfront, where you'll find plenty of public minibuses to take you to different parts of the island.

Like most Caribbean ports, Fort-de-France has had its fair share of fires, earthquakes and other natural disasters, so there are many modern structures among the more interesting 19th-century (and earlier) buildings. What hasn't changed, however, is the grid of narrow streets, which are constantly jammed with traffic. Numerous small boutiques selling the latest Paris fashions are tucked between shabby shops offering local crafts and commodities. Crossing the pedestrianised rue de la République and rue Victor Schoelcher (named after an anti-slavery campaigner) is rue Victor Hugo, where a couple of small shopping malls offer an impressive array of designer perfumes and clothing. Further up rue de la République you reach a square and a much larger shopping mall, Cour Perrinon, with a car park.

> **Diamond Rock**
>
> The Rocher du Diamant (Diamond Rock), off the south coast, an outcrop off volcanic stone jutting from the sea, was occupied by the British for 18 months in 1805–6 and renamed HMS *Diamond*.

Restaurants and markets

The centre of Fort-de-France can be explored comfortably on foot in just a few hours, and there will still be time afterwards for a leisurely meal at one of the city's many excellent restaurants (try the delicious *accras*, deep-fried fritters stuffed with prawns or salted cod). But no French town would be worth its salt if it didn't have a market or two, and Fort-de-France has its share. The busy open-air markets, which operate all day every day, are most colourful on Friday and Saturday. The fish market takes place from early in the morning until dusk on the banks of the Rivière Madame, a 15-minute walk north of the Pointe Simon terminal. The nearest market to the port, the Grand Marché, has a few vegetable stalls and vendors in Martinican dress mostly selling crafts, spices and souvenirs.

Fruit market in Fort-de-France

Metal landmarks

Occasional buildings stand out as a reminder of Martinique's long French history. Some houses have ornate gingerbread fretwork, a style imported from Louisiana in the 19th century, intricate wrought-ironwork and pretty pastel colours. Most eye-catching, perhaps, are two buildings credited to the French architect Henri Picq, a contemporary of Gustave Eiffel and, some claim, the true designer of the Eiffel Tower. The Romanesque-style **St Louis Cathedral** (tel: 596-496 60 59 00), on rue Schoelcher, hints at the architect's love affair with metal girders and joists, its steel-reinforced spire rising 60 metres (200ft) into the sky. Built in 1895 to withstand any earthquake, this strange blend of tradition and innovation, known as the 'iron cathedral', has a cool interior and fine stained-glass windows.

A couple of streets further east stands Pick's other lasting contribution to the capital's exotic architectural heritage. The imposing library, the **Bibliothèque Schoelcher** (Mon 1–5.30pm, Tue–Fri 8.30am–5.30pm; tel: 596-596 66 68 30), is a spectacular blend of Romanesque, Byzantine and Egyptian influences, again dominated by prefabricated cast-iron and steel features that nod to the design and construction of the Eiffel Tower. With ornate gables, a large glass dome and coloured metal panels, this is a truly unique building, lit up at night, and decorated with clusters of French flags and exotic tropical trees.

> ### Empress Joséphine
>
> The Empress Joséphine, Napoléon Bonaparte's first wife, was born in Martinique in 1763. It is believed she was behind her husband's decision to reinstate slavery in 1802, after it had been abolished during the French Revolution. A statue of her in La Savane was decapitated in a symbolic act of vandalism in 1991.

> **Ferry tickets**
>
> Two companies run ferries between Fort-de-France and Trois Ilets, 15 minutes away to the south. Buy a single ticket so that you can return on either ferry, otherwise you might find yourself having to pay twice for the journey.

Out of the windows you can see Fort-de-France's 'green lung', the large expanse of grass, palms and tamarind trees known as **La Savane** that contains the city centre to the east. Traditionally the place for sitting, gossiping and whiling the hours away, you can browse through the collections of T-shirts and mass-produced Haitian-style paintings in the covered craft market opposite the waterfront or just sit on one of the benches and watch the coming and going of local ferries that set off from the nearby pier. Also in the gardens is a statue of Pierre Belain d'Esnambuc, who claimed the island for France in 1635 and founded the original fort in St Pierre.

Alternatively, have a drink at one of the hotels or restaurants along the rue de la Liberté, next to La Savane.

Fort St Louis

As you sail into Fort-de-France, you cannot miss the impressive bulk of **Fort St Louis**. The citadel has been continuously occupied by the French military since the mid-17th century and is still an active naval base, but parts of it can be visited. One interesting feature is its unusually low ceilings, reputedly designed to deter attacks from taller British troops in the era of inter-European rivalry.

St-Pierre

Martinique is not a large island, but it is clearly impossible to see everything in the space of a few hours in port. Most cruise ship excursions involve a trip to a rum distillery, to some beautiful botanical gardens or to the historic town of St-Pierre, victim of the 20th-century's worst volcanic disaster. All these are definitely worth doing, although the expedition to St-Pierre takes an hour each way.

Perhaps the most evocative site in Martinique is the town of **St-Pierre**, situated on the northwest coast under the brooding volcano, Montagne Pelée. In May 1902, this volcano erupted, killing all but one – he had been thrown in jail the night before for drunkenness – of the town's 30,000 inhabitants and devastating what was known as the 'Paris of the Antilles'. Many of the ruins of this sophisticated and fun-loving place, such as its grand theatre and main church, lie just as they have for more than a century. A new town has grown up through the rubble of the old, with cafés and restaurants along the black sand beach and smart promenade, to refresh the curious visitor. There is a restored covered market on the waterfront and the local tourist office organises fascinating tours of the historic ruins. The **Musée Vulcanologique Franck Perret** (daily 9am–6pm; tel: 596-596 78 15 16) has graphic images and artefacts – such as a church bell twisted by the heat of the volcano – from before and after the cataclysm and explains how modern science has made a repetition of this natural disaster impossible.

Les Anses d'Arlet

Rum and gardens

Martinique is dotted with sugar plantations and rum distilleries, producing the world-famous *rhum agricole*, a white rum made from sugar cane juice rather than molasses. Most are open for free visits, but you will be encouraged to taste (and buy) some of the potent liquor. The **Distillerie Depaz** (Tues-Fri 10am-1pm, 1.30pm-4pm, Sat 9am-1pm, 1.30pm-4pm; www.depaz.fr), north of St-Pierre, offers a well-marked trail through each stage of rum manufacturing.

Those more interested in tropical flora should take a tour to the **Jardin de Balata** (daily 9am–6pm, last entry 4.30pm; tel: 596-496 64 48 73; www.jardindebalata.fr), on the steep, twisting **Route de la Trace**, which cuts through the rainforested mountains north of Fort-de-France to Le Morne Rouge. At their best after the rainy season at the end of the year, these gardens have a stunning collection of flowers, exotic trees and shrubs. Nearby, the **Eglise de Sacré Coeur** (tel: 596-496 64 34 18) is a smaller but almost exact replica of the Parisian original, standing among tropical foliage with spectacular mountain views.

ST LUCIA

Sandwiched between Martinique and St Vincent, St Lucia (pronounced *Loo-sha*) is the largest of the Windward Islands at 43km (27 miles) long and 22km (14 miles) wide. With a calm Caribbean coastline acting as a counterpoint to the wind-buffeted Atlantic shore, the mango-shaped island is seductively lush and has preserved its green mountainous heart with banana plantations giving way to vibrant forests. The south is dominated by the Pitons, the jungle-clad twin peaks that symbolise St Lucia.

A cultural mélange

Culturally, the island is an engaging mix, with Caribbean flair, Creole artlessness and French finesse underscored by traditional

British values. The island has changed hands 14 times, with the French and British flags alternating from 1650, when French settlers first landed. From the 1760s the island operated a plantation economy, dependent on African slave labour. St Lucia became British for good in 1814; it gained independence in 1979 but remains part of the Commonwealth. English is the official language but Kwéyòl (Creole patois) is commonplace – French and English vocabulary intertwined with African grammar.

Until recently, agriculture, chiefly bananas, was the mainstay of the economy, but recently the island has made a successful transition to tourism. St Lucia now has a variety of luxurious hotels, midrange all-inclusive resorts and low-key traditional inns for those who wish to stay on.

CASTRIES

As a port of call, **Castries** ❼ is perfectly suited to the largest cruise ships, which dock at the **Pointe Seraphine Cruise Terminal** on the north side of the harbour or at **La Place Carenage** (daily 9am–8pm; tel: 758-453 0670), Queen Elizabeth II dock, on the south side. Both sides have information bureaux, communications centres and duty-free shops. A variety of excursions are also available in air-conditioned minibuses. Taxis queue up

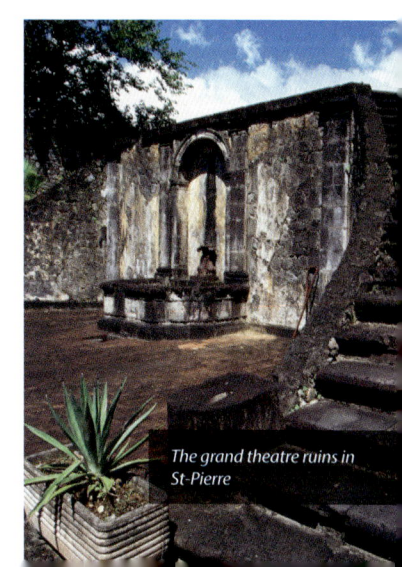

The grand theatre ruins in St-Pierre

The Pitons at sunset

offering guided trips to those who prefer to look around on their own, but it's important to remember that the ship will not wait for you.

Water taxis ply the harbour between Pointe Seraphine and La Place Carenage. The latter is right by the Vendors' Arcade and the Central Market, which is busiest on Friday or Saturday. Many old colonial buildings were destroyed in fires in 1927 and 1948 but the iron market survived, as did houses on Brazil Street and the Roman Catholic cathedral containing paintings by St Lucian artist, Dunstan St Omer.

Literary hero

The main square in Castries was renamed **Derek Walcott Square** in 1993, in honour of the St Lucian poet who won the Nobel Prize for literature. The square is shaded by a huge, 400-year-old Saman tree known locally as a *massair*; the story goes that a foreigner once asked the name of the tree and was told *massair*, which simply means 'I don't know' in Kwéyòl.

On top of the hill to the south of the town is the **Morne Fortune Historic Area** where, along with some remarkable views, you will find the old military buildings of Fort Charlotte, originally built by the French in 1768 and completed by the British over forty years later in 1814.

Southwest to the Pitons

If you head southwest and inland from town through the hills, you will come to banana plantations in **Cul de Sac Valley**. St Lucians claim that the volcanic soil makes their bananas the sweetest, juiciest ones on earth. The blue plastic bags you see covering them help retain moisture and protect them from insects and from getting too much sun, reducing the need for treating the crops with chemicals. The west coast road twists and turns southwards to the lovely fishing village of **Anse la Raye**, where trinket-sellers and fishermen cluster around the beachfront.

From here, the road skirts the lush rainforest giving glimpses of the dramatic **Pitons**, the twin cones which tower over the trees. **Gros Piton** rises more than 774 metres (2,540ft) above the sea, while **Petit Piton** stands 716 metres (2,350ft) high.

The peaks have always had a certain mystique: the Amerindians left sacred carvings on the rock, believing that the Petit Piton, the 'small' peak that dwarfs Soufrière,

Taxi minder

Taxis in Castries are well organised with an official 'minder' at the taxi rank who establishes routes, states prices and helps form small groups to visit places together. Prices are standardised for set routes but you can check at the tourist office booth located close by.

was giving birth to a baby. In the rainforest, mahogany and red cedars grow, as well as the gommier trees where the island parrots live. This part of the island was badly hit by Hurricane Tomas in 2010.

Soufrière

The quaintly ramshackle town of **Soufrière** nestles under the twin peaks and marks the gateway to a fascinating 3-hectare (7-acre) volcanic crater, **La Soufrière Sulphur Springs** (tel: 758-459 7686; http://soufrierefoundation.org). No longer active, the volcano's sulphurous vapours are believed by some to have a positive effect on the sinuses and the springs to have therapeutic value. However, most visitors are overwhelmed by the rotten egg-like smell of the sulphur. The crater, which collapsed about 40,000 years ago, has

Kayaking in St Lucia

bubbling pools of lava that steam away like an inferno.

Diamond Falls

Nearby are the beautifully maintained **Diamond Botanical Gardens and Mineral Baths** (Mon–Fri 9am–5pm, Sun 10am–3pm; tel: 758-459 7155; http://diamondstlucia.com). The gardens were created in 1785, just before the French Revolution, with funds provided by Louis XVI. While it is considered unsafe to swim in the volcanic falls, bathing in the rejuvenating mineral baths, fed by hot springs, is permissible. Among the foliage and primary colours in the garden are bold red and yellow crab's claw, ginger lily, rare orchids, trailing red heliconia, mimosa, poinsettia, and over 140 types of ferns.

The spectacular volcanic Diamond Falls

Sailing and snorkelling

An alternative way to explore the west coast is by sea, which can be organised through the cruise line or at the marina in Castries. Boat tours can include a spot of diving, snorkelling, swimming or sport fishing. **Anse Chastanet**, just north of Soufrière, is the best place for snorkelling and diving, as its reef is in a national marine park. Halfway along the west coast lies **Marigot Bay**, a magnificent steep-sided cove. The picturesque bay is full of yachts bobbing in the harbour and there are several hotels and restaurants on the waterfront.

At the beach in Barbados

Rodney Bay

To the north of Castries lie sheltered bays, beautiful beaches, hotels, a marina, historic landmarks and shopping malls. **Rodney Bay** is the main resort area, where **Reduit Beach** is one of the best stretches of sand on the island. Plenty of water sports are offered here and it is a pleasant place to spend the day. Shopping is good in the Baywalk Mall (tel: 758-452 6666; www.baywalkslu.com) at the junction of the main highway and Reduit Beach Road, with designer outlets, a supermarket and also a casino. The road is lined with restaurants, bars, cafés and ice cream parlours, as well as banks, ATMs, tour operators and cybercafés.

Further along the highway you get to the huge entrance of the **Rodney Bay Marina** with more restaurants and bars. This is also the finishing point of an annual sailing event, the Atlantic Rally for Cruisers.

At the far northern end of Rodney Bay lies the **Pigeon Island National Landmark** (daily 9.30am–5pm; interpretative centre closed on Sun; tel: 758-453 2791) and the ruins of Fort Rodney, where there is another good beach. Once used as a lookout post during the European tugs of war, the park is now the main venue for the **St Lucia Jazz Festival** (tel: 758-452 4094; http://stlucia-jazz.org) every April/May. Kayaking trips can be arranged around Pigeon Island.

A day of adventure

Active shore excursions include an aerial tram ride through the rainforest canopy followed by zip-lining through the trees, a jungle bike ride, ATV tours or jeep safaris. One of the best routes heads south to the waterfall close to Anse la Raye and visits the restored 18th-century **Sikwi Sugar Mill**. Golfers can prebook to play at the **St Lucia Golf Resort and Country Club** or at **Sandals St Lucia**.

BARBADOS

The most easterly of the Windward Islands, Barbados is a coral island, not volcanic like most of its neighbours with dramatic mountains and lush rainforests. Instead, it has open, rolling countryside with fields of sugar cane rippling in the breezes that come in off the Atlantic, which crashes in huge rollers onto the sweeping beaches of the exposed east coast.

Outside the busy capital Bridgetown, the 430-sq km (166-sq mile) island is dotted with sleepy villages and beautiful botanical gardens and plantation houses. The chattel houses, wooden shacks that were once home to plantation workers, have become an architectural feature. Painted in primary colours and pastel shades, with intricate fretwork around the windows, they often double as craft shops.

The sheltered west coast is lined with some of the Caribbean's most glamorous and expensive hotels, whose patrons return year after year. The island has gained a reputation as a millionaire's hideaway, particularly thanks to US$1,500-a-night establishments like Sandy Lane (tel: 246-444 2000; www.sandylane.com), and several smart, exclusive restaurants.

Although it is increasingly influenced by the US, Barbados has a distinctly British feel, with cricket played on village greens and red post boxes. The island was settled by the British in the 17th century and is still a member of the Commonwealth. It is clean,

> **Festival time**
>
> Crop Over starts at the end of June with Pic-o-de-Crop calypso competitions and culminates in a massive Kadooment Day parade on the first Monday in August where revellers parade the streets in eye-catching beaded costumes adorned with feather wings. This is often when politicians can find themselves at the sharp end of the calypso songwriters' pens.

friendly and regarded as safe, although the usual issues of extreme wealth flaunted in the face of relative poverty exist.

Despite years of colonialism, Barbados is flourishing and has its own colourful heritage; its annual Crop Over festival held in the summer, historically celebrating the sugar cane harvest, is rated as one of the best events in the Caribbean. The Barbados Reggae Festival in April is the biggest on the island, featuring local and international reggae artists.

A turnaround port

With ships calling daily during the high-season winter months, Barbados is one of the Caribbean islands' most visited by cruise passengers. Apart from an added gleam in the eyes of local shopkeepers, a cruise ship in town does not make a vast difference to daily life, since locals are used to tourists and the island has a well-developed infrastructure, and the many visitor attractions are well distributed.

Many cruise lines start and finish cruises here, particularly those carrying a high proportion of passengers from Europe, since the island is well served by non-stop international flights. Over half a million tourists visit Barbados every year.

It is one of the easiest destinations in which to stay on after a cruise – well worth doing, if only to sample the nightlife, which varies from fine cuisine under the stars at QP Bistro restaurant, formerly The Cliff, (tel: 246-432 0797; www.qpbistro.com) to dancing all night long at a beachfront nightclub on the south coast.

The cruise terminal is about 2km (1 mile) from the centre of **Bridgetown** ㊳, at the **Deep Water Harbour**. It has a duty-free shopping centre for jewellery, cameras and electrical goods (which are still more expensive than in the US or Europe), as well as souvenir stalls selling T-shirts. You need a passport, airline ticket or cruise line ID to qualify for duty-free prices. Visitors can also hire bikes and arrange tours at the terminal. Cars are available to rent just outside the terminal building; you will need your driving licence from home and BDS$10 for a local drivers' permit.

Other facilities include an internet café, sports bar and restaurant. **Brighton Beach** is right next to the port, where you can relax if you don't want to explore, but as always when on vacation, keep an eye on your valuables.

Rum in the sun

Also located on Brighton Beach is the West Indies Rum Distillery (tel: 246-425 9301). Close by on Spring Garden Highway, is the **Mount Gay** rum blending and bottling plant (tel: 246-227 8864; www.mountgayrum.com), which operates comprehensive signature, buffet lunch or cocktail tours, including a tasting of one of the local favourite rums.

Getting around Barbados

Barbados is quite an easy island to explore independently and is only 34km (21 miles) long, although twisting country roads make distances seem further, especially when the sugar cane is high and views are obscured. Shore excursions involve many permutations of the island tour and are usually comprehensive, but the fun of exploring is lost if you travel by coach. An open-sided Mini Moke is a better way to get around, and in a day trip from Bridgetown you should be able to get to the north and return via the wild scenery of the Atlantic coast.

Driving is on the left, and rush hour starts at 4pm. However, while all roads lead to Bridgetown, progress may be extremely slow around this time (nobody is in much of a hurry on Barbados anyway), so do allow for this – and also for getting lost, as the country roads are not well signposted.

Taxis are plentiful and line up outside the cruise terminal. Drivers are more than willing to do day trips. Fares are supposed to be fixed but there is no meter system, so always agree a price in advance. The island has a comprehensive bus network (www.transportboard.com) and the single flat fare is a bargain, but again, journeys can take a considerable time.

Palm-fringed Crane beach

BRIDGETOWN

If you have only a few hours, there is plenty to see and do without leaving **Bridgetown**. The road into Bridgetown leads down to the **Careenage**, lined with yachts and fishing boats. This is where ships used to have their hulls repaired or cleaned. Take a stoll through Independence Arch on the pedestrianised Chamberlain Bridge , which was once a swing bridge. Many local tour companies offer packages which will take you from the port through Bridgetown to many nearby beach bars, including The Boatyard (tel: 246-826 4448; www.theboatyard.com).

Walking in Bridgetown

National Heroes

Back across the bridge is **National Heroes Square** (formerly Trafalgar Square) dedicated to 10 Barbadian heroes – but no longer to Lord Nelson whose statue still stands in the centre and will be relocated one day.

At the northern end of the square the Gothic-style Parliament building dates back to 1872, while nearby **St Michael's Cathedral** stands on the grounds of the first church in Barbados, which was built in 1665.

Broad Street, off to the left of Heroes Square, is the main shopping area. Cave Shepherd (www.caveshepherd.com) and Harrison's are the principal Bajan department stores; if you don't

> **Washington's home**
>
> George Washington spent two months in Barbados in 1751, when he was 19. The house where he stayed, by the Garrison Savannah, has been restored and is open to visitors (daily 9am–4pm; 246-228 5461).

have time to leave town to shop, look out for the beautifully crafted pottery from Earthworks, which is on sale in Cave Shepherd. The Best of Barbados (tel: 246-573 6900; www.best-of-barbados.com) gift shops are a good bet for locally made souvenirs – many items for sale are produced on the island.

Driving from Bridgetown to the south coast you reach the **Garrison Savannah**, dating from the mid-17th century and once the most important military location on the island, and the home to a historic horse racing track (tel: 246-626 3980; www.barbados-turfclub.org). The area is packed with historic interest, with forts, monuments, military buildings and the world's largest collection of 17th-century cannons (tel: 246-430 0900 for a tour). The **Barbados Museum** (Mon–Sat 9am–4pm; tel: 246-538 0201) is also here, displaying everything from Amerindian artefacts to colonial furniture, and rare historical maps of the island.

THE PLATINUM COAST

The west coast, dubbed the **Platinum Coast**, is lined with smart hotels and exclusive villas hidden by trees and iron gates. Drive up Highway 1 and you'll see that Bajan life continues regardless, among the holiday paradises. There are several public paths down to the soft white sand and you can swim from the beach in front of the luxurious **Sandy Lane Hotel** (www.sandylane.com) – no one can own a beach in Barbados.

Holetown is where the first settlers landed in 1627, an event which is commemorated every February with street fairs, concerts and a music festival. There is a wide choice of restaurants and branches of the main Bridgetown stores in the shopping centre, plus gift shops in the Chattel Village.

Nearby, **Folkestone Marine Park and Visitors Centre** (Mon–Fri 9am–5pm; tel: 246-536 0648) has an underwater snorkel trail over a 11km (7-mile) coral reef (glass-bottom boats for non-swimmers) as well as changing facilities.

Speightstown

If you're in need of some solid ground beneath your feet, take a guided hike along the **Arbib Nature and Heritage Trail** (Wed, Thu, Sat 9am–2pm; tel: 246-234 9010), which starts at St Peter's Church in **Speightstown**, once a thriving port shipping sugar to England. Twinned with Charleston, South Carolina, Speightstown has a faded charm with two-storey, balconied 'shop houses' typical

CRICKET, LOVELY CRICKET…

Barbadians are passionate about cricket – it's their national game. When the West Indies are playing at the Kensington Oval, within walking distance of the port, everyone tunes in to their radios and a carnival atmosphere prevails. However, the West Indies team has been experiencing a downturn in its fortunes during this millennium and its international ranking has fallen from its heyday, which lasted from the 1960s to early 1990s.

Cricket was introduced to the West Indies by the British military more than 200 years ago to encourage community spirit. Since then Barbados has produced a long line of brilliant players, and hosted some of the matches in the World Cup in 2007. Contact the Barbados Cricket Association, tel: 246-538 1325; www.babarbadoscricket.org.

Wild green monkey

of an early Barbadian town dwelling, with the business premises on the ground floor and living quarters above. The restored 17th-century **Arlington House** (Mon–Fri 9am–5pm, Sat 9am–3pm; tel: 246-422 4064) is a fine example, and has a museum showing Barbados' early connections with the Carolinas.

Further north, the landscape becomes flatter and more desolate with remote beaches, rocky cliffs and pounding waves. Cut across to see the green monkeys and tortoises at the well laid out **Barbados Wildlife Reserve** (daily 10am-5pm; tel: 246-422 8826) and for a forest walk with fantastic views at **Grenade Hall Forest and Signal Station** (charge covers both).

Further on, you can look round **St Nicholas Abbey** (Wed-Mon 9.30am–3.30pm; www.stnicholasabbey.com), a 17th-century Jacobean mansion and one of the oldest houses on the island, where they make their own rum. A worthwhile detour is to **Morgan Lewis Mill** (tel: 246-426 2421) in St Andrew. Restored by the Barbados National Trust, it is the island's only working windmill.

THE WILD EAST COAST

Approaching the east coast from the north, you can see miles of Atlantic rollers and craggy limestone coral cliffs all the way to **Bathsheba**, an authentic village unscathed by time and popular with surfers. It is not safe to swim in the sea here but you can cool off in the many rock pools before enjoying a good Barbadian meal at **Round House (tel: 246-433 9678;** www.roundhousebarbados.com) overlooking the shore or at the historic **Atlantis Hotel** (tel: 246-433 9445; www.atlantishotelbarbados.com) in Tent Bay.

As you leave Bathsheba, the **Andromeda Botanic Gardens** (daily 10am–4pm; www.andromedabarbados.com) is a wonderful place for a rest from driving. Waterfalls splash gently through the gardens, dazzling with tropical blooms from all over the Caribbean.

Natural wonders

In the heart of the island are three fascinating examples of natural Barbados. The **Flower Forest** in St Joseph (daily 8am–4pm; tel: 246-433 8152; www.flowerforestbarbados.com) is a pretty walking trail through lush tropical gardens. **Welchman Hall Gully** (daily 9am–3.30pm; tel: 246-438 6671; www.welchmangullybarbados.com) is a deep ravine just off Highway 2, maintained by the National Trust (http://barbadosnationaltrust.org), with a trail leading through rainforest. Look out for green monkeys and colourful birds in the trees.

Close by is **Harrison's Cave** (Wed-Mon 9am-2.30pm; tel: 246-417 3700), a vast limestone cave complete with underground lakes, cascading water, stalactites and stalagmites, all of which can be seen from a small electric

Harrison's Cave

Clear waters of the Grenadines

train that carries passengers through the cave network.

Sporting chances

There are plenty of activities on offer in Barbados. The island is awash with golf courses and if you book far enough in advance you can play at the prestigious course at **Sandy Lane** (tel: 246-444 2000; www.sandy-lane.com) or at the public **Barbados Golf Club** (tel: 246-538 4653; www.barbadosgolfclub.com) in the south, also a championship golf course.

Horseriding, biking and hiking in the central highlands is a good way to feel the essence of the countryside, and as for the sea, there is windsurfing, best on the east coast in the winter months, and sailing off the south coast beaches, and the waves at the magnificent **Crane Beach** in the southeast are perfect for body boarding. Afterwards you can relax with a rum punch on the Crane Hotel's wonderful clifftop terrace (www.thecrane.com).

THE SOUTHERN CARIBBEAN

Cruising further south, it is mainly the smaller cruise and sailing ships that call at the 30-odd coral islands collectively known as the Grenadines, many of which are tinier than some of the ships. The diving and snorkelling in this part of the Caribbean are exemplary and the idyllic beaches and lagoons practically a cliché. The islands, off the Venezuelan coast, offer a fascinating mix of cultures and landscapes from South American jungle in Trinidad to desert in Aruba.

ST VINCENT AND THE GRENADINES

At 30 by 18km (18 by 11 miles), **St Vincent** is the largest and most developed of the Grenadines; remaining relatively unspoilt, it lies between St Lucia and Grenada and 160km (100 miles) west of Barbados. At **Kingstown** ㉟, the island port and capital, there are berths for two ships, linked to a cruise terminal, so it is rare that ships have to anchor offshore and tender passengers to land as they do at the other Grenadine islands, such as Bequia and Mayreau.

Built in 2001, the terminal at Kingstown has more stores, cafés, bars and fast food outlets than the town centre, where the street hawkers and shops mainly serve local needs. An indoor fruit and vegetable market (Upper Bay) and a covered fish market, known as Little Tokyo, by the dock, provide some colour.

Kingstown's Catholic **Cathedral of the Assumption** (tel: 784-456 1408) is a bizarre mixture of Moorish, Romanesque, Byzantine, Venetian and Flemish architectural styles, despite being built in the 1930s. An 18th-century fortress, **Fort Charlotte** (Mon-Sat 8am–6pm, Sun 2pm-9pm; free; tel: 784-456 1165), which stands guard above the town, has some spectacular views.

Outside Kingstown

There are plenty of taxis waiting outside the terminal, all keen to offer guided tours around the island and, if two or more of you are travelling together, a taxi tour is cheaper than a ship excursion. Alternatively, minibuses heading to specific places leave regularly from the fish market. St Vincent is a lush, forested island, and this is evident in the **Botanic Gardens** in Montrose (daily 7am–5.30pm; tel: 784-493 5824), a five- or 10-minute drive from the port. Established in 1765, they are believed to be the oldest in the

Walking up to La Soufrière

Western Hemisphere and have a breadfruit tree that dates back to the original plant brought to the island by Captain Bligh, of *Mutiny on the Bounty* fame.

Another way of seeing St Vincent is by boat from Kingstown along the Caribbean coast, past sugar and banana plantations, a former whaling village, rocky coves, black sand beaches and mountains, including the Soufrière volcano which last erupted in 1979, and round to the **Falls of Baleine**, where you can swim in the rock-enclosed freshwater pool created by the waterfall.

La Soufrière

The great advantage of visiting St Vincent is the scope for walking tours – from gentle nature hikes right up to a strenuous ascent of the 1,178-metre (3,864ft) **La Soufrière** which erupted in 2021 after decades of inactivity. The latter, however, will take a full day, including getting from Kingstown to the volcano in the island's northeast corner; whether this is feasible depends on your fitness and walking experience, the weather and the departure time of your ship.

Check with the tourist office in the terminal, where it is also possible to hire a guide. For an easier option, try the **Vermont Nature Trails** (daily 7am–5pm; www.nationalparks.gov.vc), through rainforest in the Buccament Valley, about a 20-minute drive away. Or you can take a Jeep safari tour.

BEQUIA AND MAYREAU

While St Vincent remains a real haven for nature-lovers, more cruise ships are choosing to call at **Bequia** ㊵ and Mayreau. **Port Elizabeth** is the entry point for Bequia although only the smallest cruise ships – often sailing vessels – call here, they all have to anchor in Admiralty Bay.

Once on the jetty (where the ferries from St Vincent also disembark), it is only a short walk to a group of smart shops and restaurants, and a tourist information office. There are more places to shop and eat along the harbour front (Belmont Walkway), or you could head inland for a few minutes along Front Street, where you will find an open-air market.

A water heaven

An attractive island, Bequia is really about the water. Snorkelling and scuba diving are the main reasons for coming here, and there are plenty of water taxis to get you around. The best diving sites are within the 12km (7-mile) coral reef, which has been designated a national marine park. You can also travel by boat from the main jetty to the nearest beach. And – unlike on volcanic St Vincent – the beaches are all golden sand.

Mayreau ㊶ is just 2.6 sq km (1 sq mile) of beautiful beaches and palm trees. In the past cotton and cocoa have been grown on the island. Only small cruise ships can anchor here and passengers are tendered to **Saline Bay Beach** or **Salt Whistle Bay** for a relaxing day swimming and snorkelling.

Other Grenadine islands at which some ships call include

Bequia is best

Although good diving is available off St Vincent, if you are going to Bequia, save the experience until then. With more than 30 dive sites, Bequia is renowned for its underwater scenery.

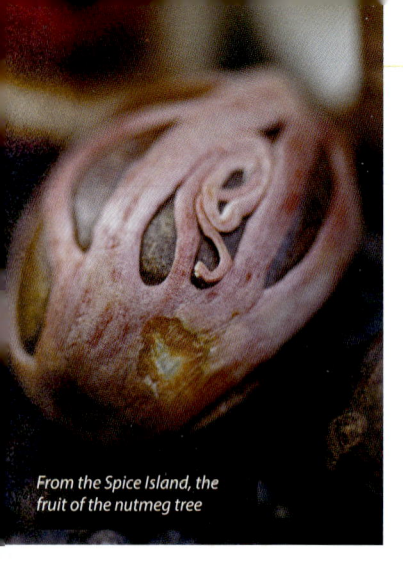

From the Spice Island, the fruit of the nutmeg tree

the five uninhabited islets of **Tobago Cays**, protected by a large reef; the idyllic resort of **Palm Island; Canouan**, with Donald Trump's championship golf course; the larger **Union Island**, a centre for sailors, and **Mustique**. On the latter there is only limited access for cruise ship passengers because the celebrities that stay here guard their privacy fiercely.

GRENADA

Known as the Spice Island, Grenada, just south of the Grenadines, is not only the world's second largest exporter of nutmeg (after Indonesia) but also grows more spices per square kilometre than anywhere else on the planet. This will be evident by the line of hard-selling spice vendors waiting to welcome you ashore at **St George's**, the island capital. However, nutmeg trees were severely damaged by Hurricane Ivan in 2004 and production on Grenada subsequently declined by about 75 per cent. Cocoa has since replaced it as the island's main crop.

Sailors down the centuries have rated St George's one of the world's prettiest harbours. Horseshoe-shaped and set in a long-dormant volcanic crater, it is a natural harbour flanked by two forts (Fort George and Fort Frederick) and has colourful French colonial-style buildings ranged along the waterfront.

Ferries and schooners can dock alongside the harbour, while cruise ships dock at **Melville Street Pier** ㊷, the other side of the promontory on which sits Fort George, where there is a visitors' welcome centre (with telephones, maps, shops and information). Just across the road and up a block is the city's market, where you can find spices, cocoa, hot sauces, jams and jellies, as well as fresh produce. This area is known as Baytown and is joined to the Carenage by a tunnel for vehicles. Pedestrians walk over the hill along Halifax Street and Young Street.

The Carenage

The harbour and promenade is known as the **Carenage**, where you find old warehouses, small shops and offices, and a selection of bars and restaurants. Many of these are on the first floor above shops, allowing the sea breezes to blow through wide open windows with a glorious view of the harbour. You will see plenty of seafood – including conch – on the menus and some traditional Grenadian dishes, made with *tatu* (armadillo), *manicou* (opossum) and iguana, from the island's forests, although these are less common now.

The cafés – like the rest of St George's – are very enjoyable. So is a visit to the ice cream parlour on the harbour front, which has a delicious range of spice-based flavours.

On Young Street, off the Carenage near the cafés, there is the small **Grenada**

Hanging heliconia

SOUTHERN CARIBBEAN

St Vincent & The Grenadines, Grenada, Trinidad & Tobago, Aruba & Curaçao (Lesser Antilles)

Location: St Vincent & The Grenadines (capital Kingstown) lie 160km (100 miles) to the west of Barbados and just north of **Grenada** (St George's), the most southerly of the Windward Islands, toward the bottom of the Lesser Antilles chain. Grenada has two small dependent territories: Carriacou and Petit Martinique. **Trinidad** (Port of Spain), lies 20km (12 miles) off the coast of Venezuela. **Tobago**, lies 34km (21 miles) to the northeast. **Aruba** (Oranjestad) and **Curaçao** (Willemstad) are the most westerly islands and with Bonaire (not a port of call) form the ABC Islands are part of the Kingdom of the Netherlands.

Time zones: UTC/GMT -4 (all the islands)

Pop: 110,000 (St Vincent & The Grenadines); 112,000 (Grenada); 1,399,000 (Trinidad & Tobago); 106,000 (Aruba); 155,000 (Curaçao). Language: English/patois (St Vincent & The Grenadines, Grenada, Trinidad & Tobago); Dutch/Papiamento (Aruba, Curaçao).

Money matters: St Vincent & The Grenadines and Grenada: the East Caribbean dollar (EC$); Trinidad and Tobago: Trinidad and Tobago dollar (TT$); Aruba: Aruban florin/guilder (Af/AWG); Curaçao: the Netherlands Antilles florin (NAf) also known as the Netherlands Antilles guilder (ANG). The islands all accept US dollars (US$).

Telephone & internet: The dialling code is +784 (St Vincent & The Grenadines); +473 (Grenada); +868 (Trinidad & Tobago); +297 (Aruba); +5999 (Curaçao). Internet is widely available.

Calendar highlights: Carnival: Trinidad (Feb/Mar), Grenada (Aug), Curaçao (Jan); Bequia: Bequia Regatta (Easter); Grenadines: Mustique Blues Festival (Jan–Feb); Trinidad: 3-day Hosay Islamic Festival (April, May or June).

National Museum (Mon–Fri 9am–4.30pm, Sat 10am–1.30pm), where exhibits include a bathtub used by Empress Joséphine Bonaparte; and Market Square, which has a lively Saturday market. The second right from Young into Church Street, leads you to the site of St Andrew's Church and the Cathedral, constructed in 1830 but destroyed by the hurricane in 2004.

Grand Anse beach

Just a water-taxi ride around the bay to the south of the harbour is **Grand Anse**, one of the finest 3km (2-mile) stretches of white sand in the Caribbean. The short, breezy journey by water-taxi, which depart regularly from the cruise ship terminal, is much more fun than going by land.

There are strict rules about any kind of development on Grenada, which applies particularly to beaches. Effectively, this comes down to nothing taller than a palm tree and nothing close to the water's edge being allowed. A selection of watersports is available here.

Dramatic sights

A drive through the interior takes in some dramatic sights – waterfalls, mountain valleys, rainforests, lakes and volcanic craters. Although the island is small, driving can be slow, hot and tiring on roads that are sometimes barely adequate, so don't be too ambitious when you have limited time. You can rent a car from agencies along the Carenage but you may prefer to take an organised tour or hire a taxi for a guided tour (negotiate the price before setting off). Local buses are slow and overcrowded but can be an interesting experience.

Most of the dive sites – coral reefs and shipwrecks – are within easy reach of the shore. Snorkellers can reach them from the beach or, occasionally, by a short boat trip. However, the dive site considered

Idyllic swimming ponds

the best – **Kick 'em Jenny**, a large submerged volcano – is further offshore.

Deep-sea fishing is big in Grenada and trips can be organised through charter companies in the harbour to catch marlin, kingfish and yellowfin tuna. The Budget Marine Spice Island Billfish Tournament, at the end of January, is a major event in the island's sporting calendar.

National parks

The **Grand Etang National Park and Forest Reserve** (tel: 473-421 4100) is a rainforest covering the mountainous backbone of the island, with a volcanic crater-turned-lake at its centre. There are hiking and nature trails, and fishing and boating in the shadow of **Mount Qua Qua**, a 700-metre (2,300ft) peak. On the way back, it's worth making a detour to the 15-metre (50ft) **Annandale Falls**.

At the **Gouyave Nutmeg Processing Station** (Mon–Fri 8am–4.30pm; tel: 473-444 8337), north of the capital, you can see how the island's most famous export is handled. The **Dougaldston Spice Estate** is a working spice plantation, growing and processing spices. Here you can buy nutmeg, cinnamon, cloves and other spices.

Belmont Estate (Sun–Fri 8am–4pm; tel: 473-442 9524, www.belmontestate.gd) is a working plantation offering tours of the organic farm, gardens, heritage museum and cocoa processing facilities. Formerly a nutmeg plantation, cocoa has since replaced it as the island's main crop. The organic cocoa produced here (and by other local organic farmers) is used to make the exquisite chocolate produced by the **Grenada Chocolate Factory** (tel: 473-442 0050; www.grenadachocolate.com). If you buy some, don't be worried about it melting in the heat of the tropics. It is so pure that it doesn't melt, but if concerned, buy their cocoa powder instead.

Along the same road, on the east coast, is the **River Antoine Rum Distillery** (tours Mon–Fri 8am–4pm; tel: 473-442 7109), where rum is still made using 18th-century methods.

In the northeast at the tip of the island, **Levera National Park** stretches inland from coral-reef protected white sandy beaches to a lake and mangrove swamp full of exotic plants and birdlife.

TRINIDAD AND TOBAGO

The southernmost islands in the Caribbean archipelago, Trinidad and Tobago are not like the other islands to the north, as they are really small chunks of Venezuela that have drifted away from the mainland. As a result, their geography, flora and fauna are more of a South American nature and has plenty of natural attractions. Tobago is still very different from Trinidad – it is much smaller, less developed and more laidback and tranquil.

TRINIDAD

Cruise ships dock at the modern complex in one of the English-speaking Caribbean's most vibrant cities. Fast-paced **Port of Spain** ⓭ is unique for its ethnic diversity and cultural richness, and mixes styles with a Latin flair arising from its proximity to Venezuela only 11km (7 miles) away. Elegant French-Creole townhouses

Small island

A few small cruise ships anchor off Carriacou, Grenada's sister island 38km (23 miles) away, an unspoilt island where wooden schooners are built by hand.

Trinidad, city of Carnival

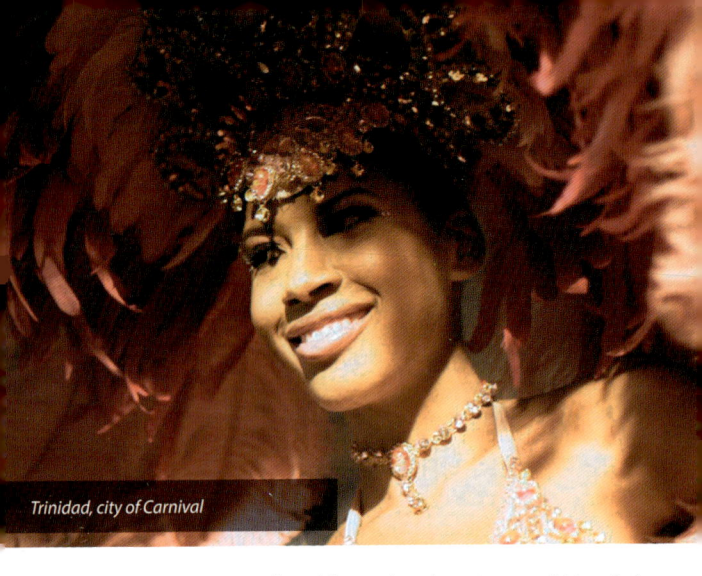

with distinctive gingerbread fretwork and ornate wrought-iron balconies nestle beneath modern, smoked-glass corporate blocks.

This is where the carnival of all Caribbean carnivals climaxes on the streets over the two days before Ash Wednesday, exploding with the colours of thousands of masqueraders driven by turbo-charged soca music, calypso and melodic steel pan.

A tour of the capital

Port of Spain and its suburbs sprawl across a plain that slopes gently from the foothills of the Northern Range down to the Gulf of Paria. On the waterfront, there are plenty of craft shops to peruse as you leave the ship. To the left, on Wrightson Road, is the Breakfast Shed, known for cheap, authentic Creole and East Indian cuisine: fresh fish, fried, stewed or served in a peppery-hot broth laced with ground provisions such as dasheen, eddoes, cassava or green figs (small green bananas) and heavy with dumplings.

Across from the terminal, the Brian Lara Promenade (named after the record-breaking Trinidadian cricketer) in **Independence Square**, is flanked by modern buildings. Here people gather to play chess or enjoy the free soca, steelpan, jazz or gospel concerts. Vendors sell coconuts and doubles – an inexpensive East Indian snack of curried chick peas in batter, garnished with mango or coconut chutney and fiery pepper sauce. Further east on South Quay, a museum in the old Spanish **Fort San Andres** (Tue–Fri 9am–5pm; free) tells the story of Port of Spain and hosts exhibitions by young local artists. The wooden terracotta-painted fort was once Port of Spain's main defence against the British troops.

Although most cruise lines offer guided taxi tours of the city and half- or whole-day excursions outside, it is more exciting (and safe) to walk around the city centre for a couple of hours during the day. For travelling out of the city, there are fixed-rate taxis at the rank

CARNIVAL IN TRINIDAD

Trinidad Carnival has earned its reputation as one of the greatest shows on earth and is the culmination of a year's worth of preparation. During the weekend before the start of Lent, a Carnival King, Queen and Calypso Monarch are crowned to great fanfare. Then from 4am on Carnival Monday until midnight on the Tuesday, normal life in the capital dissolves into one wild and euphoric party that anyone can join. Starting with J'ouvert (opening of day), revellers emerge covered in mud (or paint) portraying demons and banging tins and drums. Later the mas' bands – groups of up to 10,000 people in themed elaborate costumes – parade past the judging stands throughout the city, accompanied by ear-splitting soca, until the street party ends at Las' Lap. Then on Ash Wednesday the preparations for next year begin…

Steel pans, or drums

opposite Frederick Street on Independence Square and cheaper shared-route taxis at Woodford Square.

British-built **Fort George** (daily 9am-5.30pm; tel: 868-623 4714) is just a short taxi or bus ride into the hills above the western suburb of St James, and offers both a breathtaking panorama of the city and views of the islands off the Chaguaramas Peninsula.

Queen's Park Savannah

Frederick Street is the city's main artery, leading north to **Queen's Park Savannah**, via Woodford Square where you will find the imposing **Red House** parliament building. At the top of Frederick Street, opposite Memorial Park is the **National Museum and Art Gallery** (Tue–Sat 10am–4pm; 868-623 0339). The Savannah plays an integral part in Trinidadian life and is the major venue for carnival competitions and cultural shows. On the western flank of the Savannah are the **Magnificent Seven**, a row of early 20th-century colonial mansions, which are superb examples of idiosyncratic Trini-Creole architecture. To the north are the **Emperor Valley Zoo** (daily 8am–6pm; tel: 868-622 3530), the pretty **Botanic Gardens** (daily 6am–6pm) and the **President's House**.

A taste of the island

A choice of half- and whole-day excursions are available outside Port of Spain. West of town is the **Blue Basin Waterfall**, north of Diego Martin; **Maqueripe beach** at the end of the beautiful Tucker Valley; and the **Gasparee Caves** on Gaspar Grande island, a 20-minute round-trip boat ride from the Crews Inn Marina (call 868-634 4364 to book tours). **Maracas Bay**, Trinidad's most popular beach, is a 40-minute drive north of the capital, while to the east is the **Maracas Waterfall**, just up the valley from the original Spanish capital, St Joseph.

Other destinations include **El Tucuche**, the second highest peak (a day's strenuous hike); **Mount St Benedict** monastery, with panoramic views of the central plain; and the **Asa Wright Nature Centre** (daily 9am–5pm; guided walks available – reservations required; http://asawright.org), internationally known for birdwatching. Trinidad has a magnificent variety of bird species. Southeast of the capital is the **Caroni Bird Sanctuary**, where the national bird, the Scarlet Ibis, roosts at dusk.

SCARBOROUGH

While Port of Spain is very much a city, **Scarborough** ㊵, the capital of Trinidad's sister isle, **Tobago**, has both the look and feel of a small provincial town, and most

> ### Steel drums
>
> Steel pan music originated in Trinidad in the 1930s when it was discovered that discarded oil drums produced a wonderful sound when beaten with a stick or the hand.

> **Goat race**
>
> Buccoo is the venue for the traditional goat races that bring Tobago's Easter festivities to a close. Goats are trained, for months in advance, to run the 100 metres (328ft) to the finish line with a handler holding on to them by a rope.

of it can be explored on foot (with a few steep inclines) in a morning. After the multicultural mix of Trinidad, Tobago's predominantly Afro-Creole culture and lifestyle is noticeable, as is the slower pace.

Cruise ship passengers disembark at the modern terminal opposite the busy market, a good spot for sampling hearty Tobagonian cooking, such as curried crab and dumplings. The terminal has basic amenities, and taxis can be hired outside.

In town, the main attractions are the **Botanic Gardens**, the **House of Assembly** on James Park and the **Fort King George** complex, which houses the excellent **Tobago Museum** (Mon–Fri 9am–5pm) and has fantastic views over the town and up the coast.

As the island is only 40km (26 miles) long and 15km (9 miles) wide, it is possible to reach virtually anywhere within a couple of hours by car – idyllic white sand beaches and coral reefs teeming with marine life; superb scuba diving, snorkelling and water sports; waterfalls, volcanic hills and the Western Hemisphere's oldest protected rainforest; abundant bird and wildlife; and authentic Afro Creole culture. The latter can be found at its vibrant best in the inland hilltop villages of **Les Coteaux**, **Whim** and **Moriah**, major venues for July's Heritage Festival (www.tobagoheritagefestival.com) in which Tobago explores its cultural past with lively music and processions.

Beautiful beaches and reefs

Close to Scarborough is the developed southwest end of the island, where most tourist activity is centred round the luxury resorts and hotels at **Crown Point** and **Store Bay**. Glass-bottomed boats can be hired at Store Bay for trips out to **Buccoo Reef** and the Nylon Pool, while the beach at **Pigeon Point** has become a familiar Caribbean icon.

Inland from the windward (southern) coast the **Hillsborough Reservoir** is a favourite birdwatching spot. Further down the coast, the **Argyll Waterfall**, best in the rainy season, is a 10-minute walk from the road. Nearby, you can tour the **Tobago Cocoa Estate** (www.tobagococoa.com), learn about cocoa growing, the chocolate-making process, buy their single-estate fine chocolate and try other local culinary delights.

Divers and nature lovers head for **Speyside** and **Charlotteville**, at the eastern tip. These two fishing villages are spectacularly positioned at the foot of forested hills and are the jumping-off points for some of the best diving in the region.

The beaches to head for (both for bathing and for turtle watching) are on the northern coast: Turtle Beach (Great Courland Bay), Castara, Englishman's Bay, Parlatuvier, Bloody Bay and Man-o-War Bay are all superb.

ARUBA AND CURAÇAO

Just off the coast of Venezuela in the 'deep Caribbean' lie the small islands of Aruba and Curaçao which have a Dutch

Crossing a baby natural bridge, Aruba

heritage. Aruba has been self-governing since 1986, but since 2010, when the Netherlands Antilles was dissolved, both islands are now constituent countries of the Kingdom of the Netherlands.

Inland the terrain is hilly, providing a very different kind of flora and fauna from the rest of the Caribbean.

Aruba's capital

Excellent beaches, world-class shopping, giant casinos, stunning sea views and wild tracts of desert landscape scattered with giant boulders and exotic cacti are all within reach of **Oranjestad** ⓯, Aruba's capital – teeming with people, especially when several ships have docked at the three **Aruba Port Authority terminals** (www.arubaports.com).

Within a few minutes' walk, to the right, you will find the shop-lined L.G. Smith Boulevard, home to **Seaport Market**, and the equally extensive, **Royal Plaza**, crammed with smart shops. Straight ahead is the capital's main shopping area, **Caya G.F. Betico Croes**, where pretty Dutch- and Spanish-style buildings house stores selling cameras, jewellery and alcohol. You can also pick up Delft china, Dutch cheese, Danish silverware and embroidery from Madeira paying low levels of duty and very little sales tax (1.5 percent).

For local colour, head to **Paardenbaai** (Schooner Harbour), which is crammed with brightly painted little boats and craft stalls selling the boat-owners' wares. A few streets up in Wilheminastraad are some magnificent examples of 16th- and 17th-century Dutch architecture. Back on the waterfront is **Wilhemina Park**, a lovely tropical garden.

> ### Diverse dishes
>
> For lunch, you are spoilt for choice with Aruba's diverse population – of Portuguese, Spanish, Venezuelan, Indian, Pakistani, African and Dutch descent – offering a wide range of dishes.

Willemstad

A bet on the beach

Some of the world's best beaches can be found on Aruba. On the island's northwest coast are **Eagle Beach** and **Palm Beach**, long stretches of snowy-white sand bordered by casinos and hotels, which will (for a fee) provide all the facilities you need to swim, sunbathe and lunch in style, although use of the beaches is free. The aptly named **Baby Beach** at the southeastern end of the island has shallow waters and soft sand that is perfect for young children.

En route lies Aruba's oldest village, **San Nicolas**, a former oil refinery and port which is now full of unusual shops and alfresco cafés. Nearer the port, **Spaan Lagoen** (Spanish Lagoon) is a scenic spot which was once the haunt of pirates.

Aruba's sights

With plenty of taxis at the terminal and good tourist information available, it's easy to explore Aruba independently, but for discovering the delights of the **Barcadera Reef** and for sailing trips and jeep safaris, it's best to opt for a cruise line excursion.

The dramatic, rocky landscape of the north includes the famous **Natural Bridge**, hewn by nature from limestone albeit now collapsed (a baby bridge is also here however). Fantastical, rare boulder formations, some with Amerindian drawings on them can be seen at **Ayo** and **Casibari**, and from the 168-metre (551ft) **Hooiberg**, you have a fine view of the fields of gigantic cacti in **Arikok National Park** (tel: 297-585 1234; www.arubanationalpark.org). Bizarre rock formations can also be seen in the cave systems of **Fontein** and **Quadirikiri**.

A TROPICAL AMSTERDAM

Curaçao, 60km long by 11 km (38 by 7 miles) wide, is the largest island in the Dutch Antilles and home to more than 50 different nationalities, who give the place a liberal, cosmopolitan and welcoming atmosphere.

Amsterdam's influence is evident in the architecture of the capital, **Willemstad** ⓰. The mega cruise ships dock at the port's US$9-million terminal, a short walk from town, but smaller ships have the privilege of sailing up St Ana Bay, past the swing-aside **Queen Emma Bridge**, to the older terminal on the Otrobanda (western) side of town.

First colonised by the Dutch in the 1630s, Willemstad is resplendent with fine examples of 17th- 18th- and 19th-century Dutch and Spanish colonial architecture, the best of which are along the bay front.

Walking across the wobbly Queen Emma Bridge (or hopping on the free ferry) to the Punda (eastern) side of town you will find the colourful **Floating Market**, lined with boats from Colombia and Venezuela. As you come off the bridge, **Fort Amsterdam** is on the right, a sandstone fortress on the waterfront, which dates from

CRUISING AND THE ENVIRONMENT

With gargantuan vessels carrying up to and over 3,000 passengers docking at tiny island ports, cruising can't fail to make an impact on the environment. However, cruise lines are becoming more aware of this and there is growing recognition that land and sea must work together. Still, there is much work to do and the logistics of providing first-class services and excursions is an enormous challenge for small and under-resourced islands. Many still require major investment.

Restaurants and hotels don't benefit, as everything is provided and already paid for on the ships. Many passengers don't even disembark. Passengers don't tend to spend much on the islands except on duty-free goods, usually from internationally owned outlets.

Ships don't buy enough local produce, stocking up before they go. Ships generate a large amount of waste that pollutes the sea.

The cruise lines claim their industry provides jobs, not just on the islands but also on the ships and local tour operators and taxi companies benefit.

Cruises provide a 'taster' to many who return as land-based tourists. Modern ships now have built-in waste management systems and recycling centres, conforming to international law, which bans dumping food waste and sewage in coastal waters and plastics anywhere.

How you can help:

Disembark at every port.

Check out tours at the quayside, or sign up for locally run tours.

Use local restaurants and cafés.

Buy locally-made souvenirs and visit museums and churches.

Only take photos of people with their permission and offer a tip.

Although cruise lines are powerful, now a more conciliatory atmosphere prevails. A proper partnership benefits everyone, including the traveller.

1700 and now houses the Governor's Palace. A mid-18th century church stands nearby. At one corner of the fort and leading from the bridge is **Breederstraat**, one of Willemstad's best shopping streets and gateway to the main commercial district.

A cultural experience

The **Maritime Museum** (Wed–Sat 10.30am–3.30pm; www. curacaomaritime.com), on van den Brandhofstraat 7, Scharloo Abou, near the floating market, has some fascinating exhibits. The museum arranges harbour tours by water taxi (Wed and Sat 2pm). Also within walking distance of the Queen Emma Bridge (on Van Leeuwenhoekstraat in Otrobanda) is the **Curaçao**

> ## VENEZUELAN PORTS OF CALL
>
> **Isla Margarita** ㊼, just 40km (25 miles) off Venezuela's coast, and **La Guaira** ㊽, the main port for Caracas, 10km (6 miles) away, feature on many itineraries leaving from Puerto Rico. Margarita, once famous for its pearls, is really two islands connected by an 18km (11-mile) sandbar of broken shells. By this sandbank is the Laguna de la Restinga where you can take a boat trip through the mangroves. The western peninsula (Macanao) is fairly barren and undeveloped but has some good beaches. The main sights are in the eastern part, with duty-free shopping, a market, casinos and colonial architecture in Porlamar.
>
> From La Guaira you can visit Caracas, Venezuela's cosmopolitan capital, or view it from the top of Monte Avila. Nearby Colonia Tovar is a beautiful 19th-century town in the mountains with a good museum. If you do visit Caracas, be sure to check your government's latest safety guidance and exercise a high degree of caution, due to the risk of serious crime in the city.

Museum (Tue–Fri 8.30am–4.30pm, Sat 10am–4pm; tel: 5999-462 3873; www.thecuracaomuseum.com), a 19th-century military hospital building that holds colonial antiques and artefacts of the region's Caiquetio tribes. The **Kurá Holanda Museum** (Klipstraat 9; Mon–Sat 8am-4pm, Sun 9am-2pm; tel: 5999-462 9737; www.kurahulanda.com), on the site of a former slave yard is an anthropological museum and focuses on the African slave trade and Antillean art. Northeast of town is the **Senior Curaçao Liqueur Factory** (Mon–Fri 8am–5pm; tel: 5999-461 3526; www.curacaoliqueur.com), where you can discover the secret of the original liqueur's invention and have a taste too.

You can see orchids in Christoffel National Park

Within an hour's drive is the **Christoffel National Park** (Mon–Sat 7.30am–4pm, Sun 6am–2pm; tel: 5999-520 1685; www.christoffelpark.org), a large nature reserve in the far north of the island, with rare orchids and cacti. Its underwater equivalent is the **Curaçao Sea Aquarium** (daily 8am–5pm; tel: 5999-461 6666; www.curacao-sea-aquarium.com), which has more than 350 species of sea life.

The **Hato Caves** (daily 9am–3pm; tel: 5999-868 0379) are a network of subterranean limestone caverns, north of the capital. The caves have a mirror-like underground lake and stunning rock formations. At **San Jofat**, where members of the Dutch royal family have holiday homes, you can join a boat to go snorkelling, and see some of Curaçao's bays and inlets.

TRAVEL ESSENTIALS

PRACTICAL INFORMATION

Choosing a cruise
Types of cruise 173
Theme cruises 174
Choosing a cabin 176
Cruising with children 176
Home ports 176
Disabled travellers 177
Weddings 178

Preparing for the trip
Booking a cruise 179
Counting the cost 180
Health 181
Passports and visas 181
When to go 182
What to bring 183

Life on board
Activities and entertainment 183
Communication 184
Etiquette 185
Food and drink 185
Money 186
Ship facilities 186

Life on shore
Shore excursions 187

Cruise line information
Tourist information 189

CHOOSING A CRUISE

The first decision to make when choosing a cruise is how long do want – or can afford – to go for. Then you must consider what type would suit you best – a theme cruise, one packed with entertainment, a romantic sailing ship, or one with lots of ports of call. Most people find that a 10-day cruise is ideal: one week for exploring both on- and offshore, with three days at sea.

TYPES OF CRUISE

Do your research. Each cruise line offers a different experience: the mega ships of Carnival Cruises, Princess Cruises and Royal Caribbean provide the whole big-ship experience – Broadway-style shows, different dining options, lots of deck sports and a high proportion of balcony cabins. Many also lease or own private islands or beaches where you can enjoy a barbecue and watersports. In contrast, a small or mid-sized ship, such as those belonging to Oceania Cruises, the smaller Holland America Line ships, or the upscale vessels of Seabourn or Silversea, will be more restful.

There are small, luxurious ships that call at the harbours favoured by the yachting set – Virgin Gorda, St-Barths and St-Martin's Marigot Bay. Mid-sized ships, on which the emphasis is on the destinations as much as what's on board, may roam the Southern Caribbean, skimming the coast of South America or venturing down to the Amazon.

Star Clippers, Sea Cloud, and Windstar Cruises are the ones to choose for the romance of a sailing ship, whether it's a square rigger or floating gin palace (see page 188).

European-operated lines, such as Costa Cruises, tend to have a more international flavour, while P&O and Fred Olsen carry mainly British travellers, and US-run vessels have a predominantly American passenger list.

Know your cruise lines and ships. Although cruise lines may sound similar in their advertisements, they offer different holiday experiences at different rates. Some specialise in great food, while others have an impressivearray of onboard amenities, such as rock-climbing walls.

Once you've decided on a particular cruise line, remember that not all ships in a fleet are the same. Newer ones tend to be more expensive, but come with the latest features and more cabins with balconies. Apart from the cruise line's website, a top source of information is the *Insight Guides Cruise Guide*, which provides exhaustive reviews of 320 vessels.

Getting there. Once you've chosen your cruise, talk to a travel agent, tourist board or airline company to determine the best way to get to the embarkation point. You may wish to stay longer by buying an 'open jaw' return and flying, say, into Miami and out of Barbados.

THEME CRUISES

There is a wide range of specially designed theme cruises that cater for a huge range of interests, lifestyles, hobbies and niche markets. You name it and there's probably a cruise for it, from vampires and Goths' conventions to hard-core boot camp fitness voyages.

Theme cruises are usually arranged by cruise organisers – individuals, small companies, special interest groups, and non-profit organisations working hand-in-hand with the cruise companies – not the cruise line itself. In this sense, the ships are 'hired out' by the cruise lines to the specific groups. Affinity groups are also a natural market for niche cruises.

African-American cruises. A growing segment of the affinity market are cruises catering for African-American travellers. Blue World Travel (tel: 1-800-466 2719; www.festivalatsea.com), has earned a stellar reputation for its Festival at Sea cruises. The cruises (usually on Carnival ships), run several times a year and feature lectures on African-American culture, Motown music nights and African-attire dinner parties.

Gay and lesbian cruises. There's a thriving market for gay and lesbian cruise charters. Big organisers like Atlantis Events (tel: 1-310-859 8800 or 1-800-6-628 5268; www.atlantisevents.com) and RSVP Vacations (tel: 1-800-328 7787; www.rsvpvacations.com) can fill the world's biggest ships for exclusive gay and lesbian charters, featuring big-name gay entertainers and guest speakers, as well as a huge range of parties and excursions. Cruising is generally very gay friendly. Along with fostering a comfortable shipboard environment, these ships also stop at islands known to be welcoming to gay people.

THEME CRUISES 175

Culinary cruises. Focusing on food and wine, these cruises range from those that offer cookery demonstrations by masterchefs to others that concentrate on a regional cuisine such as Taste of the Islands cruises, which highlight French West Indian or Latin Caribbean cooking. There is also a growing trend for ships to have high-tech cookery studios on board and cookery classes under the guidance of expert guest chefs.

Educational cruises. Part of the growing trend for combining education with travel, an organisation called University at Sea (tel: 800-926 3775 in the US; www.universityatsea.com) runs an innovative series of fully accredited, continuing education courses. Many of these cruises are tax-deductible in the US.

Health cruises. There are speciality cruises devoted to yoga, bodybuilding, martial arts, meditation, stress reduction, aerobics, massage, tai chi and weight loss – including Run for Fun Cruise Tours (tel:1-833-786 4386; www.runforfuncruise.com), with organised fun runs in every port.

Musical cruises. Music is another major subject for theme cruises, with choices that include jazz, classical, opera, soul, salsa, gospel, country and western, dixieland, 1950s' retro rock 'n' roll, and big band orchestras. Check out the following cruises dedicated to specific music genres: smooth jazz (www.thesmoothjazzcruise.com), rock (http://monstersofrockcruise.com), soul (http://soultraincruise.com), country (www.countrycruising.com), blues (http://bluescruise.com) and early rock 'n' roll (http://maltshopcruise.com).

Naturist cruises are offered by several organisations, usually on smaller, privately-chartered ships. One of the more established is Bare Necessities Tours (tel: 1-800-743 0405; www.cruisebare.com).

Sporty cruises. Sport is another popular theme, with golf being one of the favourites. Fred Olsen Cruises and Silversea Cruises are renowned for their onboard golf programmes, complete with resident pro and organised rounds at the world's top courses, while other golf themes are offered by specialist tour operators, such as Golf Ahoy (tel: 1-239-344 9187; www.golfahoy.com), which will team up enthusiasts on board and arrange everything in port for a seamless golf vacation (wisely including spa treatments for non-golfing partners).

CHOOSING A CABIN

First of all, envisage how you will be spending your time during the cruise. If you love sightseeing, you may not need an expensive cabin as you won't be spending much time in it. But if you think you're going to spend sea days eating, reading and napping in the privacy of your cabin or relaxing on your balcony, then you would be advised to go for the more expensive option – a large cabin.

Sailboats, and even small cruising yachts, lean toward tiny, serviceable staterooms. Older, larger ships also tend to have small cabins without balconies that encourage guests to get out and about on the ship. Usually, the newer the ship the more spacious the cabin, and you will always have a private bathroom.

The choice will be between an inside cabin, outside cabin, balcony cabin or suite. Specific cabins can be pre-booked on all ships, although some cruise lines charge for this facility. On large ships, the least expensive cabins tend to be windowless, interior ones.

CRUISING WITH CHILDREN

Teen discos, children-only swimming pools, 'Circus at Sea' lessons and supervised, age-related activity programmes have become an intrinsic part of modern megaship cruising. Carnival and Royal Caribbean have indoor and outdoor children's facilities on their biggest ships, with huge areas dedicated to children.

The facilities on *Disney Wonder*, *Disney Dream* and *Disney Magic* are superb (with special adult-only areas for those who need a break from children), while Princess, Royal Caribbean and Norwegian Cruise Line all have good children's facilities and entertainment. Among the British cruise lines, P&O is excellent and Cunard's *Queen Mary 2* has the largest nursery at sea, staffed by highly qualified nannies. P&O and Princess ships also offer a night nursery, providing free care for sleeping infants while the parents relax.

HOME PORTS

Most of the big ships are based at Florida's three main ports: Miami (Royal

Caribbean, Carnival, Celebrity and Norwegian Cruise Line), Fort Lauderdale (Holland America, Princess, Celebrity and Royal Caribbean) and Port Canaveral (Disney Cruise Line, Carnival and Royal Caribbean).

US travellers who choose not to fly can sail to the Caribbean and the Yucatán directly from ports such as Jacksonville, Tampa, Galveston and New Orleans, often within driving distance of home. There are home ports on Caribbean islands with international airports. San Juan, Puerto Rico, and Bridgetown in Barbados are two of the busiest regional home ports. Antigua's V. C. Bird International Airport is another major hub in the region.

British-run lines, like P&O Cruises and Fred Olsen Cruises have cut back on their Caribbean fly-cruise programmes and base many ships year-round in Britain, only offering three-week Atlantic crossings and cruises in the Caribbean.

DISABLED TRAVELLERS

Cruising can be an ideal holiday for travellers with disabilities. Wheelchair users will find that most ships provide a relaxing, sociable setting while visiting lots of destinations. Take the advice of a specialist cruise travel agent before booking; make sure they provide specific information about airport transfers, boarding the ship, the facilities on board and the cabin itself.

All new ships have cabins adapted to wheelchair users, although in varying degrees. If you're uncomfortable walking long distances, consult the deck plans online, and avoid the very biggest ships, getting around with a stick or walking frame can be exhausting.

Another tip when planning a cruise is to choose a voyage with as few tender ports (those where the ship anchors outside the port and guests are ferried ashore) as possible. It is much easier for the less able to get ashore down a gangway than by climbing onto a lifeboat that is bobbing up and down.

Specialist organisations, including Wheel the World (tel: 1-6288-900 7778; www.wheeltheworld.com), or for UK cruisers, Accessible Travel (tel: 07970 073021; www.accessibletravel.co.uk), offer comprehensive cruise holiday advice.

Older cruise ships do not generally provide special facilities for those with hearing difficulties, although Crystal's two ships, the *Queen Mary 2* and some of the Celebrity fleet have special headsets in their cinemas. Newer ships have some signage in braille – on lift buttons and cabin door numbers.

WEDDINGS

Cruise lines compete with one another to offer wedding, honeymoon and renewal of vows packages, always at a price. The bigger lines have in-house wedding coordinators who will arrange everything from the flowers to the cake. Princess Cruises can hold weddings officiated by the captain, as can Celebrity Cruises, P&O Cruises and Azamara Club Cruises. On other lines, you can bring your own celebrant on board but must hold the ceremony while the ship is in port.

Many ships have wedding chapels, although these tend not to be very exciting. Ask if you can have the ceremony on the bridge or find a prettier spot on deck. Disney Cruise Line will allow couples to hold wedding ceremonies on the beach at Castaway Cay, its private island (although the official exchange of vows and paperwork must be held ashore, before the ship sails), while Holland America Line can arrange weddings at Half Moon Cay, its own private beach.

An alternative is to hold the nuptials in a romantic location on dry land in one of the ports of call and have either a reception, or a honeymoon, or both, at sea, organised by the cruise line. There are endless options for getting married ashore if you arrange it independently, but several cruise lines offer special wedding packages, and Carnival and Princess will organise a shore-side wedding with a cruise, often using one of their private islands for the ceremony.

PREPARING FOR THE TRIP

Many cruise lines don't have in-house reservations agents but they will provide a toll-free number, send brochures and put you in touch with a local representative. You can find a specialist travel agent who deals with cruises in your area through the Cruise Lines International Association (www.cruising.org).

BOOKING A CRUISE

Online
Travel websites, such as www.expedia.com, www.orbitz.com, and www.travelocity.com, all offer cruise bargains. Cruise-specific websites include www.choosingcruising.co.uk, www.cruises.com, www.cruisebrothers.com, www.cruise411.com, www.cruisecompete.com, www.cruise-compare.com and www.cruisecritic.com.

Agents in the UK
The Cruise People, 88 York Street, London W1H 1QT; tel: 44 20 7723 2450; www.cruisepeople.co.uk.

Thomas Cook Tourism (UK) Company Ltd, The Broadgate Tower, Third Floor, 20 Primrose Street, London EC2A 2RS; tel: 020 8016 3297; www.thomascook.com.

Cruise.co.uk Ltd, Grosvenor House, Prospect Hill, Redditch, B97 4DL; tel: 0330 303 8331; www.cruise.co.uk.

Marion Owen Travel, 23 Portland Street, Hull, HU2 8JX; tel: 01482 212525; www.marionowentravel.com.

Mundy Cruising, 48/49 Russell Square London, WC1B 4JP; tel: 020 7399 7670; www.mundycruising.co.uk.

Agents in the US
Cruise.com claims to be one of the largest websites specialising in cruises on the internet, tel: 888-333 3116; www.cruise.com.

Cruise Holidays has branches all over the US, Canada and the UK, tel: 866-335 8747; www.cruiseholidays.com.

Cruise Store Travel, 145 Shaker Road, East Longmeadow, MA 01028, tel: 413-525 9001; www.cruisestore.com.

Liberty Travel has branches all over the US, tel: 855-941 6294; www.libertytravel.com.

Agents in Australia and New Zealand:
Hello World Travel has branches all over Australia, www.helloworld.com.au.

ecruising.travel; Suite 202 Level 2, 89-91 Surf Parade, The Wave Building, Broadbeach, Queensland 4218; tel: 1-300 369 848; www.ecruising.travel.

Cruise Away, tel: 1-300 887 590; www.cruiseaway.com.au.

Adventure World, 131 New North Road, Eden Terrace, Auckland 1021, NZ; tel: 0800 238 368; www.adventureworld.co.nz.

COUNTING THE COST

Generally, your booking price will cover your cabin and food in the main dining room – and there are plenty of extra costs.

Hidden extras. Items *included* in the price of the cruise: all food; all entertainment; use of the gym and sports facilities (but not always all of them); transfers from the port (usually); port taxes; room service (sometimes); shuttle buses into town (sometimes); flights (usually); use of the ship's self-service laundry (usually); use of the ship's library; the captain's cocktail party.

Items *not included*: alcoholic drinks (except on Silversea, Seabourn, SeaDream, Regent Seven Seas); tips (unless stated); travel insurance; spa treatments; shore excursions; medical care; internet access and telephone calls from the satellite phone. Some cruise lines also charge extra for the following: visits to the bridge; use of some sports equipment; 'premium' exercise classes such as yoga; mineral water in cabins; room service; tea and coffee and shuttle buses. Most charge extra for dining in the 'alternative' restaurants.

Tipping. On Silversea, Seabourn, SeaDream, Regent Seven Seas and Thomson, some or all of the tips are included in the price. Many lines, including Carnival, Disney and Royal Caribbean allow, or even insist for tips to be prepaid, while others add a suggested amount automatically to your onboard account, or place an envelope for cash in the cabin on the final evening.

Regardless of tipping policy, ships carrying mainly Americans usually add a 15–18 percent gratuity to the bar bill 'for your convenience'. This is also common practice in the ships' spas. Passengers are expected to tip their waiter and cabin steward.

Travel insurance. You should always arrange comprehensive travel insurance to cover both yourself and your belongings for the entire duration of your stay abroad. Shop around as rates vary. Make sure you are covered for emergency medical care, repatriation by air ambulance (essential for international travellers), accidental death, baggage and document loss, and trip cancellation.

HEALTH

Covid-19. All ships have special Covid-19 measures in place. Check with your cruise company for extensive details.

Drinking water. In undeveloped areas away from resorts, it is best to avoid drinking tap water, especially after a hurricane when the water supply can be contaminated. In these areas, stick to bottled water, and avoid ice in your drinks.

Immunisation. No immunisations are required for travellers to the Caribbean, unless the traveller is coming from an infected or endemic area. However, it is a good idea to have a tetanus shot if you are not already covered. The main (though small) health risk to travellers on land in the Caribbean is infectious hepatitis or Hepatitis A. Although it is not a requirement, an injection of gamma globulin, administered as close as possible before departure, gives good protection against Hepatitis A. In addition, make sure you observe scrupulous personal hygiene, wash and peel fruit, and drink bottled water.

Insects. Mosquitoes are generally only a nuisance in port in the evening. To combat mosquitoes, pack a supply of insect repellent. Dengue-carrying mosquitoes bite during the day and present a small risk. The only area which usually carries a malaria risk is the shared island of Hispaniola, more in Haiti than the Dominican Republic.

Sun protection. To the uninitiated 27–32°C (80–90°F) may sound 'just like summer temperatures back home'. Don't be fooled. The sun in the tropics is more direct than in temperate regions and is even stronger at sea as it reflects off the water. Bring a high-factor sunscreen and wear it whenever you go out.

PASSPORTS AND VISAS

All passengers need a passport to travel on a cruise. It is common practice for passengers to hand over their passport at check-in until the end of the cruise, so make a photocopy to leave at home and another for the trip. Anyone wishing to visit a casino ashore may need to temporarily retrieve their passport from the purser.

Each passenger is given a cruise ship ID card, which is swiped and checked every time you leave the ship; on modern ships, it doubles as a room key and a charge card. It also indicates whether any passengers are missing when the ship is about to depart.

Visas. Usually required for visitors from Eastern Europe and Cuba. All travellers must have, upon entering the islands, a return or onward ticket, and adequate funds to support themselves for the duration of their stay.

Cruise passengers arriving via a US gateway city such as Miami or Puerto Rico have to obtain Electronic System for Travel Authorisation (ESTA) before flying or sailing. This includes citizens from all of the 38 countries that participate in the US Visa Waiver Scheme. The ESTA requires that you have more than six months remaining on your passport before its expiry date and that you have a machine-readable passport to enter the United States. The fee for ESTA is US$21 per person. If unsure, check with the passport issuing authority in your home country that your passport is still valid.

WHEN TO GO

Climate. The Caribbean islands' proximity to the equator means that seasonal temperature changes are generally limited to less than 6°C (10°F). An added bonus is the trade winds, which bring regular, cooling breezes to most of the islands. Year round, temperatures average around 27°C (80°F) throughout the region. During the winter (Dec–Mar) night-time lows can drop to about 16°C (60°F), with daytime highs reaching as much as 32°C (90°F). Rainfall varies, ranging from around 50cm (20 inches) a year in Curaçao and up to 190cm (75 inches) a year in the Grenada rainforest.

Rainfall is generally heaviest during October and November, although June is wettest in Trinidad and Tobago. The 'dry' period coincides with the peak tourist season: December to April or May.

Hurricanes. One of the most damaging and dangerous phenomena affecting the Caribbean, hurricanes can strike any time from June to November and usually last from eight to 10 days. A hurricane warning is issued when the storm winds reach at least 119kph (74mph) and storm surges are expected in a specific area within 24 hours. Cruise ships are fitted with stabilisers (fins under the water level) to reduce the pitch and roll of the ship during bad weather.

WHAT TO BRING

Bring swimwear, walking shoes (for excursions), deck shoes, a gym kit if you plan to work out, lots of sunblock, a brimmed sun hat, memory cards for your camera (expensive on board), binoculars, a small umbrella and light raincoat for sudden showers; seasickness remedies; and any regular medication you need.

What to wear. Cruising in the Caribbean can mean bringing two different wardrobes, one for the cruise and one for any overland travel afterwards. Some cruise lines, inspired by NCL's informal 'Freestyle' cruising, have done away with compulsory formal nights, although Cunard, Fred Olsen, Costa, P&O, Seabourn, Celebrity and Holland America Line are just a few that do have gala nights.

A week's cruise will generally have one or two formal nights and a mixture of casual and informal dress codes on the other nights:

Casual: Smart casual wear, but no shorts or vests.
Informal: Trousers and a smart shirt/jacket for men; cocktail dress for women.
Formal: Dinner jacket/tuxedo or dark suit for men; evening dress for women.

When away from beach or poolside, cover up – a simple T-shirt and a pair of shorts will do the trick. Nude or topless (for women) bathing is prohibited everywhere except for Guadeloupe, Martinique, St-Martin, St-Barthélemy and Bonaire. Guadeloupe, St-Martin, and Bonaire each have at least one designated nudist beach.

LIFE ON BOARD

Modern ships are as varied as resorts on land, catering for every age, taste and budget, with many of the new vessels each more innovative than the last.

ACTIVITIES AND ENTERTAINMENT

After dinner shows. The standard ship's evening entertainment, which could be stand-up comedy, a cabaret singer or a splashy Broadway-style show, includes two nightly performances, one after each dinner sitting.

Casinos. Gambling is a feature on most large ships and most casinos provide gaming lessons, as well as slot machines. Casinos in the Caribbean and on the ship tend to be more laid back than those in Las Vegas and elsewhere. Ships' casinos are closed when in port.

Las Vegas-style shows. Big 'production' shows can be spellbinding at sea, with some ships having technical facilities superior to those of a top theatre. Big-name musicals, futuristic circus shows and opera have all been staged on ships.

Live music. Ships nowadays offer everything from concert pianists to scantily clad female string quartets. Some have great tribute bands, talented jazz musicians and excellent orchestras.

Nightclubs and discos. With mixed age groups to cater for, the resident DJs generally play it safe, including old favourites in their act.

Religious services. Interdenominational services are held on most cruise ships, conducted either by the captain or an on-board chaplain. Special Jewish charters will have a rabbi on board.

Talks and lectures. Many ships have guest lecturers and guest speakers who discuss topics related to the region or a specialist interest group.

COMMUNICATION

Telephones. Making telephone calls using a ship's satellite system is expensive, at up to US$12 per minute. It is cheaper to make calls from a land line in port, or from a mobile phone with a roaming agreement. All visitors with a roaming-enabled mobile phone will receive a signal in the Caribbean. Many ships now have their own network, when the vessel is at sea and out of range, but this is extremely expensive.

Public phonecards in several denominations are available from FLOW (formerly Cable and Wireless; www.discoverflow.co) and Digicel (www.digicel-group.com) on those islands from which the company operates. Residents of the US and Canada can use AT&T USADirect public phones with a charge card, while some public phones allow European charge card holders to access their home operator.

Internet. All islands and most cruise terminals have internet cafes. All ships offer internet access although charges vary enormously. Many have Wi-Fi for passengers with their own devices and offer several internet options, including special packages for heavy users .

ETIQUETTE

Cruise lines are strict about the public areas being non-smoking, and some provide a cigar lounge for smokers.

It is forbidden to film or record any of the ship's entertainers, for copyright reasons.

If you are invited to dine with the captain, consider it an honour and reply immediately, and be sure to observe the dress code (see page 183).

Visits to the bridge are rare for security reasons, although small ships operated by SeaDream and Star Clippers may allow access.

FOOD AND DRINK

That you can eat round the clock on a cruise is no exaggeration, so try to eat in moderation. Unless there is a 'speciality' restaurant on board, all the food on a cruise is included in the price.

Bars. Ships' bars range from the sophisticated to Irish theme pubs. All drinks bought in the bar can be signed for. Be aware that many ships will add an automatic 'gratuity' of 15–18 percent.

Cafés. Cappuccino and espresso from machines are usually better than cruise-ship tea and coffee. Afternoon tea is provided on many ships, with white-glove service, dainty cakes and sandwiches.

Drinking water. Although safe, the drinking water on cruise ships is heavily chlorinated and does not taste good to most people. All ships provide bottled water, although many charge for it.

Dining and restaurants. Some ships offer from two to four different dinner sittings in the dining room, while others have 'open seating', meaning you eat when you like and sit where you like. Smaller ships, carrying fewer than 100 passengers, tend to have just one sitting where all the passengers dine together.

As well as a main dining room, many ships have speciality restaurants where a small premium is charged for a different menu and more exclusive surroundings. Vegetarians, vegans and people with other dietary requirements are usually well catered for.

Room service. Usually included in the cost of the cruise, although some lower-budget cruise lines either charge for it or do not offer it. Many ships have tea- and coffee-making facilities in the cabins.

MONEY

Cruise operators encourage guests to register a credit card at the beginning of a voyage for on-board expenses. Otherwise, a bill will be compiled to be settled on the day of departure. While on board, whether a credit card is registered or not, everything is paid for using a special card issued by the ship.

Currency onboard most ships is the US dollar, although P&O, Fred Olsen and some Cunard vessels use sterling. There is usually an ATM near the shops or casino, and exchange facilities at the customer relations desk, but rates are not competitive; use a local bank in port instead.

SHIP FACILITIES

Medical care. All cruise ships have a doctor and nurse on board (the exception being cargo ships or private). Facilities vary but a ship's doctor should be able to treat most ailments. Seriously ill passengers may be stabilised until the ship arrives in port, or airlifted off. There is a fee for consulting the ship's doctor.

Norovirus (a common gastro-intestinal virus) occurs on cruise ships, as it does in hospitals and hotels, and it can spread quickly. If you have diarrhoea, vomiting and fever, report to the ship's doctor immediately. Avoid the virus by using the antiseptic hand wipes that are handed out on board and by washing hands scrupulously.

Cinema and TV. All ships offer in-cabin TV, usually showing satellite channels, movies and the ship's channels. Many ships have a cinema, too, showing first-run movies.

Gentlemen hosts. A 'gentleman host', also known as the dance host, is a feature on traditional cruises with Cunard, Crystal, Silversea, Holland America and Fred Olsen. Personable single men in their 50s and 60s are employed to act as dancing and dinner hosts to unaccompanied older women.

Library. The ship's library provides a quiet retreat and an endless source of free reading material, from novels to guidebooks.

The Purser. The Purser's Office (also called Reception, Guest Relations or the

Information Desk) is the nerve centre of the ship for general passenger information and minor problems. This is the place to pick up DVDs, ship-compiled newspapers and the ship's programme.

Spas. Sea spas now rival land-based health facilities in terms of the services they offer. You can treat yourself to facials and massages, have your teeth whitened, consult an acupuncturist or have a Botox treatment. All this comes at a price, however. Expect to pay over US$120 for a facial, a 55-minute massage, or a reflexology session. Book ahead for treatments on sea days as they are very popular.

Water sports. Some smaller ships, namely those of Star Clippers, SeaDream Yacht Club, Seabourn and Windstar have a water sports platform which can be lowered from the back of the ship. All of these carry their own equipment. The private islands of the big cruise lines usually have a beach with water sports facilities. Waterskiing, sailing, windsurfing, snorkelling and scuba diving are available on most islands and can be organised through hotels or with independent beach operators.

LIFE ON SHORE

Common politeness is as desirable on the islands as it is anywhere else. If you need to ask directions or advice always greet the person before asking a question. And a word of advice, slow down; life operates on a different timescale in the sleepy Caribbean.

SHORE EXCURSIONS

Although expensive, shore excursions do get snapped up quickly. You can often book them at the same time as buying your cruise, but take care not to book too many tours. A crowded schedule can be punishing on the pocket, as well as physically strenuous.

Assembly times can be as early as 5am and may entail 10 hours in a bus with little time at the sight. Practically all organised excursions will schedule in some shopping time.

Independent tours. You can see and do what you want if you are prepared to organise your own excursion off-shore, and it's often cheaper to do this than go through a cruise-line tour. However, your time is usually limited in port so you need to do some research on the port of call first, bring a good map, and check that ferry and bus times coincide with the ship's arrival and departure. Remember, if you are late, the ship won't wait for you unless you are on a ship-organised tour, if you miss the boat, it is your responsibility to catch up at the next port.

CRUISE LINE INFORMATION

Azamara, US: 1050 Caribbean Way, Miami, FL 33132, tel: 305-341 0206 or 888-532 5828. UK: tel:0344 493 4016. www.azamara.com.

Carnival Cruise Lines, US: 3655 NW 87th Avenue, Miami, FL 33178, tel: 800-764 7419. UK: Carnival House, 5 Gainsford Street, London SE1 2NE, tel: 0843-374 2272; www.carnival.com.

Celebrity Cruises, US: 1050 Caribbean Way, Miami, FL 33132, tel: 888-859 7692. UK: Celebrity Cruises The Heights, 3 Brooklands Road, Weybridge, Surrey KT13 0NY, tel: 0800 240 4207. www.celebritycruises.com

Costa Cruises, US: 880 SW 145th Avenue, Suite 102 Pembroke Pines, FL 33027, tel: 800-462 6782; www.costacruises.com. UK: Carnival House, 100 Harbour Parade, Southampton SO15 1ST, tel: 0800-389 0622; www.costacruises.co.uk.

Cunard Line, UK: Carnival House, 100 Harbour Parade, Southampton, SO15 1ST, tel: 0344-338 8641; www.cunard.co.uk.

Disney Cruise Line, US: 201 Celebration Place, Suite 400, Celebration, FL 34747-4600; tel: 800-951 3532; http://disneycruise.disney.go.com.

Fred Olsen Cruise Lines, UK: Fred Olsen House, White House Road, Ipswich, Suffolk IP1 5LL, tel: 44-1473 742 424; www.fredolsencruises.com.

Holland America Line, US: 300 Elliott Avenue West, Seattle, WA 98119, tel: 855-932-1711. UK: Carnival House, 100 Harbour Parade, Southampton SO15 1ST, tel: 0344 338 8605; www.hollandamerica.com.

Norwegian Cruise Line, US: 7665 Corporate Center Drive, Miami, FL 33126, tel: 866-234 7350. UK: 4th Floor, Mountbatten House, Grosvenor Square, Southampton, SO15 2JU, tel: 0333 241 2319. www.ncl.com.

Oceania Cruises: US: 7665 Corporate Center Drive, Miami, FL 33126, tel: 855-

623 2642. UK: tel: 345-505 1920; www.oceaniacruises.com.
P&O Cruises, Carnival House, 100 Harbour Parade, Southampton, SO15 1ST, tel: 0344 338 8003; www.pocruises.com.
Princess Cruises, US: 24305 Town Center Drive, Santa Clarita, CA 91355, tel: 800-774 6237; www.princess.com.
Regent Seven Seas Cruises, US: 7665 Corporate Center Drive, Miami, FL 33126, tel: 800-886 5374 or 844-473 4368. UK: Mountbatten House, Grosvenor Square, Southampton, SO15 2JU, tel: 44 023 8082 1390; www.rssc.com.
Royal Caribbean International, US: 1050 Caribbean Way, Miami, FL 33132, tel: 866-562 7625. UK: Building 3, The Heights, Weybridge, Surrey KT13 0NY, tel: 0344 493 4005. www.royalcaribbean.com.
Seabourn, US: 300 Elliott Avenue West, Seattle, WA 98119, tel: 800-442 4448. UK: Carnival House, 100 Harbour Parade, Southampton, SO15 1ST, tel: 0344 338 8615; www.seabourn.com.
SeaDream Yacht Club, US: 601 Brickell Key Drive Suite 1050 Miami, FL 33131 tel: 800 707 4911. UK: tel: 0800-783 1373; www.seadream.com.
Silversea Cruises, US: 1050 Caribbean Way, Miami, FL 33131, tel: 800-722 9955. UK: Mezzanine Floor, 105 Victoria Street, London, SW1E 6QT, tel: 44 844 251 0837; www.silversea.com.
Star Clippers, UK: Fred Olsen House, 42 White House Road, Ipswich Suffolk, IP1 5LL, tel: 0845 200 6145 or 01473 242666; www.starclippers.co.uk.
Marella Cruises, UK: Wigmore House, Wigmore Lane, Luton LU2 9TN, tel: 0203-636 1862; www.tui.co.uk/cruise.
Windstar Cruises, US: 2101 4th Avenue, Suite 210, Seattle WA 98121, tel: 800-258 7245; www.windstarcruises.com.

TOURIST INFORMATION

For more information about what you can do on individual islands contact the local tourist offices, or the **Caribbean Tourism Organization**, www.onecaribbean.org. 7th Floor, Baobab Tower, Warrens, St Michael, Barbados 22026, tel: 246-427 5242.

INDEX

A
Ambergris Caye (Belize) 55
Anthony's Key Resort (Roatán) 56
Antigua 17, 91, 110
Aruba & Curaçao 156, 166

B
Bahamas, the 61
Baie Orientale (St Martin) 101
Barbados 12, 19, 21, 91, 141
Basseterre (St Kitts) 105
Bathsheba (Barbados) 148
Belize 53, 55
Belize City (Belize) 52
Bequia 153
Boiling Lake (Dominica) 124
Bridgetown (Barbados) 141, 145
Brighton Beach (Barbados) 143
Brimstone Hill National Park (St Kitts) 107
British Virgin Islands 91, 97
Buccoo Reef (Tobago) 165

C
Cancún (Mexico) 45
Caneel Bay (St John USVI) 95
Cane Garden Bay (Tortola, BVI) 98
Carib Indians 121, 124
Casa de Campo (Dominican Republic) 84
Castries (St Lucia) 135
Cayman Islands 71
Charlestown (Nevis) 109
Charlotte Amalie (St Thomas USVI) 93
Charlotteville (Tobago) 165
Chichén Itzá (Mexico) 46
Christiansted (St Croix USVI) 96
Colombier (St-Barthélemy) 105
Costa Maya (Mexico) 49
Costa Rica 53, 57
Cozumel (Mexico) 40, 43
Crown Point (Tobago) 165
Cuba 13, 14, 69
Curaçao 156, 165, 168

D
Dominica 91, 120
Dominican Republic 13, 14, 69, 83

E
El Luquillo Beach (Puerto Rico) 88
Everglades National Park, Florida (USA) 27

F
Falmouth (Jamaica) 78
Florida (USA) 18, 19, 21
Folkestone Marine Park (Barbados) 147
Fort-de-France (Martinique) 129
Fort Lauderdale (USA) 22, 28
Fort St Louis (Martinique) 132
Frederiksted (St Croix USVI) 95
Freeport (Grand Bahama) 64
Freeport (Jamaica) 65
Friar's Bay (St Kitts) 108
Frigate Bay (St Kitts) 108

G
Galveston (USA) 21, 22, 37
George Town (Grand Cayman) 72
Grand Anse (Grenada) 157
Grand Bahama (The Bahamas) 59, 64
Grand Cayman 69, 71
Grande Anse (Guadeloupe) 118
Grenada 154
Guadeloupe 12, 14, 17, 91, 114
Gustavia (St Barthélemy) 104

H
Havana (Cuba) 70
Honduras 53, 55
Houston (USA) 21, 22, 38

I
Indian River (Dominica) 126

J
Jamaica 12, 14, 69, 75

INDEX 191

Jost Van Dyke (BVI) 97

K
Key West (USA) 22, 39
Kohunlich (Mexico) 50

L
Lamanai (Belize) 55
La Romana (Dominican Republic) 84
La Soufrière volcano (Guadeloupe) 119
La Soufrière volcano (St Vincent) 152
Limón (Costa Rica) 58

M
Marigot Bay (St Lucia) 139
Marigot (St Martin) 103
Martinique 91, 127
Mayreau 153
Mexico 18, 19, 40, 42
Miami 21
Montego Bay (Jamaica) 76, 78
Mustique 154

N
Nassau (the Bahamas) 61
Nevis 109
New Orleans (USA) 21, 22, 36
New Providence Island (the Bahamas) 59, 61

O
Ocho Rios (Jamaica) 76, 79
Oranjestad (Aruba) 166
Orlando (USA) 32

P
Palm Beach (Aruba) 167
Paradise Island (the Bahamas) 61, 63
Philipsburg (Sint Maarten) 100
Pigeon Point (Tobago) 165
Pitons, The (St Lucia) 134, 137
Playa del Carmel (Mexico) 40, 45
Pointe-à-Pitre (Guadeloupe) 17, 115
Ponce (Puerto Rico) 88
Port Antonio (Jamaica) 76, 82
Port Canaveral (USA) 22, 31
Port Elizabeth (Bequia) 153
Port of Spain (Trinidad) 159
Portsmouth (Dominica) 122, 126
Puerto Costa Maya (Mexico) 40, 49
Puerto Rico 11, 13, 19, 21, 69, 86
Puerto Viejo de Limón (Costa Rica) 60

R
Road Town (Tortola BVI) 98
Roatán 53, 56
Roseau (Dominica) 122, 123

S
San José (Costa Rica) 58
San Juan (Puerto Rico) 21, 87
San Miguel (Cozumel) 43
Santo Domingo (Dominican Republic) 12, 84
Scarborough (Tobago) 163
Shell Beach (St-Barthélemy) 105
Sint Maarten 100
Soufrière (St Lucia) 138
Spanish Town (Virgin Gorda, BVI) 98
Speightstown (Barbados) 147
Speyside (Tobago) 165
St-Barthélemy 103
St Croix (US Virgin Islands) 90, 95
St George's (Grenada) 154
St Jean (St-Barthélemy) 105
St John's (Antigua) 110
St John (US Virgin Islands) 90
St Kitts 12, 91, 105
St Lucia 12, 91, 134
St-Martin 91, 103
St-Pierre (Martinique) 133
St Thomas (US Virgin Is) 90
St Vincent & The Grenadines 153

T
Tampa (USA) 34
Tobago 156, 161, 165
Tortola (BVI) 97
Trinidad & Tobago 156, 161

U
US Virgin Islands 93

V
Valley of Desolation

INDEX

(Dominica) 125
Venezuela 10, 168
Virgin Gorda (BVI) 98
Virgin Islands see British/US Virgin Islands 97

W
Willemstad (Curaçao) 168

X
Xcaret (Mexico) 46

Xuanantunich (Belize) 55

Y
Yucatán Peninsula (Mexico) 42

THE MINI ROUGH GUIDE TO
CARIBBEAN PORTS OF CALL

First Edition 2022

Editor: Kate Drynan
Author: Sarah Miles
Picture Editor: Tom Smyth
Cartography Update: Carte
Layout: Pradeep Thapliyal
Head of DTP and Pre-Press: Katie Bennett
Head of Publishing: Kate Drynan
Photography Credits: Alex Havret/Apa Publications 4TC, 41, 44, 46, 48, 65; Anse castanet Resort 138; Ariane Hunter 160; Aruba Tourist Authority 165; Bahamas Tourist Office 64; Barbados Tourism Authority 6T, 140, 145; Belize Tourist Board/Demian Solano 4TL; Blount Small Ship 20; Cayman Islands Dept of Tourism 72; Corrie Wingate/Apa Publications 4MC, 18, 52, 54, 55, 58; Curacao Tourist Board 167; Discover Dominica Authority 122, 125; Fotolia 4MC; Getty Images 4ML, 5M, 23, 36, 49, 61, 96, 100, 104, 114, 135; Glyn Genin/Apa Publications 13, 87, 89; Grenada Board of Tourism 6B, 158; iStock 4ML, 4TC, 5T, 5M, 7T, 7B, 25, 31, 35, 56, 62, 63, 85, 92, 94, 99, 106, 108, 117, 123, 126, 136, 144, 148, 150, 171; Jolly Beach Hotel & Spa/fotoseeker.com 112; Kevin Cummins/Apa Publications 75, 76, 79, 81, 82, 83; Luc Olivier/Martinique Tourist Board 128, 130, 133; Mary Evans Picture Library 11; Nevis Tourism Authority 109, 110; Nowitz Photography/Apa Publications 27, 29, 30, 32; Phil Wood/Apa Publications 73; Philippe Giraud for The Guadeloupe Island Tourist Board 119, 121; Shutterstock 1, 43, 116, 155; St Lucia Tourist Board 139; St Maarten Tourist Board 15; St Maarten Tourist Bureau 102; St. Vincent & the Grenadines Tourist Office/Chris Caldicott 152; Sylvaine Poitau/Apa Publications 26, 67, 71, 154; Trinidad & Tobago Tourism Development Company 162; U.S. Virgin Islands Department of Tourism 90
Cover Credits: Beach and sea Shutterstock

Distribution
UK, Ireland and Europe: Apa Publications (UK) Ltd; sales@insightguides.com
United States and Canada: Ingram Publisher Services; ips@ingramcontent.com
Australia and New Zealand: Booktopia; retailer@booktopia.com.au
Worldwide: Apa Publications (UK) Ltd; sales@insightguides.com

Special Sales, Content Licensing and CoPublishing
Rough Guides can be purchased in bulk quantities at discounted prices. We can create special editions, personalised jackets and corporate imprints tailored to your needs. sales@roughguides.com; http://roughguides.com

All Rights Reserved
© 2022 Apa Digital AG
License edition © Apa Publications Ltd UK

Printed in Turkey

No part of this book may be reproduced, stored in a retrieval system or transmitted in any form or means electronic, mechanical, photocopying, recording or otherwise, without prior written permission from Apa Publications.

Contact us
Every effort has been made to provide accurate information in this publication, but changes are inevitable. The publisher cannot be held responsible for any resulting loss, inconvenience or injury sustained by any traveller as a result of information or advice contained in the guide. We would appreciate it if readers would call our attention to any errors or outdated information, or if you feel we've left something out. Please send your comments with the subject line "Rough Guide Mini Caribbean Ports of Call Update" to mail@uk.roughguides.com.